Humpty Dumpty:
The Fate of
Regime Change

by William R. Polk

Panda Press
2013

Also by William R. Polk

Backdrop to Tragedy: The Struggle for Palestine
(with David Stamler and Edmund Asfour)
Beacon Press

The Opening of South Lebanon 1788-1840
A Study of the Impact of the West on the Middle East
Harvard

The United States and the Arab World
Harvard

The Arab World Today
Harvard

Beginnings of Modernization in the Middle East
(editor with Richard Chambers)
Chicago

The Elusive Peace: The Middle East in the Twentieth Century
St Martins

The Golden Ode
(translator and commentator)
Chicago

Passing Brave
(with William Mares)
Knopf

Neighbors and Strangers: The Fundamentals of Foreign Affairs
Chicago

Understanding Iraq
Harper Collins

Out of Iraq: A practical Plan for Withdrawal Now
(with George McGovern)
Simon & Schuster

Polk's Folly: An American Family History
Doubleday

The Birth of America
Harper Collins

Understanding Iran
Palgrave Macmillan

Violent Politics: A History of Insurgency, Terrorism & Guerrilla War
Chicago

The Diary of President James K. Polk
(editor and commentator)
Chicago

Personal History: Living in Interesting Times
Panda Press

Distant Thunder: Reflections on the Dangers of Our Times
Panda Press

Blind Man's Buff
(a novel)

SOME COMMENTS ON THE ESSAYS IN THIS COLLECTION

"This ['The Iran Crisis: Danger and Opportunity'] is a masterpiece of analysis and lucidity." —*Ambassador Dick Viets*

"Brilliant analysis. Far more comprehensive and broader in scope than anything I have seen from anyone else ..." Ray Close, former senior CIA officer.

"Brilliant article..." former Congressman and Fox News Commentator Dennis Kucinich

"Your recent essay on Libya was absolutely grand – so much that needed to be said, and you said it so well." Elisabeth Sifton, former member of the advisory board of *Foreign Affairs*.

"Your Afghan article is extraordinary in its depth, analytic power – and contemporary relevance." Patrick Seale, former chief correspondent of *The Observer*.

"A brilliant piece of reporting..." Uri Avery, Israeli commentator.

"Your paper is as good as Karl Eikenberry, Sherard Cowper-Coles, Uri Avnery and Chas Freeman say it is." David Unger, member of the editorial board of *The New York Times*.

"You have engrossed and educated me and I am very grateful." Sir James Craig, former British ambassador to Syria and Saudi Arabia

"...penetrating analysis." Yasar Yakis, former Foreign Minister of Turkey.

"A real feast! I have not read such a perceptive and profound piece of writing for ages!" Professor Ghassan Salamé, founding director of the School of International Affairs, Sciences Po, Paris.

"...brilliant and way ahead of its time." Jim Clinton, c.e.o. The Gallup Poll.

"...excellent, and perceptive, essays. I wish they could be more widely available to politicians on both sides of the Atlantic." Lord Wright, former head of the British Foreign Service, ambassador to Syria and Saudi Arabia and chairman of Chatham House.

"...splendid analysis of our dilemma in Afghanistan...you are an inspiration." —*Paul Findley, eleven times Congressman (R) from Illinois*

"...a brilliant overview." —*Tom Hayden*

""Your extraordinary essay on Libya is fascinating and extremely instructive... It's the most intelligent background piece I have read on the subject." —*Lance Murrow, Time Magazine essayist and winner National Magazine Award*

"...an extremely precisely sourced, well argued piece [on Iran]." —*Scott McConnell, former editor, The American Conservative*

"This is, of course, quite brilliant." —*Ambassador Chas Freeman, former Assistant Secretary of Defense for International Security Affairs*

"...a masterly analysis of [Afghanistan and Pakistan]," —*Brigadier (Rtd.) Yasub Dogar*

"Absolutely marvelous." —*Former US Ambassador John Gunther Dean*

First Panda Press Edition 2013
Copyright © 2013 by William R. Polk

All rights reserved under International and Pan-American Copyright Convention.
Published in the United States by Panda Press

All photographs are courtesy of the author except where otherwise noted.

The Library of Congress has catalogued this edition as follows:
Polk, William Roe 1929-
Humpty Dumpty by William R. Polk, 1st edition
ISBN: 978-0-9829340-3-6

Design & Production: Eliza Polk
Editor: Milbry Polk
Cover Design: Mary Tiegreen

www.williampolk.com

Contents

"Humpty Dumpty sat on a wall.

Humpty Dumpty had a great fall.

All the king's horses and all the king's men

Couldn't put Humpty together again."

For my grandchildren
   Adelaide, Bree & Mary;
         Alexander;
               Brenna & Tara;
                     Isabella & Leonidas

∼

With the Hope
   That you will do a better job than
               My generation with these problems.

North Africa

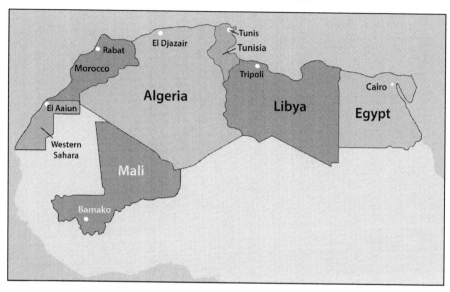

Middle East and Central Asia

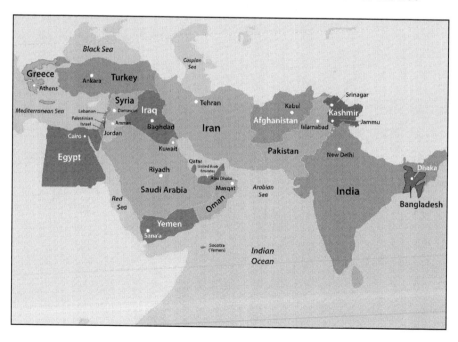

INTRODUCTION

During the four years from 2009 to 2013, wars raged from Afghanistan to Mali while in Libya, Egypt, Syria, Bahrain and Yemen regimes were either overthrown or under siege. New forms of warfare, particularly the unmanned, high-flying, remotely-controlled drone, came into use. And people almost everywhere in Africa, the Middle East and Central Asia suffered from them and from the more conventional means of causing death and destruction. In the following essays, I analyze the causes of this violent time. Taken together with my previous volume of essays, *Distant Thunder,* they provide a panorama of the contested issues, the regimes and their adversaries and the embattled societies.

I begin with a short piece I did in 2010 for *The Christian Science Monitor* on "*Lessons from Humpty Dumpty*" on the wars in Iraq and Afghanistan. A recurring theme in my thought and writing is brought out in this serious piece of satire that is usually misread as a children's rhyme. Its message is that when an established order is destroyed – knocked off the wall like Humpty Dumpty – then "all the kings' horses and all the king's men cannot put it together again."

Oblivious to this simple parable, the neoconservative advisers to the Bush administration advocated "regime change," that is knocking the existing order off the wall, as a major thrust of American policy. They justified this policy by pointing to the imperfections – and worse – of the regimes they wanted to destroy. My aim was not to justify the existing regimes but to point out that destroying them inevitably created new evils that often were far worse than what was destroyed. That certainly happened in Iraq – several million Iraqis were turned into homeless refugees, over a million were grievously wounded or killed and hospitals, schools, bridges and other facilities that had taken a generation to build were destroyed. Even more tragic was that social groups which had lived in peace and security, if not always in justice, were set at one another's throats. The fragile linkages that enabled vital activities to take place were broken. "Humpty Dumpty" was smashed.

The act of knocking "Humpty Dumpty" off the wall cost about 4,500 dead American soldiers, hundreds of thousands of wounded American soldiers, many with lifetime disabilities, and at least $1 trillion in direct costs and perhaps several times that amount in indirect costs.

Finally, as in the rhyme, despite all of our power and wealth -- all our 'horses' and men -- Americans have been unable to create a stable, peaceful new regime. So what remains? In a report on his visit to today's Baghdad, *The Independent's* Patrick Cockburn describes what happened to the Baghdad I used to know and once happily lived in, in these words,

> "I drove for miles in east Baghdad through streets flooded with grey, murky water, diluted with sewage [until] the flood waters became too deep to drive through...Theft of public money and incompetence on a gargantuan scale means the government fails to provide adequate electricity, clean water or sanitation. One-third of the labour force is unemployed and, when you include those under-employed, the figure is over half...Iraqis looked for improved personal security and the rule of law after Saddam, but this has not materialised...[during the mass slaughter of 2006 and 2007]...upwards of 3,000 Iraqis were being butchered every month [and the American-imposed regime of current Prime Minister Nouri al-Malaki carries on] with highly developed means of repression, such as secret prisons, and pervasive use of torture.

Cockburn's essay was published (Counterpunch, March 4, 2013), almost three years after my essay in this collection – when all the king's horses and all the kings men had been trying for years to put Humpty together again, at an cost -- up to then – as I mentioned above, of at least $1 trillion and with, as Cockburn and I both have said, with no discernable success.

Why is this? There are several reasons which I discuss in these essays and those I grouped together in *Distant Thunder*, but one is fundamental, yet it is so subtle that it is seldom discussed. It is an idea that occupied the thoughts of the great philosophers in Seventeenth and Eighteenth century Europe. As the French philosopher Jean-Jacques Rousseau put it, it was that the functioning of a society could be ensured only by the existence of a *contrat social*. What Rousseau meant by a social contract was that the mainly implicit understandings of what the individual owes his government and what the government owes him are the "glue" that holds society together. Thus, when they are destroyed, the whole system falls apart. This is what happened in Iraq. When the contract is broken, laws, edicts or repressions, no matter how powerful or severe, often fail to recreate the norms of human interaction. Recreating them may be the work of a generation or more. Thus, whether or not they are motivated by good will, prudent statesmen will not seek to overthrow existing systems with lethal force unless they are reliably seen to pose a mortal threat. This is not only prudence: it is the Nuremberg Doctrine that has long since become a part of American law.

From consideration of the social contract, I turn to Afghanistan. As I detailed in my book *Distant Thunder*, I first visited that fascinating country in 1962 as a member of the US Policy Planning Council. I then did a 2,000 mile trip around the country, visiting almost every area and consulting with scores of Afghans in every walk of life; the result was a draft US National Policy paper that warned of the danger of an aggressive American policy and urged instead a low-profile system of support for the then reform government. My suggestion was brushed aside because, as the American secretary of state admonished me, saying in effect that Afghanistan was not important and never would be, I should work on serious issues. I never accepted that judgment, and after I left government service I kept in close touch with events in Afghanistan and returned many times over the years.

As America sent troops into Afghanistan, following the Usama bin Ladin inspired attack on the World Trade Center and the Pentagon, I turned back to my earlier concern with what to do in or about that far-away country. I was increasingly frustrated by the superficial media accounts of what was happening there. Nowhere was the Afghan "problem" put in a historical context. Was what our government was trying to do unique? Obviously not, but every action – and every inaction – *seemed* unique to practically all of our new-born experts. Few had any interest in the Afghan experience. So I began by going back, or at least thinking back, in two jumps in time: the first was the failed British attempt roughly a century and a half before to "regime change" Afghanistan and the second was the Soviet Russian attempt to do the same in the 1980s. My account of these two failed ventures are laid out in the second and third essays.

In my second essay, I describe how the British tried to "Regime Change" Afghanistan in the middle years of the Nineteenth century. Like the Soviet Union and the Americans, the British had overwhelming conventional military power but, despite them, suffered their greatest military defeat in that tumultuous century, losing a whole army to Afghan guerrillas. And their catastrophe in Afghanistan echoed for years throughout their vast empire. Other suppressed nations took heart from the Afghan resistance and began movements with which we are still engaged.

In what the Soviet Union tried to do from 1979 to 1988 in its decade of counterinsurgency was strikingly similar to what the Americans have been trying to do from 2003 onward. I endeavored in my third paper, "*The Russians Try to 'Regime Change" Afghanistan*," to bring their policy into focus. That prospect had to be broad enough to encompass not only what happened there, but also the effects of the war on the outsiders. The Afghan war effectively "regime changed" the Soviet Union, virtually bankrupting it, causing an attempted *coup d'état* and creating massive disaffection among the people. The warning for America was loud and clear, but as I reflected on American policy I wondered if it would be heard. I find no evidence that it has been.

I had read a good deal about Afghan history over the years, but I went back over the materials I had studied, added new research and asked new questions. A quick summary of my notes is the fourth essay in this collection, "*Way off in the Wild East.*" It offers a brief account of what outsiders and the Afghans had themselves tried to do over the last century. I had watched as the reforming government of my friend, Prime Minister Muhammad Maiwandwal, set in motion a social revolution. It was overthrown and he was murdered. The *coup d'état* of Prince Daud, a cousin of the king, was as clear a starting point for the travail of our time as could be imagined.

That period of travail raised a central question that has yet to be answered: how can a government achieve legitimacy. That is the subject of my fifth essay. What I endeavored to show was the Afghan "way." This is obviously very different from the British, Soviet or American concepts of politics. However, as I report, how the Afghans get together politically and socially is not so alien from our experience as most people think. I describe, in particular, two key Afghan "occasions:" on the local level, the activities of village councils that oversee the 22,000 or so villages in which most Afghans live and the extension of the village councils to national issues through the convening of the Afghan version of a constitutional assembly and supreme court known as the *loya jirga*. Only through their actions can a sense of legitimacy be engendered, so it is dismaying to see the way in which America thwarted or perverted their actions, particularly forcing upon them a government of its choice, and to its great cost.

As costs rose, I was reminded of official communiqués out of Vietnam where "victory" was always just over the next hill and the enemy was beaten – "body counted" – beyond credibility. So, in 2010, I went to see for myself and to talk to everyone I could reach. My *"Impressions of Afghanistan,"* written after talks with everyone I could reach is the subject of my sixth essay.

I came away from my visit with the conviction -- which was shared by both the then American ambassador, General Karl Eikenberry, and the former British ambassador, Sir Sherard Cowper-Coles -- that the war was lost. There was no hope, I concluded, that we could transform the corrupt, weak and rapacious Karzai government into something that would win the support of the Afghans to survive on its own. I was reminded constantly of arguments and observations on Vietnam from my days in the Policy Planning Council.

At the end of my visit, I sat with one of the major former leaders of the Taliban, Mullah Abdus-Salam Zaeef, whose account of his *Life with the Taliban* I had read. The theme that emerged from our talk was that negotiations were imperative and that, if undertaken, they had a reasonable chance of mitigating the worst that might happen and even accomplish to an acceptable degree the fundamental objectives of the Afghans, the Americans and the others.

I found Zaeef impressive; indeed, allowing for the different circumstances I found him to be about as close as an Afghan could be to the South African warrior against apartheid, Nelson Mandela: both had shared long and hideous torture and imprisonment and both emerged from it with truly philosophical calm and sanity.

Consequently, in my seventh essay, *"Toward a Feasible Policy for*

Afghanistan," I reverted to the role I had played under President Kennedy, putting forward a policy for Afghanistan.

So much had happened, so many people had been (or were being) killed and so much hatred had been generated, and so many outsiders had been drawn into the conflict by a decade of war that I decided what was needed was less an American policy than a grand design that include all those with interests in Afghanistan. Above all, of course, was the Afghan people. To guarantee that this paper was not just a set of armchair musings; I had it read by a group of experienced and intelligent men. Among them I have already mentioned the two major Western ambassadors, Karl Eikenberry and Sherard Cowper-Coles. In addition, I sent it to Ambassador Chas Freeman, who was President Obama's choice for what is perhaps the most sensitive post in the American government, chairmanship of the National Intelligence Council, and David Unger, a long-time member of the editorial board of our "newspaper of record," *The New York Times.*

Commenting on it, General Eikenberry, wrote, "You are a very deep strategic thinker [and] I will incorporate your ideas into my own thinking about the way ahead." Sir Sherard Cowper-Coles wrote "A brilliant paper, from which I learnt much." Ambassador Freeman, wrote, "This is, of course, quite brilliant" and David Unger replied, "Your paper is as good as Karl Eikenberry, Sherard Cowper-Coles, Uri Avnery [the prominent Israeli commentator] and Chas Freeman say it is." There is no sign that the President, the Secretary of State or the Secretary of Defense read it although they received copies.

As though the problems of Afghanistan were not enough, the country is ethnically locked to Pakistan. About 14 million Pushtun (4 in 10 Afghans) live in the southern part of the country and the area the British called "the Northwest Frontier." But roughly two-thirds of the Pushtuns -- 25 million -- live in Pakistan where they aggregate about 16%

of the total population. It is in Pushtun territory where two of the major cities of both countries are found. And they are practically neighbors. The capital of Afghanistan, Kabul, is about as far from Islamabad, the capital of Pakistan, as Hartford is from New York City. The two countries were further joined as a result of nearly half a century of war: millions of Afghans fled the fighting first against the Russians and then against one another to camps in Pakistan and about two million remain in Pakistan today.

A single essay, of readable size, is obviously not the place to deal satisfactorily with Pakistan, which has a complex history and is today the sixth most populated country in the world, so I have divided my account into two parts – the forming of Pakistan which I offer in my eighth paper a view of *"The Nature of Pakistan: I The Historical Background"* and my ninth essay, *The Nature of Pakistan: II The Current Reality.*

The Sikh background and British policies have left a residue that deeply affects the country today. As they did elsewhere, the British did much that improved the conquered territory: they built dams, roads and bridges, upgraded crops and spread education. They were also adept at extracting its wealth. Consequently, much of the reason why outside commentators frequently refer to today's Pakistan as a failed state date from the century of British rule. In the name of progress, but often in their self interest, the British ruined essential features of the previous Sikh regime: they impoverished the small cultivators who had worked the agricultural land; favored the growth of huge landed estates worked by tenant laborers living as virtual slaves ("bonded labor") under a generation-to-generation system of debt to often-absent feudal landlords; bought off, subverted or exiled the old ruling class; drained off the national wealth by manipulating the currency; enlarged existing ethnic splits and created new ones; and, putting aside the existing common language, Punjabi, they imposed Urdu, a "minority language," spoken only by 1 in 12 people, as the "national" language and making English the official language. This linguistic policy was aimed at domination. That worked to a degree and for a time.

But when the heavy hand of British rule was lifted, fitting the conflicting pieces into a new whole – putting "Humpty together again"-- has proven an almost impossible task.

The task has been made very much more difficult by Pakistani fear of its even more giant neighbor, India. This led it in recent years to devote massive efforts to acquire nuclear weapons and to build and maintain one of the largest armies in the world. To understand these trends, on which the media has concentrated our attention, one must dig into the past. This the subject of my ninth paper.

In my tenth paper, I turn to Kashmir. There, as I will point out, were planted the "dragon teeth" that Greek myth told us would grow into armed soldiers.

Mainly over Kashmir, Pakistan and India have fought three wars and still engage in "war in the shadows." Struggle for dominance over its land and people has made Kashmir the "Palestine" of the East, a "cancer" of the South Asian body politic.

Ironically, for hundreds of years, Kashmir has been a haven of peace and security. Whereas other societies consecrated monuments to war, Kashmir was famed for its gardens. As the great poet-warrior Emperor Babur of India wrote, "If There Is Heaven On Earth, This Is It, This Is It!" Indian Prime Minister Jawaharlal Nehru, whose family was from Kashmir, was later to write, it was a "mixed but harmonized culture." Under the influence of Sufi Islam, which shares much with St. Francis' interpretation of Christianity, Kashmir became a cultured, open society, guided by what the Kashmiris proudly called "the way of Kashmir," *Kashmiriyat*.

But, in our lifetimes, Kashmir has become a virtual prison,

garrisoned as an enemy country by about half a million Indian troops, where between 50,000 and 100,000 Kashmiris died and thousands more were "disappeared." To understand how this came about, we need to go back to the British conquest of the Sikh empire in 1839 and the breakup of British India in 1947.

In between those events, the Kashmiris "awoke" politically and tried to break out from under conditions in which, as a British official wrote, they were "governed like dumb driven cattle." Governed, that is by the British appointed and supported *maharaja* who doomed hope for a program of moderate reform. Even as late as 1947, when the British were leaving "India," there was no decision on Kashmir. The Kashmiris wanted independence; the ruling maharaja wanted stay in power under Indian "protection" and Nehru agreed to give it if Kashmir joined the new Republic of India; and the British thought that geography and religion (the population was overwhelming Muslim) should make it a part of the about-to-be proclaimed state of Pakistan but prevented the new Pakistan government from effecting its control while allowing India a free hand. In essence, these are the issues that have dominated relations ever since and have caused four wars. If there is another, it could be nuclear.

Also in danger of war is Iran. For the last thirty-five years, since the revolution of 1979 overthrew the regime of Shah Muhammad Pahlavi, Iran and the United States have hovered close to the edge of violent conflict. Arguments about moving from the cold war of sanctions, diplomatic isolation and encouragement of dissidence, to "hot' war has been the subject of almost constant debate in America. I wrote about the danger and offered a way out of the impasse in which successive American administrations have found themselves in an essay I wrote five years ago. I reprint it here without substantive changes because I find that the dangers are still with us and that no serious consideration has been given to how to ameliorate or avoid them. *"Iran: Danger and*

Opportunity" is my eleventh essay.

Another consideration of the Iran "problem" has been on offer more recently. One of the more thoughtful analyses of policy was published in 2010 by a group of former government officials. While I welcomed an intelligent discussion of the dangers and opportunities, I found the later analysis defective and criticized its premises and conclusions. That is the subject of my twelfth paper, *"Reflections on 'weighing the benefits and costs of military action against Iran.'"* As I write, military action is again, and even more strenuously, urged.

For the thirteenth paper, I plunge into a real war much like those fought in Iraq and Afghanistan however with the essential difference that it was mainly – but not wholly -- a civil war of Syrians against one another. As I write, Syria is collapsing into ruin. Years of war have destroyed many of the villages, towns and even some cities; millions of people have been driven into exile. The delightful, friendly, welcoming people I have often visited in past years are now reduced to near savagery; their beautiful cities and monuments largely destroyed.

Some outsiders, particularly journalists, see the events as simply the "good guys" against the "bad." I find that this way of thinking usually leads to self-defeating and/or destructive action and often makes the return to peace almost impossible. So I have endeavored to dig into the Syrian "problem" to show it in its various dimensions. That is the subject of, *"The Syrian Maelstrom."* It takes off from an article by Leslie Gelb, former president of the Council on Foreign Relations, that I found better than many reports but failing to show the variety of issues the Syrian conflict brings forward and which must be dealt with, in some manner, if Syria is ever to recover.

From Syria, I move across the Islamic world to North Africa. I first visited Libya half a century ago when, as a US government official, I was charged with looking for a way to shut down the huge American base in Tripoli. I concluded that the base, however useful it was for the training of NATO pilots, was an irritant to national pride and was likely to cause a revolution. In fact, its existence stimulated the young officers whose *coup d'état* brought Muammar Qaddafi to power. Following events there over the years, I became increasingly convinced that to understand them, and particularly its "Arab Spring" revolution against Qaddafi's regime, one had both to go back into Libya's anti-imperialist struggle and its Islamic past. This is what I attempted in my fourteenth analysis, "*Whence Libya, Why Libya, Whither Libya?*"

"Whither Libya" may turn out to be the next crucial and dangerous issue. The Anglo-American-NATO decision to intervene in Libya inevitably set in motion a scramble by the defeated supporters of the Qaddafi regime for safety. Since many of them were Tuwareg – a partly Berber nomadic people -- it was natural that they would seek to return to the land of their beginning, the great Sahara desert. And, as it did to their ancestors, the desert would force them south to the waters of the Niger river. There they encountered anew their old rivals, the settled villagers, mainly Mandes, of the former French colony that had become Mali. Fighting broke out and for reasons that at least in part had more to do with French domestic politics – the newly installed French president was beset by plunging public opinion polls charging him with weakness -- than with events in Mali. For whatever reason, the French decided to intervene. As it had done to help the French in IndoChina (aka Vietnam), the United States military took a supporting role. Not wholly in jest, it might be said that the Obama administration saw a jihadi warrior, suicide bomber or terrorist on top of every sand dune.

Like some of my former government and academic colleagues and friends, I fear that America has not profited from an understanding of what went wrong in its policies toward Vietnam, Iraq, Somalia and Afghanistan and what could go perhaps even worse in the temptation to repeat those adventures in Syria, Yemen and Mali. For a while in the past and perhaps in the future Mali may justify the title of my fifteenth paper, *"Mali's Quicksand,"* a dangerous bog that I had several times encountered in the desert, in which metaphorically America could sink into a new round of expensive, endless and self-defeating commitments as had happened when the Americans "helped" the French in IndoChina.

In my sixteenth paper, *The Elusive Quest for Security,* which was written for the 2012 Washington Conference on Affordable World Security, I address what is, in a sense, the most difficult problem we as citizens face: how we can be sufficiently secure to carry on our preferred way of life and maintain our freedom.

In my seventeenth essay, *Greece, The Murder of George Polk and The Model for Vietnam,* I return to a theme that has never left my thoughts, the murder of my brother, George Polk, then in Greece as the chief CBS correspondent in the Middle East. I attempt both to put that tragic event in the context of Greek history and also to show how "cold warriors" drew from it the inspiration for what became the main strategy of the Vietnamese war.

I conclude with a sort of sales pitch for this book: we should look before we leap. This is not our usual sequence of action. Long before we even try to understand what motivates other peoples, what they have learned from their own histories, what make up their dreams and nightmares, and how they view their own "Humpty Dumpties," we often rush in to knock him off the wall. Then we spend years, lives and treasure vainly trying to put him back together.

Thus, in conclusion I circle back to what both started me on my quest for understanding of American foreign policy and the events that started American policy into the cold war and its progeny, the wars of Greece, Vietnam, Iraq and Afghanistan. It is perhaps apposite that it was the modern war in Greece that harked back to the legend of Athena telling Cadmus to sow the dragon's teeth that would grow into armed warriors, the warriors with whom we have been contending almost everywhere in Europe, Africa, Asia and Latin America during my long life.

March 7, 2013

CHAPTER 1

US WARS IN IRAQ AND AFGHANISTAN: LESSONS FROM HUMPTY DUMPTY

The CHRISTIAN SCIENCE

MONITOR

Overwhelming American force hasn't been able to restore order. Humpty Dumpty suggests why.

Humpty Dumpty sat on a wall.

Humpty Dumpty had a great fall.

All the king's horses and all the king's men

Couldn't put Humpty together again.

This rhyme that we all learned as children has had many interpretations: the defeat of a king, the explosion of a cannon, the overturn of a siege tower, and even the downfall of President Richard Nixon.

Over the years, people have found the verses memorable because, although apparently simple, they jog us to think about important truths. That is probably why they have endured and are reinterpreted in light of contemporary affairs, age after age.

For our times, "Humpty Dumpty" points to something so taken for granted that we often overlook it: the "social contract."

The social contract is the basis for a healthy, functioning society. Yet it is fragile.

1

American foreign policy in the past decade has been rooted in the notion that overwhelming force – "all the king's horses and all the king's men" – could, in fact, fix a broken social contract (Afghanistan) or create a new, improved one (Iraq).

The results have been unending and tragic costs.

Sometimes written out in constitutions, laws, and treaties, but more often just unwritten custom, the social contract is the convention in which we manage to live relatively peacefully next to one another. Whether written or not, it is based on a consensus of what we think of as "normal" or "right." In more traditional societies, it is referred to as "the way."

Historically, the idea of a social contract probably grew out of kinship. Our remote ancestors, who lived in small clans, were able to get along with one another because they were fathers and children or brothers and sisters. Few were more remote from one another than first cousins.

Then, about 4,000 years ago, clans grew into villages and towns grew into cities. Kinship became too vague or too remote to explain or enforce social peace. Some new means was required.

And, in the urban revolution, the idea of kinship was transformed into neighborhood. One was supposed to treat his neighbor as though he were a kinsman rather than a foreigner or, as foreigner often meant, an enemy.

That was not an easy transformation and is still incomplete, but over the past few thousand years, society after society has struggled with the challenge of making this notion effective.

Traditional pictures of the rhyme suggests this by making Humpty Dumpty a fragile egg.

Where societies succeeded, they created what the rhyme pictures as Humpty, sitting up on a wall, above the occasional rough and tumble, the push and shove, the give and take of daily life, but a presence that in some abstract and idealized way facilitates and brings order to the challenging process of living together.

As long as this "egg" exists and we accept it, we do not need massive and intrusive military force to keep from robbing, raping, or killing one another. Under its benign influence, we mostly continue to do what we do and refrain from what we should not do.

But if Humpty Dumpty is knocked off his perch, we lose our implicit agreement on what is right and proper.

This is more or less what the 17th-century philosophers thought of as returning to the "state of nature."

It evoked the great English philosopher Thomas Hobbes's memorable phrase in which he pictured men living outside the social contract as being in a state of war "of every man, against every man." Living in a time of great turmoil, Hobbes thought that the only way to keep order was by the application of overwhelming force.

We now know that force seldom works.

As we have seen in the attempts to impose order in Baghdad, New Orleans, and Haiti, even overwhelming military force fails. Over the past decade, we stationed a large part of the American Army in Baghdad without bringing back stability.

Indeed, history teaches us that the very act of attempting to impose security often has precisely the opposite effect.

The "trigger" of the American Revolution was the attempt of the British to impose order in Boston by military force in 1775.

The same process can be seen in the tragedy of Somalia. Today in Afghanistan, our nearly 100,000 soldiers are more targets than security forces. Once order is overthrown – Humpty is thrown down from the wall – "All the king's horses and all the king's men" are of no avail.

There is another message we can wring out of the rhyme: If Humpty's fall is not long-term, that is, people do not have time to adjust to a new reality, then he can probably be resurrected by those who have lived under his spell.

Thus, the people of New Orleans and Haiti, while they suffered catastrophes, will probably fairly soon return to living with one another on reasonably satisfactory terms. Their descent into chaos was momentary, and the effects, while horrifying, will probably be self-correcting. This is because, as the usually pessimistic Hobbes tells us, people everywhere really want peace.

But if, on the contrary, the social contract is shattered and remains inoperable for a long period of time, relations of groups of people – particularly if they are easily identified by racial or religious differences – become fixed in new modes and the old shared order is virtually irreparable.

We rather deprecatingly refer to them as "failed societies" and attempt ourselves to impose order or to support warlords or dictators who promise to do so.

That is a danger America would be wise to avoid. The best way to do it is by avoiding pushing Humpty off the wall.

By shattering the social contract, invading and changing a regime (even one we regard as tyrannical) to a new "better" model, we run the risk of leaving in our wake anarchy over which we have no control and which will be a breeding ground for the very forces we thought we were taming. Then the costs to society, both ours and theirs, will be virtually unending.

We would do well to ponder the message of Humpty Dumpty.

June 28, 2010

CHAPTER 2

THE BRITISH TRY TO "REGIME CHANGE" AFGHANISTAN

"The enormous expenditure required for the support of a large force [in Afghanistan] in a false military position at a distance from its own frontier and its resources will no longer be the policy of this government...The British armies in possession of Afghanistan will now be withdrawn [and] will leave it to the Afghans themselves to create a government.

A statement like that would certainly make the headlines in every newspaper in the western world today. But, it would not be "news." It was issued on October 1, 1842 by Britain's Governor-General of India, Lord Ellenborough.

Ellenborough was quicker than the Soviet or American invaders a century later, but even then he was too late. Before he had a chance to reassess what was later to be called the British "forward" policy – an early version of the policy advocated by the neoconservatives today -- insurgency had spread throughout Afghanistan. Wherever British troops were found, they spurred hatred among the Afghans. Finally, the British decided that the cost was too great and the chance of "victory" too small so they began to withdraw. Of the last 16,500 soldiers, civilian men, women and children who retreated from Kabul down the Khyber Pass through what is today known as the Federally Administered Tribal Areas, only one survivor made it to the first British outpost, Jallalabad, the summer capital of Afghanistan.

In the First Afghan war Britain suffered its worst military defeat in the Nineteenth century. And perhaps even more importantly, the defeat "destabilized" the world order. Rebellions against British rule broke out in Sindh (in what is now Pakistan), several British-controlled Indian princely

'Remnants of an Army' by Elizabeth Butler portraying William Brydon arriving at the gates of Jalalabad as the only survivor of a 16,500 strong evacuation from Kabul in January 1842. http://en.wikipedia.org/wiki/File:Remnants_of_an_army2.jpg

states were in turmoil and anger began building against the British in the decaying Mughal empire toward the great "Mutiny" of 1857. The dramatic defeat in Afghanistan convinced other European powers, some of the still unconquered parts of the Indian subcontinent and even Britain's colonies that Britain's "day" was over.

II

So who were these empire-wreckers, these Afghans?

The short answer was that they were the inhabitants of one of the few countries that were not incorporated into an empire in the age of imperialism. They remained independent because Afghanistan was simply too remote, too barren and too poor to be colonized. Composed of deep valleys, rugged mountains and high plateaus, scattered along one of the world's great mountain ranges and huge, salty deserts with patches of quicksand in the south and west, it is a vast area about the size of Colorado and New Mexico combined. Afghanistan is *rough* – with lands rising from 258 meters above sea level to 7,485 meters -- *brutal* – with torrential wind,

6

rain and snow interspersed with searing heat and drought -- *dry* – with less than 12 percent of the land even partly arable -- and *warlike* – with every man armed and eager for a fight.

An aerial view of mountains in Afghanistan April 23, 2008 U.S. Air Force photo

Few foreigners tried to conquer it, but over the centuries some used Afghanistan as a highway – the Chinese made pilgrimages across the deserts and mountains to the seats of Buddhist learning, Alexander the Great and his successors gingerly picked their ways through deep defiles toward the subcontinent and Mongol conquerors stormed through its passes in pursuit of world domination. Just to the south lay the rich, densely populated collection of kingdoms we know today as India. It was India that drew Alexander, Tamerlane, Babur, Nadir Shah, Ivan the Terrible, Tsar Alexander, Napoleon, Queen Victoria, Kaiser Wilhelm and Stalin toward it. Few invading armies managed to stay long, but most left behind graves to mark their passage.

What made Afghanistan resistant to conquerors paradoxically made it a refuge. Many of today's people are descendants of Central Asians who first fought and then fled from the relentless Russian invasions begun by Ivan the Terrible and carried forth under the later Tsars and Commissars. Others are relics of passing armies – some claim descent from Alexander the Great's Macedonian legionnaires, the *pezhetairoi*, and others from Genghis Khan's Mongol horsemen, the *ordu*. Keeping their customs and languages, today's Afghans are divided among twenty-one ethnic/cultural communities, speaking an extraordinary variety of tongues derived from the Indo-European, Semitic and Ural-Altaic language families. The languages themselves encapsulate Afghan history.

These ethnic and linguistic divisions appear to be the most significant ways to think of Afghan society, but they are not. There is a more fundamental

7

division that has shaped Afghan history and the people's response to outsiders. This division arises from the fact that no group, tribe or village could become very large because water is almost everywhere in desperately short supply. So most people lived in communities that rarely numbered more than a few hundred men, women and children. Living apart in small clefts in the mountains and separated from other communities by often impassable terrain, they were able to maintain cultural differences. So, each of Afghanistan's 22 thousand or so villages functioned as a tiny nation-state.

When I first traveled throughout Afghanistan as an American government officer in 1962, I visited numbers of these villages, met many of their headmen and observed how they ran their affairs. It seemed to me then that one could visualize Afghanistan as a rough field covered by 22 thousand Ping-Pong balls. Each "ball" was autarkic, discrete, inwardly focused. No single ball depended upon or could dominate the others, and no village elder seemed to know much about events or conditions among nearby but often inaccessible neighbors. His mandate was strictly local.

The little communities, villages or subdivisions of tribes, clung as tenaciously to their few fertile acres of land as the ancient Greek "warring states" had clung to theirs. They had to because the alternative was starvation. Life was grim, resources were scarce and almost each day brought an actual or potential battle for survival.

Like later American visitors, I brought with me to Afghanistan preconceived and rather simplistic ideas. At that time in Washington one "buzzword" (then much favored by the Defense Department) was "impact package." An impact package was a donation that supposedly would win natives' "hearts and minds." The Defense Department had recently put one together to win back the Algerians whom we had been helping the French to kill. Providing the drums and trumpets for a military band was at best a joke and didn't work with the Algerians, but would a better one work in Afghanistan? We had been trying to find one that would. Roads, airports and irrigation projects didn't seem to make much difference then – nor do they today. But I was told to keep looking.

Stopping one day near a tiny village, I was invited, indeed almost kidnapped, to a meal. As I tried to bite into a piece of what vaguely resembled chicken – a great luxury for my hosts – I got the idea that our AID program might do as well providing these wretchedly

HERAT, Afghanistan--The view of a western Afghanistan village (ISAF photo)

poor people with a simpler, cheaper but more meaningful impact package – tender, fat, hybrid American chickens -- as building expensive and then little used highways. I was soon brought to reality. One of my more experienced companions, a road builder from Texas, looked at me with scorn: "why do you think those chickens look like that?" He asked. "Hell, nothing but eagles could survive up here."

He was right. To survive, even the Afghans themselves had to be eagles. So every experience, every instinct, turned them inward to their small group of close relatives (their *qawm*). Just beyond the next hill were enemies, even if also cultural or biological kinsmen, whose hand was always raised against them. Hands did not stray far from trigger or handle.

I was struck, as all visitors have been, by the fact that the Afghans, who had so little to hold life together, were fiercely independent. In their three attempts to conquer the Afghans, the British lost heavily and lashed back in fury, even burning whole villages and massacring the inhabitants. In the decade-long war they began in 1979 the Russians found that, with their tanks, helicopter gunships and bombers, they could crush any number of "ping pong balls," but they could never negotiate more than a temporary truce, village by village, and so tried to crush them all. They killed about a million people and drove another three million out of the country. But

9

Afghanistan, this collection of thousands of tiny city-states, outlasted them. Worn out, the *Shuravi* – as the Afghans called the Russians -- gave up in February 1989. As they crossed the Amu Darya river north into the Soviet Union, they left behind the bodies of about 15,000 of their soldiers. The Afghans did not then know it, but they had also killed the Soviet Union.

III

Unlike the more cynical British invaders, whose "education" in imperialism came from India, the Soviet leaders believed that the Afghans really wanted to adopt their way of life. They had some reason in addition to ideology for this belief. The Soviet record in Central Asia was, objectively speaking, better than the British record in India. Neither power had allowed significant political freedom, but the Russians had provided better health, better working conditions and more useful education than the British.

So, the Soviet leaders and their local acolytes were sure that, even if only secretly or vaguely, the Afghans wanted what they wanted, that in every Afghan heart was a potential Communist. In more recent times, Americans have adopted the same way of thinking: Afghans are potential American-style democrats. We only had to create conditions where their true selves could be expressed and their true desires be fulfilled.

This is an old theme in political philosophy: Rousseau was willing even to force men to be free – that is, to be like us -- a thought for which he was attacked by the Jesuit and monarchist philosopher Joseph de Maistre in a memorable epigram[1] that the Russians and the Americans should have heeded: if people do not do as we think and act like we think they should, perhaps acting as they do is mandated by their particular culture or, as de Maistre would have it, by their nature. As he criticized Rousseau's desire – and anticipated both the Russians and our attempts -- "it is as if one were to ask why sheep,[2] who are born carnivorous nevertheless everywhere nibble grass." The Afghans, like people everywhere, were (and are) guided by their own beliefs and customs.

---

1   I am grateful to Isaiah Berlin for drawing my attention to it.
2   De Maistre's simile was more apt than he probably knew: the British and the Ottoman Turks both referred to their subjects as sheep (*ryot*, in the British Indian vocabulary).

The British would have none of this nonsense. Implicit in their doctrine was the sure belief that sheep eat grass. Period. No point was to be gained by hoping (or fearing) that they would rise above that level. So the wise policy was to give them enough grass to keep them from trying to become carnivores. It was a simple policy and it worked pretty generally for quite a while. Military power was exhibited to fence in the fields where the sheep were allowed to graze and was used, usually reluctantly and economically, to punish those who otherwise might stray. "Grass" was money. The British were quite open and direct in using it. Repeatedly, in the accounts of their dealing with the Indian states, the Iranians and the Afghans, would be rebels were paid off. But, as the British and the Russians found, when the Afghans believed that their way of life was being violated, every man prided himself on his willingness to fight.

In the daily course of events, some problems could not be solved by gun or knife. This was particularly so with close relatives. So the Afghans, like many peoples, developed a system of arbitrage. The adult males of each community would gather in what they called a *jirga*. In that meeting, their problems would be discussed under the supervision of a respected elder, a *khan* or *malik*. Such figures were known in the Greek Resistance in World War II as "responsible men," *ipefthinos*.

Finally, in a way remarkably similar to the practice of the "Long House" of the Native American Iroquois, in days or even weeks of talk, tensions would be worked off and a consensus finally reached. After the consensus was reached, life could go on because it was considered sinful to oppose the decision of the *jirga*. Anyone who did risked losing his membership in the community and, on being forced out, would become, literally, an outlaw.

Since not all problems were local, *jirgas* were occasionally assembled among neighboring groups. This was particularly the custom when tribes or villages felt threatened by foreigners. Again, we can see the custom as one familiar in Western experience. The Americans, the French and the Russians formed similar groups during their revolutions – known respectively as Committees of Safety, *Comité de salut public* and *Soviets*. Even the short-lived Republic of Texas set up "Committees of Safety and Correspondence"

11

in 1832. Such groups were both administrators of customary law and political forums.

On rare occasions in Afghanistan, a great assembly, a *loya jirga*, would convene to deal with "national" issues. This assembly, rather than what we think of as executive departments of government or a sitting parliament, is still today the ultimate Afghan constitutional assembly.

Particularly in tribal societies or societies divided by natural barriers – both of which are evident in Afghanistan -- *jirgas* were not always successful. So, ultimately each man was the guardian of his individual honor and protector of his individual rights. Thus, he might act alone, in company with his close kinsmen or under the guidance of a revered leader to protect against or avenge an insult, a theft of property or the killing or wounding of a member of his group. Vengeance remained an imperative.

Countervailing forces had to be powerful to overcome this intense inward and violent custom. And they were. As I found on my first visit in 1962, people living in a poverty no one in the Western world had ever experienced would literally starve themselves to entertain guests. That chicken I had such trouble swallowing was the symbol of *melmastia*. *Melmastia* (roughly, hospitality) was the absolute obligation of every man, no matter how poor. And *melmastia* did not stop with food. As a guest, I was under the protection of my hosts who would have defended me to their last breaths.

That is why, even when the American government offered as a "dead or alive" reward for Usama bin Ladin a sum beyond the dreams of avarice, no Afghan came forth to surrender him. The offer was not so much tempting as insulting to the Afghan code of honor (the *nang-i Pukhtun*). To have accepted would have brought shame (*sharm*). So I turn to Afghan beliefs and customs.

IV

While the British and the Russians could never benefit from it, the "ping pong balls" did have a pattern. Overarching the collection of autonomous communities are shared beliefs and customs. Although there are regional, religious and ethnic variations, they interweave to form, symbolically appropriately for Afghanistan, a virtual "carpet" in which society and culture become durable even under incredible adversity.

The strong backing, the "warp," of the social carpet is a shared code of custom. Along the southern frontier, this is known as the *Pushtunwali*. With local variations, this body of custom is shared throughout the land and tightly binds each individual to a sense of duty and right.

By the *Pushtunwali* each individual has the absolute obligation to defend his kinsmen and guests. Should he fail in this duty, he must take vengeance (*badal*) against the aggressor or his kinsmen. If he does not, he loses his sense of self esteem (*meranah*) and becomes despised even within his family. In theory, since there is no effective police force, the certainty of *badal* defends the lone traveler; in practice, it has made Afghanistan an armed camp in which the finger of every man rests on the trigger of his rifle. Feuds over real or imagined insults or attacks fester for generations. Afghanistan is the true land of the Hatfields and McCoys.

This shared code enables us to understand why today's drone bombings and the practice of night raids and torture produce the opposite effect than those who do them expect: every time a person is harmed, his immediate family, his clan and his whole tribe have the absolute obligation to avenge him. This, of course, is what makes today's "targeted assassinations" self-defeating. Every person killed brings forth the hatred of all his relatives, just as it did in Scotland where societies resembled in some ways the Afghans. One bitter result of this was the Afghan vengeance against the British in 1841; the whole "tribe" of the English paid in blood for the sins of their leaders.

As I observed all over Afghanistan -- in the center of the vast Hindu Kush, down in the salt deserts and quicksand of the southwest and up along the northern frontier -- every man, woman and child is knotted into the Afghan "carpet."

And, just as the "warp" of a rug is strengthened by the "weft," so Afghan society is braced by religious belief. In no Islamic country have I seen people so uniformly and comprehensively religious. Long before anyone in the West heard of today's Taliban,[3] about one Afghan man in each dozen thought of himself as a *mulla* or lay preacher. And in the 1840s, almost everyone thought that the only way to fight the English was to unify under Islam.

This was a traditional concept. The religious leader of the little state of Swat in the North West Frontier district of what is now Pakistan is reported to have then addressed a *jirga* of tribal leaders, saying[4] "The British are fast laying the foundations of their rule deep in our homelands…It is, therefore, the prime need of the hour that we should form an Islamic state, which, besides being a religious obligation, can safeguard our interests and secure us from their subjection." A century later, one of guerrilla leaders in the war against the Russians told an English visitor in the same spirit, "the most precious thing we have is our faith; without it we have nothing."

Overarching ethnic groups, linguistic divisions, and mutually hostile communities is the commitment to Islam. Like the other aspects of Afghan culture, it is both divided and shaped by history, geography and mission. Along the western frontier, where Iranian influence has been strong, Shiism predominates, but there, as well as in the high valleys of the Hindu Kush range, where the Aimaq and Hazara peoples live, and in the far northeast, near Tajikistan, Shiism takes on a distinctively Afghan cast; in the north on the plain between the Hindu Kush and the Amu Darya river (the modern frontier with the former Soviet Union), the Afghans are mostly speakers of a dialect of Turkish and like most Turks practice Sunnism. The largest group of Afghans are the Pushtun who occupy virtually the whole of the country south of the Hindu Kush mountains. They are Sunnis and think of themselves as "pure" or fundamentalist Muslims although the Islam they practice is deeply influenced by what must be pre-Islamic customs. Indeed, some of their practices of customary law (*ravaj*) violate Quranic injunctions.

---

3   The earliest reference I have seen to the Taliban referred to the followers of the religious leader, the Akhund, of the little state of Swat in what is now Pakistan. He put together a militia of Afghan *taliban ul-ilm* (students of religious knowledge) in 1835 to support the then Afghan king against the Sikhs of the Punjab. André Singer, *Lords of the Khyber*, 180.
4   Quoted in Singer 183.

Islam arose in an Arab tribal society and tribal Afghans adapted to it easily. The aspect we focus on today is the concept of religious struggle (*jihad*) and propensity of Afghans to see themselves as warriors of the faith (*mujahidin*). That is the way most Afghans saw their fight against the Russians in 1979-1989 and see it in their fight against us today; it was the way the Afghans saw their fight against the British in 1841. So knowing what happened should provide valuable lessons. I now turn to the British experience.

V

Before Lord Ellenborough issued his order to quit Afghanistan, the Afghans and the Sikhs of the Punjab had wrestled with one another over the lands in between -- Kashmir, Sindh, Baluchistan and what came to be called "the Northwest Frontier." Fear of the disciplined and well-armed forces of the great Sikh leader, Ranjit Singh, caused the then Afghan ruler, Dost Muhammad, to request British intervention in their dispute. He made the mistake many Indian princes had made and thereby had lost their independence.

Trained by a century of experience with the ambitions and fears of the myriad Indian principalities and the Mughal empire behind them, the British were initially cautious. So Lord Ellenborough's immediate predecessor, Lord Auckland, took the high road of morality: Britain did not interfere in the affairs of other states, he said. The reality was that the British were not yet ready to take the next leap forward in their move toward empire. They soon perceived a threat which gave them both a reason and an opportunity, and they took it.

The reason and the opportunity were partly the gift of the Tsar. Like the British, the Russians had long been expanding their empire. It was inevitable that their outward thrusts – the Russians to the south and the British to the north -- would clash. Some encounters were armed while others were diplomatic; some with troops and others by single individuals. The struggle for the ancient city of Herat offers examples of each form of conflict.

Using the Iranians (a.k.a. the Persians) as proxies, the Russians added a "stiffening" of Russian troops. The Russians obviously saw Herat as both a base for further moves and as a way to win the Iranians as allies. The British got involved when a young English artilleryman, Eldred Pottinger, then on a spying mission, turned up to offer his advice on the city's defense. Pottinger became the "media" hero of the day in England when the Iranians and Russians failed to take the city.[5]

For the Russians, Herat was an affordable but not crucial gamble, and they had already decided to go around Herat by sending a diplomatic mission, protected by an escort of Cossacks, direct to Kabul. The mission was led by Captain Ivan Victkevich (a.k.a Jan Witkiewicz), a Polish officer in the Tsar's army,[6] The British weighed Victkevich's mission in the scales of their own actions – that is, as preparation for a Russian move "forward" -- and were furious. Success at Herat seemed to be about to turn into defeat in Kabul. So on March 6, 1838 they issued a most undiplomatic ultimatum to the Afghan ruler, Dost Muhammad Khan:[7]

> You must desist from all correspondence with Persia and Russia; you must never receive agents from [them] or have aught to do with him [sic] without our sanction; you must dismiss Captain Vickovitch [sic, the Russian agent] with courtesy; you must surrender all claims to Peshawar on your own account, as that chiefship [sic] belongs to Maharaja Runjeet Sing [sic]; you must also respect the independence of Candahar [Qandahar] and of Peshawar, and co-operate in arrangements to unite your family.

While the loss of territories must have been infuriating to Dost Muhammad Khan, it was British intervention in family rivalries that were

---

5   The major cause of the Irano-Russian defeat was not his action but a British armed incursion into western Iran; the British were determined to stop the Russians and the already shaky Iranian regime wisely ducked the threat by withdrawing from Herat. As William Dalrymple points out in his excellent recent book, *Return of a King*, Pottinger's role is at least questionable.

6   On the "players" in the Great Game, see Peter Hopkirk, *The Great Game*, 165 ff. For a drawing of Vickovich see William Dalrymple's, following page 152. Dalrymple is unique among historians on Afghanistan in using Persian-language sources.

7   *Parliamentary Papers, 1959,* 177, quoted in Louis Dupree, *Afghanistan,* 371-372.

most disturbing to the Afghan ruler. With long experience in dealing with Indian dynasties the British had put their finger on the most sensitive issue in oriental politics, the rivalries between half brothers.[8] Dost Muhammad Khan had little control over "your family" whom he realized the British could use against him and certainly none over the former king, Shah Shuja, the exiled leader of the rival tribal confederacy whom the British would install as "their man in Kabul." Moreover, it would be hard to find a statement more insulting to a man guided by *Pushtunwali* than outsiders, and worse, Christian foreigners, dabbling in the family affairs. Thus, in his turn Dost Muhammad Khan was furious and publicly received the Russian agent. That was the move that determined the fate of Afghanistan.

The then Governor General of India, Lord Auckland, like today's Neoconservatives, determined to "regime change" Afghanistan. His advisers, also like today's Neoconservatives, thought could it could be done easily and cheaply. But, unlike today's "hawks," the British could draw on cheap Asian warriors. It was with a British-commanded "Army of the Indus" made up of Indians, Nepalese, and Punjabi Sikhs that they set out for Afghanistan.

It was to be a difficult journey. Between British India and Afghanistan were long stretches of desert, narrow passes through the mountains and hostile people. The great Sikh ruler, Ranjit Singh, refused permission for the British troops to pass through his kingdom. He was wise to do so because, living off the land as armies then customarily did, they destroyed crops, pillaged towns and disrupted tax collection. So the main British column was forced to swing south through Sindh and Baluchistan. The parallel to the American supply problem in Afghanistan today is evident: Pakistan has been an unwilling conduit for American troops, equipment and food, forcing the Americans also to use another, more difficult and more costly route. America could, of course, use aircraft, but the British army had only elephants and camels. And, as the American demands on Pakistan created a new set of enemies, so did the British demands on Sindh and Baluchistan.

---

8   Already nearly 1,500 years before, the Indian counterpart to Machiavelli and Sun Tzu, Kautilya (aka Vishnagupta) wrote in the *Arthasastra* that a ruler's most dangerous enemies are his relatives, the half-brother products of multiple marriages whose mothers pit them against one another. As he wrote, princes "like crabs have a notorious tendency of eating their begetter." See my *Neighbors and Strangers* (Chicago, 1997) 231-232.

Troops at Kandahar in 1880
http://en.wikipedia.org/wiki/
File:Troops_at_Kandahar_1880.jpg

As the English chronicler of the war, John Kaye, has written,[9] "the British Government had not only announced its intention to assist the long-exiled monarch in his attempt to regain his crown, but had encouraged him to assert long dormant claims, and had announced its intention to march an army into the country of the Ameers [Sindh] , to plant a subsidiary force there, to compel the Princes of Sindh to pay for it, to knock down and set up the Princes themselves at discretion, to take possession of any part of the country that might be wanted for our own purposes – in fact, to treat Sindh and Baloochistan [sic] in all respects as though they were petty principalities of our own.

That the Ameers thus struggling in our grasp, conscious of their inability openly to resist oppression, should have writhed and twisted, and endevoured to extricate themselves by the guile which might succeed, rather than by the strength which could not, was only to follow the universal law of nature in all such contests between then weak and the strong.

In short, the campaign began badly. It would end worse. In between, as Kaye continued, "Throughout the entire period of British connection with Afghanistan, a strange moral blindness clouded the visions of our statesmen…"[10]

The Anglo-Indian "onslaught" was one Kipling would have described as of "more-than-Oriental splendour." In addition to the actual fighting men, initially about 9,500 and rising to 21,000, most of whom were Indians, came nearly 40,000 camp followers (wives, mistresses, whores, seamstresses, moneychangers, tailors, cooks, grooms, butlers, handymen, priests, *mullas*, magicians and children), each with his own baggage and carried by about 30,000 camels. The British officers needed scores of camels and some even used elephants – the commander carried his "kit" on 260 camels. And the kit

---

9   In his classic 1890 *History of the War in Afghanistan*, I, 402-403.
10 *History of the War in Afghanistan*, I, 402-403, 423.

was what a British officer in India demanded: crystal chandeliers, a portable bathtub, a mobile wine cellar, multiple uniforms and ball dresses, an orchestra and all manner of sports equipment, including of course cricket bats, to be cared for by dozens of servants. Even a junior officer was allowed to bring six servants.

Much of the task of provisioning this vast multitude was carried out on by contractors to whose tender mercies and voracious appetites they entrusted, as we do today, much of their comfort and safety. The British expeditionary force was a city in motion.

Obviously, the officers put a higher priority upon comfort and style than upon food and fodder. They would soon pay the price for this choice in the desolate sandy wastes of what is now southwestern Pakistan. As food and fodder were used up, with no other source of supply within reach, and with the baggage camels dropping dead "by the scores on the desert," the troops were put on quarter rations. An Asian soldier got half the ration of the European soldier and camp followers got only half of that. They had no option but to stagger on. The "road" got worse. It took the army ten days to pass through the 60-mile-long daunting Bolan Pass. Then, as Kaye wrote, "Starvation was beginning to stare his [the British general's] troops in the face."

Entrance to the Bolan Pass from Dadur by James Atkinson, 1780-1852 from *Sketches in Afghanistan* (sic).As the Superintending Surgeon of the Army of the Indus, Bengal Division he accompanied the troops into Afghanistan for the First Afghan War and witnessed the 1839 capture of Kabul. His fortuitous recall to India before the winter of 1840 saved his life.

Poor planning and ignorance of the country was magnified by faulty intelligence on the people. Like both the later Russians and the Americans, the British believed what they wanted to believe rather than what they saw and heard. The army commander wrote that "Notwithstanding all the croaking about Shah Soojah's want of popularity, [I] feel certain that my prediction will be verified, and that his Majesty will be cordially welcomed by all classes of the people... [the entry into Qandahar in April] was received with feelings nearly amounting to adoration [and] the best feeling is manifested toward the British officers by the entire population here..."

Reality came slowly and was deferred or hidden as long as possible. But even the senior political official, the Envoy, Sir William Macnaghten, admitted in a letter to the Governor General of India, as the troops slowly marched toward Kabul – reaching which took four months -- that "Our officers and our measures are alike unpopular in this country." Based on Macnaghten's unpublished letters, Kaye wrote[11] that

> "It was becoming clearer to him [Macnaghten] every day that the Afghans regarded the intrusion of the British into their dominions with the strongest feelings of national hatred and religious abhorrence...They were not to be bought by British gold, or deluded by British promises...not to be reduced to loyalty by Douranne Kings [the British appointed rulers-to-be], nor to subjection by foreign bayonets."

At each occasion when they had expected an enthusiastic popular turnout, they saw instead, as one of the British officers wrote, a "most mortifying indifference." When Shah Shuja was to be reinstalled by the British as king in a suitably grand occasion, "barely a hundred Afghans had been attracted, either by curiosity or by loyalty..." The Afghan view of the Karzai regime in contemporary American-controlled Afghanistan offers a similar lack of commitment that has been witnessed by almost all the Western ambassadors and journalists.

So what could the British do? Arms were one answer; money was the other. Based on his experiences, talks with surviving British officers, their

---

11 *History of the War in Afghanistan.* Volume I, Book III, 451.

correspondence and official reports, Kaye wrote[12] that to prepare the way for their man in Kabul,

Two Afghan soldiers (one Kohistani and one Hazara) poses with their jezail rifles in Kabul, Afghanistan, circa 1878/80. Photo by John Burke

From Kashmir to Kabul The Photographs of John Burke and William Baker 1860-1900.

> Money had been freely scattered about; and the Afghans had already begun to discover that the gold of the Feringhees [the Christian Europeans] was as serviceable as other gold, and that there was an unfailing supply of it. Early in the campaign, [Sir William] Macnaghten had encouraged the conviction that the allegiance of the Afghans was to be bought – that Afghan cupidity would not be proof against British gold. So he opened the treasure-chest; scattered abroad its contents with an ungrudging hand; and commenced a system of corruption which, though seemingly successful at the outset, wrought, in the end, the utter ruin of the policy he had reared.

Force of arms was the other option the British had. Their disciplined sepoy soldiers were backed by artillery, a weapon that few Afghans had or knew how to use effectively. But in other weapons, they were not well served. The British infantrymen and Indian sepoy were equipped with the "Brown Bess" musket which dated from the Napoleonic wars and had a range of little more than a hundred yards whereas the Afghans' armed themselves

---

12   *History of the War in Afghanistan* I, 435-436. As has long been widely believed and has been confirmed in recent days (*The New York Times*, April 28, 2013; *The Guardian*, April 30, 2013, and Gary Collins (sortilegus@hotmail.com), America embarked on essentially the same policy. (Mr. Collins is Senior Adviser, Program Manager for Criminal Justice at United Nations Office on Drugs and Crime in Kabul.) The articles, editorials and Mr. Collins confirm the passing of "ghost money" from both the US and Britain "in the tens of millions" to Afghan Prime Minister Hamid Karzai. Whereas the costs of the British campaigns were borne by India, the costs of the American campaign were borrowed from China.

with a 75 caliber, flintlock, muzzle-loading musket dating from the American revolution. The Brown Bess was more modern, but the "long rifles," which the Afghans called the *Jazail*,[13] had a range of about a mile. British troops were literally outgunned. American troops in Afghanistan would similarly later complain that their modern, light-weight rifles were under a similar disadvantage when compared with the old weapons the Afghans had seized from the Russians.

At some point in the fighting, the British developed the favored counterinsurgency device of our times, the improvised explosive device, the IED.[14] There is no indication that the Afghans then used it; they later learned about it from their fighting with the British.

The British problem wasn't only in equipment; the Afghan warriors were valiant. In the fighting later in Kabul, the Ghazis even broke the British square – then considered the ultimate defense tactic, dating back to Waterloo. While not so disciplined as the British soldiers, the Afghans defeated them in several formal battles. And, in terms of morale, particularly toward the end of the occupation, the Afghans realized that they were fighting for their homeland; the Indian sepoys and the English troops were not.

After a series of battles for towns in the Helmand valley, the British entered Kabul in August 1839. There, they and their choice as ruler, Shah Shujah, were boycotted by the whole population. But, the by then disheartened king, Dost Muhammad, concluded that his people were not yet ready to repulse the British onslaught and, after a desperate retreat all the way north to Bukhara, where he was briefly imprisoned in a dungeon, he meekly surrendered to the British envoy to be sent off in exile to India.[15]

Having taken over Kabul easily, the British made themselves at home. The British chief political officer Alexander Burnes wrote to a friend about

---

13 The *jazail* was the original counterinsurgency weapon; it was developed to put down the American insurrection. I have one in my study, with the stock remade in Afghanistan and the English-made barrel marked "Amory 1779." As General Sir Andrew Skeen, who spent most of his life fighting the Afghans, wrote in *Passing it On*, "The accuracy of these people's shooting is sometimes astounding... I saw four men knocked out by one sniper, known to have been fifteen hundred yards [almost a mile] off..."
14 For the IED see *Passing* it on 9-10.
15 His surrender is described by George Pottinger, *The Afghan Connection*, 107.

the life he lived and the table he kept with "smoked fish, salmon gills, devils and jellies [washed down with] champagne, hock, Madeira, sherry, port, claret, not forgetting the hermetically sealed salmon and hotch potch, all the way fra [sic] Aberdeen. And deuced good it is..."[16]

Had Burnes stopped with the delights of his table, he would probably have lived longer, but he also amply supplied his bed. Like other British officers who had not sufficiently supplied themselves from India, he found willing consorts among the female population. Although already an experienced veteran of "the Great Game," he cast aside what he knew of Afghan customs and created for himself a *zenana* (harem) of courtesans like the British had enjoyed in the early days of their residence in Calcutta. Apparently, he went further and dallied with the daughters and wives of the Afghan notables.

As William Dalrymple has written,[17] "...In this way he made himself the hate figure he remains to this day in Afghanistan; and it was this, according to the Afghan accounts, that helped spark the final fatal explosion in Kabul and his own gruesome death on 2 November [1841]."

After a particularly lurid episode during which Burnes took in a favorite slave girl of one of the principal tribal leaders and had the retainers of her owner beaten for coming to his house to retrieve her, a *jirga* was assembled to decide what to do. The furious jilted lover addressed his fellow notables, saying,[18]

> Now we are justified in throwing off this English yoke; they stretch the hand of tyranny to dishonor private citizens great and small: fucking a slave girl isn't worth the ritual bath that follows it: but we have to put a stop right here and now otherwise the English will ride the donkey of their desires into the field of stupidity, to the point of having all of us arrested shortly and deported into foreign imprisonment. I put my trust in God and raise the battle standard of our

---

16 John Kaye, *Lives of Indian Officers*, II, 282-283, quoted in Dalrymple, *Return of a King*, 201.
17 *Return of a King*, 260.
18 *Return of a King* 261, quoting from the account of Mirz Ata, *Naway Maavek* "The Song of Battles", 215-220.

Prophet Muhammad, and thus go to fight: if success rewards us, then that is as we wished; and if we die in battle, that is still better than to live with degradation and dishonour."

By then, after the Afghans had murdered Burnes, it was probably too late, but in the weeks and months before the final break, the Afghans continued to propose that they negotiate an end to the British occupation. In a letter to Sir William Macnaghten, on behalf of tribal leaders, a confidant and distant relative of the British puppet king, set forth the proposed terms[19], "...their sole desire," wrote Lt. Vincent Erye, "being that we should quietly evacuate the country, leaving them to govern it according to their own rules, and with a king of their own choosing.

By that time, fighting between the Afghans and the British had become general. The British had laid out their encampment in the same spirit as their food, drink and women: not minding the topography of Kabul, they picked the lower ground, overlooked by excellent sniper locations, and exposed their troops to guerrilla tactics. As casualties mounted and food reserves diminished, morale of the Indian and English soldiers collapsed. Soldiers refused orders, began to fight one another, ran away and, as I mentioned, even allowed their ultimate defensive disposition, the square, to be broken. At their wits end, the commanders began to consider how to get out.

The British military commander, General Elphinstone advised Macnaghten to negotiate, pointing out that they had been in a state of siege for three weeks, that the whole force was surrounded, that winter was approaching, that food and ammunition were running low, that there was no prospect of resupply or reinforcement, and "with the whole country in arms against us."[20]

It was already too late. The Afghans had tasted the blood of the hated invaders and knew they were winning. When the British delayed, the Afghans upped the ante. As Lt. Erye summarized the Afghan demand, it was

---

19   Erye, *The Military Operations at Cabul,* 122. Erye was there and apparently read the letter dated November 26.
20   Erye, *The Military Operations at Cabul,* 123 ff for this and following quotations including the British offers and the Afghan replies.

"That we should deliver up Shah Shoojah [the British-installed ruler] and his whole family; lay down our arms; and make an unconditional surrender; when they might perhaps be induced to spare our lives, and allow us to leave the country on condition of never returning." That was on November 27.

Macnaghten refused those terms and both sides fixed on battle. The engagements around the British positions used up ammunition but failed to create any security. Still Macnaghten delayed. Then, after two weeks, he again sought the advice – in writing and in a public letter, presumably to protect his reputation – of General Elphinstone. Also in writing, the General was emphatic: negotiate on how to get out.

Parenthetically, I must draw attention to three aspects of this exchange in comparison with practice in our times: first, the men on the spot were necessarily required to act on their own since they could not be guided from afar. Today, particularly non-military officials are guided even on small matters by remote control; second, regardless of rank or the nature of their appointment, military commanders usually then and today take precedence over political or diplomatic officials and, third, even in the most desperate conditions, most men, like Sir William Macnaghten, worry at least as much about their reputations as their lives. Afghanistan offers us close parallels today to events in 1840.

So Macnaghten went out of the British lines on December 11 to meet with the Afghan chiefs – whom he said "might be considered the mouth-piece of the people," that is, although he did not use the term, a *jirga* – to propose new terms.[21] He proposed "that the British should evacuate Afghanistan [sic]" that "no British force should be ever again sent into Afghanistan unless called for by the Afghan government, between whom and the British nation perpetual friendship should be established on the sure foundation of mutual good offices." The British contingent would be allowed to return unmolested to India. Money was to be paid and "amnesty should be granted to all those who had made themselves obnoxious on account of their attachment to Shah Shoojah and his allies, the British." (Would something like this issue figure in any negotiations following the American withdrawal and the collapse of the

---

21 It is perhaps more than a historical coincidence that I was told by one of the former senior leaders of the Taliban movement that "if you do not negotiate, they [the Taliban] will take it all."

Karzai regime today, one should ponder.) The former king, Dost Muhammad Khan and all other Afghans in exile would be allowed to return. Finally, "all prisoners should be released." (Again, this will probably be an issue in any end to the war today; today, of course, prisoners pose a far more complex issue since they are held not only in various prisons in Afghanistan, but in Guantánamo and elsewhere, are of various nationalities and are regarded as operating against the West in a number of other countries.)

Macnaghten hedged some of his terms, leaving them for later detailed negotiations – obviously after the British aim of getting its expeditionary force safely out of the country had been accomplished – and sought to include an advantage for British policy by proposing that Britain should "enter into a treaty with Russia, defining the bounds beyond which neither were to pass in Central Asia." That would make such ventures as the Herat battle and the mission of Captain Victkevich impossible or at least less likely.

Most of the Afghan chiefs agreed, but not the son of the exiled king. He apparently did not trust the British to allow his father freedom to return from exile and expected them to renege on promises if their fortunes changed. He was at least partially right: the British would later take a terrible vengeance on the Afghans.[22]

Two more weeks were taken up with running battles between the dwindling forces of the British and the rapidly gathering Afghan tribesmen and religious devotees, then often called the *ghazis*. Each side thought the other treacherous: the British clung to the hope that a fresh force would arrive from Qandahar or Jalalabad so that they could overwhelm the Afghans and they tried to divide the Afghan leaders against one another[23] with the promise of money and enhanced positions; as Erye observed, "The strength of the rebels had hitherto lain in their unanimity; the proposed stroke of policy

---

22   During the British invasion the next year, in November 1841, after vicious fighting around Qandahar when ghazis wiped out a British detachment of 130 men near Ghazni the British "slaughtered every man, woman and child" within the village of Killah-Chuk, (John Kaye *History of the War in Afghanistan*, iii, 138, cited in Dupree, *Afghanistan*, 395) The British then forcibly cleared most of the population from Qandahar. When his forces retook Kabul, General Pollock ordered the destruction of the great bazar in Kabul and the charming nearby resort town of Istalif. Dupree, *Afghanistan*, 398.
23   As Macnaghten wrote in a secret dispatch (quoted in Dupree, *Afghanistan*, 386) "I have been striving in vain to sow 'nifak' [dissension] among the rebels and its I perfectly wonderful how they hand together."

would at once dissolve the confederacy, and open a road by which to retrieve our ruined fortunes." Macnaghten also worked out a plan to ambush the tribal chiefs[24] but his plan failed because the British forces were by then too disheartened and weak to move.

On their side, the Afghans were in no hurry to implement what they had initially agreed to since they had the British firmly in their grip. Having waited too late to negotiate – with the growing desperation of the British and the growing enthusiasm of the Afghans -- the partially agreed terms were put aside. Violently. In their final meeting, Macnaghten was seized. As Captain Colin Mackenzie wrote to Eyre, the khans tried to protect Macnaghten's staff, but "a crowd of fanatic Ghazees [Ghazis], who, on seeing the affray, had rushed to the spot, calling aloud for the blood of the hated infidels, aiming at them desperate blows with their long knives and other weapons, and only deterred from firing by the fear of killing a chief...[then] determined not to disappoint the public expectation altogether, -- influenced also by his tiger passions, and remembrance of his father's wrongs [that is, wrongs done to his father], -- Mahomed Akber [Muhammad Akbar] drew a pistol, the Envoy's [Macnaghten's] own gift a few hours before, and shot him through the body, which was immediately hacked to pieces by the ferocious Ghazees..."

In these hate-filled events, even Muhammad Akbar was constrained by the Afghan code of *melmastia*. When one of the British officers, Captain Mackenzie, grabbed his stirrup – the sign of demanding protection – "Muhammad Akbar Khan drew his sword and laid about him right manfully [while his retainers] were obliged to press me up against the wall, covering me with their own bodies, and protesting that no blow should reach me but through their persons." Muhammad Akbar Khan, wrote MacKenzie, "then turned round to me, and repeatedly said in a tone of triumphant derision,

'Shuma moolk-i-ma me geered!' (*You'll* seize my country, will you!")[25] But, after this outburst, astonishingly, Muhammad Akbar Khan disguised MacKenzie in Afghan clothes and allowed him to return to the British

---

24   Letter by the Military Secretary to Macnaghten, Captain G. St. P. Lawrence, reprinted in Erye, *The Military Operations at Cabul*, 173 ff.
25   In a letter to Lt. Erye printed in *The Military Operations at Cabul*, 167-168

fortifications unharmed. *Melmastia* was dominant over anger, a personal imperative, but it did not extend to other foreigners.

After Macnaghten's death, the officers who had been with him were accused of treachery -- particularly of trying to split the Afghan khans as Macnaghten was known to be doing – and were told "that they would now grant us no terms, save on the surrender of the whole of the married families as hostages, all the guns, ammunition, and treasure." A *jirga* was assembled and offered the British slightly more favorable terms: families would be allowed to leave if hostages replaced them and 1.4 million (14 lakhs of) rupees[26] were paid over to the Afghans with the help of Hindu money lenders.

Finally on January 6, as Lieutenant Vincent Erye put it, "the fatal morning dawned" after the siege of two months, with most of the British, particularly their Indian soldiers and camp followers, already near starvation and wading through the deep snow. About 4,500 soldiers were still alive and were joined by some 12,000 camp followers "besides women and children." Some 2,000 pack animals carried such supplies as the British forces still controlled. But they could hardly move. The "mingled mob of soldiers, camp-followers, and baggage-cattle" in some 17 hours of painful march made only five miles. Meanwhile, Afghan tribesmen followed close behind to loot supplies and pick off stragglers. From the hills, other tribesmen "maintained a harassing fire" with their *jazail* long rifles. For those who experienced or read about the French fleeing Paris in 1940 trying to escape the German army, as they were harassed from the air, would have found the scene familiar. Erye's words ring true for both: the civilians "from the very first mile [were] a serous clog upon of our movements, and were, indeed, the main cause of our subsequent misfortunes." Day after day, as their numbers diminished, the survivors slogged on.

Finally, the "monstrous, unmanageable, jumbling mass" was purged as a few officers, women and children were made over to the Afghan general as hostages and were thus protected while officers, soldiers and the camp

---

26 Roughly £1 million in the currency of the time. Currency equivalents are usually based on buying power of selected items, but of course many of those items did not then exist. Labor is another measure, but there was a vast disparity between India and Europe. We would probably not be too far wrong to say it was roughly £50 million. Other costs, I will mention below were, as today, far beyond the cash outlay.

followers lined "the road with bleeding carcasses...The sick and wounded were necessarily abandoned to their fate...[as *jazail* snipers] marked off man after man, officer after officer, with unerring aim..." The thousands who had started the retreat were reduced to only one British officer who managed to reach the British post at Jalalabad.

VI

The cost of the First Afghan war, like the cost of the later Russian and American campaigns, cannot be reckoned only in money, but William Dalrymple calculated[27] that the direct monetary cost to the British was the equivalent of "well over £50 billion in modern currency." As he points out, the real costs were different: he paraphrases the report of the commander-in-chief Sir Jasper Nicholls: the war was an "unparalleled disaster...exhausting the Indian treasury, pushing the Indian credit network to the brink of collapse and permanently wrecking the solvency of the East India Company. The loss of maybe 40,000 lives, as well as those of around 50,000 camels; and after

Afghan fighters. Cover of James Atkinson's (1780-1852) *Sketches in Afghaunistan* (sic); published by H Graves & Co, London, 1842

alienating much of the Bengal army, leaving it ripe for mutiny, the British had left Afghanistan much as they found it..."

Like the American Neoconservatives, British strategists read the lesson of failure to be that more force was needed; neither group understood the fierce desire of people to be independent, to run their own lives, to live according to their own cultures. What the neoconservatives advocate today was foreshadowed by what is known as the "Forward Policy." Laid out by Sir Henry Rawlinson in 1868 and adopted by Prime Minister Benjamin

27   Page 419. For another calculation see Thomas Barfield, *Afghanistan,* 120.

Disraeli in 1874, it aimed to incorporate Afghanistan into the British Empire. It quickly led to what is known as the Second Afghan war of 1878-1880. Like the First War, that war was precipitated by a reaction to Russian diplomacy; like the first involved the murder of the British envoy; and, also like the First War was a failure. But again the lesson was not learned and Britain invaded a third time, in 1919, also without beneficial or lasting effect.

The most uncompromising view of these failed ventures was given in the *Report of the East India Committee on the Causes and Consequences of the First Afghan War.*[28] Like some Americans today, the authors of the Report charged that the war was initiated "...evading the check played by the Constitution on the exercise of the prerogative of the Crown in declaring war. It presents, therefore, a new crime in the annals of nations – *a secret war!* It has been made by a people without their knowledge..."

Moreover, the war then like ours in Iraq and Afghanistan today was nearly ruinously expensive. It caused the jewel of the British empire, India, "the exhaustion of her flourishing treasury; complete stop to internal improvement; loss of the lives of fifteen thousand men (loss of camp-followers not known); destruction of fifty thousand camels; abstraction of her circulating medium of the country; loss of at least £13,000,000 [now estimated from £17,000,000 to £20,000,000]; permanent increase of the charges on India of £5,500,000; paralyzation [sic] of commerce; diminution of the means of culture, of transport and of revenue; chilling the affections of the native army, and the disposition to enlist; loss of England's character for fair-dealing; loss of her character of success; the Mussulman [sic] population is rendered hostile; causes of rebellion developed by the pressure of taxes and the withdrawal of troops [leading to the 1858 Indian 'Mutiny'] and finally, the other political part in England is committed to the continuation of such deeds, after they are recognized by the people of those islands to be criminal, and after they had brought upon our heads disaster and retribution."

May 15, 2013

28: Quoted in Dupree, 400-401 from Henry Bathurst Hanna, *The Second Afghan War.*

CHAPTER 3

THE RUSSIANS TRY TO "REGIME CHANGE" AFGHANISTAN

As some of you know, I have long been a student of Afghan affairs. I first went there in 1962 when I was a Member of the Policy Planning Council. During that visit, I made a 2,000 mile trip around the country during which I managed to talk with dozens of village elders, government officials and the diplomats and advisers from all the main states. The result was a policy paper I presented to the Secretary of State's policy committee.[1]

The main argument in my paper was that the wisest policy for America was a modest and discrete involvement designed to help the Afghans manage their own affairs. To accomplish this goal, I proposed various ventures in education, health and infrastructure.

Above all, I proposed, America should avoid actions that were likely to restart the "Great Game," the competition for control of Afghanistan between Imperial Russia and the then British-dominated South Asia. Neither we, nor the by-then Soviet Russians, nor the by-then independent South Asians – and certainly not the Afghans – would gain. What the British called a "Forward Policy" had long since proven wasteful, sterile and self-defeating. Its modern version, proclaimed by Secretary of State John Foster Dulles, was likely to repeat in Afghanistan what he and his brother Allan, then director of the CIA, were already doing in Iran: ultimately nullifying attempts, slow and weak as they were, toward increased national capacity and improvement of life.

Secretary of State Rusk was complimentary of my effort but cautioned me not to waste my time: Afghanistan was not then and would never be

---

1: It is reproduced in my collection of essays under the title *"Toward a Feasible Policy for Afghanistan"* in *Distant Thunder: Reflections on the Dangers of Our Times.*

of any significance. Believing this, we phased down from the Dulles policy because we were distracted by urgent considerations in Vietnam. The Russians, similarly, eased their activities because they too were distracted by other events, notably in Eastern Europe. And, onto this relatively open field, the Afghans began a program of national enhancement. The university took the lead. Ideas, programs and even new styles of social interaction and dress appeared. It was as though the Afghans had heard Chairman Mao say, "let a hundred flowers bloom." They -- not he -- meant it.

But the modernization movement was shallow and weak. It needed all the help it could get. What I had urged we do might have made a crucial difference, but our policy machine had only two settings, full speed ahead or stop. No moderation. We didn't quite stop, but we came close. And we drifted with events so when the King's cousin, Daud Khan overthrew the various and competing reformers and radicals, and installed a rightist dictatorship, we hardly noticed.

Neither, at first, did the Russians. In fact, they were quite content with the Daud dictatorship. As the former British ambassador to Moscow, Sir Rodric Braithwaite, in his excellent study of Soviet policy[2], has observed,

> "Because the Soviet government valued its relationship with the Daud government, the Ambassador and the Chief Soviet Military Adviser were instructed to have no dealings with the PDPA [Communist Party] leaders."

As we did in Iran and elsewhere, they conducted their more sensitive relationships through their intelligence channel. The message they sent along that channel was dispiriting to the Afghan Communists: stop fighting among

---

2 *Afgantsy: The Russians in Afghanistan 1979-89.* I have relied extensively on this work since it is the only comprehensive source based on the Soviet government archives and also because Ambassador Braithwaite is a shrewd and experienced observer. Other sources I have also perused are more limited. Lester W. Grau and Michael A. Gress (editors and translators), *The Soviet-Afghan War* give us the accounts and views of the Soviet General Staff. Similar is the collection of Soviet officers' reports on the tactics of the combat in Lester W. Grau's *The Bear Went Over the Mountain.* Aleksandr Antonovich Lyakhovskiy,s *Inside the Soviet Invasion of Afghanistan and the Seizure of Kabul, December 1979* gives the views of a highly regarded Russian military historian on the pivotal event in the beginning of the Russian intervention. Gilles Dorronosoro, *Revolution Unending* is excellent on the Soviet withdrawal. Finally, Gregory Feifer's *The Great Gamble: The Soviet War in Afghanistan,* is a perceptive journalistic account.

yourselves support President Daud.

The Afghan Communists did not listen. Few though they were – Braithwaite suggests only about 1,500 -- they were determined to seize power. Although we do not know much about their thinking, it is likely that they were driven rather than inhibited by recognition of their weakness. As they watched Daud purge one after another of his initial allies, they must have realized that if they did not seize power, Daud would imprison or kill them too. And, because they were split between an urban, university-oriented faction (known as Parcham) and a rural-based faction (known as Khalq), Daud found them an easy target. He took the initiative and began on April 25, 1978 to arrest the leaders, some of whom he had executed, but he purged too casually: from prison, the would-be rebels managed to get their junior military officer allies to strike on their behalf.

The coup itself, as coups often are, was the easy part. But the inexperienced young Party chiefs and their army colleagues soon overplayed their hands. Even when their objectives were laudable, as some were, they were unpopular among the generally conservative society. So eleven months after the coup, the army mutinied. Russian officers were killed and the regime teetered.

What the Russians then faced sounds very familiar to us today with just the change of a few names and dates. What, the Russians leaders wondered, was their real interest: if they moved to protect their Afghan allies, they might disrupt the Russian-American détente which, despite Soviet repression of revolts in Eastern Europe, Leonid Brezhnev thought of as his "page in the history books." Was Secretary Rusk right? Was Afghanistan not important, or at least not important enough to risk other policy goals? And what response might a new "Forward Policy" draw?

The Soviet government had reason to worry about a possible American reaction. Even though Afghanistan was not a major American concern, neighboring Iran was. And there the American position, the very keystone of the then American Middle Eastern policy, the Shah's regime, had been rudely overturned by the January 1979 Revolution. As the Russians were reacting to the revolts in Eastern Europe, it must have seemed to them not inconceivable that the Americans, motivated by their belief in the "Domino Theory" (that when one ally falls, the others are likely also to fall), would react to their Iranian fiasco by invading Afghanistan. Even if they did not send in troops, the Russians must have considered, the Americans might seek to establish intelligence-gathering bases to replace those they had operated in Iran. Worse, in the context of the Cold War, they might get themselves into position to engage in espionage among the restive Muslim population of Central Asia. Suddenly Afghanistan seemed significant.

Not, of course, as significant as Eastern Europe. So wise statesmen exercise what they believe to be prudent. But in strategy what passes as prudence is sometimes the first step in a process that soon becomes i"to fight their war for them." The Russians were equally blunt in talks with the Afghans. Alexei Kosygin lectured the Afghan president, a fellow Communist, that 'If we sent in our troops, the situation in your country would not improve. On the contrary, it would get worse. Our troops would have to struggle not only with an external aggressor, but with a part of your own people. And people do not forgive that kind of thing.'"

Another argument must have been in the minds of those aging men. Although it is hardly known outside of the Kremlin, there was a precedent to make the Soviet leaders hesitant. This Russian intervention would not be the first. In 1929, Stalin had sent a task force of a thousand men, dressed in Afghan army uniforms, to help the then ruler keep his throne. They failed. Amanullah Khan fled and the military mission was withdrawn. Subsequently, the officer who had led the mission was shot. In high stakes Soviet leadership, it was prudent to remember the past.

But probably the deciding cause was that even in the Politburo few people had any idea of what might be involved. As Braithwaite writes – similar words might have written about America's wars in Vietnam, Iraq and Afghanistan -- "Needless to say, the experts who actually knew about Afghanistan – and there were many of them in the Soviet Union in those days – were neither consulted nor informed." Instant experts came to the fore while seasoned officials were shunted aside: "no one in authority bothered to debrief [the very able Soviet ambassador who had spent 7 years in Afghanistan] or ask his opinion.... When the crisis peaked, the senior Soviet officials in the Afghan capital were men with little or no experience of the country."

What differed from Vietnam was that, unlike the American generals in Vietnam,[3] the Soviet Army leaders were strongly opposed to intervention. The chief of staff argued all the way to the Politburo:

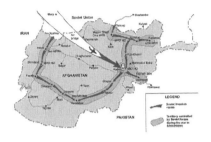

Soviet bases in Afghanistan
http://en.wikipedia.org/wiki/
File:SovietInvasionAfghanistanMap.png

"The Afghan problem had to be settled by political means; the Afghans had never tolerated the presence of foreigners on their soil; the Soviet troops would probably be drawn into military operations whether they liked it or not. His arguments fell on deaf ears..."

When the decision to intervene was made by the civilian Party leadership on Christmas day 1979, a powerful military force that ultimately numbered over a hundred thousand men and women, supplemented by various paramilitary formations, raced toward Kabul.

Powerful though the Soviet army was, as the chief of the Soviet General Staff had warned, its power was insufficient. In my government experience, I never met a general who believed he had enough men or equipment. Counterinsurgency theory, based on the Vietnam War, held that the ratio of soldiers to natives needed to be about 20 or 25 per thousand. The Soviet forces always would fall far short of that. The 100 thousand they could muster gave a ratio of about 3 soldiers per thousand. (The American ratio has varied around 2 per thousand.)

---

3   At this time, I lectured twice at the National War College to a class of the US armed forces' "best and brightest," then mostly colonels, many of whom went to be generals. They were gung-ho for the war and were hostile to my arguments on why we would lose it. The Joint Chiefs of Staff repeatedly told Presidents Kennedy and Johnson that victory was just around the corner and would be assured by another of what the Obama administration christened a "surge."

To supplement what their own personnel could do, the Russians soon moved to create or reform existing organizations in the military and police. Their efforts with the Afghan army were, at best, of limited success. On paper, it was a formidable force, and the Russian-trained officer corps was actually reasonably competent, but the soldiers were mainly "Shanghaied" villagers. They not only could not be relied upon to act independently (as is true in Afghanistan today despite years of training and billions of dollars committed to this goal) and ran away when under fire (as our troops today complain Afghan soldiers often do), but also about two in each three deserted with their weapons. Many joined the resistance or turned over their weapons to it.

The more entrepreneurial of the peasants-become-soldiers learned to turn desertion to a profit. They took advantage of the offer of a bounty to enlist. "Renting" tribesmen was a Soviet policy copied twenty years later in northern Iraq by General Petraeus. As he said, "money is my most important ammunition in this war." While it made Petraeus's reputation, it did not work for him any more than it did for the Soviets. Many Iraqis and Afghans pocketed the money and when convenient walked home. The Afghans may have been shrewder military-businessmen: as the Russians learned, some "soldiers" changed sides time after time, picking up a bounty each time.

The Russians were more successful with the *Kashad* (roughly the gendarmerie), *Kashad* and the political police, *Khadamat-e Etela'at-e Dawlati*, (KhAD, which were partially patterned on the Soviet *SpetsNaz* and the KGB's special forces, were more effective or at least more long lasting. Although their brutality created masses of new enemies for the Russians, they continued to employ them. After renaming them, President Karzai today continues to use them.

Unlike the Americans, the Russians did not use foreign mercenaries or Russian "contractors." In 2009, the 60,000 American regular troops were overmatched by some 68,197, often third-world, mercenaries. Blackwater, aka Xe, has become a major contractor with an income of about $ billion. It is not alone. Most American installations are now guarded by private armies.

Almost from the beginning the Soviet forces engaged in counterinsurgency tactics. The Russians learned that they could get better intelligence, and so win battles and avoid ambushes, if they performed "civic action." Instead of money, they offered services. Inspired by the Médecins Sans Frontières, they trained intelligence officers in rudimentary medical skills – as American forces later did -- before sending them out into the villages.[4] They undertook large-scale programs also in education, government reform, social affairs including women's rights, irrigation and road building. Remarkably, they trained over 70,000 workers in relatively modern techniques. But, as Braithwaite pointed out,

> "They discovered...that most Afghans preferred their own ways, and were not going to change them at the behest of a bunch of godless foreigners and home-grown infidels. The Russians did not, and could not, address this fundamental strategic issue."

At the urging of the neoconservatives, the American government would later fall into the same trap: the history they did not heed proves that, while the reforming of a government is sometimes possible, the restructuring or recasting of a whole society is almost certainly beyond the capacity of foreigners. It must evolve internally or it will not evolve at all.

More pointedly, if reform of any sort or the provision of aid is tied to the tactics of foreign control, it will be regarded by the natives not as beneficial but as the very front line in the war. Neither the Russians nor the Americans have learned this simple truth.

After five years of warfare, a new Soviet government under Mikhail Gorbachev began to try to negotiate and scale back. In November 1986, it arranged to install a new, still Communist-dominated but more broadly based, government in Kabul. As in Hamid Karzai's Afghanistan today, Muhammad Najibullah's government then set out a two-pronged policy: build up the army

---

4   American forces went even further, offering the headmen of villages not only aspirin, antibiotics and bandages but also Viagra, a "weapon of war," not available to the Russians.

Anti-Soviet guerrillas 1987

and gendarmerie but proclaim a policy of national reconciliation. To enhance Najibullah's prestige, the Russians increased their aerial bombing of areas they did not control.

Meanwhile, the guerrilla war continued. As Braithwaite makes clear, the toll on the Soviet forces, particularly on helicopters, was only a small fraction of the cost to America during the Vietnam war. And he dispels the myth that the American provision of the "Stinger" SAM was what turned the tide: "Gorbachev had decided to withdraw a full year before the first Stinger was fired."

Another myth attributes a particularly sinister tactic to the Russians: the seeding of rebel areas with bombs disguised as toys or cattle food. As Braithwaithe points out, these devilish devices were copies of bomblets first used by Americans in Vietnam.

Gorbachev decided in 1986 to get out of Afghanistan and began, as President Barak Obama was later to do, by withdrawing a part of the Russian contingent. He quickly discovered that getting out was slower and harder than going in. Chief of the Soviet General Staff Sergei Akhromeev summed up the failure:

> "In the past seven years [600,000] Soviet soldiers had had their boots on the ground in every square kilometer of the country. But as soon as they left, the enemy returned and restored everything the way it was before. We have lost this war."

The Russians finally turned to diplomacy, but they were too late. Not having opted to negotiate, they found that the insurgents, having victory in sight, were in no mood to give up any advantage. Thus, they refused to sign the agreement formalized on April 14, 1988 in Geneva between the Afghan government and Pakistan (which was involved both because it was sheltering millions of Afghan refugees and because it was the conduit of aid to the insurgents) and guaranteed by the United States and the USSR.

That was nearly but not quite the end of the Communist regime. Even with its 300,000-man army, it rapidly gave up most of the country. As did the Saigon regime, it lasted a further three years without external support. Finally, in 1992 it literally ran out of gas: the weapons the Russians had left behind could not be used against the rebels who steadily consolidated their gains. The real price of the war was then to be paid, first by the Afghans and then by the Russians.

The insurgents had proved unbeatable partially because they were not unified; now the lack of unity made it impossible for them to govern. With the Russians gone, they turned on one another, tore the cities – particularly Kabul -- into rubble and caused about a quarter of a million more Afghans to flee or die.

Russian withdrawl from Afghanistan
http://en.wikipedia.org/wiki/File:Evstafiev-afghan-apc-passes-russian.jpg

The price the Russians paid, like that being paid by America, was to be measured in shattered lives, wasted treasure and warping of institutions. Post-traumatic stress disorder was not then so well understood in Russia, and the Russian government was less sympathetic or helpful to its veterans. But, recognized or not, about one in two soldiers suffered from it. Malaise reached every corner of Russia and played no small part in the collapse of the Soviet system. America is today far stronger, but the final tab of America's Afghan adventure – in money, institutions and beliefs -- has yet to be paid.

February 19, 2013

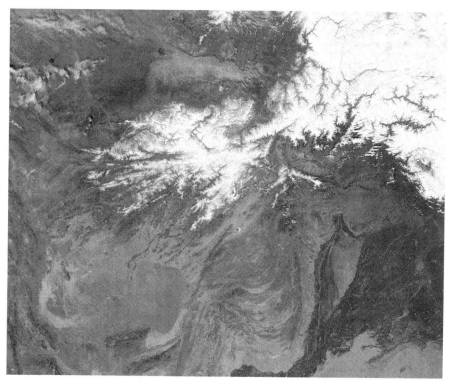

A dense pack of snow and ice covers the rugged, mountainous landscape of Afghanistan
February 27, 2006 (U.S. National Park Service)

CHAPTER 4

WAY OFF IN THE WILD EAST

When I first went out to Afghanistan fifty years ago, few Americans had ever heard of the country. Those who had, knew of it as the place where the wild warriors we know from Kipling's tales came from or where a handful of intrepid British officers were holding the line against imaginary hordes of galloping Russian Cossacks in "The Great Game."

No sensible government sent its men to Afghanistan for its own sake. It was just a "no-man's mountain" separating the cold, arid Russian steppe from the warm, rich lands and cities of India. Invaders – the list is long and goes back to before Alexander the Great -- hurried through as fast as they could lest they get caught in avalanches or ambushes. Those who tarried often paid terrible prices. The British in 1842 suffered their worst defeat in that warlike Nineteenth century just outside Kabul, losing their entire expeditionary force: of some 16,000 men, women and children, only one man escaped. After two more wars, the British gave up in 1919.

The Russians did not. Whatever their aggressive intentions may have been toward India, they also saw Afghanistan in defensive terms. They thought that British use of it as a base would pose a danger to their own empire. History showed they were right: the Russians never invaded India, but during the Russian Revolution the British did invade Russian Central Asia. More important, and certainly more long-term, was the Russian fear that an independent and perhaps militantly religious Afghanistan might stir revolts among the related Muslim peoples of what later became the republics of Kirghizstan, Uzbekistan, Turkmenistan, Kazakhstan and the always turbulent and only partially subdued Muslim peoples of the Caucasus. In short, the Russians were motivated by their own version of the "domino" theory that so mesmerized Western strategists after the Second World War. While Winston Churchill, fearing that one pro-Western government after another was on the brink of toppling, warned of the spread of Communism, Josef Stalin echoed his Tsarist predecessors in dreading the incitement of "Panislamism" among the subject peoples of his empire. He had reason. After all, it was in conjunction with Islam that the nationalist movements of the Caucasus and Central Asia had fought the advance of the Russian state for centuries. So, in their turn, the Russians in 1979 were sucked into the quick sands of the Dasht-e Margo (the Desert of Death) and the mountains known as the Hindu Kush (the Killer of the Hindus).

Khyber Pass 2007
NASA satellite image

Until the Russians made their move in 1979, no one in the American government paid much attention to Afghanistan. In the 1950s and 1960s, it was a wretchedly poor little country, far away, without significant natural resources and inhabited by only about 12 million people, most of whom were illiterate, "medieval" in custom and living on the edge of starvation. But it was positioned next to the Soviet Union so that great Cold Warrior, Secretary of State John Foster Dulles, saw its strategic importance, as the British had long before him seen it, as a barrier against the Russians. Even though the motivation of the British, to protect their Indian empire, had ended in 1947 with Indian independence, Dulles a decade later thought the United States should try to win Afghanistan over to "our side" or at least to keep it out of Soviet control. He was not willing for America to do much, but he was willing to make gestures. Those gestures, in the custom of the 1950s, meant giving the Afghans an airport, a road and an agricultural scheme. Weighed in the scale of what the Eisenhower administration was then doing in what Mr. Dulles saw as the "central front" – the Iraqi, Iranian and Pakistani members of the Baghdad Pact -- what was set in motion in Afghanistan were mere tokens. And they were done in a haphazard fashion without much thought or direction.

That was the situation in Afghanistan when the Kennedy administration came to Washington in 1961. Then, new eyes were focused on what we were doing all over the world. Of course, Afghanistan was not a high priority – it was still poor, faraway and medieval. But after all, Dulles had a point: it was still cheek to jowl with the Soviet Union. In 1961, at the height of the Cold War, its position gave it at least some strategic importance.

So Chester Bowles, a former governor of Connecticut and then Under Secretary of State, thought he should go and have a look for himself. He was probably inspired by his friend, Justice William Douglas of the Supreme Court, who had a sort of love affair with what he called in the title of one of his books, *Strange Lands and Friendly People*. Bowles was sure that however strange the lands might be, the Afghans must be friendly. He thought that about nearly everybody. And, quite apart from the Cold War, he believed that Afghanistan was one of those places where America should hold out a helping hand. Particularly, he felt, the Kennedy administration needed to reexamine Mr. Dulles' legacies. So, as soon as he had made the appointments he thought would start the process of reform of the State Department in Washington, he decided to set off, and he asked me to go with him.

At that time, I had just left Harvard, where I was a young Assistant Professor and a member of the Center for Middle Eastern Studies. Thanks to Bowles and also to McGeorge Bundy, the former dean of the faculty at Harvard and newly appointed director of the National Security Council, and, of course, President Kennedy, I had been commissioned a member of the Policy Planning Council.

The Policy Planning Council was the new name given to the organization Secretary of State George Marshall had founded in 1947. Marshall, America's senior general, had been horrified when he moved across the Potomac from the Pentagon to find that the State Department had no general staff. So he immediately created one. That was the Policy Planning Staff with the acronym S/P. Under George Kennan, it was the group that designed the Marshall Plan to resurrect war-shattered Europe and also envisaged the concept that shaped American foreign policy for the next twenty years, "containment" of the Soviet Union. S/P was Marshall's brain trust.

Marshall's followers lacked his vision and felt little need for a staff; so like the State Department as a whole, S/P withered. By 1961, it was a shell of its former self. But Kennedy thought that it could be resurrected. He was desperate to reform the State Department and thought that a revitalized general staff might become the yeast to leaven the then virtually moribund department. So rather than abolishing it, he renamed it from "staff" to "council," and upgraded the posts to the civil equivalent of general officer. Now called "members" instead of "staff," those who were appointed were expected to be independent of the main divisions of the Department and so were given sufficient rank to make some difference in status-conscious Washington. Kennedy had great hopes for it and its new members. To lead it, he chose as its chairman a man for whom he had great respect, Walt Rostow, then a professor of economics at MIT and a distinguished planner of wartime and postwar policy in Europe. Rostow's task was to recreate the organization that General Marshall envisaged and George Kennan personified.

Rostow was blocked during the crucial first year of the new administration; Washington still cowered under the shadow of McCarthyism and Kennedy feared that he could not get Rostow confirmed by the Senate.

So he remained in the White House at the National Security Council, but I was brought "aboard," as Washingtonians liked to say, in June 1961.

I was to advise on how the United States could do a better job of protecting American interests and accomplishing American objectives in most of the Islamic world and to focus particularly on North Africa, the Middle East and West Asia.

When I "read myself into" the files that my predecessor at S/P had left behind, I found why Kennedy had been worried. The information and policy advice "heritage" locked away in safes was thin gruel. I remember asking, to annoyance of the security officers, why anyone bothered to safeguard it. The files made evident that my predecessor knew little about the area. But, to be honest, I was not in much better shape myself. My knowledge was spotty. My training, research, teaching and writings had been focused primarily on the Arab part of the vast area for which I had become "responsible." True, I had visited most of the other countries, but I had never been to Afghanistan, so I jumped at the chance to go with Bowles.

When we reached Afghanistan, we found the American embassy in disarray. If the State Department was moribund, the embassy was the smoldering ruins of a sort of soap opera battlefield. It was torn by internal feuds, the staff was dispirited and everyone was determined not to do anything that might disrupt his career. So, as experienced bureaucrats, they realized that the best thing was to do nothing. Anyway, who in the American government cared? Assignment to Afghanistan was nearly a punishment; it was certainly not what an ambitious officer judged would ensure promotion. As one man told me, he expected that when he was next considered for promotion or being "selected out" (that is, fired), he thought that the board would ask themselves, "why was he put out there?" Then they would surmise that there must be something wrong with him.

The embassy was also leaderless. The ambassador had left under a cloud of gossip among the more senior (and aged) embassy wives for allegedly having affairs with the junior (and younger) embassy wives. The CIA station chief was so exposed, never even being invited to embassy functions, that everyone in the small and ingrown Kabul diplomatic corps (and presumably in the Afghan government) laughed about his "cover" as a vice consul. Much worse, the aid director turned out to have never been outside the capital city, Kabul. He admitted to Bowles and me that he had never visited any of the programs for which he was responsible.

It showed. The programs begun under the Eisenhower administration, with much hoopla and the raising of Afghan expectations, languished for lack of direction, follow-on funding and key personnel: as I was to find, a dairy was begun for inexperienced sheep herders with no veterinarian and the $100 million irrigation project in the Helmand valley for recently settled nomads had no irrigation specialist to help them learn how to farm. Failures, theirs and ours, I was constantly told, left the stale taste of disappointment in the mouths of our Afghan friends. This was to be demonstrated much later in 2010 when, ironically, the site of our great agricultural venture in the Helmand valley, then called Marja, became the redoubt of our Taliban foes. Far from winning hearts and minds, we had planted the seeds of Afghan disillusion.

Governor Bowles was horrified by what we heard at the American embassy and asked me to drop out of his mission and undertake a thorough review of the country and what we were doing – and not doing – there. "What a mess," he said. "No one here has a clue what we are doing or what we should be doing. It seems to me that they have got it all wrong. So why don't you take off and go everywhere, see as many people as you can, listen to them and then come back to Washington to present a new National Policy Paper outlining what we should do?"

I remember jumping up and starting out the door of the office we shared. He laughed and called me back, saying that perhaps we should talk it over first. Also laughing, I retorted, "No, the President told me to follow your instructions. I have left. Goodbye! I'll see you in Washington." He managed a last "good luck" as the door closed behind me.

So it was that I took a 2,000 mile trip by jeep and airplane with an occasional side venture by horseback, during which I sipped tea and chatted with scores of Afghan officials all over the country. During my trip, I met a dozen provincial governors along with un-counted numbers of village headmen, university professors, students, foreign ambassadors and, to be honest, almost anyone I could get to help educate me. For several weeks, I behaved like a hungry man at a loaded buffet table. So engrossed did I become that Rostow, who by then had moved over to the Policy Planning Council, sent me a three-word message asking, "are you lost?" And, inspired by a private joke we shared on loquacious diplomatic messages, I replied simply, "no." I was enjoying every minute, even digging my jeep out of the sand.

Since much has happened since that trip and I have been engaged in many other issues, occasionally revisiting Afghanistan and certainly never losing my fascination with it, but to keep close to what I then found, I will fall back on the report I wrote immediately upon my return to Washington and presented to Secretary of State Dean Rusk's policy meeting on March 27, 1962.

My first point in the U.S. National Policy Paper was that American policy should be modest. No more talk about "winning." I wrote that the "pre-eminent U.S. policy objective in Afghanistan is maintenance of Afghan neutrality and independence." I stressed that America should not act in ways that the Soviet Union might regard as a threat and so move against Afghanistan. But, I ended by saying that "if we drift as we are now doing, Afghanistan is likely to slide into the Soviet orbit over the coming decade or so." That is exactly what happened. But, I also pointed out that U.S. intelligence had discovered no evidence of a Soviet intent to take over Afghanistan so we should not provoke the Russians. Therefore, "if we wish to do so, and act intelligently, we can maintain this buffer...Doing so successfully will depend far less on money than on intelligence and tact."

The key element in "intelligence and tact" was to realize both what the Afghans wanted and what they feared. From generations of balancing on the summit of Asia – beleaguered by the Russians to the North and the British to the south – the Afghans knew that they must live on a precarious foothold above their greedy great power neighbors. So any attempt to "win them over," as John Foster Dulles would have liked to do, could "only weaken the Afghan ability to survive." A wise American policy would aim at helping them keep independent of all outsiders, including us. With some carefully planned and administered aid -- and much forbearance -- we could assist them, but, I stressed, "The key is the Afghan will to survive."

Fortunately, my trip offered proof of that will. As I observed, "The Afghans are a proud and sturdy nation. Living in deep and widely scattered valleys and on high plateaus, scattered along one of the world's great mountain ranges, a vast area about the size of Colorado and New Mexico combined, they are today and historically a mosaic of ethnical, religious, and linguistic groups who share the characteristics of mountainous life, are inured to hardships and are proud of a glorious past." The Hazara peoples, who inhabit the central mountain region of Hindu Kush, may be descendants of Chingis Khan's legionnaires while the inhabitants of what is now called Nuristan claim descent from the Macedonians of Alexander the Great. The Pushtuns (aka the Pathans as the Indians renamed them), who are scattered all over the country as villagers but whose main concentration is in the south, have an even more obscure heritage. Some scholars allege, because of their common names and some of their customs that they be one of the lost tribes of Israel. More likely is that their ancestors were one of those nomadic groups driven across Asia by history's first "domino effect."

It is worth taking a minute to describe the "falling dominos." I recount it because it is, in a real sense the seminal process of Central Asian history and accounts for much of Afghan society today. It is also perhaps the only real "domino" in the human experience. What seems to have happened – I say "seems" because the early and causative great events happened beyond the purview of Western observers and are only partly recounted in Chinese records – is the following:

Roughly 2,000 years ago, after having suffered repeated raids from their northern nomadic neighbors, the Chinese hit upon a complex but highly successful policy to deal with them. What they did may have been history's only successful counterinsurgency.

Knowing that the fortifications we call the Great Wall were not the answer, the Chinese baited a trap for the nomads. Instead of trying to drive them away, they lured the people they called the Hsiung-nu[1] into a corrupting relationship. Rather than using the wall as a barrier, the *Ai*, (its name in Chinese), they set up markets along it and flooded those markets with opulent goods. Where the nomads had been content with wool and skin, the Chinese provided silk; where they had made do with goat meat and camel milk, the Chinese provided all manner of delicacies. Their aim was to weaken the hardy tribesmen with luxury. At the same time, they even provided the nomad chiefs with wives from among their young princesses so that the habits and customs of a richer life entered the nomads' tents and helped shape their children. This was obviously a long-term strategy, but when the time was ripe, the Chinese themselves crossed the great wall to attack the Hisung-nu and drive them out of their traditional grazing lands.

Reeling from the attack, the Hsiung-nu in turn fell upon another nomadic group, whom the Chinese called the Yüeh-chi and whom Western classical writers such as Ptolemy knew as the Tochari. These people, in turn, were driven in mortal fear from their grazing- grounds, and as they fled westward, they fell upon a third great tribal confederation, the Wu-sun. We don't know much about these great events, but we know parts of the end of the story. The last domino to fall was probably the displaced nomads whom the ancient writers called the Scythians. They moved into Afghanistan and are believed to have become the ancestors of today's Pushtun peoples.

Wherever they came from and however they got to Afghanistan, the Pushtun people embody a long and embattled heritage. Not surprisingly, like the other peoples who ended in Afghanistan, they sought niches in the little valleys scattered along its vast stretches of mountain where they could defend themselves. And, clinging precariously to a hazardous life, they espoused customs that emphasized valor, hardihood and violence. War became their way of life. Their ideal man was the warrior. They would not have felt alien in the England of King Arthur or Beowulf.

Over the centuries, the Pushtun people occasionally fought in the

---

1   These people may have been the "Huns" who played havoc with the Roman empire in later times.

armies of the neighboring empires but compressed into the tiny valleys of their mountain fastnesses they constantly fought with one another. The Europeans they most closely resembled were the Scots who also lived by a warrior code and who bedeviled the English for centuries. It was thus a sort of historical symmetry that brought the English into conflict with these "Eastern Scots" when they added India to their empire.

Frontier warfare was to occupy the British invaders of Afghanistan for more than a century. Even with poison gas, aircraft, armored cars, the machinegun, artillery – none of which the tribesmen had – the British could not "pacify" them. Why they could not has been told to us in *Passing It On*,[2] one of the first manuals of counterinsurgency, by a man who was perhaps the British master, General Sir Andrew Skeen. Fighting them all his life on the North West Frontier, he described why the British could never win. The people, he wrote,

> are probably the finest individual fighters in the east…They come down hillsides like falling boulders, not running but bounding, and in crags they literally drop from foothold to foothold…These men are hard as nails; they live on little, carry nothing but a rifle and a few cartridges, a knife and a bit of food, and they are shod for quick and sure movement… killing…is the only way to make the tribesman feel defeat.

The British killed and killed. To little avail. The tribesmen were then and are today, as General Skeen wrote 80 years ago, "firm believers in living to fight another day, however often it may mean bolting like rabbits; and it is quite impossible to 'pin them to their ground.'" In short, they fought as guerrillas. As they still do. Skeen's troops found, to their pain, that the Pushtuns were superb at their task: "The accuracy of these people's shooting is sometimes astounding…I saw four men knocked out by one sniper, known to have been fifteen hundred yards [almost a mile] off."

---

2   Gale & Polden, Aldershot (England), 2nd edition, 1932.

So the British tried another tactic, one at least as old as the Roman Empire: divide their enemies. To this end, they sent a survey mission under Sir Henry Durand into the southern mountains to draw a new frontier along the crest. This is the Durand Line which they forced the then Afghan ruler to accept in 1893 and which is today the frontier between Afghanistan and Pakistan. It is the reason why Pakistan now has a Pushtun population of nearly 30 million and Afghanistan has about half that many.

But for the Pushtuns the Durand Line was merely a figment of the British imagination. What mattered to them were the customary grazing and migration grounds of the tribes into which they were divided and to which they owed their allegiance. These grounds spanned the frontier as indeed they must because the animals of the nomads had to move with the seasons. Trying to stop them was the task at which men like General Skeen took on and failed.

So the British tried buying off the tribal leaders, but as General David Petraeus would find almost a century later in Iraq it was not a purchase. Paying blackmail – a term incidentally that originated along the Anglo-Scottish border hundreds of years earlier – was never more than a short-term "rental." The price today is higher and the terms differ, but the game is still the same.

Not so wild as the mountains and deserts along the Durand Line are other areas of Afghanistan. A part of the reason for social cohesion is, of course, geographical. Afghanistan is mainly mountain and desert, so tight little groups – gathered in some 22,000 villages -- huddle around and defend with all their skill and might places where water makes life possible. These conditions give rise to cultural traits. Indeed, like the Scottish *clanns*, Afghans live by a code of revenge (*badal)* that in the quest for security makes for unending hostility. Like the Scots, the Afghan villagers and tribesmen were dirt poor but had a self-esteem (*meranah),* indeed a pride of nobility, that is always breath-taking and can sometimes be life-taking. No slight is ever forgotten even after generations. Vengeance is the absolute requirement. This, of course, is what makes today's "targeted assassinations" self-defeating.

Every person killed brings forth the hatred of all his relatives, just as it did in Scotland and among the Scots Irish in America.

But a cultural imperative balancing hostility was made evident to me in my trek around the country in 1962. Everywhere I went, I went, as a guest. And the code by which all Afghans, as particularly spelled out by the Pushtuns in their *Pushtunwali*, absolutely requires that every self-respecting man be a host. People living in a poverty no one in the Western world had ever experienced would literally starve themselves to entertain me. *Melmestie* (hospitality) was the absolute obligation of everyman, no matter how poor. And *melmestie* did not stop with food. As a guest, I was under the protection of my hosts who would have defended me to their last breaths. That is why, even when the American government offered as a "dead or alive" reward for Usama bin Ladin an amount literally beyond the dream of avarice, no Afghan would think of surrendering him. Our offer was not so much tempting as insulting to their code of honor (the *nang-i Pushtun*). To have accepted would have brought everlasting shame (*sharm*).

Most of the social code is operative not just in the now-war ravaged south but also in the mountainous center and the plain land beyond the Hindu Kush. There, other ethnic groups live – still live even when they have put aside village life for life in the cities -- by a code that was in many ways similar to the *Pushtunwali* and guard their independence just as fiercely. And for good reason. Many of them had painful memories of the cost of refugee life. The Uzbeks and other Turcoman groups in the north were descended from ancestors who had fled from the Tsarist Russian or Soviet armies in a desperate attempt to preserve their independence. For some, the flight from oppression began hundreds of years ago, many fled after both the Whites and the Reds acted to crush the "Pan-Turanian" movement around the First World War and others suffered internal exile under the Soviet occupation in the 1980s. Like the Pushtuns who had been separated from kinsmen by the Durand Line, these Turkish peoples were separated by their cousins, but the Russians today like the British in past times feared their influence through militant Islam and the siren call of nationalism.

Between the Turks in the North and the Pushtuns in the South are other groups including the Hazara, most of are holed up in tiny, isolated valleys in the almost impenetrable mountain wall that divides Afghanistan in half.

Overarching the collection of autonomous communities, Afghanistan's 22,000 villages, are shared beliefs and customs. While there are regional and ethnic variations, they interweave to form, symbolically appropriately for Afghanistan, a virtual "carpet" in which society and culture become durable even under incredible adversity.

The strong backing, the "warp," of the social carpet is a shared code of custom. And, just as the "warp" of a rug is strengthened by the "weft," so Afghan society is braced by religious belief. In no Islamic country have I seen people so uniformly and comprehensively religious. Fighting foreigner invaders is an old tradition and is motivated by devotion to Islam. About one man in a dozen thinks of himself as a *mulla*. As one of the guerrilla leaders in the war against the Russians told an English visitor, "the most precious thing we have is our faith; without it we have nothing." So, as the foremost American student of Afghanistan, Louis Dupree once told me, "you can't cast a stone anywhere here without hitting the shrine of a holy man." As I observed in the center of the vast Hindu Kush mountain range, down in the salt deserts and quicksand of the southwest and up along the northern frontier, every man, woman and child is knotted into the warp and weft of Afghan culture and Islam.

Overarching ethnic groups, linguistic divisions, and mutually hostile communities is the commitment to Islam. Like the other aspects of Afghan culture, it is both divided and shaped by history, geography and mission. Along the western frontier, where Iranian influence has been strong, Shiism predominates, but there, as well as in the high valleys of the Hindu Kush range, where the Aimaq and Hazara peoples live, and in the far northeast, near Tajikistan, Shiism takes on a distinctively Afghan cast; in the north on the plain between the Hindu Kush and the Amu Darya river (the modern frontier with the former Soviet Union), the Afghans are mostly speakers of a dialect of Turkish and practice, like most Turks, Sunnism. The largest group of Afghans are the Pushtun who occupy virtually the whole of the country south of the Hindu Kush mountains. They are Sunnis and think of themselves as "pure" or fundamentalist Muslims although the Islam they practice is deeply influenced by what must be pre-Islamic customs. Indeed, some of their practices of customary law (*ravaj*) violate Quranic injunctions.

Islam arose in an Arab tribal society and tribal Afghans adapted to it easily. The aspect we focus on today is the concept of religious struggle (*jihad*) and propensity of Afghans to see themselves as warriors of the faith (*mujahidin*). Already in 1835, students of [religious] knowledge (*Taliban-ul-ilm*) functioned as a militia. Devotion to Islam formed the basis for their resistance to South Asian Hindus and Sikhs, to imperial Englishmen and more recently to the "Godless" Russians. Now it forms the basis for Afghan resistance to us.

So, what was Afghanistan in history and the one I got to know half a century ago and how did those two Afghanistans relate to the Afghanistan we know today?

Visitors, including me, have been struck by the diversity of the Afghans in mode of living (urban people, settled villagers, nomads), religion (Sunni and Shia Islam), language (Pashtu, Dari, Baluchi, various Nuri languages, Azari and other Turkish dialects and a number of smaller groups of languages), ethnicity (Pushtuns, Tajiks, Hazaras, a variety of Turkish groups, and the people of Nuristan along with a scattering of Sikhs, Arabs and Jews). Yet, as I found in my travels and wrote in my policy paper, "There is certainly more to 'Afghanistan' than a collection of peoples." They share much although their rugged terrain, and particularly the great mountains, have divided them over many centuries and have made possible the survival of diverse groups of refugees.

The Afghanistan I experienced in the 1960s was nearly the country known to invaders over the centuries. As I reported, much of the country is accessible only on horse or camel. Other areas I could reach by jeep but at speeds at less than six miles an hour. Even the main 'roads' are little more than trails: 318 miles from the capital to Qandahar required 15 hours of hard driving and the 168 miles from Farah to Herat took seven hours. On one of the "roads" through the mountains, the jeep in which I was being carried could not make some of the "switch-backs" without stopping, backing up and then turning. Inches away from the wheels was a drop of 1,500 feet into jagged rocks. Skeletons of pack animals could be seen far below. Even on some of the straight stretches, grades rose at 25 percent. To judge from photographs taken all over the country today, those driving conditions have hardly changed. Even by plane, travel was problematic because of frequent bad weather over the mountains.

It wasn't – and isn't – only the mountains. Afghanistan contains some of the most difficult deserts in the world. Much of it, as in the "Desert of Death" (the Dasht-i Margo) contains vast areas of marsh where thin veneers of salt crust cover quick sand. My route led me right through this desert. In a four-wheel jeep, it was hard and dangerous going; by camel or donkey, it was virtually impassable.

For the physical attributes of their country, the Afghans have paid a terrible price. What I found in 1962 was that per capita income was about $50. Life expectancy was probably as low as 20 years. Infant mortality about 500/1000. There are very few public services. For example, in Badakhshan Province, with a population of approximately 350,000, there was one doctor and in Kataghan Province, with a population of one million there were seven doctors. Malnutrition was almost universal; bread was the staple and rice was regarded as a luxury. Nowhere in Afghanistan, even in the capital, was there a supply of safe drinking water; everywhere it was taken from open ditches. Consequently some 60,000 children died each year from diseases spread by polluted water. Spot checks by the WHO representative in the north indicated that tuberculosis affected over 50% of the people and intestinal diseases were almost universal. Since an antibiotic pill cost three-days wages for a laborer, most people just suffered.

Those figures have hardly changed. Except to be multiplied. The Afghan population was 12 million in 1962; today it may be, for no one really knows, about 30 million. But such statistics as we have are still horrifying: More than one in three Afghans subsists on the equivalent of less than 45 cents a day and more than one in two preschool children is stunted because of malnutrition. They are the lucky ones; one in five dies before the age of five. That is, in terms of child mortality, the second highest in the world. Diarrhea, hepatitis, typhoid, malaria are still rampant because most people do not have sources of clean water. In fact, 60,000 children die each year from drinking polluted water. Like nearly everyone today, my little party had to draw our drinking water from open ditches. And one young embassy officer who accompanied me died as a result of contracting dysentery – as millions of Afghans have. Perhaps the only bright health note is that Afghanistan appears to have almost no HIV/AIDS because of its rigid "medieval" social code.

I found that in 1962 we were doing nothing about these problems. What interested my predecessors among American planners were grandiose schemes. Two stood out. The first was an airport at Kandahar. At $25 million in 1950s dollars – today's $500 million – it was a monument to blindness. The town population was then made up of 80,000 poor farmers –- little or no opium was exported in those far-off days! -- and until the American army arrived there were no foreigners. Certainly no tourists. All aviation fuel had to be trucked in from Pakistan or Russia. The airport was just a monument until the Russian air force arrived to use it.

What had never occurred to our officials was to say to the Afghans that we wanted to help them with their transport problems and were prepared to spend, say, the equivalent of that airport, so we should jointly consider what made sense. Instead, we opted for grandiose, showy and ultimately wasteful projects. The biggest of all was the Helmand Valley Authority.

The Helmand Valley Authority, as the obvious pattern of the initials HVA, indicates, was begun as a major social engineering project on the model of the TVA. The Helmand Valley for over a thousand years had supported flourishing civilizations but invasions, depopulation and neglect have led to the breakdown of its ancient canal system. While the area was not capable of sustaining a vast TVA-like development, it offered the only major area of potential growth of Afghanistan. Reclamation of the land and draining of the swamp areas could significantly boost Afghanistan's productivity, would allow the Afghan Government to achieve its objective of increasing its earning of foreign exchange and, if properly devised, could foster the growth of a stratum of small holders which would give the country more stability. Those developments, in turn, the Eisenhower administration calculated, would win the Afghans' "hearts and minds" and prevent them from slipping into the Soviet orbit.

Up to 1962 only the upper Helmand Valley had been subjected to intensive development. The project, on which the U.S. by 1960 had spent more than $100 million (in today's currency and conditions perhaps $2 billion) had been the butt of much criticism over its obvious short falls: since it was begun on inadequate studies of water and salt conditions, some land had been lost while other land had been reclaimed at exorbitant cost. The plan was to settle nomads to work the land, but they were given little or no training for the tasks they faced. Land was parceled out to families, but each plot was too small to provide a family sufficient income to feed itself, purchase fertilizers and acquire good seed. No credit facilities were created so the farmers were forced to borrow from money lenders at as much as 100% interest. Chronically in debt, they often could not plant and were forced to allow land to lie fallow on alternate years. And without expert guidance, the recently converted nomads mismanaged the little they had. Irrigation water was given free and not sufficiently controlled so, having spent their lives in thirst, they naturally used excessive amounts. As the American-trained governor of the province told me, "they are like alcoholics given the key to package store." Yet, as I was repeatedly told, "With this project the American reputation in Afghanistan is completely linked." As I have written, it is perhaps not surprising that it was precisely in this area, now called Marja, that the Taliban created their most secure base.

After 1962 I made many more trips to Afghanistan, the last of which – to a very different Afghanistan -- was in 2010. Then the country was overflowing with Americans. The American embassy I had first seen with about 20 officers had grown to well over 1,000. The lanes through the charming little city of Kabul with its bustling markets had been converted into man-made canyons between high blast walls. The villages in which I had been welcomed, fed and housed, were scenes of manifestations of hatred toward Americans. And those Americans who visited were fitted out like medieval knights with body armor, helmets and arms. The outlay on Secretary of State Dulles's "gestures" had grown to expenditures of at least $100 billion a year. And no one seemed to know how to do anything other than the failed tactics General Sir Andrew Skeen had "passed on" from the British experience almost a century before.

Many tragedies were played out in Afghanistan after my first venture in 1962, but when I returned to Washington and presented my analysis and recommendations, they lay in the unknowable future. After listening to my report, Secretary of State Dean Rusk was personally kind but dismissive: "Bill," he said, "you did a good job and what you say is interesting, but Afghanistan is a waste of your time. It is unimportant and never will be. So I advise you to return to serious matters."

That was advice I was incapable of following. I was never to get Afghanistan out of my sight. Having grown up on a ranch in Texas with the memories of the Wild West, I found Afghanistan to be "the Wild East."

October 14, 2010

CHAPTER 5

THE LEGITIMATION CRISIS IN AFGHANISTAN

In the media celebration of our "victory" over the Taliban in the Helmand Valley,1 little attention has been given to the nature of insurgency: the proper tactic of guerrillas is to fade away before overwhelming power, leaving behind only enough fighters to force the invaders to harm civilians and damage property. This is exactly what happened in the recent fighting in Marja. Faced with odds of perhaps 20 to 1, helicopters, tanks and bombers, the guerrillas wisely dispersed. Victory may not be quite the right description.

That battle will probably be repeated in Kandahar, which, unlike the agricultural area known as Marja, is a large and densely populated city. Other operations are planned, so the Marja "victory" has set a pattern that accentuates military action. This is not conducive to an exit strategy--it will not lead out of Afghanistan but deeper into the country. Indeed, there is already evidence that this is happening. As the *Washington Post* reported shortly after the Marja battle ended, not far away the "Marines are constructing a vast base on the outskirts of town that will have two airstrips, an advanced combat hospital, a post office, a large convenience store and rows of housing trailers stretching as far as the eye can see."

Since the Helmand Valley is the focal point of the military strategy, it is important to understand its role in Afghan affairs. The Helmand irrigation project, begun in the Eisenhower administration as a distant echo of the TVA, was supposed to become a prosperous island of democracy and progress. As a member of the Policy Planning Council in the Kennedy administration, I visited it in 1962. What I found was deeply disturbing: no studies had been made of the land to be developed, which proved to

---

1   This paper was written in 2010 when it appeared that the American army was winning the Afghan war.

Helmand Valley (UK Forces Media)

have a sheet of impermeable rock just below the surface that caused the soil to turn saline when irrigated; the land was not sufficiently leveled, so irrigation was inefficient; nothing was done to teach the nomad settlers how to farm; plots were too small to foster the social engineering aim of creating a middle class; and since there were no credit facilities to buy seed, settlers were paying 100 percent interest to moneylenders. In short, after the buildup of great expectations, disappointment was palpable.

Was it a portent? It seems likely. At the least, it's striking that precisely where we carried out our first civic action program is where the Taliban became most powerful.

So what should that experience have taught us? That we should learn about the Afghans, their country and their objectives before determining our policy toward them. There is much to be learned, but I will here highlight what I believe are the three crucial issues that will make or break our relationship.

The first issue critical to evaluating US policy is the way the Afghans govern themselves. About four in five Afghans live in the country's 20,000-plus villages. During a 2,000-mile trip around the country by jeep, horseback and plane half a century ago, as well as in later trips, it became clear to me that Afghanistan is really thousands of villages, and each of them, although culturally related to its neighbors, is more or less politically independent and economically autarkic.

This lack of national cohesion thwarted the Russians during their occupation: as I have said, the Russians won many military victories, occupied at one time or another virtually every inch of the country, and through their civic action programs they actually pacified many of the villages, but they could never find or create an organization with which to make peace. Baldly put, no one Afghan group could surrender the rest. Thus, over the decade of their involvement, the Russians lost about 15,000 soldiers – and the war. When they gave up and left, the Afghans resumed their traditional way of life, what might be called "the Afghan way."

That way of life is embedded in a social code (known in the Pashtun areas as Pashtunwali) that shapes the particular form of Islam they have practiced for centuries and, indeed, that existed long before the coming of Islam. While there are, of course, notable differences in the Pashtun, Hazara, Uzbek and Tajik areas, shared tradition determines how all Afghans govern themselves and react to foreigners.

Among the shared cultural and political forms are town councils (known in the Pashtun areas as *jirgas* and in the Hazara area as *ulus* or *shuras*). The members are not elected but are accorded their status by consensus. These town councils are not, in our sense of the word, institutions; rather, they are "occasions." They come together when pressing issues cannot be resolved by the local headman or respected religious figure. Town councils are the Afghan version of participatory democracy, and when they act they are seen to embody the "way" of their communities.

Pashtunwali demands protection (*melmastia*) of visitors. Not to protect a guest is so grievous a sin and so blatant a sign of humiliation that a man would rather die than fail. This, of course, had prevented the Afghans from surrendering Osama bin Laden. Inability to reconcile our demands with their customs has been at the heart of our struggle for the past eight years.

As put forth in both the Bush and Obama administrations, our objective is to prevent Al Qaeda from using Afghanistan as a base for attacks on us. We sharpened this objective to the capturing or killing of bin Laden. That is popular with US voters, but even if we could have forced the Afghans to surrender him, it would have alienated the dominant Pashtun community. Thus, it would have probably increased the danger to us.

But it is unnecessary, since a resolution of this dilemma in our favor was available for years

While Pashtunwali does not permit a protected guest to be surrendered, it allows the host, with honor, to prevent the guest from engaging in actions that endanger the host. In the past, the Taliban virtually imprisoned bin Laden, and they have repeatedly offered--provided we agree to leave their country--to meet our demand that Al Qaeda not be allowed to use Afghanistan as a base. Although setting a withdrawal date would enable us to meet our objective, we have turned down their offers.

The second crucial issue in evaluating our policy is the way the people react to our civic action programs.

Afghanistan is a barren, landlocked country with few resources, and its people have suffered through virtually continuous war for thirty years. Many are wounded or sick, with some even on the brink of starvation. The statistics are appalling: more than one in three subsists on the equivalent of less than 45 cents a day, almost one in two lives below the poverty line and more than one in two preschool children is stunted because of malnutrition. They are the lucky ones; one in five dies before the age of 5. Obviously, the Afghans need help, so we think they should welcome our efforts to aid them. But independent observers have found that they do not. Based on some 400 interviews, a team of Tufts University researchers found that "Afghan perceptions of aid and aid actors are overwhelmingly negative." We must ask why this is.

The reason, I think, is that the Taliban understand from our pronouncements that civic action is a form of warfare. The Russians taught them about civic action long ago, and Gen. David Petraeus specifically proclaimed in his Iraq days, "Money is my most important ammunition in this war." Thus many ordinary citizens see our programs as Petraeus described them--as a method of control or conquest--and so support or at least tolerate the Taliban when they destroy our projects or prevent our aid distribution.

To get perspective on this, it is useful to look at Vietnam. There too we found that the people resented our efforts and often sided with our enemies, the local equivalent of the Taliban: the Vietminh, or, as we called them, the Vietcong. The Vietminh killed officials, teachers and doctors, and destroyed even beneficial works. Foreigners thought their violence was bound to make the people hate them. It didn't. Like the Kabul government, the South Vietnamese regime was so corrupt and predatory that few supported it even to get aid. When we "inherited" the war in Vietnam, we thought we should sideline the corrupt regime, so we used our own officials to deliver aid directly to the villagers. It got through, but our delivering it further weakened the South Vietnamese government's rapport with its people.

Is this relevant to Afghanistan? Reflect on the term used by Gen. Stanley McChrystal when his troops moved into Helmand: he said he was bringing the inhabitants a "government in a box, ready to roll in." That government is a mix of Americans and American-selected Afghans, neither sent by the nominal national government in Kabul nor sanctioned by local authorities.

How did the Afghans react to McChrystal's government? President Karzai was at least initially opposed, seeing the move as undercutting the authority of his government. We don't yet know what the inhabitants thought. But we do know that when we tried similar counterinsurgency tactics in Vietnam, as the editor of the massive collection of our official reports, the Pentagon Papers, commented, "all failed dismally."

If we aim to create and leave behind a reasonably secure society in Afghanistan, we must abandon this failed policy and set a firm and reasonably prompt date for withdrawal. Only thus can we dissociate humanitarian aid from counterinsurgency warfare. This is because once a timetable is clearly announced, a fundamental transformation will begin in the political psychology of our relationship. The Afghans will have no reason (or progressively less reason, as withdrawal begins to be carried out) to regard our aid as a counterinsurgency tactic. At that point, beneficial projects will become acceptable to the local *jirgas*, whose members naturally focus on their own and their neighbors' prosperity and health. They will then eagerly seek and protect what they now allow the Taliban to destroy.

If under this different circumstance the Taliban try to destroy what the town councils have come to see as beneficial, the councils will cease to provide the active or passive support, sanctuary and information that make the Taliban effective. Without that cooperation, as Mao Zedong long ago told us, they will be like fish with no water in which to swim. Thus, setting a firm and clear date for withdrawal is essential.

This leaves us with the third issue, the central government. We chose it and we pay for it. But as our ambassador, Gen. Karl Eikenberry, has pointed out in leaked reports, it is so dishonest it cannot be a strategic partner. It is hopelessly corrupt, and its election last year was fraudulent; General Petraeus even told President Obama that it is a "crime syndicate." It is important to understand why it lacks legitimacy in the eyes of its people.

For us, the answer seemed simple: a government must legitimize itself the way we legitimize ours, with a reasonably fair election. But our way is not the Afghan way. Their way is through a process of achieving consensus that ultimately must be approved by the supreme council of state, the *loya jirga*. The apex of a pyramid of village, tribal and provincial assemblies, the *loya jirga*, according to the Constitution, is "the highest manifestation of the will of the people of Afghanistan."

Like the Russians, we have opposed moves to allow Afghanistan to bring about a national consensus. In 2002 nearly two-thirds of the delegates to a *loya jirga* signed a petition to make the exiled king, Zahir Shah, president of an interim government to give time for Afghans to work out their future. But we had already decided that Hamid Karzai was "our man in Kabul." So, as research professor Thomas Johnson and former foreign service officer in Afghanistan Chris Mason wrote last year, "massive US interference behind the scenes in the form of bribes, secret deals, and arm twisting got the US-backed candidate for the job, Hamid Karzai, installed instead... This was the Afghan equivalent of the 1964 Diem Coup in Vietnam: afterwards, there was no possibility of creating a stable secular government." An interim Afghan government certified by the *loya jirga* would have allowed the traditional way to achieve consensus; but, as Selig Harrison reported, our ambassador at the time, Zalmay Khalilzad, had a bitter 40-minute showdown with the king, who then withdrew his candidacy." We have suffered with the results ever since.

Could we reverse this downward trend? If we remove our opposition to a *loya jirga*, will the Kabul government respond? Probably not so long as America is willing to pay its officials and protect them. But if we set a clear timetable for withdrawal, members of the government will have a strong self-interest in espousing what they will see as the national cause, and they will call for a loya jirga. Indeed, President Karzai already has.

Would such a move turn Afghanistan over to the Taliban? Realistically, we must anticipate that many, perhaps even a majority, of the delegates, particularly in the Pashtun area, will be at least passive supporters of the Taliban. I do not see any way this can be avoided. Our attempts to win over the "moderates" while fighting the "hardliners" is an echo of what we tried in Vietnam. It did not work there and did not work for the Russians in Afghanistan. It shows no sign of working for us now. As a 2009 Carnegie Endowment study of our occupation and the Taliban reaction to it laid out, even after their bloody defeat in 2001, "there have been no splinter groups since its emergence, except locally with no strategic consequences."

Nor, as I have shown in my history of two centuries of insurgencies, *Violent Politics*, are we likely to defeat the insurgents. Natives eventually wear down foreigners. The Obama administration apparently accepts this prediction. As the *Washington Post* reported this past fall, it admits that "the Taliban cannot be eliminated as a political or military movement, regardless of how many combat forces are sent into battle."

A *loya jirga* held soon is the best hope to create a reasonably balanced national government. This is partly because in the run-up to the national *loya jirga*, local groups will struggle to enhance or protect local interests. Their action will constitute a brake on the Taliban, who will be impelled to compromise. Today the Taliban enjoy the aura of national defenders against us; once we are no longer a target, that aura will fade.

65

If we are smart enough to allow the Afghans to solve their problems in their own way rather than try to force them to adopt ours, we can begin a sustainable move toward peace and security. Withdrawal is the essential first step. Further fighting will only multiply the cost to us and lead to failure.

April 1, 2010

CHAPTER 6

IMPRESSIONS OF AFGHANISTAN

*the*Atlantic

> *This essay was written in the summer of 2010 so some of the persons (e.g General McCrystal) are no longer there, but the essential information is, unfortunately, still in date.*

KABUL, AFGHANISTAN—One of the advantages of being an "old hand" in the Middle East or Central Asia is that almost anything one does conjures up memories that make for interesting contrasts. My first visit to Afghanistan back in 1962 began by car, driving up the Khyber Pass from Pakistan. I was accompanying Governor Chester Bowles, then "the President's Representative for Europe, Asia and Latin America," that is, the holder of a title but with no real authority. As befit his title, we had an American military airplane but, as governed by the reality of his lack of power, it had broken down. So we drove. I liked that better since I had pored over Kipling as a boy, and the Khyber was, of course, where the wild tribesmen hung out.

They still do. I didn't then see any of them, but I read the signs of the passing of the British and Indian regiments carved into the rocks. It was a wonderful way to reach Kabul. And it was a portent of the future.

In those days, Kabul was a rather sleepy little city of about 50,000, roughly the size of the 1930s Fort Worth, Texas, into which I was born. Fort Worth was cleaner, but, despite the distant memories of the Wild West in Texas, Kabul was far more interesting. And it had the most marvelous rug stores. It was also the jumping off place for my 2,000 miles trip around the country by Jeep, horseback and the occasional plane. I fell in love with

Afghanistan from the first. To me it is "the Wild East."

My second visit was a decade later. Kabul had hardly changed, but the regime had. Afghanistan was in a sort of golden age of reform. Everyone was full of hope. The markets were full of furs, rugs and those delicious melons that the great conqueror and poet Babur Shah thought worth more than all of India. Hippies, then known as "world travelers," flooded into the country, equipped with their parents' credit cards to the delight of local merchants. But what was really impressive was the university. Filled with earnest young men and bright, alert and daringly dressed young women, it had an air of excitement.

Today's entry into Kabul is not less exciting but is stunningly different. The "advised" way to go these days is by air from Dubai. The take-off point, Dubai airport, is a huge shopping mall, almost entirely manned by Filipino expatriates, with attached airlines from every part of the world. So large is the terminal that I was taken from the lounge of the feeder airline, Safi, to the gate by one of those little electric carts that are now standard airport transport. Even the speedy cart took a quarter of an hour to make the trip.

Settling back in my seat on the Safi plane, a modern Airbus with pilots of dubious background (one moved over from, as he put, "Libya, you know Qaddafi") I flipped through the airline magazine. There, instead of the usual ads for perfume and watches, were advertisements for fully armored cars:

> You are moving in a dangerous region, you find yourself in the wrong place at the wrong time, within a matter of seconds; your vehicle has become a target. Not a problem if you have to have an armored vehicle from GSG...GSG's armoring provides you with valuable time, enough for you to grasp the situation, assess the threat and be able to react appropriately. (GermanSupportGroup.com)

If this was not enough to make tourists want to rush to Afghanistan, the airline magazine also provided enticing pictures of shattered, bombed-out buildings.

My reading complete, I was ready for Kabul's "International Airport." It was even more spartan than the airport I knew in the 1970s, but this time, as we moved toward the terminal, we paraded past dozens of planes of other airlines. To judge by the tarmac, it was bustling. What was particularly striking was that Kabul is the "hub" of a United Nations virtual airline of helicopters and jets. And, although the Americans run a far larger airport at Bagram, their planes and particularly their jets, overflow into Kabul. Nothing like that was to be seen in my earlier trips.

When we got into the terminal, I found the Afghans to be still the same polite and welcoming people I had known in previous trips. Then signs began to appear of the ugliness of civil war. I would see many such signs in the days ahead, but a hint came in the first minutes. I was met outside the customs by an American embassy expediter. He had been expecting me, he said. We shook hands; then he sat down. Or rather squatted since there were no chairs. Why were we not walking out to the car? I waited for him to speak, but he just motioned me to sit. Slightly annoyed, I asked what we were waiting for. He replied that he had seven other arriving Americans to escort into Kabul. They were just a trickle in the daily flood. Indeed, it appeared that half Kabul was made up of new American arrivals. However, the expediter, seeking to assuage my impatience, rather proudly said that I had been honored with a special car. Then why, I asked, could I not just get in and go. "Ah," he said, "it is not that easy." It turned out that not even embassy cars were allowed to within about two hundred yards of the terminal, so everyone had to walk from the exit to the guarded car park. And, naturally, as "nature" is defined these days in Kabul, one could not do that without an escort.

First lesson: nothing in Afghanistan is easy.

Before I got to Kabul, I had received an email from the escort officer assigned to me, saying that since Kabul is a "high danger" area, the embassy wanted me to rent from a private security company known as "Afghan Logistics" an armored Toyota "4 Runner" and hire both an armed security guard and a bullet proof vest at 20,000 Afs (roughly $450) daily. I was to be reassured that the rates included the driver's salary, fuel and taxes. No bullets were stipulated. I guess they were extra. However, the daily rate was only for 8 hours and overtime was at double rate, Kabul being presumably more dangerous at night. But my embassy escort officer said, these arrangements were both necessary and standard procedure, and with them I would thus be reasonably well protected.

I declined. My doing so was not a sign of bravery but a calculation that such a display would mark me as a worthwhile target.

Flashing through my mind were memories of experiences in other "high danger" areas. I had arrived in Algiers in 1962 shortly before the return of President-designate Ahmad Ben Bella (and met him at the airport with our ambassador-designate). During that confused and nearly frantic week, when the French had more or less completely pulled out and the "external" army of the Provisional Algerian Government had not yet taken over, the "internal" or *wilayah* guerrillas were not only settling scores with the French and the Algerians who had collaborated with them, but also with one another. The *wilayah* underground fighters were impressive fellows; they had fought an army 30 times their size and had worn it down, but almost none of them could read. So documents were more objects of suspicion than passes. A smile and a handshake were better than passports.

But many people, particularly those associated with the Organisation Armée Secrète, had little experience in smiling and if their hands shook it was because they were carrying heavy weapons. Not surprisingly, CIA sources indicated that in those few days some 16,000 people were "disappeared." Yet, I felt safe walking around the city. Two years later in Saigon, I watched a fire-fight one night from the Embassy roof, standing next to former Vice President and then Ambassador Henry Cabot Lodge. Everyone even then knew that the Viet Minh "owned the night." But, during the day, I felt no hesitation in walking about the city.

Kabul today provides a very different experience from those. First of all, signs of danger are all about. Thousands of armed private security guards from many nationalities as well as Afghans are scattered throughout the city on virtually every block. Cars are checked at intersections by Kalashnikov-wielding Afghan policemen or men who I assumed to be police although some I saw were not in anything resembling a uniform. Never mind the "bad guys," gun-toting policemen, many said to be high on drugs and virtually all untrained, were enough of a menace.

Most Kabulis feel that menace, since Kabul is said to be now under the control of President Karzai's police, and the police are rough with civilians and often shake them down. But the 140,000 American and American-led troops and the scores of thousands of mercenaries and private security guards pay no attention to the police. Nor, as I was to find, do various privileged Afghans. Anyone who counts has his own private army. So, taken as a whole, the 50,000 or so "security" forces constitute a new virtual nation – or actually nations, plural -- as they come from everywhere, Gurkhas from Nepal, Malays, Samoans, various Latinos and Europeans with a mixture of what looked like a delegation from an American weight-lifting club -- alongside of Afghanistan's already complex mix of nations.

Pashtuns, Tajiks, Hazaras, Uzbeks, Turkmen, Aimaqs, Kirghiz, Nuris, Baluchis and others rub shoulders; no one group is the majority of Afghans. Each tends to congregate with its own kind in discrete areas, but there is much mixing. This is particularly evident here in the capital, but happens village by village throughout the country. So, as some have suggested, dividing Afghanistan along ethnic lines would either be impossible or would cause continuous conflict.

President Karzai would like to rid Afghanistan of the "private security forces," whom he accuses of fostering corruption and committing human rights violations. He announced, as I began my tale on August 17, 2010, that he will abolish these private armies, withdrawing their visas, expelling them and closing down the 50 or more firms that hire them, but he probably cannot do so. They are "embedded" with our military and with all the diplomatic missions and the Afghan power elite. Even the American army uses foreign mercenaries for protection.

Without any sense of irony, diplomats and generals admit that they hire these guards to protect not only themselves but even their soldiers. Our ambassador, to cite one example, travels with a guard of mercenaries rather than one of Marines who, in my days in government, were charged with guarding the embassies. British Deputy Ambassador Tom Dodd told me, with what I thought was a flash of pride, that the British had a ratio of 1 mercenary for each Englishman whereas the American ratio was 3 to 1. With numbers so large, I asked him to account for them. "Money," he replied. "They are cheaper than regular soldiers."

I find that hard to believe. It must be a toss-up. Each soldier costs us $1 million a year, but foreign (as distinct from Afghan) mercenaries earn $1,000 or more day just in salaries, not counting housing and food, transportation several times a year back and forth to their homes and, perhaps most significant, life insurance.

So much for the foreigners, so why do Afghans hire bodyguards? Partly prestige, no doubt, but also because of a genuine fear of private vendetta or assassination by one or other of the scores or even hundreds of warlords. These men cannot, or at least do not, trust the regular police to protect them. Having a dozen or so gunmen is also the road to riches. And, most believe, it is the best way to stay alive to enjoy those riches.

But it isn't just the rich and powerful whose *condottierri* lord it over the ordinary Afghans: assorted other gunmen, including unemployed young men and even off-duty policemen, routinely shake down passers-by, shop keepers and even households. Scruffy fellows they may be, but loaded down with Kalashnikov machineguns, grenades and pistols, and cavalier about reading government documents, they pose an implicit threat to almost everyone. The "on-duty" police can do nothing about them because no one can tell who they are or who stands behind them – ministers, heads of government departments, bigger warlords or even the Taliban.

Let me dilate on just the Taliban. We think of the Taliban as a coherent unit. No doubt it is partly that. But it is diversified in command structure because of the weakness of its embattled communication system. So whatever the "center," which is presumed to be far away in Quetta, Pakistan, decides may not be known in a timely fashion, if at all, by more or less isolated cadres. Moreover, the organization has many, perhaps not always wanted, part-time volunteers. Although they may operate in the name of the Taliban. Many of these people are not auxiliaries but opportunists. Because of an insult or the presence of a target, groups of young thugs often carry out assaults or kidnappings on their own. Such events are different from the well-planned attacks (like the one a few years ago on the hotel in which I stayed) involving suicide bombers and commando units. The aim of the independents is not political; it is either revenge or money, or both. This makes their danger unpredictable.

Unpredictable it is but it is more or less ever-present. It comes not only from these casual thugs, the Taliban or even other major insurgent groups. Indeed, almost anyone with enough money or willing kinsmen can set himself up as a "power broker." A staff report to the Congress entitled "Warlord, Inc., Extortion and Corruption Along the U.S. Supply Chain in Afghanistan," described what must be a fairly typical minor strongman who was described as "an illiterate, hashish-producing former warlord who directs a semiofficial police force…he is also a key partner of US forces." He has 40 "soldiers" and rules only about 4 square miles. So you have all the elements: drugs, protection money, command over a small piece of the supply route – and alliance with US forces.

Groups like this are all over the country and in the aggregate the payoff to them is huge. An American Congressional investigation entitled "Warlord, Inc., Extortion and Corruption Along the U.S. Supply Chain in Afghanistan," published in June this year, showed that to implement a $2.16 billion transport contract the US military is paying tens of millions of dollars to warlords, corrupt public officials and (indirectly) the Taliban to ensure safe passage of its supply convoys throughout the country." Dexter Filkins of *The New York Times* (who incidentally won a George Polk Award) put it bluntly, "With U.S. Aid, Warlord Builds an Afghan Empire." He described "an illiterate former highway patrol commander [who] has grown stronger than the government of Oruzgan Province, not only supplanting its role in providing security but usurping its other functions, his rivals say, like appointing public employees and doling out government largess. His fighters run missions with American Special Forces officers, and when Afghan officials have confronted him he has either rebuffed them or had them removed." How did he do it? Money. Filkins points out that his company charges $1,200 for each NATO cargo truck to which it gives safe passage and so makes about $2.5 million a month. How does he get away with it? As Filkins wrote, "His militia has been adopted by American Special Forces officers to gather intelligence and fight insurgents."

Afghanistan today is somewhat like medieval Italy, a land of warlords. The big ones are just the more impressive of hundreds if not thousands of small bosses, some with only a dozen "guns," who operate in a single neighborhood or along a short stretch of road. While many are involved in the drug trade, others draw their funds from offering protection or engaging in casual kidnapping. They are known to work with or at least around the police or even, themselves, may be part-time members of the police force and/ or private security details. I imagine that every Afghan knows who's who in his neighborhood, but an outsider can easily blunder into a messy situation. Canny outsiders, like the members of the resident press corps, as Dexter Filkins later told me, feel relatively safe because they know where not to go.

In two ways, this is a very old system in the Middle East. In the cities, merchants kept a sort of peace because they wanted people to visit their shops, and Nineteenth century European and native travelers in outlying areas often "rented" free passage from local lords. Payment for passage is common – and very profitable, as the Congressional study made clear -- today in Afghanistan. Trucks moving fuel or supplies, even for the American Army, almost anywhere in the country do so by paying off the local strongmen. The American command is criticized for this practice, but it is notable that even when they supposedly ruled Afghanistan, the Taliban engaged in the same practice. What is new is that this system has spread to the cities. Even restaurants are fenced in with huge concrete walls and steel gates and "rent" protection.

I went one evening to a little Lebanese restaurant called "The Taverna" for dinner with Dexter Filkins. I found it to be packed with people. The owner happened to be from the Lebanese Shuf mountains. On a silly impulse, I asked him if he were a Junbalti or a Yazbaki. He looked astonished and asked how I knew of such things. When I replied that I had written a book on his land, he sent over dish after dish, "on the house." Nevertheless, the meal was fairly expensive. The reason was obvious: four armed men, in fact moonlighting policemen, were guarding the entrance. They are the new thing – not bouncers but "doorstops."

The biggest doorstop of all, of course, is the American embassy. Embassy is hardly the right word. It is a vast urban fortress, a city in its own right. Indeed, it is now the largest in the world with roughly 1,000 civilians and is flanked by a military garrison that is far larger and a comparable but unmentioned CIA complex. The American "city" has its own water purification and electrical system, roads, dormitories, offices, shops, coffee houses and an "eating facility." (It would be libelous to call it a restaurant). Virtually every piece of the American bureaucracy – representatives of more than 60 agencies -- is in residence. And by residence I mean working, eating, sleeping, exercising, and being entertained. I spoke to several people who had left the grounds only a few times in their one- or two-year tours of duty. They are not allowed to walk anywhere in Kabul (or elsewhere) but must go only in armored cars, wearing a full suit of body armor and helmet. The Embassy compound is less than a mile from the airport, but to get there is to run an obstacle course through a man-made valley of high, concrete blast walls. Every few yards is a steel telegraph poll to be raised, a group of security guards to be satisfied, a guard dog to sniff the car's contents, a mine detector to be run under it. Then, as each barrier is passed, the driver zigzags, like a giant slalom skier, around massive concrete blocks to the next check point. I counted half a dozen. At each check point the identification procedure starts all over again to satisfy a new group of sober-faced, heavily-armed mercenaries. I particularly noted that in addition to their weapons, each man carried in his flak jacket at least a dozen extra clips of bullets – ready, no doubt for a prolonged siege. Overhead, a sausage-shaped balloon equipped with sensors keeps watch on the entire city and helicopters circle frequently. Armored cars and machinegun nests are discretely scattered about. No wonder the Afghans believe they are under occupation and that the Americans intend to stay behind walls. Not your typical happy neighborhood.

I had been invited to spend my first night as a guest of Ambassador Lt. General (rtd.) Karl Eikenberry and his charming wife, Ching. I will come back to them in a few moments, but I want first to continue with the physical aspect of life in Kabul.

Since Senator John Kerry had swooped in, unannounced until the last minute, I had to move over to a hotel on the morning of my second day in town. Getting there was not easy, but (obviously to clear the way for the Senator – my threat to vote Republican did not save my bed!) the embassy "speeded" me on my way in an armored car with an American-employed Afghan guide.

Mr. A (who requested that his name be withheld, fearing vengeance as an American "quisling") is a graduate student of law in Kabul University who works for the US AID mission, As we drove toward the hotel along the nearly empty Kabul River, he pointed out the window at the swirling, densely packed, but surprisingly polite mass of people, many obviously poor but to my eye with no beggars among them, and said, "this is our problem…"

My first thought was that he meant that they or we were in peril from the chaotic torrent of trucks and cars. That seemed a good guess since many showed the scars of previous encounters. Then I thought he might have meant that we could be caught in a riot, like an Embassy car, driven by contractors from the mercenary firm DynCorps, was last month, when they ran over and killed four people. In that instance the latent anger of the Afghans boiled over with a crowd shouting "death to the Americans." We might be lynched if we ran over one of the pedestrians. That also seemed highly likely. It was obvious that anger was there, just under the surface and that it could easily be set off.

The explosive mixture was at hand: Neither pedestrians nor cars paid any noticeable attention to one another. No give was offered at any point by anyone, but somehow each driver knew when he was defeated just before a collision would have happened. The men and often-*burqa*-clad women pedestrians performed as though in a Spanish bullfight. The "bulls" tore along, dashing around or between one another when they could, diving into temporary gaps, passing on both sides without any notion of on-coming traffic or of the presumed lanes into which the road might be divided, while the pedestrians, like toreadors, nimbly dodged in and out (or, if old, blind or one-legged, as a number I saw were, entrusted themselves to God's mercy).

Accidents were surprisingly few; I saw only two in a quarter of an hour. Sitting often in jams when traffic congealed with both streams head to head with one another, it struck me that if the Taliban attacked, they would have no chance to get away. Traffic may be Kabul's most effective security force.

But I was missing Mr. A's point. He was giving me my second lesson in Afghan politics. It wasn't traffic regulation but the rule of law that he was thinking about. He went on: "...we have laws, very good laws, but no means of enforcing them. These people," he gestured toward the closed and locked window, "don't even know that we have a constitution and certainly don't know what their rights are, while the rich and powerful, who do know that we have a constitution and laws, don't pay any attention to them. They just do what they want and take whatever they like. And there is no one to stop them."

I asked if this was also true in Taliban-controlled areas. Without the slightest hesitation, he said, "no. It is not. There is no corruption where the Taliban are in control."

When we arrived outside the Serena hotel (which incidentally is owned by the Aga Khan), we were stopped by the first group of armed guards outside its battlements. The walls were more tightly spaced but even more impressive than those at the embassy. Blankly before us was a wall made of a 30 foot-high steel gate. As we were identified by a group of guards, the gate was slid back on its rollers. Slowly we drove in. There we were stopped by a steel poll and faced a second high steel gate.

Then the outer gate was rolled shut. There was just enough space between the two gates for a large car. Locked securely from behind and in front, the car was checked with a mine detector for bombs. Then the pole was raised and the second steel gate was opened. We were in, or at least the embassy armored car was in. Then the steel panel at the rear of the car was opened to reveal my suitcases which, in turn, were passed through a detection system. My little camera was particularly worrying to the security guard, but finally he shrugged and let it (and me) through.

Then to the "front desk" to register. Despite the view through the glass window of the dozen or so guards, laden with their weapons, milling around the driveway and five others more or less discretely, but with bulging double-vented suit coats, standing around the hall, everything began to seem just like a normal hotel. Except, as I scanned the parking lot, I could see that the gates were fixed to even higher concrete walls. They were, I guessed, 40 to 50 feet high. I would later have a chance to see that the whole hotel and its charming Persian-style garden, an area of perhaps ten acres, was surrounded by a similar wall of which most was capped with additional barriers or razor wire. The Serena Hotel, whatever else it may be, is a castle.

Mr. A accompanied me to my room. I thought this showed a somewhat excessive concern for my security since we were surely as safe as walls and gates and guards could make us, but his move turned out to have another meaning -- as so much in Afghanistan these days seems to have. This is Ramadan, the month of fasting, and Mr. A could not eat or drink in public so he asked, rather sheepishly, if I would be so kind as to order him a sandwich and a Coca-Cola in the privacy of my room. I was glad I did because this gave us a chance to talk rather more freely than in the embassy car which, I presume he thought was bugged. He told me that while the Shiis, of which sect he belonged, also keep the fast of Ramadan, he did not. He did not explain but from other experiences I gather this was in part his way of saying that he was a modern, educated man.

As we waited for the sandwich, he told me a bit about his life. He could not, he said, admit that he worked for the Americans. And certainly not for the Embassy. So he told his family that he worked for a private construction firm. He was afraid to visit his native province, in the Tajik area, because even a Tajik relative might denounce him to the Taliban for collaboration with the Americans. However, he said, since his wife was from the same area, he sometimes had to return, but he dreaded each visit.

I asked about his roots. His father, he said, had been a doctor who was chased out during the Russian occupation; so Mr. A grew up a refugee camp in Peshawar, Pakistan like hundreds of thousands of other Afghans. When the Russians pulled out of Afghanistan in 1989, his family moved back and settled in Kabul. Since Kabul has grown from a city of about 50,000 in 1980 to 5 million today, his is a common experience.

I shamelessly used our wait for the sandwich and coke to pursue our talk in the car about the rule of law. What about property? I asked. "There is no security in property," he said. "If a person owns, for example, a house, and the local strongman wants it, he just tells the owner to get out. The owner has no choice. If he does not obey, he is apt to be beaten or killed. There is no recourse through government even if the owner has all the proper papers." But much "private" property, he explained, is not registered. It is either what people took over during the civil wars or is owned by custom, perhaps generation after generation. Under the circumstances of lawlessness, however, the distinction between registered and unregistered property is meaningless since neither can be upheld by any authority.

This is true, he continued, even of government property. If the "intruder" is powerful enough, that is well enough connected to one or other of the inner circle, he can simply take over government lands or buildings. Then even government officials can do nothing to make him vacate. In fact, he may be a minister himself, a member of the "inner circle."

The inner circle was bluntly described by members of the American press corps in their meeting with Senator John Kerry as Afghanistan's native mafia. The "families" include the Hazara Vice President, Karim Khalili; Kabir Mohabat, an Afghan with American citizenship; "Marshal" and now Vice President Muhammad Qasim Fahim, a Tajik; and "Marshal" Abdul Rashid Dostum, the Uzbek warlord who disdains any government post but is the President's "right hand." (Dostum deserves an Olympic gold medal for opportunism. A leader of the Uzbek people of the North, he fought the Russians, then joined them to fight the insurgents; then he joined the insurgency to fight the Russians; next he joined the Taliban; then he switched sides again to join the anti-Taliban "Northern Alliance" and is infamous for suffocating in steel lift vans in the sweltering summer captured Taliban soldiers. Now – for how long? – he is a supporter of President Karzai.) It also includes Zara Ahmad Mobil who ran what is regarded as the most corrupt organization in Afghanistan, the Ministry of Interior, and (as an editorial in *The Guardian* put it) "is now in charge of the opium industry;" and, certainly neither last nor least, the Karzai family.

President Karzai was himself described, in two dispatches in November 2009 from our Ambassador to Secretary of State Hillary Clinton (which were leaked to *The New York Times* and published in January 2010), with great diplomatic caution, as "not an adequate strategic partner." After being dressed down by President Obama for doubting Karzai's integrity or rather not being willing to overlook it in order to get on with the war and to get along with General McChrystal, Ambassador Eikenberry, maybe here is a place to put in a sentence to say he was replaced. now is even more cautious. At least in public. As I will later point out, in our late night chat on the embassy terrace, he was more realistic. But, he the points out that Karzai is all we have as an alternative to the Taliban. In short we are in a position not unlike the one we faced in Vietnam.

As a general, Eikenberry was a previous commander of the then smaller American force in Afghanistan. Prior to that he was the military attaché in the American embassy in Beijing, where he knew my friend, Ambassador Chas Freeman. Eikenberry's charming wife, Ching, is from China's far northeast and so is of partly Mongol background.

A scholarly, intelligent, hard-driving and honest man, Eikenberry tries to be optimistic; that goes with the job. He has to be optimistic no matter what he feels to keep up the spirits of his staff, but in his confidential dispatches of last November, he wrote, "The proposed troop increase [the "surge"] will bring vastly increased costs and an indefinite, large-scale U.S. military role in Afghanistan, generating the need for yet more civilians. An increased U.S. and foreign role in security and governance will increase Afghan dependency...and it will deepen the military involvement in a mission that most agree cannot be won solely by military means...Perhaps the charts we have all seen showing the U.S. presence rising and then dropping off in coming year in a bell curve will prove accurate. It is more likely, however, that these forecasts are imprecise and optimistic."

Here I do not want to go into detail on our private talk on the Embassy roof, which lasted until midnight, because I am writing a paper for him, based on my study and my talks here, on what I think we must now do. Let me just say that I do not believe he has changed his November assessment. Indeed, both he and all the knowledgeable people with whom I have talked believe the situation is far more dire now than last year. It is not just the statistics on casualties and wounded, although they show an accelerating downward trend and the wounded, in particular, are much more numerous than is reported and their wounds are both more grievous and much more expensive to compensate for. (A person with a head injury will cost the Treasury over his lifetime about $5 million in medical bills over his lifetime. Such costs are not figured into the figures given out by the Defense Department on the cost of the war.) But, it is clear that we do not have a coherent or long-term strategy and are trying to make up for that deficiency by throwing money – and people – into the fray more or less without any way of judging whether they help achieve or prevent us from achieving our vague objectives. Meanwhile, the Afghans appear to be sick and tired of Americans.

So back to my first informant, Mr. A. when I asked him about the local feeling toward the Americans he was so guarded that I did not press my question. All he felt he could say was that there are too many and their constant presence and display of power are galling. But Ambassador Eikenberry, he said, was personally very popular. Why? I pressed. "He goes everywhere without a big escort, and the Afghans like that," was his reply. Eikenberry later told me that he tried to appear often even in the supposedly unsafe market area with only a couple of bodyguards whom he kept as unobtrusive as possible. I don't know whether the Afghans admired his bravery or were just happy that he was not flaunting his power. But, whatever the reason, I was to hear repeatedly that he is indeed popular.

In my day with him, I was astonished by his performance. It was the very embodiment of the Washington adage: "the urgent drives out the important." Managing his vast staff, including four subordinate ambassadors (talk about bureaucratic inflation – I have never heard of an American embassy with more than one ambassador!), over 60 US agencies (over many of which he is not in ultimate command) and a thousand people, meeting daily with General Petraeus and his senior officers, holding frequent conferences with the Afghan press and influential Afghans, giving sometimes several speeches a day, escorting and briefing visiting VIPs like Senator John Kerry, meeting with, listening to and admonishing President Karzai, and touring the ubiquitous trouble spots and even, while I was there, walking the four-mile perimeter of the embassy walls to personally check out the security arrangement, he is run ragged. I sat in on the briefing of his "country team." There he was the coach, trying to build morale; the teacher, urging the men and women from agencies not under his control to get "out into the field" and to show more sensitivity to the Afghans; and the diplomat, complimenting each person by name for some act he had heard about. It was a remarkable performance. Then he rushed off to meet Kerry, flew with him to a remote post, assembled the American press corps for a briefing, and in the evening held a dinner for the entire Afghan television station owners and reporters at which he gave another speech. As I chided him, he never has time to sit back and think about what all our frantic activities are really all about. He must have been alarmed to hear Senator John Kerry say in an interview here in Kabul on August 19, "We have to remember that this is the beginning, just the beginning…"

From reflecting on our, the American, problems, I went to pay a call on Dr. Sima Samar. She is the head of the Afghanistan Independent Human Rights Commission (AIHRC) and a highly articulate, intelligent and well informed person. She also must be physically and morally brave because the environment in which she operates is incredibly difficult and she has no real power.

As I was getting used to doing, I arrived at her office gate which, like so much of Kabul today, is massive and steel. A peep hole, like one might see on the cell door of violent inmates in a prison, was pushed open several inches so I and my embassy guide could be scrutinized. Several minutes passed. Then a section of the massive gate was swung open to let the two of us inside. Once we were identified, the full gate was swung back to enable our embassy car, also identified, with suitable painted messages and a sort of inside license plate in place of a sun visor, to be driven in. Then the gate was rolled shut.

As in most of the other buildings, heavily armed – Kalashnikov automatic rifles, hand grenades, pistols, flak jackets, helmets, radios, etc. – guards eyed us balefully. They were Afghans. Then an unarmed civilian appeared, half bowed, shook hands and said *hoda hafez*. Turning, he led me, but not my Afghan companion, Mr. A, up a narrow flight of stairs onto a non-descript and rather threadbare landing. It was in stunning contrast to the massive "security" outside. My first thought was 'all this protection for so little!'

Then Dr. Samar emerged, seized my hand and led me into her crowded office. She is an impressive woman, bright eyed, with a ready smile, of (I guess) 55 years. She had somehow read about me so our preliminaries were very brief, just the mention of mutual friends, particularly the grand lady of Afghanistan, my friend Nancy Dupree, who had particularly urged me to see her. Then without the usual offer of tea (since it is Ramadan), we got down to business.

The situation here, she said, is really neither black nor white. In some ways it is better than it was a few years ago, but the real opportunity was missed in 2002 when the Taliban had been defeated. Had a relatively small American force been left here then, an acceptable level of security could have been created and maintained. Today, she went on -- as I found in most of my talks, everyone began on an optimistic note and soon this faded into a somber mood -- today, the real casualty is hope. People today do not believe that an acceptable level of security can be achieved. The fundamental problem, she said, is the warlords. They are so deep into the drug trade, are making so much money, and are so tied into the government at the very top that there is little hope for any sort of reform. Putting in more troops will accomplish nothing.

But, then, to my surprise, she went on to say that the Afghan army and police force are really improving. They need time. Will they get it? She asked me. I said that I doubted that, despite US government statements, the American commitment was open-ended. Indeed, America itself is so beset by financial problems that the mood is shifting. She nodded and sighed.

Then our conversation virtually began anew. From warlords and improvement of the security forces, she shifted to what obviously is the bottom line: the issue of corruption. Can the regime survive? Many people here -- but not she, she matter-of- factually said – have dual nationality. They send their children abroad, a son in England, another or a daughter in the US or Canada, etc. – and perhaps their wives as well. They also send along with them or at least to foreign banks as much money as they can. The reason why they do so is simple, they have little trust in the existing government and less in the future. Why not? She asked rhetorically. They have nothing to fall back on. What they are doing is personally prudent even if it is nationally disastrous.

As I listened, my mind went back to Vietnam. Afghanistan is in so many ways Vietnam redux. Everyone is preparing his bolt hole and wants to be sure that it is well padded with money. Afghan Minister of Finance Umar Zakhilwal admitted that during the last three years over $4 billion – billion! -- in cash had been flown out of Afghanistan in suitcases and footlockers (like I thought only Mexican drug dealers used) destined for private accounts or persons abroad. While money in those amounts has a serious effect on the faltering Afghan economy, what is even more important is that it shows that commitment to this regime and to Afghanistan is fragile and declining among the inner circle, Afghanistan's power elite.

Back to Dr. Samar. What else, could she put her finger on? I asked.

"Foreign corruption," she said. "Oh, of course, it is not the same kind. But when a contract is awarded to a foreign company and it then either does a bad job or does not finish its work and yet exports 80% or 90% of the contract funds, is that not also corruption? We would understand even 50% but few take that little. Is that not corruption too? But you Americans pay little attention to it; yet it serves as a model for our people.

"Even when corruption is not involved," she continued, "there are two tendencies that undercut the benefit your actions might have brought. The first is the use of machines. Of course, I know," she went on, "machines are faster and may even do a more beautiful job, but they displace labor. And unemployment is one of our most serious problems. It would be far better to use shovels and give people jobs.

"Also bad is the tendency of your contractors to draw on labor from outside the place where a project is undertaken. Of course, contractors draw on the cheapest source of labor. So they might use Tajiks to do a project in a Hazara area, for example. Then the local people have no sense that it is theirs. We see this often. But, if a road, for example, is built in a village by local people, they feel it is somehow theirs and will take care of it. But Americans show no sensitivity to Afghans and their way of living."

Nothing was to be gained, she said, by adding more troops. There are already probably far too many. Each new soldier gives rise to a new Talib. And troops do not address the core issue.

But, she was not in favor of a total withdrawal at this time. Time , she said, must be given to enable the police force, at least, to improve. That, she agreed, was not much solace but it was the best that could realistically be offered from here.

I next went to see the Deputy Special Representative of the UN Secretary General, the former German Ambassador to Iraq, Martin Kobler. His immediate superior, Steaffan de Mistura, a friend of my good friend and neighbor, Samir Basta, who was his boss had told me that he is an excellent man and here, I found he is said to be one of the best informed men in town Unfortunately, he was away on leave, so Ambassador Kobler filled in.

Ambassador Kobler's headquarters, UNAMA, was understandably

under massive protection. No UN person could forget the killing of the UN team in Baghdad, including my dear friend, Nadia Younes, who had just been appointed Assistant Secretary General for the UN General Assembly. How and why this tragedy happened is a story I will tell at another time, but here it is memorialized in concrete, steel and a small army of guards.

Ambassador Kobler launched into our talk by emphasizing how the UN people moved out around Afghanistan. He did not say it, but almost everyone else I spoke to did: the Americans stay huddled in their compounds. Even when they are in "the field," they don't get out and around very much. It is mainly to move its workers around that the UN maintains the "airline" I saw when I landed in Kabul. Kobler himself, he said, tries to make at least one trip a week, often two, outside of Kabul to one or more of the 40 some odd project headquarters the UN maintains.

As most of the officials I met were to do, Kobler started rather sanguine about the current situation, but slowly retreated into major worry about how to reconcile the two, and contradictory, objects of the essentially American policy -- the thrust to build up a central authority (which, as he said, violates the national genius of the Afghans) while working with the manifestations of local autonomy (which is the Afghan tradition). The Americans, he commented, are trying to swim against the tide of Afghan history by their emphasis on central authority. Afghanistan always had a weak central authority that allowed the provinces much freedom of action.

But the Americans are even carrying out their own policy ineffectively, he said. About 80% of all aid funds flow outside the control of the central government so effectively the American program (as in Vietnam) substitutes itself for the central government and so in the eyes of the public diminishes it. Later I was to hear from the director of our AID program, Earl Gast, that actually 92% of aid money bypassed the central government. It was now down to 80% and his, Gast's, objective was to reduce it to 25%. It is cleaner that way, of course, but it shows Afghans that they do not have a government other than us. We faced and were defeated by the same problem in Vietnam: using American officials we got aid to the people but doing so showed them that their titular government was worthless.

Kobler continued: since the American military has virtually all the disposable money, and the Afghans regard America as intending to dominate the country into the future, they regard all foreign aid efforts as a tactic of the war -- as General Petraeus is endlessly quoted as saying, "money is my main ammunition." These thoughts led us into the issue of our Afghan traditions versus ours. To work here in any capacity, he said, we must be sensitive to Afghan traditions, which we often are not. Every time our soldiers bang on a door, or break it down, and enter a house to search for an insurgent, going into the women's quarters and even checking on, or otherwise manhandling the women and children and opening up their private closets etc., which they feel they must do as an insurgent (who might kill an American the next day) may be hiding there, the soldiers (or more likely the Special Forces) inevitably lose that family to the Taliban or at least make them hate the Americans.

But, at the same time, he went on, we must stand up for the values we hold. We do and must absolutely oppose such awful acts as stoning to death people who violate Sharia laws. There can be no give on this issue.

Perhaps the most interesting piece of information Kobler gave me was on the Taliban reaction to last week's UN Report on Taliban killing or injuring Afghan civilians. Although the Taliban denounced the report, and the UN for making it, their press release contained what Kobler thought was a major new development: they called for the creation of an international tribunal including the Taliban to investigate the charge. Kobler rightly saw this as a ploy to give the Taliban a sort of recognition as a quasi-governmental "player," but admitted that it may have lifted the veil slightly on a form of cooperation. He said, of course, the Americans, and therefor the UN, would not agree.

I objected, wondering if there were not a way to use this demarche. Perhaps we should remember, I said, a precedent of the Algerian war. He laughed and said that of course no one remembered any precedents from previous wars. He (and later others including the Russian ambassador) agreed. Everyone said that at the start of each new year we throw away all our memories of the actions and reactions of the past year and start all over again.

But what did I have in mind? He asked.

It was not a complete analogy but some adaptation from the Algerian war might be useful to consider. Toward the end of the Algerian war of independence, America had a crippling diplomatic problem: we were closely allied to France which was fighting the Algerians, but we were emotionally on the Algerian side and thought that, in any case, they would prevail. The State Department was torn apart: the European Bureau wanted to have nothing to do with the Algerians while the African Bureau was keen to recognize them. President Kennedy hit on a typical Kennedy solution: use his family. He sent Jackie Kennedy's half-brother, Hugh Auchincloss, up to New York to hang out at the UN. He had no official title, but he was to be there as a friendly presence. Identified as he was with JFK, his job was to make representatives of the Provisional Algerian Government, which had observer status at the UN, feel welcome. I wondered if some sort of adaptation might open up contacts with the Insurgents. Was there no way that at least the beginnings of foundations for future bridges might be laid?

He said he doubted it.

From each of my forays, I found it a relief to return to the hotel. Again, tradition: Inside the forbidding walls was a delightful "Persian" garden, where two fountains playing into water channels which were flanked by beds of roses. I felt back in "my" Middle East. Alas, the one of fading memory. Then, I had dinner in the hotel courtyard, listening to traditional Afghan music. Suddenly came the distant call to prayer. The drummers were silenced, but the moment the call ended, they took up their drums, not concerned about prayer time but only about the announcement of prayer. The Taliban would have been outraged. And, as the Russian ambassador later told me, the ambassador from the UAE certainly was: the accent in Arabic was terrible and the several calls to prayer across the city paid no attention to timing. In the UAE, he said, they pushed a button and the whole country heard one call!

At noon the next day, I drove over to the British embassy to see Deputy Ambassador Tom Dodd. To say the least, this is an unusual British embassy. It is the UK's largest, although dwarfed by the American establishment. It echoed the Americans in its elaborate security but, to me more striking, was the abrasion of Foreign Office formality. The email I received from one of the clerks setting up the appointment was addressed, "Dear William," and saying that "Tom" would be happy to see me. I thought how the formal British ambassadors I had known of old would be turning in their graves.

Mr. Dodd – Tom – is a new arrival, and not, I inferred from his rather vague remarks about his background, a regular Foreign Office man. He was indeed a civil servant but of what kind I could not tell. He was more optimistic than most of those I met. He said that while the situation in Kandahar was the worst, some of the other cities, such as Mazar-i-Sharif, Herat and Kunduz, were better. What distinguished them? I asked. He said it was simply that the local warlords were more willing to share their loot with their followers. So there was a sort of "trickle down effect," but in Kandahar the President's half-brother was stingy. I laughed to think how the phrase "trickle down," coined by my former colleagues, the Chicago economists, was applied to Afghanistan "security."

Not noticing my reaction, he said that if the programs of his government, the US and the Afghans have five years, the situation in Kandahar would be better. Not much gain for five years in that word "better," I replied. Moreover, I thought a more realistic time frame was 6 months to a year. And I pointed out how a number of the very people who fervently advocated the war, like Richard Haass, the current president of the Council on Foreign Relations, have now turned against it. As he wrote in the July 17 issue of *Newsweek*, "We can't win and it isn't worth it." I didn't feel that this registered.

When he got on to the military aspects, Dodd said he did not interface with Petraeus, but he went on to say one positive and one negative thing: the positive thing is that apparently there are many fewer Special Forces night raids, although, he said, he is not privy to them. (That too rather surprised me. As the UK's acting senior representative, I should have thought he needed to be privy to everything that affected the UK's position.) The negative thing is that the policy of killing off the Taliban old guard (he pointed out that here "old" means 50) is bringing forward younger and more violent men who have none of the experience or subtlety of the older generation. This cannot be good, he said. I would later hear much the same from a former senior Taliban leader, Mullah Abdus-Salam Zaeef, although he would tell me that much of the old guard is still alive and in command.

One interesting aspect of the government of Karzai, Dodd said, is that he can pick up a mobile phone and call almost anyone in the country and connect within half an hour, and, he said, "the Afghans love to talk." So presumably Karzai is in contact almost continuously with people all over the country.

Despite the fall in public support in the UK for the British position here, he said, Britain has a more important stake than America since it has about 1 million Pakistani and 3 million Indian residents/subjects in the UK. But, he said, with I thought something like wry amusement, in the event of any sort of settlement, interim or otherwise, "Britain has no money for projects of any magnitude. When it leaves, as it inevitably must, it will be able to maintain its special forces and a training mission for the army or police. Nothing more." When we got onto the cost of the war, to my surprise, he misspoke or was totally misinformed: he said that the American war effort here was, after all, "cheap." I must have looked astonished because he went on to clarify his remark: it was only $7 billion a year. That is even less than the published figure – perhaps half the real cost – not for a year but for a month.

Speaking of money leads me to my meeting the next day, Wednesday, August 18, with US AID Mission Director Earl W. Gast, America's senior man on the Afghan economy.

Gast was refreshingly candid. Also relatively new to his job, he was proud of what he was doing. His favorite program, he said, was the "Afghanistan's National Solidarity Program (NSP)," which is described as "the largest development program in Afghanistan and a flagship program of the Afghan government." It was begun in 2003 and claims to have financed over 50,000 projects in all of Afghanistan's 34 provinces. In the words of its MIT-led evaluation team, the program "is structured around two major village-level interventions: (1) the creation of a gender-balanced Community Development Council (CDC) through a secret-ballot, universal suffrage election; and (2) the disbursement of grants, up to a village maximum of $60,000, to support the implementation of projects selected, designed, and managed by the CDC in consultation with the village community. NSP thus seeks to both improve the access of rural villagers to critical services and to create a structure for village governance on democratic process and the participation of women."

Nation building in high gear! But as a jaded old hand in reading government handouts, I asked Gast if it really made any difference. By way of a reply he gave me the report of a study group sponsored by MIT under contract to AID. The contractors did a random survey in 250 areas and gave a mixed report. Their report was, indeed, the opposite of what I would have expected: they found a strong impact on selected aspects of village "governance" but none on economic activity. Reading closely both what they said and what they did not say, I doubted that the program had much impact on anything except on our feeling that we were doing something.

Doing something, Gast said, was his major problem. He is under intense pressure from Washington to show actions of almost any sort. Before he arrived, he said, one of the big efforts at doing something was down in the newly conquered province of Marja. The US military had run the Taliban out -- or so they thought -- and General McChrystal was bringing in a "government in a box." Perhaps the most important piece "in the box" was to be the creation of jobs. So AID set up a program to hire 10,000 workers – virtually all the adults in a local population of about 35,000 people – but only about 1,000 took up the offer. Why? The answer was simple: the local people knew more about guerrilla warfare than the American army did. From years of experience, they knew that the guerrillas had done what guerrillas are supposed to do, fade away when confronted with overwhelming force and come back when the time is right. They are back. And, as other insurgents have done in all the insurgencies I studied in my *Violent Politics*, they have punished those they regarded as traitors. The 9,000 Afghans who turned down the AID offer were what Chicagoans would call "street smart."

Did we learn anything from this experience? To get another opinion, I met with Dexter Filkins, an "old" – that is, not old in my terms but at least a

91

decade old -- Middle East hand, who has spent years in repeated assignments here, in Iraq, India and Pakistan and who is one of the few who really gets about the country, on his own, not "embedded," and not loaded down with flak jacket, body guards and minders. He is just young enough and daring enough to see a different picture, I thought. I was right.

First, he said, the Kandahar operation is already in full swing. It isn't just the assassination squads of the "Special Ops" (aka Special Forces) but large-scale regular army action although the Military here, known as ISAF, are not talking about it. And it is essentially, as I wrote in June on "changing the guard but not the drill," the same as the Marja operation, just bigger. The failed Marja campaign is the template for the Kandahar campaign. And it too will fail, Filkins predicted. Filkins said that Petraeus was essentially trying to apply what he did in Iraq to Afghanistan without much thought that the two countries are very different. I disagreed: it was a deeper mistake. As I have written, Petraeus is replaying not only what the Americans did in Vietnam but even what the French tried to do in Vietnam.

To my surprise, Filkins was relatively complimentary about the military high command and particularly about Petraeus. What he found most favorable was that, unlike all the civilians holed up in the embassy fortress, the military does get out into "the field." Had Ambassador Eikenberry heard this, he would have agreed. Much of his admonition to the members of his Country Team meeting was to get out and see.

But, is this really such a good idea? I wonder. Almost everyone with whom I spoke mentioned how disturbing it was to the Afghans to see so many Americans. True, there are large areas of the country with no American military or civilian presence, but from Kabul west, south and east, Americans are thick on the ground. Would adding more be beneficial? And particularly adding more when decked out in helmets, flak jackets and goggles – like my escort officer, a nice American woman – had to wear even up in the supposedly "secure" northern city of Mazar-i-Sharif. Not speaking any of the local languages, almost entirely new to the country (very few have little preparation before they come, stay here longer than a year and have little contact or, apparently, interest while they are here) and prone to tell the locals how to manage their lives, they conjure the phrase common among even our close friends and allies, the English during World War II, about the Americans, "over sexed, over paid and over here."

To get a non-American and "historical" view on foreign intervention in Afghanistan, I arranged to have a dinner and long talk with Russian Ambassador Andrey Avetisyan. Since we had not met before, I asked him to tell me about himself. He is a Pashto language specialist who has served in the Russian Foreign Office, in Belgium and for three stints here including once during the Soviet occupation. I met him courtesy of my old friend Evgeny Maksimovich Primakov, the former Russian Foreign Minister, Director of the KBG and Prime Minister.

Avetisyan and I covered much the same ground as I did my previous talks with, obviously, different angels of vision. I will report only the differences here.

Avetisyan was quite categorical in saying that there was no hope of winning the war militarily. Then he went into a bit of the history of the Soviet campaign. Two things he particularly singled out were ones that, he thought, the Russians did rather better than the Americans. First, they separated economic and military actions. Their "civic action" projects, unknown to most outsiders, actually accomplished a great deal. We discussed my favorite, the vast plantations of olives and the production of oil (both casualties of the civil wars in the 1990s) from which the memory lingers to this day. He is often approached, he said, by Afghans, even former anti-Russian fighters, who compare the Russians favorably to the Americans.

The second aspect of the Russian economic program he thought was better was that the Russians did not provide cash to the Afghans. Of course, he said, they paid salaries, but they brought in the equipment that was needed and paid, directly, for work done with it. So, he believed, the problem of corruption of the Afghan government then was far less than today.

The military policy of the Americans, he said, was roughly comparable to the Russian. That is, except that it was more simple then: you either fought

93

or you collaborated. Today, the mixing of civic action, counterinsurgency, military occupation and special operations makes a complex combination. However, reliance on the military did not work for the Russians and, he believed strongly, would not work for the Americans today.

What about the Russian involvement today? I asked.

There are two aspects, he replied. First, the Russians are worried about the Central Asians and Caucasians who have come to fight for the Taliban. What are they going to do when they go home? He wondered. "Some people," he said, "think that they will have just grown old and become tired of war. But I am not so sure." They are hardened veterans, and maybe they will take home what they learned here. The second aspect, he said, is that if the Taliban win, they and their version of Pan-Islamism will make an impact on the republics of former Soviet Central Asia.

I laughed and said, "the Domino theory in reverse." He nodded.

"However," he continued, "wherever the al-Qaida people are today, it is important to remember that they were here before the Taliban arrived. The Taliban found Usama bin Ladin already here. I suppose their getting together was a matter of money. The Taliban had almost none and the Saudis had a lot. It was a natural alliance."

I commented that I understood that about a year ago, the Taliban put Usama under what I guessed could be called "cave arrest." Avetisyan laughed and said "there are many reports. Unquestionably, there have been severe strains in their relationship. I do not think that they will exercise major influence on the Taliban. Nor will the Taliban give them a free hand."

Returning to my major interest, I pressed about how and when one could think of getting out. He said that it would take at least 5 years to develop an Afghan army, and that to get out quickly now would probably plunge the country back into civil war.

I pursued the point. Should we consider early negotiations or wait?

He replied that to negotiate now would be difficult because the Karzai government is so obviously weak. The Taliban, he said, have their men in every office of the government and there are no secrets from them. I mentioned that after the Vietnam war ended, we discovered that the South Vietnamese President's chief of office admitted to having worked for the Viet Minh throughout the war. "Well," he said, "it is even more pronounced here. The Taliban are everywhere."

I mentioned that I was hearing that there are three options: get out now or very soon; pull out the main military forces but leave behind "Special Ops" forces; or negotiate.

He replied that, of course, we must negotiate. Indeed, he said, his information was that it was now on-going among the Afghans, but that the Pakistanis were disturbed when the Afghans tried to do it alone. He mentioned the Pakistani arrest a couple of months ago of two senior Taliban who were involved in negotiations. (This was reported and variously interpreted in the Western press.) But we could and must help the negotiation process, he said. He felt that in the context of negotiation, it would be possible to begin to pull out, but that it should not be precipitous.

The worst of all, he said, was what I had set out as the second option: to take out the regular military and leave behind the Special Forces which operate like the Soviet *SpetNaz*. It would be far better to keep the regular army even at the high point it has reached (which is larger than the former Soviet force level) than to rely on the Special Forces. The Special Forces are particularly hated by the Afghans, as were the *SpetNaz*, and, actually, are responsible for most of the really glaring abuses here. They would ruin what reputation we have left. That would not be good for anyone, Russia included, he continued.

I remarked that of course we could not control negotiations. He agreed and said that he thought the Afghans could handle that when they decided that they had to.

Could we not create that condition? I asked. That is, by setting a firm

95

date for withdrawal? That was what his government had done when it was intent on withdrawing. It would probably – or at least possibly -- not undercut our position. Moreover, it might have little effect on Taliban strategy. After all, I pointed out, assuming that they are reasonably in touch with the outside world, the Taliban leaders will know that support for continued military action here has dropped to near zero in much of Europe and is in free fall among those Americans who previously were the war's main advocates. As an example I mentioned the recent Newsweek article by Richard Haass (the president of the Council on Foreign Relations, which I have mentioned above) under the title, "We can't win and it isn't worth it."

What setting a date would do, I argued, would take us to the position he had just mentioned the Russians were careful to create, separating the economic from the military policy. The purpose of what I had in mind, I went on, was to change the "political psychology" of the war. Then, or gradually, village *shuras, jirgas* or *ulus* would come to see that the opening of a clinic or building a canal was not a tactic in the war. Rather, it was a benefit to the villagers. They would want those things and would protect them. Then, if the Taliban opposed, they would lose the support of the people. He said that he absolutely agreed with this. "It is the only way."

I then laid out what I would like to see happen here: the reassertion, with suitable modifications, of the traditional idea of the state. That is, a central government with sufficient military power to protect itself and punish aggression but with most emphasis on the economic and cultural means of integration. For example, using foreign aid, controlled by the central government through something like the American Corps of Engineers to undertake the major infrastructure projects. Under this arrangement, the central government would control foreign affairs including the encouragement of foreign aid while the provinces would handle their local affairs in accordance with their cultural traditions. Over time their policies would be influenced or swayed by the central government through the offer of opportunities for technical training and education and funding for development projects. Fairly rapidly, I thought, people in the provinces would be attracted to the things the central government could offer. Again, he agreed, saying that is the only real hope for the country.

"One can see," he amplified my thought, "that we have done far too little on education. There is no point in doing more big projects if the Afghans do not know how to handle them and do not regard them as their own."

We finally came to an issue on which he thinks we could beneficially cooperate. The Salang Pass through the Hindu Kush mountains needs to be rebuilt. It is the only feasible, economically viable passage between Central Asia and the Indian Subcontinent. It would enable the Afghans to ship their goods more cheaply to the outside world. It also is the supply route for the American army. And, perhaps most important of all, it could be a joint Russian-American project which would both symbolize and effect the transition from the still-remembered Cold War to a new era of peace and stability. I promised to discuss it both with our AID director here and with friends in Washington. I think it could really be the best thing to come out of Afghanistan in many years.

Sadly, I was not able to see either the former Minister of Finance, Ashraf Ghani, or the current Minister of Finance, Omar Zakhilwal, both of whom are out of the country. Ghani, I am told, really ran Afghanistan for several years until President Karzai became jealous and decided to get rid of him. Zakhilwal, I was told, is not of his caliber but is also an able and intelligent man.

Always seeking balance in what I was hearing, I arranged to have dinner with the Afghanistan correspondent of *The Guardian* and *The Economist*, Jon Boone, and the correspondent for *The Times*, Jerome Starkey, at a little restaurant with banquets in place of tables and chairs, the Afghan style, called "the Sufi." I was wary about going there because the name sufi means "woolen" and is applied to that group of Muslims who most closely resemble the mendicant followers of St. Francis of Assisi – and they certainly did not care much about the quality of their food! It actually turned out to be a very pleasant place – that is, after one passed through a cordon of armed guards and the metal detector -- with an Afghanesque seating arrangement on rugs with cushions. But after an hour, I began to feel my legs, tucked up underneath me, grow numb. No longer am I the man who rode a camel

97

across Arabia! I could not be sure quite what I was eating in the dim light, but the food, very Afghan, was very tasty. Anyway, I was not there for the food but to listen to their opinions on the current situation.

Their opinions differed. Boone, an Oxford man who has been here three years, thought that any serious move toward evacuation would throw the country back into civil war while Starkey thought that a descent into civil war much less likely and that, since leaving would happen anyway, it was a good idea to begin negotiation soon. Both agreed that the current government is hopelessly corrupt and not really reformable. Boone placed his hopes on the police, which he thought would take five years to get in shape. He thought parts of the army, particularly the Afghan Special Forces, some of whose officers had been trained at Sandhurst, were relatively sound, but the regular soldiers, he and Starkey agreed, were at best unmotivated and at worst would swing quickly to the Taliban.

Both commented on the massive flight of money, which I have discussed above. Boone remarked that the amount being exported shifted, depending on the Afghan evaluation of the length of the American commitment. He also pointed to an aspect of the Karzai policy I had not been aware of: the government goes into the market place, here literally a market place, once a week and buys up Afghan currency (Afs) with dollars. This has the effect of driving up the price of the local currency, and so enables those who want to take out dollars to buy them more cheaply and giving them a profit even before the money gets abroad. In short, Afghan government financial practice was subsidizing the flight of currency to the benefit of the inner circle and the warlords.

What do the Americans know about this? I asked. Probably everything, both men replied, but this thought led them to comment on the fact that practically no American ever leaves the Embassy compound. That was only in part a criticism as both Boone and Starkey thought it was probably better that the Americans were less evident because, decked out in their body armor and helmets and surrounded by guards, they were not popular. Both said the most disliked were the Special Forces (aka "Special Ops") who are believed to carry out at least a thousand raids a month (!) and often with considerable brutality and always with little regard for Afghan customs. Both remarked that until WikiLeaks published some of records, no one even here had any idea about the scale or impact of this intrusion. Both regarded these raids as a major cause of hatred of Americans and a great danger to the American strategy.

My last journalist contact was Joshua Partlow of *The Washington Post*. He very kindly invited me to his house – which he more or less inherited when an attack on the UN guest house induced the UN to make all of its personnel leave outlying houses. The house, by American standards, was modest, but like all the buildings I entered, it mustered its complement of armed guards and the double door entry. As I walked in, I mused on what percentage of our income is today devoted to "security." Here in Afghanistan, it must just about match the amount paid out in bribes.

In the living room, I saw a huge double bass in the corner. How wonderful, I thought, for a young reporter way off in the Wild East to have brought this monstrous fiddle with him. What a task that must have been! He must be really devoted to music. When I asked about it, he laughed and said, no, he did not play and did not even know where the fiddle came from. It was in the house when he moved in, perhaps abandoned by some previous occupant. Now, he said, it was just decoration.

In shared the house with several other people including another *Washington Post* reporter, David Nakamura and Victoria Longo, a young woman working at the UN office here. Also joining us for dinner were Keith Shawe, a English botanist who worked for The Asia Foundation, an organization that was already active in Afghanistan when I first came here in 1962, and a young Chinese-American woman, fresh from working at the USAID mission in Kandahar.

To my astonishment, Partlow produced a rare bottle of wine, and powered by the unusual event, we unraveled the Afghan predicament. Of course, that meant going over much the same ground as all my other conversations, violence, corruption, the question of how much or little the official Americans saw or understood of the country, and where this is all heading. In summary, I found that they were just as pessimistic as the better informed of my other contacts. The young Chinese-American woman, Bayfang, had worked as a reporter before joining AID to work in Kandahar. So she had experienced both the freedom of the reporters and the "security" of the officials. She remarked on how hard it was to get permission to go out of the guarded compound where, as in Kabul, all the official Americans lived, and then only in body armor and with guards. No wonder, she said, the Americans could not understand the country. They hardly saw it. The reporters, of course, used local transport, mainly taxis, and usually went by themselves to call on Afghans or foreigners in pursuit of their stories. The evening turned into a sort of college bull session. They were all pessimistic. Things are going downhill.

Now I have the last and most interesting of all my talks to relate. Mullah Abdus-Salam Zaeef was the Taliban's head of the central bank, deputy minister of finance, acting minister of defense and ambassador to Pakistan. In short, he was one of the most important men in the Taliban establishment.

William Polk interviews Mullah Abdus-Salam Zaeef who was the Taliban's head of the central bank, deputy minister of finance, acting minister of defense and ambassador to Pakistan, one of the most important men in the Taliban establishment. Kabul 2011.

When Pakistan withdrew its recognition of the Taliban government in 2001, he was abducted, "sold" to the CIA and packed off to Bagram prison, to another prison in Kandahar and finally to Guantánamo. Among them, as he recounts in his autobiography, *My Life With The Taliban*, he was humiliated, repeatedly tortured, almost starved, sat upon, spat upon, pissed upon, cursed, almost always deprived of a chance to pray, had his Qur'an sullied and was deprived of sleep for days on end. Finally after four years he was released in 2005 without charges and allowed to return to Afghanistan. He now lives, more or less under house arrest, in Kabul.

Arranging to see him also brought back memories for me: many years ago in Cairo, I met and got to know Prince Abdul Karim al-Khatabi, the leader of the failed Rif war of liberation against the Spaniards and the French. He too was packed off to exile and held incommunicado by the French during the entire period of World War II. Khatabi's and Zaeef's lives and personalities and social background were very different, as were their experiences – Prince Abdul Karim was treated with respect whereas Mullah Abdul Salam was tortured -- but both were leaders of their national revolts. So, I approached this opportunity with excitement. I thought I could learn a great deal from him.

By taxi, I went to see Mullah Abdus-Salam with a translator. It took about an hour to reach his neighborhood. The taxi driver wandered about for a long time, unable to find the house. The district had been virtually destroyed in the civil war and the area where his house showed all the effects of both war and Afghan poverty. The streets were flanked by the usual open sewers (*juis*) and almost blocked by rubbish and the remains of collapsed buildings. When we arrived, I went into the doorway past the usual collection armed guards and up a modest flight of cement steps, then, as custom required, after taking off my shoes, I went into Mullah Abdus-Salam's bare, but sofa-encircled reception room. Rising, Mullah Abdus-Salam greeted me shyly. I was not surprised. After all, I was an unknown American and from his book and the comments of my journalist new friends, I expected that he would be at least wary if not hostile. I wasn't sure what language we would use so I said to my translator to say how much I had looked forward to meeting him after reading his book. The translator spoke a few words to him, paused and then said, "sir, he wants to speak in English." Since Pashto is Zaeef's native language, my Farsi-speaking translator was perhaps in as weak a language position as I.

So, during our talk, we went back and forth between English and Arabic which, as a religious scholar, he spoke very well. Mullah Abdus-Salam is now 42 years old and was born in a village near Kandahar. His father was the imam of a village mosque and the family, probably even more than any of his farming neighbors, was very poor. His mother died when he was a baby, of what he does not know, perhaps in childbirth. His older sister died shortly thereafter and his father, when he was still a child. As he recounts in his autobiography, his youth was grim. He was shunted from one relative to another and had to struggle for the little education, both religious and secular, he got. When the Russians invaded in 1979, he joined the great exodus of millions – ultimately 6 million or about one Afghan in each two – to Pakistan where he lived in several of the wretched refugee camps. At 15, he ran away from "home," if one can call a refugee tent that, joined the resistance against the Soviet invasion, fought as a guerrilla, was caught in some nine ambushes and was severely wounded. During this time, he joined the Taliban, as he told me, because it was more honest, less brutal and more religious than the other resistance groups. By the time, he joined it, Mullah Muhammad Umar had become the Taliban leader. At the end of the Soviet occupation, the various guerrilla factions split, fought one another and, in the desperate struggle for survival, becoming "warlords," preyed upon the general population. Meanwhile, the leaders of the Taliban, as he recounted, had stood down or, more accurately, had returned to their schools and mosques. Finally, in reaction to the warlords' extortions, rapes and murders, the Taliban coalesced and reemerged. Then began a period of negotiation, missionary activity in the name of Islam and finally fighting that led the by-then greatly expanded Taliban into control of most of Afghanistan and catapulted Mullah Abdus-Salam into its most difficult civil tasks.

Today, those difficult times, and his even worse years in prison, hardly show. He has just been removed from the UN and US "blacklist," and now, as I found, lives modestly in Kabul. He is a big man, not fat but portly, with penetrating black eyes and a modest black beard. I was at some pains to establish at least the beginnings of trust between us and must have succeeded because we spoke with some humor (always a good sign) and candor. In our talk, I found no sign of animosity toward me or even, as I expected from his autobiography, toward America and Americans. After preliminaries, I asked what he saw ahead and how the Afghan tragedy could be solved.

In reply, he said, "it is very hard to devise a way, but we should know that fighting is not the way. It won't work. And it has many bad side effects such as dividing the people from the government."

Given his background I was surprised by his concern for Karzai's government. But as we talked, it was clear that he was thinking in terms broader than Karzai. He meant that the Afghans must have an accommodation to government, *per se*, if they are heal their wounds and improve their condition.

The only realistic way ahead, he went on, "is respect for the Afghan people and their way whereas America is now relying wholly on force. Force didn't work for the British or the Russians and it won't work for the Americans."

(I doubt that Mullah Abdus-Salam could have heard of it, but his opinion was borne out by the commander of one of the US strike forces in southern Afghanistan, Lt. Col. David Flynn, a career officer who also had served in Iraq. He told a reporter from *The Mclatchy Newspapers* on August 19, "We've killed hundreds and thousands of Taliban over nine years, and killing another thousand this year is not going to be the difference.")

The word "respect" often figured in his remarks, as from my study of Afghanistan and the Arabs and Iranians, I knew it would. But instead of working toward peace, he said and I paraphrase, America has created obstacles to peace which only it can remove. Here, he said, was a complete block: America has put the Taliban leaders on a black list, a "wanted" list, and they know that they will be killed if they surface to negotiate. Without their removal from the "capture or kill" list and a guarantee of safety from kidnap or murder, they cannot negotiate; trying to make contact with the Karzai regime is sure to get them killed. Perhaps they have even tried. He said that he did not know if Karzai and any of the Taliban leadership were in contact, but under these circumstances, he doubted it.

While he stressed (and the Taliban have announced) that he is not authorized to speak for Mullah Muhammad Umar, he thought that the American troops did not need actually to pull out before negotiations could begin. If it was certain that they were going to do so, then negotiations could be got underway. That seemed to contradict some of the Taliban pronouncements, demanding withdrawal before negotiation, but it is, I believe, itself a negotiable issue.

So how do the Taliban see a post-US-controlled Afghanistan? I asked.

He replied that "it all depended on how it comes about. If it comes through negotiation, then probably the Taliban will be content with genuine participation in the government, but if it comes through force, then the Taliban will take everything."

I asked about what he has been doing since his autobiography was translated. He perhaps did not quite understand my question and said that he was in Guantánamo until he was released. He suddenly asked me how old I am and, when I replied with my august status, he said "good. There was a man in Guantanamo who also was old and he was gentle with me. The younger men were not."

That brought up the question of the American policy of targeting and killing the leadership. I said that I thought that such actions would open the way for younger, more radical men. Yes, he agreed, that would certainly happen but the senior, "old," leadership is still intact, living, he said, off somewhere in Pakistan. The usual guess is in the city of Quetta, which historically was a part of Afghanistan.

I turned to the issue of al-Qaida, saying that their activities, their composition and their relationship with the Taliban were what really interested most American politicians. He confirmed what the Russian ambassador had told me: Usama bin Ladin was already operating in Afghanistan before the

Taliban came into power. Of course, Mullah Abdus-Salam said, almost echoing the words of the Russian ambassador, the Taliban needed money and Usama was almost the only available source. All the Afghans, he pointed out, have the tradition of granting sanctuary (*melmastia*) to a guest. It is mandatory. Moreover, Usama was the enemy of the enemies of the Taliban. So there was an understanding. But after 2002, he said, "that understanding lapsed, asylum for Usama was withdrawn and the Qaida fighters, including Usama, are no longer in Afghanistan. [American military and intelligence sources have publicly confirmed this.] They will not come back. The Taliban will not allow them to return."

When Mullah Abdus-Salam returned to Afghanistan, he said, he three times met with President Karzai who asked him to participate in the great national assembly, the *loya jirga*. He said he told Karzai that it was not proper to have a *loya jirga* during occupation by foreign forces and urged him not to hold it. He also told Karzai, he said, he personally could not, under the circumstances, participate.

I asked if he saw Americans. Yes, he replied an American general once came to call on him, asking what was the best way to arm Afghans to fight the Taliban!

He didn't laugh, as I expected he would.

What about the American AID program? I asked.

Granting aid, he said, had a bad effect "because it split families. If a man took American money, making him a traitor to Afghanistan and to Islam, his own brother was apt to kill him." But, I said, in other circumstances would it not be good? "Oh, certainly," he replied. So, I added, then we must change the circumstances. He nodded. Musing, he said he was often asked to compare the Russians and the Americans. On the good side, he said, the Russians came by invitation from an existing government whereas the Americans invaded. But, on the bad side, the Russians were far more brutal than the Americans, bombing whole villages, killing perhaps a million people. On their side, he went on, the Americans at least brought the UN with them and that was a good thing for Afghanistan. The Americans, however, were here only in opposition to the Russians and when there was no Russian threat they left. I was surprised by what I inferred was almost nostalgia in his remark. It was nearly what I had heard from Dr. Samar on the role America could have played in 2002.

I then raised the issue of the brutality of the Taliban. I did not mention the recent UN report on the injuries inflicted by the Taliban on Afghan civilians as I am sure he would think that these are inevitable in a guerrilla war. Instead, I raised the issue of the execution by stoning of an Afghan woman. I remarked that such barbaric practice gave a horrible image of the Taliban even though such executions were authorized by both the Old Testament and the Qur'an. But we no longer believed in it. Can the Taliban modernize? I asked.

He shrugged. "What can you expect now? The Taliban are completely isolated, under constant attack, and naturally this throws them back onto old ways. They cannot afford to relax even on such matters."

I asked about his own religious observance. It being Ramadan, he was of course fasting. I asked if he went to the little mosque I had seen nearby in his capacity as a mullah. Oh no, he said, he was not allowed to for his own safety. That remark also surprised me. Was he afraid of the Taliban? I asked. He rather ducked that question, saying only that he did go to the mosque for the Friday congregational prayer. But, although he did not specify, it was clear that in the circumstances of Afghanistan today, as I saw everywhere I turned, almost anyone of any standing was unsure where danger might arise. Also, the government would probably not approve his attendance at a place where he might influence the population. Better to pray at home.

He said he has written a second book, also in Pashto, somewhat like his first. The publishers of his autobiography, he said, refused to pay him royalties as he was on the black list. So he asked that they just hold the money, but, in the end, they refused to give him anything. I suggested that he should write an article on how to end the war and plan to contact Rick MacArthur to see if *Harpers* would be interested.

Mullah Abdus-Salam has been invited, he said, by the European parliament to visit Europe. But he had not applied for a visa. He said he had only recently been free to do so, and he had to remember that he was a guest in the country and must not do anything that might embarrass his hosts.

As I was leaving, he said that he was expecting the German ambassador. And, indeed, as I went out, there were four big armored cars with a dozen or so men armed with wicked looking machineguns, eyeing me suspiciously, and a small group of German diplomats, waiting to go in.

I was amused that they did not even look sheepish when, by myself without armed guards, I walked passed them to my taxi.

August 24, 2010

Ethnolinguistic Groups in Afghanistan

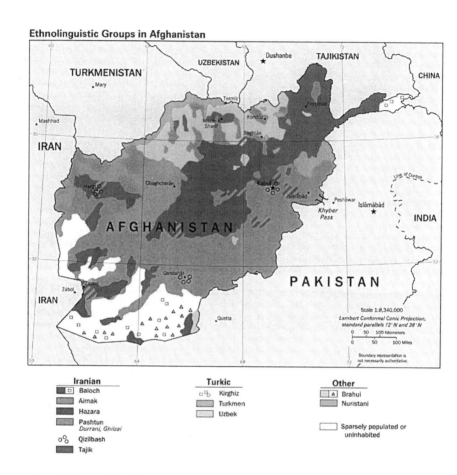

Ethnic Diversity Map

CHAPTER 7

TOWARD A FEASIBLE POLICY FOR AFGHANISTAN

Too much of what we read in reports and analyses on Afghanistan is based on wishful thinking. It is late, but not too late, to move toward an affordable and sustainable policy. To arrive at such a policy, we must begin by considering historical, geographical, ethnic and economic realities on the ground rather than merely focusing on what the Afghans, the Americans and other nations desire.

The Basic Facts

Afghanistan has a surface area of 6.5 thousand square kilometers (about the size of Texas or the combination of France, Belgium, The Netherlands and Denmark) of which 85% to 90% is mountainous and/or desert. The central massif, broken by deep valleys, rises to a maximum height of nearly 8 thousand meters and much of the south and west is sand, rock or salty marsh. Thus, the economically "usable" Afghanistan is comparable to just Florida or the combination of Belgium and The Netherlands. The country has few proven resources. Energy has been particularly lacking. Water power is hampered by erosion, causing generators to disintegrate and storage lakes to fill with sediment. Both oil and coal have been found but have only begun to be developed. Timber is in very short supply, with forests covering less than 5% of the surface; much of the earlier forest areas have been denuded (destroyed by war or cut for fuel). Ground water almost everywhere, except in the far north, is unavailable while rain falls heavily and creates often devastating floods in March-April. Other floods come when snow melts in mid summer. These times are inappropriate for most agriculture; so Afghanistan cannot feed itself. The reality is that Afghanistan is and will remain a poor country.

The population has risen over the last half century, from perhaps 10 million in 1962, when I first went there, to 31-33 million in 2012. Today, over half of the Afghanis are below the age of 18, so a major upsurge of population can be anticipated in the years ahead. Before the Soviet invasion and occupation, the population was at least 80% rural: most Afghans were settled peasant farmers, living in some 22,000 villages, but perhaps 1 in each 8 or 9 was a nomad. Religiously, about 5-6 people in each 10 are Sunni Muslims and somewhat more than 3-4 in 10 are Shia Muslims. Ethnically, the population is divided into at least two dozen communities of which the Pushtuns (aka Pathans) (4 in each 10), the Tajiks (3 in each 10) and the Hazaras (1-2 in each 10) are the largest. These groups speak off-shoots of the Indo-European family of languages, mainly Dari, a dialect of Farsi (Persian). Smaller Turkish and Mongol groups speak languages in the Ural-Altaic (or East Asian) family while other, even smaller, communities speak languages in the Semitic family of languages. Thus, Afghanistan is culturally, socially and politically diverse.

While, the diversity of the country is evident, it is important not to exaggerate its effects. The inhabitants of the cities, towns and villages share shaping influences of means of earning their livings, religious belief and practice and historical experience. The best known traditional code of life is the *Pushtunwali* of the Pushtuns, but similar "social contracts" are echoed in the other communities; Islam in Afghanistan, like Christianity in Europe and America, is divided, but overall there is an intense loyalty to it; and the experience of nearly all Afghans, shaped by generations of warfare, set them apart, they fervently believe, from all foreigners. At minimum, the Afghans have a unity in their difference from others.

Throughout history, central governments have functioned only intermittently and in sharply limited spheres except in the few cities. Effective government is traditionally primarily a function of village communities: each village runs its own affairs under its own leaders; its inhabitants were economically virtually autarkic, making most of their clothing and tools and eating their own produce.

This lack of national cohesion thwarted the Russians during their occupation: they won almost every battle and occupied at one time or another virtually every inch of the country, and through their civic action programs they actually pacified many of the villages, but they could never find or create an organization with which to make peace. Baldly put, no one could surrender the rest. Thus, over the decade of their involvement, the Russians lost about 15,000 soldiers – and the war. When they gave up and left, the Afghans resumed their traditional way of life, what might be called "the Afghan way."

"The Afghan way" is today manifested in three aspects of government: first, the central government is weak. Its writ is hardly noticed, much less obeyed, outside of downtown Kabul and a few other cities. Religious law, outside the control of government, is supreme. Secular law exists only on paper. Those who can read it are usually powerful enough not to have to pay any attention to it. Many of the powerful, rich and well-connected have their own private "armies." Indeed, the most striking characteristic of Afghanistan is that it is a country of private armies. Thus, as Thucydides wrote of the ancient Greeks, "the strong do what they can and the weak suffer what they must." Poorer Afghans live in fear of theft, kidnap or murder. Their only recourse is the payment of protection money. It follows that such government as exists, at least outside village communities, is corrupt at every level, from the traffic policeman to the president. A UN study in 2010 found that officials and thugs "shake down" their fellow citizens each year to an amount equal to about a quarter of the country's gross domestic product. The sometime US commander, General David Petraeus, described the ruling institution as a "crime syndicate."

A June 2010 report to the US House of Representatives Subcommittee on National Security and Foreign Affairs entitled "Warlord, Inc." detailed one aspect of extortion and corruption to show how millions of foreign assistance dollars are funneled into the crime syndicate. As the report makes clear, there are four major results of this activity: the crime syndicate becomes overwhelmingly powerful; the action of the Karzai family and associates demeans the very concept of government; the participants in the scam will do anything to continue the flow of money into their hands; but, they are hedging their bets by moving their new fortunes and their families abroad with all deliberate speed and in full public view. As President Karzai himself already admitted in a well-publicized speech in November 2008, "The banks of the world are full of the money of our statesmen." Consequently, virtually no Afghan acknowledges the legitimacy of the Karzai government or its edicts. Most competent observers believe that once American troops are withdrawn, the existing government will collapse. Those now in power obviously agree with this assessment as shown by their rush to get their fortunes and their families abroad to safe havens.

The traditional Afghan means of achieving political legitimacy is not by the system the central government, partly at American insistence, has employed: election. Even if it were, election is discredited today as fraudulent. The traditional Afghan way to achieve legitimacy is by consensus. Every social group, beginning in each village, comes together in a council. In the Pushtun areas, these councils are known as *jirgas;* in the Tajik area, *shuras;* and in the Hazara area, *ulus.* These councils are not, in the Western sense of the word, institutions; rather they are "occasions." They are called into being when some locally pressing issue cannot be resolved by the local headman or a respected religious figure. The members are not elected but are accorded their status by popular acclamation. Often the members are religious leaders. The code they enforce is what the local people see as their "way." That is, what they believe to be fair, right and proper. Throughout Afghanistan the definition of these attributes is Quranic in an Afghan way.

While such councils seem exotic to Americans, they are, in fact, remarkably widespread – the wartime Yugoslav partisans created *odbors* for similar purposes; as did the Greek EAM *andartes.* In Greece then, as in Afghanistan today, they were led by men regarded by their neighbors as *ipefthinos* or "responsible men." Similar needs gave rise to *juntas* in revolutionary Spain; "councils of public safety" in revolutionary America; *comités de salut public* in revolutionary France; and *soviets* in revolutionary Russia. None of these groups came about in elections; indeed, it is the electoral process itself that is exotic in most of the world. It still has not taken root in many places including Afghanistan.

As broader areas perceive common issues, local assemblies then give rise to "elevated" councils. In Afghanistan, local councils joined in regional councils to deal with shared concerns and ultimately coalesced into a single national council, known as the *loya jirga*. The loya jirga shares characteristics with constitutional assemblies. Its role in Afghan life was never fully understood by either the Soviets or the Americans. That role is described in the current constitution as "the highest manifestation of the will of the people of Afghanistan." Its will was thwarted by US interference behind the scenes to impose Hamid Karzai as interim president of the country in 2002. Consequently, the working of the loya jirga was regarded by many Afghans as corrupted by foreign forces.

Third, virtually all Afghans share a deep commitment to Islam. In fact, Afghanistan is perhaps the most religious of all the Muslim lands. Religion permeates all aspects of life, literally from the cradle to the grave. And the most common Afghan version of Islam, a variation of the Hanafi School of law, is the most rigid now being practiced. We think of the extremists as members of the Taliban (literally "religious students"), but they would have little power if what they enforced was not what Afghans believed to be proper.

This perception is demonstrated by Afghan history. Twice in the last half century, Afghan governments tried to lead their citizens into a modern (read: "Western") program of reform. In the 1960s and 1970s, the government of Prime Minister Mohammad Maiwandwal seemed to be on the way to turning Afghanistan into a progressive modern state with heavy emphasis on the liberation of women, the spread of education and openness to foreign influences. His administration was easily overthrown; a decade later, the culturally more progressive of the two Communist parties, the urban-based Parcham, took power and set in motion an even more radical modernization program. In reaction, large units of the army went into rebellion, butchering "modernists" and their Soviet advisors. Huge uprisings broke out all over the country, even in larger towns and cities where reformist ideas were more acceptable than in rural areas.

When it conquered most of Afghanistan in 1996, the Taliban government enforced the strictest form of Islam practiced in modern times;

many of its draconian actions were derived from the Old Testament and are proclaimed but not practiced in Ultra-Orthodox Judaism and in some obscurantist Christian sects. For implementing them, the Taliban regime has been widely criticized not only by non-Muslim foreigners but also by most non-Afghan Muslims. To our eyes, the Taliban was seen as imposing an ugly, retrograde, "Medieval" rein of terror, but it was not so regarded by many, possibly even most, Afghans. Thus, two of the things to be determined in Afghanistan's future are how rapidly and how much such attitudes can be expected to change. Many intelligent Afghans, including former senior members of the Taliban organization, have told me that such change will come but is unlikely so long as the country remains under foreign occupation.

Afghan society is also notable for its poverty. That has always been true, but during the brutal Soviet invasion and occupation and in the devastating civil war that followed, nearly 1 in each 10 Afghans was killed or died and about 5 million people fled to Pakistan or Iran while other millions – no one knows how many – lost their homes but stayed in Afghanistan. Most living inhabitants have known no time of peace or even minimal security. Large numbers are sick or suffering from wounds and lacking in skills needed to improve their condition.

Public health and education are both near the bottom of the world scale: more than 1 Afghan in each 3 lives on less than the equivalent of US $0.45 (45¢) a day and more than 1 in each 2 preschool children are stunted because of malnutrition. They are the lucky ones: 1 child in 5 dies before the age of 5. Life expectancy is about 45 years. On education, nearly 90% of Afghan women and nearly 60% of Afghan men are illiterate. Only 1 in each 5 Afghan children attends primary school and from ages 7 to 14 at least 1 in each 4 drops out of school to work.

Both the Soviet and American occupation forces have mounted "civic action" programs with the proclaimed purpose of raising the standard of life of the Afghan people. Obviously, the Afghans need help, so Americans – and the Russians before them – have thought that they should welcome efforts to aid them. But independent observers have found that they do not. Based on some 400 interviews throughout the country, a team of Tufts

University researchers found that "Afghan perceptions of aid and aid actors are overwhelmingly negative." We must ask why this is.

The reason appears to be that the Afghans, and particularly the insurgents, understand from published pronouncements that "civic action" is a form of warfare. In their decade of occupation, that is the way the Russians used it; that is also the way the American government uses it today. The official position was neatly summed up by General David Petraeus as he fought in Iraq: "Money," he said, "is my most important ammunition in this war." The Afghans take him at his word.

Related to this perception of the actions of foreigners, Afghans generally suffer from what might be called an "invasion complex." Throughout history -- with rare exceptions -- Afghanistan has been more acted upon than acting upon others. In the long period of pre-history, it was the route by which Central Asian invaders (probably the founders of the ancient Indus River civilization and certainly the later Indo-European tribesmen who founded India's later kingdoms) reached the sub-continent. Afghanistan was the route across which Alexander the Great's Macedonians, various other East Asians fleeing from China and invading Turks plunged into South Asia. More recently, it was the scene upon which the conflict between Tsarist Russia and British India, the so-called Great Game, was played. Finally, Russia invaded in 1979 and occupied the country for a decade. A vicious civil war followed until the Taliban took control of about 90% of the country in the late 1990s. Their government was overthrown by the US in 2001. Supported by some NATO military contingents, America has occupied the country ever since. This long experience has left a residue of fear and even hatred of foreigners that permeates Afghan society.

The country is landlocked, about 500 kilometers from the nearest sea, and is surrounded by Iran, Pakistan, China and the former Soviet Union with frontiers aggregating some 5.4 thousand kilometers. The capital, Kabul, is only about half as far from the Pakistani capital, Islamabad, as New York City is from Washington D.C. The area in between, which the British called "the Northwest Frontier," is the homeland of the Pushtuns, a Pashto-speaking, Sunni-Muslim people. Roughly one-third of them --14 million

-- live in Afghanistan (where they make up about 40% of the total Afghan population) and the other two-thirds -- 25 million -- live in Pakistan (where they aggregate about 16% of the total population).

Afghanistan's neighbors have undeniable interests in the country: when it is weak, foreigners intrude and when it is strong it reaches into their domains. Particularly in religion, it interacts strongly with both South and Central Asia and Russia where 1 in each 7 is a Muslim and are rapidly increasing. Pakistan's interests are the closest, but it is not alone: India seeks to use Afghanistan to backstop its policy toward Pakistan and Kashmir; China has a new interest in Afghan energy production; the Russian Federation wants to prevent encouragement of Muslim disaffection in its Central Asian provinces and its allies; Iran shares Shia Islam with a major ethnic community, the 1 to 2% who are Hazaras, has deeply influenced Afghan culture including the language of the majority of Afghans and seeks to choke off the pernicious drug trade originating in Afghanistan.

The roles of foreigners have undergone major changes in recent years and these changes will increasingly affect what is possible for outsiders to accomplish. First the Soviet Union and later America and the European Union have each fought for a decade against Afghan opponents. Neither has "won." And, in the course of warfare and occupation, new interests have been created. Among these is the almost desperate need of their leaders to avoid admitting failure.

Foreigners find failure easy in Afghanistan. It is known as the graveyard of empires. The British lost a whole army there in 1842 and two subsequent campaigns ended in failure; a Russian invasion in 1929 was a near catastrophe, and in the 1979-1989 occupation as mentioned above, the Russians lost about 15,000 soldiers. The American invasion and occupation, as of October 2012, has cost over 2,100 casualties and perhaps five times that many gravely or even permanently wounded. Few believe it can succeed.

These are the key facts forming the pattern in which policies must be accommodated; so what is possible to do that is acceptable to the Afghans and foreigners?

II

The *Essential* Objectives of the Afghan People and The World Community:

The fundamental objective shared by the Afghans and foreigners is a peaceful and secure country, able and willing to manage its own affairs and to act as an independent member of the world community.

This objective is brought into sharp focus by the insistence of the member nations of the NATO alliance that Afghanistan, under any government, prohibit the use of its territory or other facilities for acts of terrorism or subversion in member countries and their allies. This, after all, was the justification for the overthrow of the Taliban regime in 2003. This is the second objective;

The third objective is particularly important for, but not necessarily understood by, Americans. It is not only to eliminate or cut down on the vast expenditures of money (much of it borrowed) and human resources (much of it wasted in battle or used in unproductive ways) but also to avoid a "blowback" by the warping or degradation of their institutions, comity and laws caused by fear, apparent necessity for drastic action and excessive concern with "security";

The fourth objective of the member nations of the NATO alliance and particularly of the United States is to end or at least diminish the costs to them of the war. Member nations of the NATO alliance are already acting to accomplish for themselves this objective. Afghans generally do not share it: the Taliban movement, fractured though it may be, is determined regardless of cost to induce the foreigners to leave and to reestablish something like the regime that was destroyed by the American invasion. The Karzai government wavers between the NATO/American and the Taliban objectives. In principle, it seeks total independence but its power brokers (aided and abetted by influential outside participants) are making vast amounts of money off the occupation and are in no hurry to end it. That is to say, there is a small but significant area of agreement on the objectives but not on timing, on the means to achieve them and on whom will control the action.

III

Objectives *Desired* By The Afghan People and The World Community:

Although, in current conditions they have not uniformly or vigorously articulated it, we may assume that a desired objective of all the Afghan people is a more adequate standard of living with both an improved diet and an enhanced level of health as well as a level of education that will enable them to achieve and sustain a strong economy;

Both the majority of the Afghan people and concerned foreign powers desire a level of stability sufficient to prevent civil strife and invite further foreign intervention;

Member countries of the NATO alliance as well as China and Russia would like for Afghanistan to take a place suitable to its capacities in legal world trade. Specifically, they would like to profit from Afghanistan's mineral resources, to make use of its routes of trade and to get its help in interdicting the drug trade;

Since some aspects of Afghan society, notably the position and role of women, appear to outsiders as ugly and "medieval," they would like to foster the "evolution" of the society along contemporary Western lines. This objective is not widely shared in the country today although, briefly in the 1960s and 1970s, it was the policy of the then Afghan government and was approved by a wide swath of urban society. Under conditions of peace and independence, especially if these are brought about through negotiations, it is likely gradually to re-emerge.

IV

Accomplishment of These Objectives:

Accomplishment of these objectives will be, at best, a complex task and can be accomplished only gradually. Rarely throughout its long history and only briefly in the last century have the Afghans had the opportunity to set their own agenda or to mobilize themselves to accomplish their own aims. Moreover, even discounting for the handicaps under which they have lived, they have not made satisfactory use of the opportunities they have had. (That is, except in the paramilitary field where they have taken on and essentially defeated both the Soviet Union and the United States.) Unless or until the Afghans gain the necessary scope of action to manage their own affairs and even to commit their own mistakes, they are unlikely to make significant progress in non-military endeavors. This scope can come only after an end to foreign control of their affairs. Therefore, the necessary but not sufficient step is true independence.

Costly and disappointing experience should have taught Western governments, and particularly the United States government, that the successful "engineering" of another country's government by foreigners is rare and that the beneficial recasting of an exotic society is even more rare. Foreign powers can contribute only marginally to local initiatives. To succeed, action must be modest.

V

Means of Action:

The United States government must acknowledge, as does the Karzai government, that the Taliban claim to a major degree of participation in whatever government evolves cannot be successfully denied. This will be politically difficult for Western governments, but the sooner they, and particularly the United States government, recognizes this fact, the stronger will be its means of action. We must assume that the Taliban knows, as did the Vietminh in their war against the American occupation in Vietnam, that time in on their side. While painful, the Taliban struggle is sustainable at acceptable cost and is fought in their neighborhood while the NATO and American campaign is enormously expensive, not popular with their own peoples and is remote from their concerns. Thus, a wise American policy would seek negotiations at the earliest feasible time.

Negotiation is the most efficient, fastest and least costly way ahead. The elements that will arise in negotiations are not many but are fundamental.

First is the revamping of the central government to include the Taliban. Absent this, there will be no productive negotiation. President Karzai himself has called for their inclusion. Before negotiations are undertaken, precisely what would be involved cannot be made clear. Hints have suggested participation in a sort of government of national unity with each side staking a claim to spheres of influence or control. The Taliban want more; Karzai wants to give less. This, of course, is the essence of negotiation. Neither Karzai nor the Taliban trusts the other to abide by the deal they make. So a careful step-by-step process will be required and probably some form of guarantee will have to be devised to overcome the lack of trust.

Second is the structure of the state. Probably some sort of federal configuration will be necessary, but, at all costs, the country should not be "balkanized." This is because Afghanistan's several ethnic/religious/linguistic communities are so mingled that splitting the country into pieces, as some have suggested, would set off a panic flight that would create millions of new refugees; moreover, the resulting mini-states would be too weak to sustain themselves and so would invite perennial intervention.

Probably the negotiators will agree to continue the traditional, ethnicity-based arrangement of provinces. Exact boundaries may prove difficult to determine but something like the Pushtun south, the Tajik northeast, the Turkic north and the Hazara central massif will constitute the major elements. Afghans will probably agree to keep the current freedom of movement among the provinces; indeed, it probably could not be effectively curtailed.

In this somewhat loosely unified state, the negotiators will probably easily agree that area around Kabul should be a federal district, as it historically has been, administered by the central government. The foreign negotiators and donors of aid should endeavor to get agreement on making the federal district the leader in modernization. For example, strengthening of the university with such associated professional schools as the medical training college, augmented by European and American universities and foundations, acting like the Rockefeller Foundation did in China, will attract potential leaders from the provinces and help to integrate the country. Such a policy will be difficult to sell to the Taliban.

Third, and more difficult to be agreed will be the allocation of military power. Today, it is of two very different kinds: the Karzai regime has, at least on paper, a standing army while the Taliban has, effectively, a guerrilla army. If negotiations are delayed beyond the withdrawal of the foreign, mainly American, forces, it is likely that the standing army will simply implode. Soldiers will just go home. That is what happened in many revolutionary situations, most recently in neighboring Iran. This is another reason, obviously, to undertake negotiations sooner rather than later.

What negotiators should aim to achieve is the creation of a relatively small standing army. It should be small because such limited human and monetary resources as the country has are desperately needed elsewhere and a large army, absent other vigorous public institutions, which do not yet exist, would likely lead to a military take-over and derailment of the development program.

Fourth is the role of the government of national unity in other aspects of rule. Control of foreign affairs would give the central government the means to negotiate with and encourage donors and investors. Since external aid would pass through its hands, the central government could allocate aid projects among the provinces and so exercise a subtle but considerable influence over their policies. Continuation and strengthening of a uniform currency, under control of a central bank, will also help to unify the country, but given the level of corruption and flight of money, this may be stoutly resisted by Karzai's supporters; the Taliban will be less concerned with this issue.

Fifth is the crucial issue of the smaller-scale structure of the state: village assemblies are the backbone of Afghanistan. Their role is absolutely

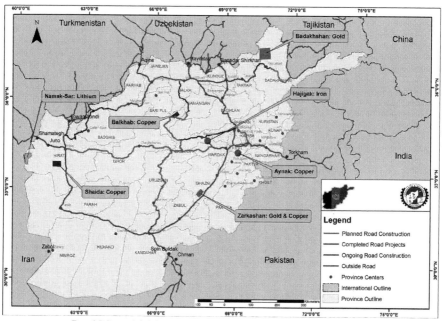

Road Map of Afghanistan identifying major resources.

crucial. It should be easy to convince a government of national unity to support them. One way to do this is to give them authority over local aid projects. First on the list could be small, inexpensive, locally-built, farm-to-market roads (to connect with the ring road (see map) so that farmers can get their produce to market before it spoils. Such a program was highly successful even half a century ago, when I first observed it, but it was aborted by invasion, civil war and the break-down of rural order. Such a program in the aftermath of a negotiated end of war would meet locally-perceived needs, give a much-needed example of success and engender a new sense of "ownership." Thus, the village assemblies will be empowered, encouraged to support peace and make a serious attack on the current massive unemployment.

VI

Dangers and Costs of Negotiation and Non-Negotiation:

Since, obviously, negotiations that include the Taliban will be politically costly, the United States government and particularly the current administration is likely to delay or even to avoid action. Given this contingency, a second category of action must be considered. What would it entail?

The first step would be the setting of a clear, firm and reasonably proximate date for the evacuation of foreign forces. Moves have been made in this direction, but they have been weakened by hedging on timing and numbers. So they have not had the effect on the Karzai regime, the Taliban or the general public that is needed. It is important to understand exactly why clarity and determination are crucial. In summary, it is because they are necessary to change the "political psychology" of the Afghans. And only if such a change is brought about can progress can be made on either the essential or the desired objectives stated above.

Consider the reaction of the Afghans. The Taliban is committed to continue fighting until foreign forces evacuate the country. It is unlikely that they will accept a partial or long-delayed evacuation. If not, the war will continue. The Karzai regime shows two responses to lack of a clear policy: on the one hand, its "power brokers" continue at a truly astonishing scale and speed to profit from the occupation and, on the other hand, they are withdrawing their assets and families to safe havens abroad. Meanwhile, the general population can make no significant contribution to peace but, in part, helps to continue the insurgency by passively allowing or actively helping the Taliban.

The evidence of this is made clear in the way the way the Afghan community has viewed the war. At the present time, the Taliban can not only move virtually at will and draw support from the people but can destroy even such foreign donations as clinics, schools, bridges, etc. The reason, as stated above, is that the Afghans regard these results of foreign activities as part of the military tactic to dominate them. Americans and Europeans with a sense of history will recall that in the 1950s, the Vietnamese also acquiesced in guerrilla tactics, allowing free passage and providing support, but also destroyed the works of the French (and later the Americans). The Vietcong murdered even doctors, nurses and teachers. Other insurgent groups have followed the same policy.

So, if we believe it is to our shared interest to move Afghanistan toward a degree of security which would allow an American administration to withdraw without a politically unacceptable defeat, we must change the context in which our actions are judged: that is, we must disconnect military tactics – our self-defeating counterinsurgency action -- from developmental programs.

If a firm date in the reasonably near term is believed, the Afghans can feel that their principal, shared objective has been achieved: the foreigners have agreed to leave. At that point, the village assemblies – *jirgas, shuras* and *ulas* -- will *begin* to view the construction in their neighborhoods of a clinic, the opening of a school or the laying of a farm-to-market road as intrinsically valuable; they will want these things for themselves and their fellow villagers.

Will the Taliban and/or local militias under the command of warlords continue to do as it is now doing to thwart this process? Probably. But if they do, they will gradually but inexorably lose the support of the villagers on whom they rely. (Thus, in Mao's often quoted phrase, the "water" will dry up around the "fish.") In this new context, they will be seen as operating against the public good in ways that can no longer be justified as opposition to foreign domination. In short, their cause will have become redundant and their opposition to foreign-financed and conceived beneficial activities will come to be seen as unpatriotic and anti-social.

VII

Anticipated Results:

Over time: Afghanistan can evolve into a relatively peaceful society in which citizens will have a chance for a considerably improved standard of living and, in the context of Afghan cultural norms, will come to share an acceptable form of participatory democracy. More Afghan émigrés, now constituting a drain on neighboring countries and needed at home to replace the over 1 million Afghans killed or died in the wars, will return as about 6 million already have. While results within Afghanistan itself will be modest, the benefits to outside powers will be immense: the enormous drain on the financial resources of the US and other powers will end, the wounding and killing of their soldiers will cease; and the dislocations of their societies in reaction to their perception of threats of terrorism and subversion will lessen as Afghanistan can no longer be used as a launching pad for actions against them. In short, the program laid out here is to the interest of all parties and should be undertaken with all deliberate speed.

This paper was written in 2010 at the request of the then US Ambassador to Afghanistan, General Karl Eikenberry. A few minor and mostly stylistic changes were made for this final version on January 8, 2013.

January 8, 2013

NASA Satellite image of Pakistan showing the Indus River
System 2002.

CHAPTER 8

THE NATURE OF PAKISTAN:
I: THE HISTORICAL BACKGROUND

Corrupt dictatorship or democratic ally, failed state or improving society, den of terrorists or haven of freedom fighters, rogue state or lynchpin of the Free World alliance -- is reality like beauty also only in the eye of the beholder? Or is Pakistan, like all states, a mixture of actions and beliefs that come to the fore in different circumstances? In this essay, I consider the "nature" of the country. In Part I, I begin with the past in order to bring out fundamental features behind events of the present time in Part II.

This NASA satellite image of the Indus valley shows the enduring reality of Pakistan with waters flowing down from the glaciers of the Himalayas, Karakoram and other high mountains into what otherwise would be the desert of Pakistan.

It was in what is now Pakistan, the land of the Indus river, where one of the three great ancient civilizations – along with Egypt and Mesopotamia – was born. Sadly, we know little about it both because we cannot read its script and also because in more recent times the British-Indian empire found the bricks that made up its great cities too valuable to leave to archaeologists and dug them up to use as the road-bed for a new railway line. From what remains, scholars have been able to discern a civilization that built a municipal water supply, sewers, drains, wide streets and other major public works that today's inhabitants would envy. But some time, probably over generations, around 1800 BCE, Indo-European speaking Aryan invaders plunged down from Central Asia, destroying the economic basis for the Indus civilization and driving the Dravidian-speakers survivors off their lands. Under their blows, as the Rig Veda tells us, the Indus people sank "down into obscurity.""[1]

The invading Aryans destroyed the great water works and stole the cattle of the Indus people. Indeed, they not only lifted the cattle but appropriated the very idea of cattle. That is, they traded their totem animal, the horse, the proper talisman of their nomadic life, for the cow of the settled natives. And they proudly cloaked their policies in the new and evolving religion of Hinduism. Although there can be no proof, it appears that it was the progeny of the survivors who formed the "pool" from which Pakistan's and India's Muslim population mainly comes.

The conquered Dravidian-speaking natives, known as the *Dasa*, were not only defeated but also damned. Because of deeds in a former life, according to Hinduism, their suffering had a transcendental justification and could not be escaped. Thus, their descendants, the "untouchables," (*sudras*) were condemned to everlasting humiliation and misery by fate (*karma*). For them, conversion to Islam was liberation. Because millions converted, India today has a huge Muslim minority and Pakistan is almost entirely Muslim. Thus, unconsciously and with no memory of the past, today's Hindus and Muslims were prepared, virtually preordained, for strife.

The Aryan invaders were followed by a variety of other Asian peoples. Turks, Mongols and Arabs swept in, had their periods of glory and left behind genetic and linguistic legacies that can be identified even today. Some of the migrants were benign, some actually improved the land and enriched the inhabitants, but others devastated the land and massacred the natives. Particularly after the Mongol invasions, much of the Indus valley fell into a dark age.

*   *   *

Awakening from this dark age was a slow process as also it was in Europe. In both places the revival of agriculture and trade played a part and, as in Europe, people sought both solace and justification for their actions in religion. Probably there were earlier reformers, like Gautama Buddha, who

---

1   I have dealt with this period in my study *Neighbors and Strangers: The Fundamentals of Foreign Affairs* (Chicago University Press, 1997).

sought to overcome worldly and supernatural tyranny, but it was not until about the close of the Fifteenth century of our era that Hinduism itself experienced serious moves toward toleration if not exactly humanism. In what later was to become the core of Pakistan, the Punjab,[2] three religious revival movements announced themselves: Bakhti Hinduism, Sufi Islam and Sikhism. The most powerful at least at first was Sikhism. It was a new faith based on Hinduism. The word *sikh* comes from the Sanskrit for "teaching," and its teachings were proclaimed by the teacher or *guru*, Nanak Singh.

Like Islam's Muhammad, the Sikh prophet Guru Nanak proclaimed the oneness of God. He set his new faith apart from both Islam and Hinduism by proclaiming that "God is neither a Muslim nor a Hindu." As the historian of the Sikhs, Khushwant Singh, wrote,[3] "Sikhism was born out of a wedlock between Hinduism and Islam after they had known each other for a period of nearly nine hundred years. But once it had taken birth, it began to develop a personality of its own and in due course grew into a faith which had some semblance to Hinduism, some to Islam, and yet had features which bore no resemblance to either."

Reading the Guru's sayings and reflecting on the practices of the early Sikhs, I have been particularly struck by similarities to Islam: the central feature was monotheism. Reforming Hinduism, particularly Bakhtism, had moved toward that belief, so alien to classical Hinduism, but transformation did not go very far. The multiplicity of the gods and the Hindu worship of them in the form of stone idols was what so disturbed the Muslims. Guru Nanak shared that feeling. Refusing to worship Hindu statues, Guru Nanak told his followers that "If God is [just] a stone, I will worship a [whole] mountain." Human beings, he asserted are brothers (*bhai*), members of a brotherhood, (*khalsa*) just as in Islam, Muslims are *ikhwan,* members of a religious "clan," the *qawm*.

Indeed, Guru Nanak went even further: to him all mankind was equal. It followed that the Hindu caste system (*varna*) was tyrannical and sinful.

---

2 Its heartland was defined by five rivers (*Punjab* comes [not come] from the Persian words for five -- *Panj* - and the word for rivers or water - *ab*. These form the Indus river system.
3 *History of the Sikhs*, Oxford UP.

To counter caste segregation, he opened communal dining facilities (*langars*) in the temples he founded, open to all comers – rich and poor, Muslim and Hindu, men and women, upper and lower castes and even the untouchable (*sudras*). They were welcomed, fed and encouraged to engage along side of Sikhs -- and one another -- in the singing of hymns. But to protect their community and faith, the *Panth*, his followers were enjoined to be ready to engage in religious war, *charm-yudh*, as Muslims are obliged to struggle in *jihad*. The Sikhs also formed militias, *misls*, similar to the armies with which Islam conquered its empire.

Strikingly also, Guru Nanak asserted a personal communication with God. God is said to have given "him a cup of *amrit* (nectar) to drink and charged him with his mission in the following words: 'Nanak, I am with thee. Through thee will my name be magnified. Whosoever follows thee, him will I save. Go into the world to pray and teach mankind how to pray. Be not sullied by the ways of the world....'"

But Guru Nanak was also instructed to be realistic about humanity. While, over time, people could be expected to lead reasonable lives, they should consult guides, *gurus*. Reason was the key word: Nanak did not favor withdrawal, *udas*, or asceticism. As Khushwant Singh has written, "Spiritual life did not demand an ascetic denial of food, company, and sex, for a citizen discharging his obligations to his family and society had as good a chance of attaining salvation as a hermit or a monk." In short, what Guru Nanak did was to lay the religious basis for a new society.

That society, although always a small minority, was vibrant and successful generation after generation. It remained for his ninth successor as Guru, Gobind Singh, to create a larger, more unified and more warlike community and thus to lay the basis for a powerful new state. That state was to be the life mission of one of the most remarkable statesmen of South Asian history, Ranjit Singh. Taking power in the Punjab – which still today is the heartland of Pakistan -- when he was nineteen in 1799, Ranjit Singh blocked Britain's imperial march across India.

During Ranjit Singh's youth, northern India was largely under the control of Sikhs, but they were split into religious and militia factions. Thus, his first major task was to unify the country. Next he expelled the Afghan tribesmen who had formed the main fighting forces of the Punjabi factions. Then he conquered most of the dozens of principalities and fiefdoms that a century later would become Pakistan. Finally, in 1819, he conquered Kashmir. How he managed to turn the formerly divided and weak Punjab into a powerhouse had, it seems to me, three important causes:

First, he drew into his service not only Sikhs but also Hindus, Muslims and Christians. He was able to do this because of the ecumenism that had been so distinctive a feature of Sikhism since the time of Guru Nanak. He chose his closest advisers on skill rather than community background. His prime minister was a Sikh; his finance adviser, a Hindu and the man in charge of foreign affairs, a Muslim. Other officials and provincial governors and fief holders might be of any religion.

Second, he undertook what was, for the time, a massive transformation in the wealth of the country. Under Ranjit, the state provided rewards, subsidies and tax reductions to those who brought new lands into cultivation, improved old lands and dug water wells. Irrigation canals were cleaned. The condition of the peasantry was improved by distribution of lands formerly held by large (and often absentee) owners. Many landless sharecroppers became owners and their traditional form of "participatory democracy," village councils (*panchayats*), was confirmed. Education spread into the countryside and a sort of literary renaissance occurred in the cities. In short, he created something like a social, economic and psychological new "middle" class.

Third, having seen the power of the East India Company, Ranjit threw himself and his state into military affairs. To survive, as the East India Company inexorably gobbled up the other states, he realized he must, at least militarily, become British. For the traditional Punjabis, the "queen of battle" was the cavalry, and as people of the vast plain of Punjab, in this arm they excelled. But, Ranjit realized that cavalry could be only ancillary: what increasingly counted was artillery. Although cannon were first used massively by the Ottoman empire, the development of guns and tactics had become European. So he had to get weaponry and knowhow from Europe or from the British in India. As the historian J.S. Grewal has written,[4] "The men who initially served in these units of the army were mostly deserters from the army of the East India Company..." On this basis he built what was to become one of the most powerful – and certainly one of the most modern -- armies in Asia. Militarism would become the central feature of his reign. And would be passed down to his Pakistani heirs.

But, there were two black holes in Ranjit's universe; the one was that his quest for modernity and particularly for military power required much money. He could get what he needed only from the tillers of the soil and so, inevitably as he built his army, he squeezed them regardless of the effect on the peasants' well-being. Linked to this policy was a turn away, in the middle years of his reign, from the humane thought of the Sikh prophet and the reassertion of a repressive policy that in some ways echoed the Indo-European conquest of the Indus Valley and the Hindu repression of the native peoples, many of whom, by this time, were Muslims.

The results of these social, economic and military measures were, predictably, accentuation of the split between the Muslims and the Sikhs who increasingly lapsed into Hinduism. As Khashwant Singh summarized the results, the Sikhs again:

> Worshipped Hindu gods alongside of their own *Granth* [faith], venerated the cow, went on pilgrimages to Hindu holy places, fed Brahmins, consulted astrologers and soothsayers, and compelled widows to immolate themselves on the funeral pyres of their husbands [that is, committing *sati*]. Among certain sections, notably the Bedis, the caste to which Guru Nanak had belonged, the practice of killing female children on birth had been revived.

In short, they abandoned the ecumenical society that Guru Nanak had spent his life building. The Sikh regime no longer reached out in friendship to Muslims but laid ruinous taxes on them (causing the first of many famines);

---

4   *The Sikhs of the Punjab*, Cambridge University Press.

Ranjit banned the distinctive Muslim call to prayer and closed down the major mosques; and the Sikhs again pushed to the fore the distinctive totem animal of the Hindus, the cow, punishing slaughter of it with death.

In summary, this was the condition of the Punjab when the British arrived on the edge of what is today Pakistan in 1820.

*   *   *

Having by 1820 been educated by generations of experience dealing with and conquering dozens of Indian states, the British recognized the strategic and economic potential of this last great piece of the subcontinent. So they were anxious to take it for themselves and to protect it from their rivals. Curiously, among others they feared that their former colonists, avaricious, land-hungry and pioneering Americans, might come and settle on the rich lands along the banks of the great Indus river. The Americans, of course, were only an imaginary threat -- they were much too busy settling North America. But the British did have real if only potential rivals in the Russians.

The Russians were moving inexorably toward the south. Following the 1552 first step by Ivan the Terrible, the three "greats," Peter, Catherine and Alexander, advanced through the Muslim khanates of the Caucasus and Central Asia toward India. In English and British-Indian imagination, the Russians took the shape of hordes of Cossacks, galloping southward through the mountain passes and across the vast deserts toward India. There was some truth in this image. Although their armies were decimated by hunger, thirst and disease, the Russians did reach the north of what is now Afghanistan in the middle of the 1800s. And their British contemporaries concluded that the Afghans were not capable of stopping them. Nor, judging by their own policies, would the Russians stop on their own. As a later Tsarist foreign minister, Prince Aleksandr Gorchakov, put it,

> the difficulty is to know where to stop...in the interests of security [a powerful state must] exercise a certain ascendancy over...undesirable neighbors [so it must advance] deeper

and deeper into barbarous countries…irresistibly forced, less by ambition than by imperious necessity…"

Getting the Russians to stop became a central aim of British rulers of India as much later, during the Cold War, it would become the key objective of American policy. To protect India, the British government of India adopted what was later called the "Forward Policy."

The Forward Policy, long before the title was coined, was the contemporary British equivalent to the foreign policy projection of the more recent American neoconservatives: aiming not just defend to but to take over strategic countries, establish client governments and use the countries as barriers against the Russians. But before they were in a position to move forward to confront the Russians in Afghanistan, the British had to conquer the last remaining obstacle to their rule, the Punjab.

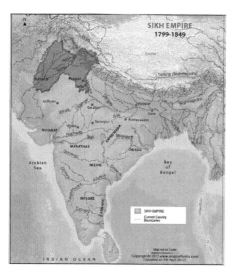

The Sikh Empire.
Map courtesy of "Maps of India."

The Punjab would prove a difficult obstacle. Although theoretically a part of the Mughal empire, the Punjab under Ranjit Sikh was really an empire on its own. It comprised a large part of northern India.

As happened in each of the Indian states the British had taken over, the power of Ranjit's Punjab could not be sustained. The British had mobilized one of the world's largest and best equipped armies, mainly made from Indian soldiers under English officers, and backed by a "stiffening" of separate units of Englishmen. Their first major test came in the First Anglo-Sikh War six years after the death of Ranjit Singh at the battle of Ferozeshah.

Those six years made all the difference. The army fought furiously and well – the British came close to surrendering – but it was sold out by its commanders. The successors and courtiers of Ranjit Singh turned on one another to try to snap up the spoils of his state. With his firm hand removed, the Sikh government and high command literally fell apart. As was typical of Islamic monarchies, where multiple marriages gave birth to half-brothers, envy, ambition and fear produced ugly and bitter fights over inheritance. Often the losers were blinded, strangled or killed in battle. In Punjab, after the death of Ranjit, a lesser solution was found in corruption and lechery. The British political agent summed it up by saying that "At Lahore they are quiet, drinking and intriguing politically and amorously...I sometimes feel as if I were a sort of parish constable at the door of a brothel rather than the representative of one government to another."

After two more hard-fought battles, in which thousands of Sikhs and hundreds of British troops were killed, the Sikhs fought as guerrillas with "hit and run" (*dhai phat*) tactics. Then they laid down their arms. The British immediately followed their victory with a "politico-military" strategy: demobilizing what was left of the Sikh army, confiscating its artillery and disarming the peasant militia. Then came the political strategy: Ranjit's followers were bought while others were humiliated or exiled.

Finally, the British installed their own regime. As the British conqueror, Lord Hardinge, wrote in another context, "the native prince is in fetters and under our protection, and must do our bidding." So, by 1849, the Punjab, the largest part of today's Pakistan , was firmly in British control. As Lord Dalhousie, the Governor General, put the British policies, "I can see no escape from the necessity of annexing this infernal country..."

* * *

Annex they did. For almost a century in a variety of ways they laid the basis for what is today Pakistan in the image of British India. How they did this is crucial to understanding the country of today.

In economic, social and education affairs, the British began to do what they had done to the army [put a colon, not a semi-colon]: they wiped out native activities. They virtually monopolized foreign trade and rigged the currency exchange in their favor while they siphoned off a large part of the revenue. Other measures led to the decline of the prosperity of the mainly Muslim farmers in favor of mainly Hindu moneylenders. As Naved Hamid has found,[5] "...at the end of British rule...less than four per cent of the agricultural population owned more than 50 per cent of the land while poor peasants, landless sharecroppers and agricultural labourers accounted for 80 percent of the population... [whereas before the colonial period landless] tenants hardly existed. [Thereafter] The moneylender, freed from the control of the village communities, was able to charge usurious interest and manipulate the account in his favour, so that once in debt the peasant could seldom escape." Everywhere, the British took the side of the money lender. In just four years, from 1880 to 1884, the British authorities arrested some 44,874 or 5% of the peasant farmers for debt. These policies created massive famines. Moreover, they greatly increased hatred between the Muslim and Hindu communities.

Village notables and assemblies (*panchayats*) were overruled by English officials, customary law was replaced by colonial edict and taxes, which previously had been imposed in kind and varied according to the harvest, were made payable in cash and were fixed regardless of the yield. Meanwhile, the educational system, as in the rest of the British Indian empire, was shifted away from the traditional medium of Arabic and Persian to English.

In short, under British rule, native, mainly Muslim, culture came to be viewed as subversive.

The British governor general had announced this policy immediately after the last major battle: as he put it, it was to effect "the entire subjection of the Sikh people and destroyed its power as an independent nation." This was to be done primarily by force. So the British built a supplementary armed force and police that numbered about half the size of Ranjit Singh's army.

---

5 Naved Hamid, "Dispossession and Differentiation of the Peasantry in the Punjab During Colonial Rule, *Journal of Peasant Studies*, Vol 10 #1, Oct, 1982. Also see M.L. Darling, *The Punjab Peasant in Prosperity and Debt*, Oxford 1925 and S.S. Thorburn, *Musalmans and Moneylender of the Punjab*. Blackwood, 1886.

Sikh soldiers, on being disbanded and having neither land nor commercial skills, often were forced into *dacoitism*, operating in robber bands that preyed on the mainly Muslim peasantry, but some turned their hostility on the English and their puppets. In response, the British increasingly relied on repression through the military, secret police (*khufia*) and spies (*jasuses*).

After half a century of such oppressive rule, the British-Indian (by this time no longer the Company but the Empire) government grew worried by the economic and security effects of its own policy and tried in the 1900 "Punjab Alienation of Land Act" to prevent city merchants from taking over the lands of working owners. Belatedly and half-heartedly, the government made attempts to satisfy the peasants' hunger for land. But, the accumulation of many grievances led to a wide-spread feeling that Britain was destroying rather than protecting local traditions and culture. Mass meeting and inflammatory leaflets began to stir popular resistance. Unable or unwilling to consider the causes, the British increased military, paramilitary and police action, exiling agitators, banning meetings and seizing printing presses. An atmosphere of rebellion was created and the British set what would become a persistent theme for the rest of their rule – suppressing grievance by force. Everywhere they looked, they found what they regarded as disloyalty or sedition. As N. Gerald Barrier found,[6] "police informants in the Punjab – whose continued employment in effect depended upon their ability to unearth or to fabricate sedition – sent in incredible tales of impending mutiny and an Afghan-Russian-Punjabi entente to seize the border districts." The British reacted to the craze. By 1921, the Punjab had become essentially an occupied enemy state.

What is truly remarkable is that many of the inhabitants, particularly those who were better educated and materially better off, not only accepted British rule but adopted its forms and practices, even those that were most oppressive or humiliating, as their own. Yet, at the same time, the British sought not to live in India and certainly not with the Indians but in the scores of segregated "little Englands" with which they dotted the Indian countryside. While they had a grudging respect for the wild tribesmen and

---

6   "The Punjab Disturbances of 1907: The Response of the British Government in India to Agrarian Unrest," in David Hardiman's *Peasant Resistance in India*, Oxford, 1992.

were indifferent to the wretched poor, the British despised the Anglicized Indians who affected English manners, wore English clothes, spoke English, studied in English schools and thought of themselves as at least British if not wholly English.

Luckily for the British, this new class of Indians mostly attempted assimilation rather than revolt. But, step by step this new class was pulling or being driven apart. As it became increasingly frustrated, it still did not strike back but took up non-violent, English-style protests. Violence was almost entirely on the part of the British controlled police, soldiers and hired thugs. But a change in expectation was spreading. What decades earlier would hardly have been noticed then began to be seen as illustrations of British contempt for Indians. And, whether by design or inadvertence, incidents of the breakdown of public order drove wedges not only between the population and the British but also among the Hindus, Sikhs and Muslims. Each was finding leaders, organizations and voices.

*   *   *

Part of the reason for the new politicization of the Muslim population in the core areas of what became Pakistan was that it had come to view the Sikhs as just another variety of Hindus, many of whom the Muslims knew only as money lenders and whose practices, supported by the British authorities, enforced by imperial edict and justified by English law, they found abhorrent.

Another part of the agitation was caused by a sense of deprivation of land. For years, money lenders had managed through foreclosures on debt to acquire peasant lands. As of 1921, 60% of the land-owning farmers possessed too little (less than five acres) to support their families while a total of 86% owned just enough to be barely above the level of hunger. And, other than sullen withdrawal, they found no means of getting the British to change the system. Desperate, small holders and landless workers began to murder Hindu – and increasingly Sikh – money lenders. Fear of insurrection motivated the British to retaliate with increased violence. In these conditions, a failure of the monsoon rains tipped society into famine. Each step led to the next. Humiliated, angry and on the brink of starvation, the Muslim poor struck back – thus seeming to prove the charge that they were, after all, just terrorists.

At first, these events do not seem to have been inspired or shaped by religion. True, the poor at least in Punjab were mainly Muslims. And some of their religious guides were fundamentalists, known in the Punjab as in Arabia as Wahhabis, but their calls for resistance were faint. The next move was made by the privileged rather than the poor and while it defined itself in religious terms, it was primarily a political reform movement. It was that cut of Indian Muslim society, rather than the religious establishment that took the lead. It was they who began to join the newly formed "All India Muslim League."

Caught between the British and the Hindus, Muslim leaders like Muhammad Ali Jinnah[7] began to demand a voice. Theirs was overwhelmed by the more numerous Hindus. To be heard, they insisted on separate electorates or at least designated seats on public institutions. So, after the "Reform Act" of 1919, much of the agitation over the next twenty five years was diverted from the British and focused instead on the "weightage" (proportional representation) awarded to each community.

The triangular nature of the nationalist movement -- Muslim against Hindu, Hindu against Muslim and both against the British was played out all over India in the press, in massive demonstrations and in the meetings of the Hindu-dominated Congress.

Among both the Hindu and the Muslim leadership, there were remarkable men. They were similarly influenced both by the way of life of British India and England. How they differed was more in their objectives than in their means of action.

One stood apart and towered above all the others -- Mohandas Gandhi. Although, like most of the other leaders, he was deeply attached

---

7 A sidelight on the interwoven complexity of Indian politics is that the native language of both Muhammad Ali Jinnah and Mohandas Gandhi as well as other of the Indian Hindu leaders were Gujaratis of Sindh. Gujarati is an Indo-European language, related to Hindi, while the modern official language of Pakistan, Urdu, is strongly Persian- and Arabic-influenced in vocabulary and script.

to England where he had studied and to English law which he practiced, he purposefully rejected everything associated with the styles of British India and, indeed, of England. He approached the problems of Indian politics and society by literally dressing not only his body and pronouncements but also his philosophy in the style of the Indian "common man." Gandhi's political persona was particularly remarkable because he had returned to India relatively late in life after twenty years of practicing law in South Africa. But the Indians of both religious communities almost immediately recognized him as the "great soul" (*mahatma*) of India.

The English did not. He baffled them. More than baffled, infuriated. He could not be bought off or frightened. Like the British Indian officialdom, Churchill loathed Gandhi, referring to him as a "half-naked *fakir*."[8] Viceroys in India arrested him, but feared that in the ultimate act of defiance, he might starve himself to death and set off uncontrollable riots not only among Hindus but also, uniquely for a Hindu among Muslims. So, in his last incarceration, they installed him in a palace rather than a prison. When it came his turn to deal with Gandhi, the Viceroy, Field Marshall Lord Wavell, grew increasingly angry. He found Gandhi to be "exceedingly shrewd, obstinate, domineering, double-tongued, single-minded politician, and there is little true saintliness in him."[9]

Undeterred by imprisonment or disagreement, Gandhi marched to his own drumbeat, no one else's. He certainly played a crucial role in the attempt to subvert British policy on the Muslims, but, at the very end of his life, he had become so disillusioned by the actions of his own (Hindu) community and his companions in the Congress leadership, that he denounced them and even contemplated moving to Pakistan.

Weighed in his scale, the other leaders were lesser men although by any other standard they also were remarkable. Without going into excessive detail, what particularly strikes me is that whereas Gandhi merged himself, his emotions and his philosophy into his vision of "Mother India," the leaders of both the Hindu-dominated Congress and the Muslim League cast

---

8   A fakir (correctly, a *faqir*) is a mendicant – a man like St. Francis – who carries religion to the downtrodden. Churchill meant to imply that Gandhi was just a faker or fraud.
9   Stanley Wolpert, *Jinnah of Pakistan*, Oxford University Press, India paperback edition, 2012, 276.

themselves in an English mold. Focus on three leaders: Jawaharlal Nehru of the Hindus, and Muhammad Ali Jinnah and the Aga Khan of the Muslims. They must have appeared to their fellow countrymen as exactly what the aspiring, relatively affluent and educated members of their communities most wanted to be, perfect English gentlemen. Each was more at home in English than in any Indian language, all three dressed mostly to Savile Row tastes and, more importantly, each saw his relationship to England as the trump card in their struggle for India. Nehru carried it to the logical extreme by having a love affair with the wife of the last Viceroy, Lady Edwina Mountbatten. The London *Mail on Line* of September 26, 2009, called it "a spicy *ménage a trois*."[10]

Spicy or not, the affair was used by Nehru to further his single-minded determination to make India into "Hindustan." While he perhaps benefitted from what he could learn "from the pillow" about British policy and also from having suggestions passed to the Viceroy by his wife, relationships with England on the Muslim side were less intimate. But Muhammad Ali Jinnah and the Aga Khan found their own ways. What typified their approach was the recognition that ultimately British India was controlled by England. It was essential, therefore, to carry their message to England. Whereas in British India, despite his wealth and considerable intelligence, the Aga Khan was disparaged by even junior officers and civil servants as just a "Wily Oriental Gentleman," a *WOG* -- or even more insultingly in other ways -- in England, he was often a guest of the royal family. Without pressing the point, I think he shrewdly hit on a way to use his wealth: learning that English royals were addicted to horse racing, he made himself the leading member of the "horsy" circle around the royals, with Ascot as his embassy and his stud as one of England's prides.

By origin a fellow Ismaili, Muhammad Ali Jinnah lacked the Aga Khan's wealth and wit, but by education and profession he was drawn into a different cut of English society and politics. An outstanding lawyer, he could deal effectively with the people who ultimately controlled British

---

10: Not only Lord Mountbattan but many others knew of the affair through having gotten hold of her love letters or copies of them. Some were passed to Jinnah who, as the perfect English gentleman, returned them, allegedly unread. On the affair see Alex von Tunzelmann's *Indian Summer*. For local knowledge of it see Sapan Kapoor in the March 29, 2013 issue of the Pakistani *Express Tribune*.

policy toward India, the "mandarins" of the civil and foreign services. It is only my interpretation, but I believe that both the English and the British felt more "at home" with him than with any other South Asian leader. He was reliable, a gentleman, almost "one of us." The feeling was reciprocated: he supported Britain when it counted in the Second World War so, while the Hindu leadership was imprisoned, Jinnah was left free to promote his position within the Muslim community and, indeed, to sharpen its sense of itself. This comfortable relationship ended abruptly when the Labour Party came to power in London and Lady Mountbatten's husband became Viceroy in India.

*　　*　　*

Already during the 1930s, at least emotionally, India was already being partitioned. In 1933, the man who might be called the Pakistani Herzl, Choudhary Rahmat Ali, wrote a pamphlet called "Now or Never" on the need for a Muslim homeland. Like Herzl, he coined a name for the hoped-for homeland. The name he created was "Pakistan." As Herzl did with *Judenstaat,* Choudhary Rahmat Ali he built his program into the name. He formed the name from the letters of the areas assumed to be united under Islam: *P* came from Punjab; *A* from the Afghan North West Frontier province; *K* from Kashmir, *S* from Sindh Province and *istan* from Balochistan. The Persian word *pak* also had the advantage of meaning "pure" or "clean" so Pakistan was to be the land of the true believers.

Neat though the play on words was, the reality was far from supportive. The central province, Punjab, was about half Hindu or Sikh; Kashmir had a Hindu *maharaja* lording over a still politically unsophisticated Muslim population; and millions of Muslims were scattered across the rest of India. Only Bengal, which Choudhary Rahmat Ali did not mention, was a mass Muslim community. Some Muslim leaders, notably Muhammad Iqbal, were still willing to have their community be part of a loose Indian federation as a British Empire dominion. As much as they disagreed with their British rulers, they trusted them more than the Hindu Indians.

That proposed accommodation was immediately undercut when the

English government declared war on Nazi Germany.[11] Without consulting any of the Indian leaders, the then viceroy, Lord Linlithgow, declared that India also was at war with Germany. While they were outraged at not being consulted on this fundamental "national" issue, the leaders of both Hindus, and Muslims hoped that the British would use the occasion to graciously proclaim their independence. They were quickly disabused. Linlithgow summoned Gandhi and Jinnah to inform them that there would be no further discussion of devolution until after the war. Churchill rubbed salt into the wound of Linlithgow's statement two years later when he informed Parliament that the ringing declaration of the Atlantic Charter, meant to proclaim a brave new world of freedom, did not apply to its empire in India.

Nevertheless, the Muslim leaders pressed ahead for some form of autonomy or independence. This culminated in the early days of the Second World War in the March 23, 1940 Lahore Resolution calling for a two-state solution. Perhaps another unconscious parallel to Arab-Israeli affairs, it broke down before the ink was dry. The leaders of the Congress refused to accept the Lahore Resolution and the British had already closed off discussion of any settlement until after the war.

Disappointed by the British refusal of their demands for liberty and annoyed by Muslim separatism, Congress voted to begin a "quit India" campaign using non-violence (*satyagraha*). Their decision was met by a severe British crack down in which, among other things, the British enforced an embargo or diversion of food supplies that is estimated to have cost about three million Indian lives.[12] They also arrested all the Congress leaders they could catch including Gandhi. One who they could not reach, although they tried to assassinate him, was Subhas Chandra Bose. Bose made his way back from Europe to Asia, first in a German submarine and from Madagascar onward in a Japanese submarine, rallied the 30,000 Indian troops whom

---

11   This and other parts of the account on the wartime and postwar negotiations is most accessibly set out in Stanley Wolpert's excellent *A New History of India*, Oxford University Press, 1977 ff and in his *Jinnah of Pakistan*, Oxford, 1984 ff..

12   The causes of the famine, which particularly affected the Muslim population of Bengal (later Bangladesh) were initially natural (severe storms, tidal waves and a cyclone) but were accentuated by the tax structure, distribution failures, hording and government failure to act. Churchill personally refused to allow diversion of shipping to alleviate the famine in 1943. Both he and Lord Linlithgow insisted, in the face of the facts that there was no shortage of food there. So millions died.

the British had surrendered to the Japanese at the fall of Singapore and organized them into an army that in March 1944 attacked the British in India.[13] Frightened by the prospect of this assault, the British reversed course and offered the Indian leaders the prospect of eventual limited liberty. Both the Congress and the League found this inadequate.

Then a remarkable thing happened. With most of the Congress leadership immobilized and presumably out of communication, two leaders who had not been imprisoned, the Muslim Liaquat Ali Khan and the Hindu Bhulabhai Desai, carried on secret negotiations that resulted in a plan to form a coalition government and, ultimately, a single state with the Muslims agreeing to give up their demand for Pakistan in return for participation in government. When word was leaked of their negotiations in 1945, the newly freed Hindu Congress leadership immediately repudiated it. It was one of those fascinating "might have beens" which occasionally enliven history. Perhaps it could have saved India and the tragedy of partition.[14]

*   *   *

During the war, Muhammad Ali Jinnah disagreed with the Hindu leadership on tactics and objectives. While continuing to demand independence, he supported the Allied side and, being out of prison, used the war years to enhance the power of the Muslim League. Among other efforts, he founded the first "Pakistani" newspaper, *Dawn*, which is still a major voice of that country.

In almost every town, village and city Muslims and Hindus were increasingly pulling apart so that the physical as well as the emotional bases were being laid, reluctantly on both sides at first, for the real partition in 1947. A last ditch effort was made to stave it off. Two leaders who had not been

---

13: The so-called Indian National Army was made up of the 30,000 troops that the British surrendered at the fall of Singapore; Bose had been, along with Nehru and Gandhi, one of the leaders of the Indian nationalist movement and was regarded as still very popular, perhaps even more popular than Nehru, in India where he was known as the Netaji or "Respected Leader." The attack was also aided by the Burmese leader, Aung San, the father of Aung San Suu Kyi. The attack reached India but petered out in 1945. Captured senior officers were put on trial, but the trial turned out to be a lesson in Indian patriotism and the indicted officers became national heroes. On Subhas Chandra Bose see Sugata Bose, *His Majesty's Opponent*, Harvard U.P., 2011.

14   See Jaswant Singh (2009). *Jinnah: India, Partition, Independence*. Oxford: Oxford University Press, 2009 and "Story of Pakistan", http://storyofpakistan.com/desailiaquat-pact/2007.

imprisoned, the Muslim Liaquat Ali Khan and the Hindu Bhulabhai Desai carried on secret negotiations that resulted in a plan to form a coalition government and, ultimately, a single state with the Muslims agreeing to give up their demand for Pakistan in return for participation in government. When word was leaked of their negotiations in 1945, the newly freed Congress leadership immediately repudiated it.

Then openly, and under the sponsorship of the British viceroy, the whole senior leadership of Congress and the League met at the summer resort of Simla to consider a new round of proposals. That meeting broke up when the Congress leaders demanded that Congress -- not the League -- must choose the Muslim delegates. Thereafter the positions of both sides hardened: Congress leaders denied the right of the Muslim League to participate in government and the Muslim League replied by reaffirming their demand for the creation of a separate state. The British proposed what the British-Indian and the English governments thought was a compromise – again much as the British had done in Palestine. In India it was to be a unified nation-state in which military and foreign affairs and a few other shared issues would be handled by a central government and the provinces would have the option of leaving the Union. The Muslim League accepted but the Nehru-led Congress rejected it.

At their wits end, the newly elected Labour Party English government decided to transfer power to two "dominions," India and Pakistan. Where populations were mixed (including Punjab and Bengal) plebiscites would be held. Remarkably, the new Viceroy, Lord Mountbatten, got Nehru, Jinnah and the Punjabi Sikh leader together to announce the deal on the radio. Pakistan was about to be born.

June 1, 2013

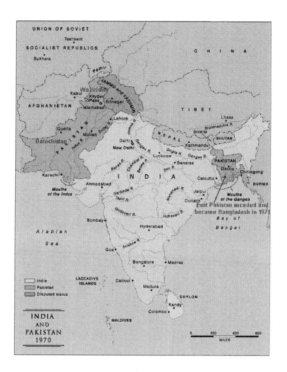

Map showing the partition of the Indian Empire into
Pakistan and India. The Durand line is the current
border between Afghanistan and Pakistan.

CHAPTER 9

THE NATURE OF PAKISTAN:
II: THE CURRENT REALITY

Much too late, the British tried vainly in 1946 and 1947 to head off the collapse of British India by riot and murder. A Parliamentary commission again suggested a federal structure where the rights of both communities could be protected under British control. And, to make the case, it warned the Muslims that partition would create a small Pakistan which would be "dependent on the good will of [the much larger] Hindustan." By then, the British effort was also too little: the Congress leader Jawaharlal Nehru thought the plan unworkable and unacceptable while the Muslim League leader Muhammad Ali Jinnah dismissed it as British double dealing. No strong leader was prepared to endorse the concept of Britain remaining in India in any guise. A dead end had been reached.

Order rapidly broke down with the first intercommunal "Great Killing" occurring in Calcutta in August 1946 and echoed throughout India in the following weeks. The British found that most of the casualties were Muslims, killed by Hindu thugs, but the action unnerved the British government. Essentially giving up its attempts to work out a compromise, its reaction was to invite Nehru to form an all-India government. In response, millions of Muslims decked their houses with black flags, the signs of despair and anger, and prepared for the worst. It soon came.

While not yet official, India was already irredeemably partitioned. As the historian Stanley Wolpert has written,[1]

> There was no reconciliation, no solution to the problems
> of fundamental mistrust, suspicion, fear, and hatred. Too
> much blood had been let, too many knives buried in too

---

1 *Jinnah of Pakistan,* Oxford University Press, Indian paperback edition 2012, 294.

147

many backs, too many unborn babies had been butchered in their mother's wombs, too many women raped, too many men robbed, people were fired to irrational hatred by the sick reflections of their communal neighbors in the house or village next door."

In the "Great Killing," the British governor reported that "Almost all casualties have been Moslems and it is estimated that of these 75% have been women and children." That was the trigger. In the partition of India, nearly a million people were killed or died and over 9 million Muslims crossed from India into lands that became Pakistan while roughly the same number of Hindus and Sikhs crossed into India or into that part of the Punjab that was joined to India. Jinnah aside, Indian Muslims voted for the creation of Pakistan with their feet.

The scars of this vast movement of peoples, mostly done under horrific circumstances, have shaped Indian-Pakistani relations and the political culture of Pakistan ever since. Fear, anger and what I have called the post-imperial malaise still dominate both states and have led, among other things, to the decision of both states to acquire nuclear weapons and to maintain huge conventional armies.

The logical first task before the leaders of the new states should have been to create the structures of government; however, both Pakistan and India inherited from the British Empire not only prefabricated organizations – armies, ministries, law courts, civil services, postal systems etc. -- but also the codes of management required to run them, Thus, Pakistan was born in full flight. It could not escape its past in almost any respect. However much it thought of itself as new, it was also "British" and in part even "English." Thus, the new Governor-General, Muhammad Ali Jinnah, who had spent this life arguing for an Islamic homeland, astonishingly proclaimed to the constituent assembly what only an English trained lawyer, not a refugee from intercommunial killings, could have said,

> You are free to go to your [Hindu] temples. You are free to go to your mosques or to any other place of worship in this

State of Pakistan...you may belong to any religion or caste or creed. That [your creed or community] has nothing to do with the business of the State.

To me, with the prejudice of a historian, Jinnah's proclamation sounded like an echo of the Sikh community as envisaged by Guru Nanak Singh over four hundred years earlier. It was both ecumenical and bold. But, as happened to the Sikhs under Ranjit Singh, the Pakistanis would have to try to find the means to protect themselves from the huge power coming out of India. Like the Sikhs, the post-independence Pakistanis sought it in militarism.

*   *   *

Militarism, as I have written in the previous paper was the style set by the "ancestor" of Pakistan, the Punjab, and it was further emphasized when the East India Company took over the area. Britain always relied on a native army, the *sepoys*, under English officers and "stiffened" by English regular troops. The British regarded the Sikhs as one of India's "martial races," so a military way of life was built into the Punjab and through it into Pakistan.

Pakistan is often said to be a military state by inheritance. That is, it inherited the British Indian army (whereas India inherited the bureaucracy). This is an exaggeration. Pakistan got what is usually considered[2] about a third of the old army "but only a sixth of its sources of revenue. From birth, therefore, Pakistan was saddled with a huge army it could not pay for..."

As it emerged from the bitter days of partition, Pakistan was in about the same proportion to India as Mexico to the United States. By every criterion, India overshadowed Pakistan and still does. In 2011, according to the World Bank, there were 1.2 billion Indians and only 177 million Pakistanis; the gross domestic product (GDP) of India is about $1.9 trillion as compared to Pakistan's $210 million.

Size mattered, but more important was strategy. Pakistan's leaders

---

2: Husain Haqqani, "Breaking Up is not Hard To Do," *Foreign Affairs*, March/April 2013.

believed, with good reason, that India's leaders had not given up their often repeated aim to reincorporate Pakistan into India as the Nehru government was then doing with other breakaway or potentially breakaway provinces. Reading the pronouncements of the Hindu Indian leaders and watching their acts, not only officers but also civilian leaders, journalists, civil servants and the citizenry at large then concluded (and mostly still believe) that there really is a wolf at Pakistan's door.

Pakistan's British masters (first) and advisers (later) concurred in this belief. As I mentioned above, the 1946 Parliamentary commission had warned that small Pakistan would be "dependent on the good will of [the much larger] Hindustan." It also seemed to the Pakistanis confirmed by the swift military Indian response to the bungled attempt by Pakistan to take over Kashmir. Later, the breakaway of East Pakistan (Bangladesh) shifted even further the balance of power toward India. Following the terrible riots and killings of the Partition, Pakistan engaged in trial after trial of strength with India. It lost them all.

As one informed observer summarized,[3] they "have fought wars in 1947, 1965, 1971 and 1999, as well as significant skirmishes in 1984, 1985, 1987 and 1995, and have almost come to blows on numerous other occasions." Pakistan's repeated defeats were inevitable. In addition to other advantages, India fields an army about twice the size of Pakistan's 600,000.[4] Only in nuclear weapons and delivery systems is there a rough parity. However, nuclear weapons can be set aside in the equation since neither side can use them without committing suicide; their real value, if any, is deterrence but even that has not prevented wars or lesser clashes.[5] Pakistan has lost each encounter; thus, the "security mindset," so evident in Pakistan, is grounded in the reality of the overwhelming power of India. Fear of India was palpable from the beginning of Pakistan and remains today a dominant aspect of Pakistani politics. Pakistan sees India as an existential threat to its survival as a state.

---

3   Haviland Smith, former CIA station chief and chief of its counter terrorism staff, http://rural-ruminations.com/
4:   International Institute for Strategic Studies, *The Military Balance 2013.*
5   On Pakistan's "miscalculation" on the value of nuclear weapons as a deterrent during the Kargil crisis of 1999, see Owen Bennett Jones, *Pakistan; Eye of the Storm,* Yale University Press, 2002.

Pakistan's view of this threat is a key element in the three issues on which world attention has been focused by the media in recent years – the turbulent North West Frontier, Afghanistan and Kashmir. Since I have written extensively about them elsewhere, I will here simply summarize the main points:

Pakistan and Afghanistan are genetically linked across the frontier the British imposed in 1893 to divide Pakistan's North West Frontier Province from Afghanistan. The people on both sides are Pushtuns; indeed, about 15% of Pakistanis and 40-45% of Afghans are Pushtuns. They dominate Afghanistan and have played a major role in Pakistan. President Ayub Khan was a Pushtun as is the prominent Pakistani sportsman Imran Khan who contested the presidency of Pakistan in 2013. The Pushtun territory on the Pakistani side of the frontier is about the size of Nebraska while the Afghan Pushtun area is roughly the size of Florida.[6]

Pushtuns saw the Durand line as an example of "divide and rule" and in 1949, an Afghan national assembly (*loya jirga*) declared the Durand Line illegal. Then and during the 1960s, there was a move to create a single "Pushtanistan." Both Afghanistan and Pakistan opposed this move. For Afghanistan, the Pushtun area virtually was the state and for Pakistan any further loss of territory (particularly after the loss of Bangladesh) might be fatal. Just as Nehru feared -- and fought against -- the loss of any of India's diverse provinces, so has Pakistan.

There is a second aspect to Pakistan's Afghan policy. It is fear of encirclement. The Pakistanis, uniformly I find, see Afghanistan as protecting Pakistan's flank. Any increase of Indian influence over Afghanistan is viewed with alarm. In this sense, Pakistan sees even such actions as the opening

---

6   Roughly the area comprising today's North West Frontier Territory was seized by the Sikh leader Ranjit Singh from the Afghans about 1820. The British first tried to conquer it, fighting 24 major engagements and innumerable firefights between 1852 and the First World War. In their "modified forward policy," the British occupied the tribal area with forts and carried out punitive raids (known as "butcher and bolt") while the tribesmen fought back as their descendants do today, having learned to make what are today called improvised explosive devices (IEDs) In the so-called third Afghan war, the British employed 340,000 troops and 185,000 transport mules, camels and elephants. Then they gave up and more or less let it alone except for punitive raids. It was incorporated into Pakistan in 1947. On the invention of the IEDs see General Sir Andrew Skeen, *Passing it On: Short Talks on Tribal Fighting on the North-West Frontier of India,* Aldershot, 2nd edition, 1932, 9-10.

of Indian consulates, visits by prominent leaders and provision of aid as something like the British Nineteenth century Forward Policy. The "Great Game" is alive and well in Central Asia.

Moreover, the wild Pushtun area of Pakistan is as difficult to control by Pakistanis as it has been by the British, Russians and Americans. It has bred its own species of Taliban and marches to the beat of its shared *Pushtunwali*. Pakistan has found that it cannot be controlled militarily at an affordable cost; nor, indeed, since it wishes to keep Afghanistan within its orbit, does it wish to defeat the Pushtuns. Despite frequently repeated pronouncements and some limited military actions, its long term interests are shaped by its belief that a Pushtun-controlled – which will probably mean a Taliban-controlled -- Afghanistan offers Pakistan what has been termed "strategic depth" in its ongoing confrontation with India. Thus, Pakistan is unlikely to bow to American pressure, or even drone bombings and Special Forces raids, to undertake large-scale and determined action against the Pushtuns or the Taliban.

Kashmir is both a more emotional and a clearer issue for the Pakistan government and people. "Saving" Kashmir was the first objective of the new state and it failed. All it was able to hold onto were the offal and the bones, the relatively poor, cold highlands, while India grabbed the lush valley. And the population is fellow Muslim. Protecting the Muslims from Hindus was, as we have seen, the raison d'être of Pakistan, and Kashmir, whose very name built into the newly coined name of the country, Pakistan, was felt to be due the same protection.

Pakistan's military leaders have learned that their army cannot successfully fight India, but, as they watched the campaign against the Russians in Afghanistan, they learned that big armies are vulnerable to guerrillas. And, as the Indians beat down, imprisoned and killed increasing numbers of Kashmiris, they created enemies. With relatively minor investments in equipment and training, the Pakistanis thus found natural and dedicated allies for a clandestine fight against the Indians. That fight has now gone on for two generations and shows no signs of ending.

Apart from the emotional issue of Kashmir as a natural part of Pakistan, Kashmir is the source of life for Pakistan. Without the waters flowing down from Kashmir's glaciers Pakistan would be a desert.

But uncontrolled water can be, and recently has been in Pakistan, more devastating than any war so far and rivals the horrors of the 1947 Partition. As an aspect of global climate change, Pakistan was hit in the summer of 2010 by unprecedented monsoon rains. Floods swamped an area larger than England, turning about 20 million people into refugees, submerging villages, drowning about 2,000, killing livestock precious to the peasant farmers and destroying the

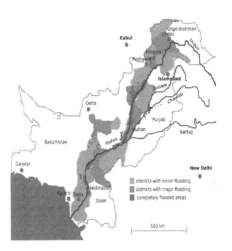

Map of the 2010 flooding of the
Indus River Valley
http://en.wikipedia.org/wiki/File:Indus_
flooding_2010_en.svg

results of decades of construction of infrastructure. About 5,000 miles of roads, railway lines and bridges and 7,000 schools were washed away. The floods were a mammoth setback to the country.[7] They were the worst ever recorded. They demonstrated both how thin a veneer is the modernization of the economy and at the same time how resilient in the face of disaster is a relatively unsophisticated economic structure. Pakistan survived and its military leaders perhaps drew the lesson that it could survive even a devastating nuclear war.

In the context of repeated defeats, it has been impossible even for the few civilian leaders who wished to trim the role of the military to do so. The military was always ready to step in if they tried. Generals Iskander Mirza, Ayub Khan, Zia ul-Haq and Perviz Musharaf each made military

7 See *The Magazine of the International Red Cross and Red Crescent Movement*, 2010, Alex Wynter, "Natural Disaster," *The New York Times*, June 27, 2010, Carlotta Gall, "Pakistan Flood Sets Back Infrastructure by Years" and *The Washington Post*, June 27, 2010, Brian Vastag, "Devastating 2010 Pakistan floods…"

coups d'état and put the country under military rule nearly half of the years since independence. Realizing their weakness, civilian governments rarely opposed and often abetted the ambitions of the military.

Ironically, it is the very failing of the military system that gives it both its strength and its justification. Because Pakistan's army has lost all of its campaigns against India, it convincingly argues that it needs more resources. That the heavy allocation of resources has thwarted growth of prosperity is held to be inevitable; that it made the functioning of political parties, the judiciary and the press more difficult is justified by the need to give full support to the forces of national security; and that it has delayed or derailed attempts to uplift Pakistan's poor is explained as a consequence of the threat of war.

How this "security mindset" will play out in the coming months is the key question confronting the new Nawaz Sharif government. Arguably today, getting along with, containing or controlling the military is mainly a domestic political issue, but in the formative years, Pakistani militarization was aided and encouraged from abroad.

Beginning already in the Truman administration and greatly increased in the Eisenhower administration, American policy, aided and abetted by Great Britain, has been to build the capacity of the military to act in an anti-Soviet role, first to participate in CENTO and SEATO, second, to provide a secure base for anti-Soviet insurgency in Afghanistan and, third, to enable Western intelligence to monitor Soviet nuclear tests in Central Asia with communications and electronic intercepts and overflights by the famous U-2. [8]

Government after Pakistani government rose to the bait that was put out to entice cooperation. To interface with the CIA, the Pakistan government created the Inter-Services Intelligence (ISI) which became virtually a state

---

8   In pursuit of its own strategic interests, China also aided and abetted Pakistani militarism. It has furnished military equipment, constructed a naval base at Gwadar and offered credits. The Pakistanis are pushing the use of the highway and pipeline linking the port to Islamabad and on to Kashgar. For the latest moves see *South China Morning Post,* June 30, 2013, Teddy Ng, "Xinjiang-Gwadar port economic corridor tops Pakistani leader's China agenda."

within the state. In payment for its anti-Soviet role – a recreation of the Nineteenth century policy of British India – Pakistan received about $40 billion. To ensure compliance with Anglo-American policy, the United States alone has "lent" or given Pakistan more than $30 billion (of which about half was military related) since 1948.[9]

During the same time, the Pakistanis have learned that their newly trained and expensively armed but surplus military units have become a valuable resource, almost like the produce of an oil field, to be exported to Middle Eastern countries that lacked their own military prowess. And, as with the oil-rich states, the existence of virtually unaudited vast sums received in these ways promoted vast corruption.

*   *   *

Corruption has been damaging but what is even more significant is that, while the military component of the money coming from abroad helped to build the capacity of the military, it did not and could not build such countervailing institutions. Foreign aid could supply tanks, aircraft and training missions but not an independent judiciary, a dedicated parliament or a vigorous press. Such institutions had not been allowed to develop firm roots under British rule and after independence grew only slowly, sporadically and with frequently setbacks. The resulting imbalance has prevented Pakistan from developing into a stable state. That the military is the only institution with cohesion, power and mobility -- even with public acceptance of its claim to honesty and patriotism -- is evident from the fact that the military have taken over the government in repeated coups, ruling in 1958-1971, 1977-1988 and 1999-2008. "Politics," almost universally regarded as corrupt, self-seeking and opportunistic, is just what happens between military coups.[10]

Naturally, the army command used its power to demand what it thought it needed to defend the country or what it wanted to reward itself. It has done so handsomely. Senior officers live "behind high walls, in

---

9   Congressional Research Service, "Pakistan: U.S. Foreign Assistance," October 4, 2012.
10: See Aqil Shah, "Getting the Military Out of Pakistani Politics," *Foreign Affairs*, May/June 1911 and Pew Research, May 10, 213, Richard Wike, "What Pakistan Thinks,"

manicured compounds of a luxury unimaginable to the average Pakistani."[11] For years, this has amounted to upwards of 70% of the government budget. As I will stress, this outlay is unlikely to diminish by much.

The military is not alone in undermining the capacity of the government. Concentration of wealth in the hands of people powerful enough to avoid taxes continued after independence. Prime Minister Zulfiqar Ali Bhutto's attempts to rein in corruption were certainly among the reasons for his overthrow and execution; his daughter Benazir and her husband, Asif Ali Zardari, (both subsequently prime ministers) were well aware of this danger and not only went along with "the system," but were outstanding practitioners of graft. Both spent periods under indictment for allegedly illicitly collecting more than a billion dollars.[12] Zardari set a style. In Zardari's later government, neither his prime minister nor any other members of his cabinet paid any taxes. Some would not even pay their utility bills.[13]

Corruption and militarism have cost the country not only stability but well-being. The government is crippled by its own poverty. Less than one in each hundred citizens pays an income tax.[14] Cabinet ministers and members of Parliament routinely avoid even charges for their utilities. Most of government revenue came (at least during the 1990s) from customs duties. These were famously circumvented or underreported with the loss to government of well over a billion dollars a year. So, particularly during the periods of power of Benazir Bhutto (1988-1990 and 1993-1996) and her husband and successor Asif Ali Zardari (2008 to 2013) the government could not perform services needed by the vast majority of Pakistan's 187 million

---

11 *The New Yorker,* September 19, 2011, Dexter Filkins, "The Journalist and the Spies." To be fair, senior Chinese and Russians even under Communist regimes lived in comparable luxury.

12 I should tell the reader that I had a rather intimate relationship with the Bhuttos. My daughter Milbry Polk was very close to Benazir and her brother Mir when all three studied at Harvard. She was invited to Pakistan and lived with the family in the summer of 1973. During that time, Prime Minister Zulfiqar Ali Bhutto and I corresponded. Finally, just before the hanging of his father, Mir consulted with me on what if any action he might take to prevent it. On the corruption issue, see *The New York Times,* January 9, 1998, John F. Burns, "House of graft: tracing the Bhutto millions". Also see *The Hindu,* March 27, 2004, A.G. Noorani, "Benazir in Swiss courts."

13 On the tax issue see *The New Yorker,* September 19, 2011, Dexter Filkins, "The Journalist and the Spies," quoting the Pakistani journalist Umar Cheema. On utility bills non-payment see *The London Review of Books,* June 20, 2013, Tariq Ali, "The Filthy Rich Election."

14 *The London Review of Books,* June 20, 2013, Tariq Ali, "The Filthy Rich Election."

people. As *New York Times* correspondent John F. Burnes reported[15] at the end of Benazir Bhutto's primeministership, the nation was so poor that

Perhaps 70 percent of its [then] 130 million people are illiterate, and millions have no proper shelter, no schools, no hospitals, not even safe drinking water. During Ms. Bhutto's five years in power, the economy became so enfeebled that she spent much of her time negotiating new foreign loans to stave off default on $62 billion in public debt [but apparently far more time generating a billion dollars] in illicit profits through kickbacks in virtually every sphere of government activity – from rice deals, to the sell-off of state land, even rake-offs from state welfare schemes.

By the end of Zardari's presidency in May 2013, Pakistan's foreign currency reserves were down to just one and a half month's of what was absolutely required for imports; this is, just half of what the IMF regards as the bare minimum.[16] Everywhere, as The New York Times correspondent Declan Walsh wrote,[17]

Chronic electricity shortages, up to 18 hours per day, have crippled industry and stoked public anger. The education and health systems are inadequate and in stark disrepair. The state airline, Pakistan International Airlines, which lost $32 million last year, is listing badly. The police are underpaid and corrupt, and militancy is spreading. There is a disturbing sense of drift...This failure is the legacy of decades of misadventure, misrule and misfortune under both civilian and military leaders, but its price is being paid by the country's [then] 180 million people.

Decades of exploitation, corruption, theft, mismanagement and waste followed the almost desperate attempt by Mrs. Bhutto's father, Zulfiqar Ali Bhutto, to uplift the Pakistani poor. If any single Pakistani leader could be

---

15 *The New York Times,* January 9, 1998, "House of graft."
16 *The Washington Post,* June 1, 2013, from *the Associated Press.*
17 *The New York Times,* May 18, 2013, "Pakistan Rusting in its Tracks."

said to embody Pakistan, after the "Father of the Country," Muhammad Ali Jinnah, it was he. Moreover, his period in public affairs both encompasses most of Pakistan's experience as an independent country and suggests the dangers and the possibilities of its future. I now turn to him.

* * *

Zulfiqar Ali Bhutto in 1975
http://sv.wikipedia.org/wiki/
Zulfikar_Ali_Bhutto

Zulfiqar Ali Bhutto was born into one of the wealthy, feudal families of British India. His father had been the chief minister of Junagadh (now Gujarat) then a collection of more than a hundred mainly Muslim principalities which was seized by India during Partition. So he had the experiences both of a privileged childhood and of the collapse of a former high status. As a young man, he was educated at the University of California (Berkeley) and Christ Church College (Oxford). Like Muhammad Ali Jinnah, he was then trained as a lawyer in London at Lincoln's Inn. He became active in national affairs from 1957 when he was made a member of Pakistan's mission to the UN; the next year, aged 30, he appointed to the first of several cabinet posts before becoming in 1963 foreign minister; then, from 1971 to 1977, he dominated Pakistani affairs as president or prime minister. Overthrown by the military commander he had chosen, General Zia ul-Haq, he was put into prison and hanged, possibly already dead after a last-minute torture to attempt to extract a confession from him, in April 1979.[18]

Before discussing what he tried to do during his twenty years in office, I will first tally the resources with which Pakistan was then endowed and with which he had to work. The first was agriculture.

---

18 *The Daily Express* correspondent, Robert Eddison, on May 21, 1979 wrote in "Was Bhutto's hanging a cover for murder?" That he was already dead when taken to the gallows. In the classical language, his name was *Dhu'l-Fiqar* the name given to the sword of Ali, the 4th caliph, produced an unintended double entendre forecasting his terrible end: it means "endowed with misery."

Agriculture, enlivened by the five rivers coming down from the mountains and glaciers of Kashmir to the Punjab plain, had long been the basis of Pakistani wealth. It was what made possible the ancient Indus civilization and was the basis on which Ranjit Singh built his empire.

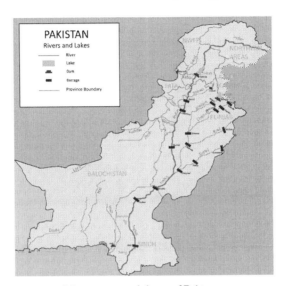

Major rivers and dams of Pakistan.
http://en.wikipedia.org/wiki/File:Pakistan_Rivers.PNG

Cotton was the traditional export crop, but grain was literally the staff of life. Poor seed, exploitation of the peasants by government, big landlords and usurers made for small yields. As a result, most peasants subsisted on the edge of starvation. Then in the years after the Second World War came the development of "Miracle Wheat and Rice" in the Green Revolution.[19]

Better seed and better methods made possible a ten-fold increase in production and because the new seeds took shorter growing periods multiple cropping became possible in some areas. But the genetic breakthrough quickly ran into three major problems: excited by the great opportunity, the long-hungry farmers used far too much irrigation water so about 15% of their lands became waterlogged and saline.[20] Second, large landowners took half or more of the produce and gave their tenants little incentive to improve.

19 *Wessels* [York, Nebraska], June 18, 2013, Bill Ganzel, "Farming in the 1950s & 70s."
20 UN FAO, UNDP and UNEP, *Land Degradation in South Asia,* 1994. Chapter 5.

As the World Bank investigators found[21] "This system had all the trappings of an exploitative feudal culture... [leaving the peasants] without legal protection." Bluntly put, they did not have the margin of security or strength to gamble on a new technology. And, third, the peasants were insufficiently educated to make effective use of the Green Revolution.[22]

Industry was far less developed than agriculture and faced a more difficult challenge in reaching world markets. Textiles, based on domestic cotton production, were the leaders, but most producers were small-scale. Rug production, with better access to world markets, was a cottage industry. Most shops employed fewer than ten workers. Little use was made – indeed, there was little awareness of the presence -- of minerals or other natural resources. Energy was everywhere deficient and unpredictable. So, during Bhutto's time, industry as a whole provided less than a quarter of Pakistan's gross domestic product. To achieve growth, Pakistan had to change.

Change was Bhutto's mantra during his twenty years in office. Some of his policies were beneficial; about some problems he could do little or nothing; in others he acted in ways that were precipitous, ill-conceived, grandiose and harmful to Pakistan. I note first, those of his policies that harmed Pakistan.

Bhutto encouraged a costly war with India over Kashmir in 1965. He was complicit in driving Bengal into a rebellion that caused another war with India in 1971 and split the new state of Bangladesh off from Pakistan. That war was humiliating for Pakistan – resulting in the surrender of some 93,000 Pakistani soldiers. Bhutto got India to release them in 1972, but he was widely blamed for their capture. The loss of Bengal further weakened Pakistan vis-à-vis India and was one of the causes of the military's demand for increasing amounts of the state's assets and later for the overthrow of his government

---

21 Ishrat Husain, *Pakistan: The Economy of an Elitist State.*

22: At the request of President Kennedy in 1961-1962, the then head of the Scripps Institution of Oceanography at La Jolla, Roger Revelle, made a study of the salting problem of the Indus valley. He and his colleagues found that it resulted from water logging and that relatively simple and inexpensive measures – regulating water flow and digging shallow wells -- could considerably increase agricultural production. It is a sidelight on my theme in this paper, but partly as a result of this study, Revelle went on to pay a major role in environmental studies. One of the men he influenced in the course of his teaching at Harvard on Global Change, was Al Gore. So, in part, public awareness of the dangers of global climate change can be said to have been begun in Pakistan. I first learned of his work in 1962 when he came to talk to the members of the Policy Planning Council on his work on the Indus river.

and his murder. Realization of Pakistani weakness caused Bhutto to push Pakistan to become a nuclear power and to acquire nuclear weapons. In 1965, he famously said to his government collaborators that if India builds the bomb, we "will eat grass, even go hungry, but we will [I cannot do it, but the lines across the page should be removed] get one of our own. We have no other choice." India exploded its first nuclear weapon in 1974 near the Pakistani frontier. Pakistan did not follow until 1998. Realization of Pakistani weakness caused Bhutto to push Pakistan to become a nuclear power and to acquire nuclear weapons. In 1965, he famously said to his government collaborators that if India builds the bomb, we "will eat grass, even go hungry, but we will get one of our own. We have no other choice."[23] India exploded its first nuclear weapon in 1974 near the Pakistani frontier. Pakistan did not follow until 1998.

The argument that Bhutto's decision to "go nuclear" will prevent future wars is problematic and that Pakistan will benefit from access to state-of-the-art technology has yet to be proven. But what is certain is that the nuclear program has diverted vast amounts of money from badly needed social welfare and infrastructure projects. And, of course, if India and Pakistan fail to keep any future conflict limited, the chances are good that both societies will suffer immense harm from nuclear weapons. Neither side appears to have ever seriously considered the possible benefits of joint nuclear disarmament. But, unless disarmament were comprehensive, giving up its nuclear component would put Pakistan at a serious and permanent disadvantage. It is thus highly unlikely.

Bhutto's approach to industry was precipitous and more guided by ideology (he regarded himself as a socialist) than by what was needed to make it more productive. In 1972, he began a two prong equalization program: he moved to nationalize such industry as Pakistan then had and he ordered the confiscation of about a million acres of farm land to be turned over to

---

23   In his book, *The Myth of Independence*, Bhutto alludes to an aspect of the quest for nuclear power by the emerging states that is often overlooked -- the desire to participate in the latest developments in science and technology. He feared that if Pakistan stood aside, doing so would "impose a crippling limitation on the development of Pakistan's science and technology." To try to avoid this, he created a world-class Institute of Theoretical Physics in 1967. When, in 1972, the nuclear scientist Abdul Qadeer Khan returned to Pakistan, work on weaponizing atomic research was speeded up.

landless agricultural workers. Later he added the banks to the state-owned sector. These moves caused a temporary fall in production and inevitably widened the scope for corruption. Despite these misadventures, production rose dramatically in the following years, with GDP rising from $7.7 billion in 1972 to $24 billion in the year of his overthrow.[24]

Bhutto was by no means a civil libertarian and did not gracefully or even legally brook opposition. When the leaders of the province of Balochistan balked at his policies, he dismissed them from office and sent in the army to put down public protests. Several thousand protesters were killed. When the army commanders refused to act against the police in another incident, Bhutto cashiered them. Attempts at breakaway by Sindhi and Pushtun separatists were brutally put down. Worse was his agreement to insert a clause in the 1973 Constitution declaring that members of the Ahmadiyah[25] community would no longer be considered to be Muslims.

About some issues, he could do little or nothing – neither beneficial nor harmful. Corruption was one. Corruption was then, and remains today, the cancer of the Pakistani body politic. Already deeply embedded in society and government from at least the time of Ranjit Singh, it remained a way of life throughout British times. Bhutto realized that for Pakistan to change from a backward, weak and poor country into the dream he had for it, he had to root it out. But all he could do was to remove the 2,000 or so most flagrantly involved officials. Corruption has remained impervious to all "medicine."

Far worse still was the plight of the children of Pakistan's very poor. As a US Department of Labor study pointed out,[26]

Millions of children in Pakistan suffer under a system of

24: "Gross Domestic Product (GDP) of Pakistan, 1970-2011" Ivan Kushnir's Research Center, http:// kushnirs.org/macroeconomics/gdp/gdp_pakistan.html

25 The Ahmadiyah movement is an off-shoot of Islam. Like the Sikh movement, it combines elements of Islam, Christianity and Hinduism. Founded in the second half of the Nineteenth century it has spread, mostly in Pakistan but also abroad. Like the Baha'i movement in Iran, it has been vigorously persecuted in Pakistan for unbelief (*kafariyah*) and has moved its mission abroad. Effectively outlawed in an amendment to the 1973 constitution, it is remarkable for the number of prominent Pakistanis who follow its creed including senior military commanders and the key figure in the development of Pakistan's nuclear program.

26 *Bureau of International Labor Affairs*, no date indicated.

bonded labor. The bonded labor system consists of giving advances of "peshgi" (bonded money) to a person. As long as all or part of the peshgi debt remains outstanding, the debtor/worker is bound to the creditor/employer. In case of sickness or death, the family of the individual is responsible for the debt, which often passes down from generation to generation. In the case of children, the peshgi is paid to a parent or guardian, who then provides the child to work off the debt...

Bhutto's approach was mainly indirect: he attempted to raise the level of agricultural workers' standard of living so that they would not have to "sell" their children. But there were too many poor people and too many children for this attempted reform to work in the few years of his administration.

Reform was mandated in 1988 by the Pakistan Supreme Court and in 1992 by Parliament, but nothing was done to actually stop the practice; it continues and is estimated to blight the lives of up to 19 million children, many below the age of seven, who literally slave away for up to twelve hours a day, subsisting on one meal a day, being frequently beaten for lapses in work quality or exhaustion, in brick kilns, carpet weaving huts and cotton fields.[27] The system remains intact, impervious to reform while poverty rules.

Neither Bhutto nor his successors have changed this tragic aspect of Pakistani poverty.

However, what Bhutto did accomplish was truly revolutionary. Realizing that Pakistan needed a fundamental overhaul, he moved the National Assembly to create in 1973 a new constitution, believing that it would foster conditions that would make the overthrow of a government and the aborting of a social welfare program impossible. He could not, in the few years he had to carry out his program do much more than announce it because, as I have argued, Pakistan lacked the institutions and habits needed to balance the power of the very rich and the military. Realizing this, Bhutto put heavy emphasis on the fundamental weakness: lack of education.

---

27 *The Atlantic*, February 1996, Jonathan Silvers, "Child Labor in Pakistan."

Put simply, he sought to create a progressive society through education. In an address to the nation, he took pride[28] in having created "6,500 new primary schools, 900 middle schools, 407 high schools, 51 Intermediate Colleges, 21 Degree Colleges...[and] four new Universities...The People's Open University is another innovative venture which has started functioning from Islamabad." These ventures alone would have sufficed to secure him a major place in Pakistani history.

He recognized that improvement in education alone, while fundamental, would not work unless the Pakistanis could rise above absolute poverty. So he undertook several other ventures that resulted in a rise of the standard of living. For an agricultural society, access to land was critical. But, as I have pointed out, the heritage of the British era was the conversion of productive peasant owners into serfs. So he passed a law to break up large holdings, putting a 150 acres limit on the amount of irrigated land one farmer could own. Realizing that the new owners would quickly fall into the hands of usurers, he forced the banks to make available credit on sustainable terms to small holders. Investment in the economy more than doubled.

These actions and others aimed to enhance industrial workers' rights resulted over the years after his tenure in office in a shift of nearly one Pakistani in each two (about 46%) living in "absolute" poverty to less than one in three (30%). The poverty line has hovered near there ever since.[29] Over the years, his policies can be credited with raising about 25 million people out of poverty. (It should be recognized that in this venture, he and successor governments were aided massively by the émigré Pakistani work force which sends remittances from abroad.)

Bhutto recognized that what he was trying to do would not be popular with many of his countrymen, particularly in the military, so he organized a political party in 1967 to give himself what he hoped would be the power to carry out his plans. His Pakistan Peoples Party (PPP) survived his death and

---

28   Prime Minister's address to the Nation, December 20, 1975.
29   Report from the Pakistani Sustainable Development Policy Institute in *The Statesman,* September 25, 2012. That equates to nearly 59 million people. Thus his action raised roughly 25 million out of poverty; but still today about three in each four rural households in Balochistan live below the poverty line. *Dawn,* October 15, 2012, Ashfak Bokhar. "Skewed land ownership, chronic rural poverty."

was taken over by his daughter Benazir and her husband with results that, I believe, would have deeply disturbed him. It is the PPP, corrupted as it had become under his daughter and her husband, that Nawaz Sharif defeated in the 2013 election.

It wasn't only internal opposition with which he had to contend. A key element in his foreign policy was, understandably, finding a counterpoise to India. The logical choice was China. So he reached out to China, settling a long-standing border dispute by turning over to China some 750 square kilometers of Pakistan-occupied Kashmir in 1963 and advocating China's takeover of the seat then occupied by Taiwan on the Security Council. This policy in turn so infuriated President Lyndon Johnson that he warned the then Pakistani dictator, Field Marshall Ayub Khan, that the Bhutto policy would make US aid to Pakistan unpopular with Congress and hinted that, to continue to receive American aid, he should remove Bhutto as foreign minister.[30]

Despite his advocacy of wars with India over Kashmir and Bangladesh and his promotion of the nuclear weapons program, Bhutto was a practitioner of accommodation in foreign affairs. He worked with Indian Prime Minister Indira Gandhi to set out a cease fire in Kashmir. He even risked an attempted military coup by visiting Bangladesh to atone for its casualties in their war. And, above all, he negotiated with Indira Gandhi the 1960 Indus River water sharing treaty. This was of fundamental, indeed vital, importance to Pakistan.

*   *   *

The attempt to solve the Indus river system water problem is a base from which we can look ahead at Pakistan's danger and hope for the future. I see this falling into three interrelated issues: water for agriculture, population growth and perennial tension caused by the danger of war.

Since Pakistan is an agricultural country, with limited sources of water and a rapidly rising density of population, the 1960 Indus River Treaty could

---

30   Robert J. McMahon, "The Foreign Policy of Lyndon Johnson with its Asian Allies," in H.N. Brands (ed), *The Foreign Policy of Lyndon Johnson,* Texas A & M Press, 1999, 171.

only temporarily alleviate the water problem. That problem has since gotten worse:[31] today farmers in some of the most productive areas of the country face "desertification." They are drawing down their only other source of water, aquifers, at a rate that cannot be sustained. Already in some areas, the water table is falling as much as 3 meters (10 feet) a year so that traditional tube wells can no longer reach water; in them, the water table has fallen to as much as 300 meters (1,000 feet) below ground level. So, access to acceptable amounts of the waters of the Indus system has become literally vital.

Distribution of the Indus water is something Pakistan cannot solve on its own or even under the terms of the Indo-Pakistani treaty because India also is desperate for water. The Indian National Commission on Water predicted that by 2050 Indian demand will exceed all available sources of supply. In India too, the water table is falling. As it does, millions of Indian farmers will no longer be able to draw water from traditional tube wells. Deeper fossil aquifers will also become depleted so that even powerful pumps will not produce water. Eventually, and in some areas today, farmers cannot grow food and are abandoning lands. As the Indian Minister of Finance told a World Bank mission, India is already struggling to contain "a growing set of little civil wars over water." So, in what appears to be a violation of the treaty and its amendments, India has continued, long after Bhutto's time, to build dams on rivers leading to Pakistan.[32]

Thus, potentially, what have been "little civil wars over water" could become international wars. This is the strategic danger I see facing whatever the new Pakistani leadership tries to do in the coming years.

How likely is a serious clash?

31: John Briscow and Usman Qamar, *Pakistan's Water Economy: Running Dry*, World Bank, 2006.

32 As *The Statesman* pointed out on February 24, 2011, Indian acts violated the Indus Water Treaty and as *The Deccan Herald* editorialized two days later new dams will give India the ability to virtually turn off Pakistani access to water at the critical phase of the agricultural season. The Lahore Chamber of Commerce asked for American intervention because, it said, "...without water, 20 million acres of otherwise fertile land would dry up in a week and tens of millions of people would starve. No army, with bombs and shellfire could devastate as thoroughly as Pakistan could be devastated by India by cutting off river flows." Also see *The International Herald Tribune*, July 21, 2010, Lydia Polgreen and Sabrina Tavernise, "Kashmir dam raises tensions." India did cut off water to Pakistan once before., shortly after Partition began.

Over the longer term, I do not see any way to avoid it unless one of three unlikely developments happens – either change from the agricultural basis of the economy and so relieving the water problem, or stopping the growth of population or a reunification of Pakistan with India.

Today, even in cities, most sources of income are agriculture-related and the creation of new industry, given deficiencies of power, resources and skills will be difficult. Since about 36% of the Pakistani society is below the age of 14, population growth is almost unstoppable.

Since India faces comparable problems, a clash could come about *strategically* as population increases in both countries and the need for additional water becomes more acute. It could also come about *tactically* as happened recently. In 2010, the former World Bank expert on South Asian waters, John Briscoe reported,[33] "India chose to fill Baglihar [Hydroelectric Power reservoir in Indian occupied Kashmir] exactly at the time when it would impose maximum harm on farmers in downstream Pakistan...If Baglihar was the only dam being built by India on the Chenab and Jhelum [rivers], this would be a limited problem. But following Baglihar is a veritable caravan of Indian projects."

The third possibility, reunification, sounds the least likely of the three, but, as Germany shows, there are precedents that also seemed unlikely. In favor of it is the fact that India is home to more Muslims than Pakistan; opposed to it are a number of factors including (1) the disparity of living standards;[34] (2) deep bitterness and fear of Hindu domination on the part of the Pakistanis; (3) almost certain opposition by the Pakistani civilian and military leaders. For opposition to be overcome, some catastrophic event would probably have to happen. But when such events have happened in the last (for example, the defeat of the Pakistani army in Bangladesh or the massive floods of 2010), there was no move toward unification. Conceivably,

---

33: John Briscoe, "War and Peace on the Indus." The South AsianIdea Weblog, June 25, 2013. Also see Dawn, February 3, 2010, Khaleeq Kiani, "Five dams being built in occupied Kashmir" and The National, July 28, 2010, Shaukat Qadir, "India's new dams threaten Pakistan's farming sector."

34: In 2012, India had a gross domestic product of $1,492/capita and Pakistan of $1,296 but these figures are skewed by the much larger spread of wealth in India while, statistically, India is rising faster than Pakistan.

a nuclear clash between the two states might produce enough desperation to move them together. But, even in that circumstance, I find it unlikely.

Presuming that the military/security establishment of Pakistan is aware of these or similar projections for the future, it undoubtedly will insist that government continue the heavy outlay of resources on the army, air force and the nuclear weapons program. In recent years, Pakistan has been spending 15 times as much on the military on education and 44 times as much on the military as on health. Unless these figures are readjusted, the Pakistan of the future will be a poor, overpopulated, environmentally ravaged state.

The newly elected Nawaz Sharif government will probably seek to change the context of Indo-Pakistani relations to make such a readjustment possible, but given the realities of water and population in both countries, the scope for such changes will be narrow. How Indian and Pakistani leaders attempt to cope with these fundamental issues will determine the issues of war or peace for the years to come.

June 15, 2013

CHAPTER 10

A GLANCE AT KASHMIR

Kashmir can be thought of as the Palestine of Central Asia. Like Palestine, it is the scene of a deadly conflict between resident societies and the focal point of regional conflict. Both have led to several wars. Also, like Palestine, Kashmir is the meeting ground of some of the world's most powerful religious forces: in Palestine, Islam, Judaism and Christianity; in Kashmir, Islam, Hinduism and Buddhism. Both Kashmir and Palestine are the heirs to fascinating historical experiences. Thus, while the focus of statesmen and journalists alike is on the present simmering conflict between Pakistan and India, we cannot understand Kashmir or reach a guess on what might be done about it without attention to the past. So, I will begin this short note with Kashmir's geography and history.

I

Before the fourteenth century Kashmir was populated by both Hindus, who had moved up from the subcontinent, and Buddhists, who had moved westward from neighboring Tibet. The Hindus were mainly in the south in the fertile Vale of Kashmir – which is about the size of Rhode Island -- while the Buddhists inhabited the poorer, mountainous area in the northeast known as Ladakh. The far, northeastern, portion of Kashmir known as Aksai Chin,[1] now occupied by China, which is a frozen desert at varying altitudes up to 16,000 feet. Around the northern edges are the high Hindu Kush, Pamir and Himalayan mountains where no permanent settlements existed.

---

1   A personal note: when India and China clashed over this area, I was serving in the Policy Planning Council and, being ignorant of the area, convened a group of people I thought might know more than I. Immediately, I asked for maps. The government, I was told, had none. Perhaps *The National Geographic* might have some. Anyway, the experts said, it was so high and so deep in snow, maps would not help much. As it turned out, there was little snow as the area was a desert. No one, not even the Indians, knew. The Chinese walked in on the frozen, bare ground. They are still there.

Vale of Kashmir (NASA Satellite image)

Then, in 1320 AD the area was invaded by one of the Mongol armies Genghis Khan had hurled across Asia. The upper class, which had the means to flee, fled while many of those who were left behind were slaughtered. The old Kashmir, like societies in many of the lands conquered by the Mongols, collapsed. After a century or so of misery, hunger and disease -- a true dark age -- the grandchildren and great grandchildren of the older Kashmiris gradually emerged from their hiding places and began to put their lives together again. Theirs was a very different Kashmir from the one their ancestors had known. As one scholar of Kashmir history put it,[2] the old order of Hinduism, which depended on the caste system "lay in ruins, for its basic law – the law of marriage – had been violated by men and women who had mated during the Mongol cataclysm and gave rise to a homogeneous, casteless society. The future history of Kashmir will be unintelligible to anyone who fails to

---

2   R.K. Parmu, *A History of Muslim Rule in Kashmir, 1320-1819*

comprehend this basic fact."

In the years that followed the exodus of the Mongols, a new ruler, a Hindu, came to the fore, but he soon was converted by a Sufi mystic to Islam. As in other areas devastated by the Mongols, Sufi Islam seemed an answer to contemporary misery. It spread widely in the Middle East and Central Asia. Its message was appealing and seemed logical to the sufferers: Sufis believed that the world is a place of desolation where those who search for a richer life will find only despair. The solution to wretchedness, they believed, is rejection of materialism and seeking solace in the millennial claims of religion. In following generations, most of the Kashmiris followed the ruler into Islam. Most converted to Islam through Sufism which was known in Kashmir as *Rishism*.[3]

Over the following years, under the influence of *Rishism*, some Hindu practices faded away -- idols were melted down, widows were no longer burned in *sati* beside their dead husbands and the symbol of Hinduism, the *qashqa*, was no longer drawn on the forehead -- but the Islam that evolved in Kashmir was deeply influenced by Hinduism.

Under the rule of a tolerant Muslim prince and following the message of Sufism, Kashmir became again a cultured, open society, which, the Kashmiris proudly called "the way of Kashmir," *Kashmiriyat*. As Jawaharlal Nehru, whose family were Pandits from Kashmir, was later to write, it was a "mixed but harmonized culture." Less realistically he went on to say that *Kashmiriyat* "is so evident even today in Kashmir." That was certainly not true when he spoke; nor, as I will detail, is it true today. Indeed, the concept of *Kashmiriyat* is one of the casualties of the violence of the last half century. During that time, upwards of 100,000 Kashmiris have been killed, thousands more have been raped and still more wounded while tens of thousands of others were "disappeared" or left to rot in prison. The "mixed but harmonized culture" was replaced by conditions almost on the scale of the Mongol invasion.

By Nehru's time, about 8 in 10 Kashmiris were Muslim but were

---

3   Mohammed Ishaq Khan, *Kashmir's Transition to Islam: The Role of Muslim Rishis.*

ruled by the 1 in 10 who were Hindus, supported by the 500-800 thousand-man Indian army of occupation. And Hindus still dominated the Kashmiri economy. Hindus and Muslims lived in conditions that were separate and unequal and, after roughly 1990, as the struggle for independence became more violent and the Indian security forces more brutal, the two communities grew further apart in fear and anger. Increasingly, as the Scots journalist for the BBC and *The Guardian* Isabel Hilton reported[4] from lengthy interviews with Kashmiris, to them the Indian security forces "look and behave like an occupying army." One of Hilton's informants,

> A tremulous sociology professor described to me the social effects of the long war – migration, unemployment, broken families, a startlingly high rate of suicide. It's the constant fear...torture, tension. Even at home, the security forces can arrive at any minute. We used to be a leisured people. Now, all our entertainment has gone. It's out of the question to go out. Education had deteriorated...young women cannot find husbands, married women are widowed and destitute [and especially the poorer people] subject to constant cordon searches...[and had pointed out to her the graves of] professionals – lawyers, teachers, doctors – and [other] men who had died under torture...[with] each act of violence generating a new response that generates more recruits...The Kashmiriyat is now a forlorn memory, and has been replaced by the cult of the gun...Scarcely a family in the valley is untouched.

To clarify today's Muslim-Hindu, Kashmiri-Indian and Indian-Pakistani tragic relationships, I must first focus briefly on the major events in the Nineteenth and Twentieth centuries when Kashmir was swept first into the Punjabi Sikh empire and then into the British Indian Empire and began, haltingly, to acquire a taste for independence.

---

4   "Letter from Kashmir," *The New Yorker,* March 11, 2002.

II

As the Nineteenth century opened, Kashmir was split among some 22 small principalities which owed allegiance, as they had for centuries, to the Mughals of India or the Pushtuns of Afghanistan. Then in 1819-1820, they were conquered by the great Sikh ruler of the Punjab, Ranjit Singh and incorporated in his empire.

As I describe in "The Nature of Pakistan," Sikhism began in the Sixteenth century as a reform movement. The founder, Guru Nanak, sought to mingle Muslim and Hindu beliefs, rituals and populations. He rejected Hindu polytheism and affirmed the Islamic insistence on monotheism (*tawhid*); he proclaimed the brotherhood (*bhaism*, in Sanskrit or in Arabic, *ikhwaniyah*) of mankind; and he made a personal example against the caste system by himself sharing living quarters and meals with Hindus, Muslims and untouchables (*sudras*). Emphasis on ecumenicalism made Sikhism popular over a wide area of India and fit the *Kashmiriyat* philosophy of life. But gradually over the three centuries following the death of Guru Nanak, Sikhism turned away from his welcoming of Islamic beliefs and practices and reverted to the Hinduism from which it had evolved. As a minority of the population of the Punjab, the Sikhs apparently needed a more strident, assertive set of beliefs than those set out by Guru Nanak. For this the Kashmiris were to pay a heavy price.

The price paid by the Kashmiris was particularly onerous in the early years of the Nineteenth century. In summary, what happened was this: reacting to the advance of the British across India, the Punjabi emperor, Ranjit Singh, built a formidable army

Vale of Kashmir with Nanga Parbat in the background. http://sxc.hu/browse

173

with which he blocked the British advance, drove the wilder Afghan tribes away from the plains and expanded his reach into Kashmir, absorbing its 22 principalities. In 1809 the British not only recognized him as the sole ruler of more or less what is now Pakistan and much of northern India but also agreed that they would stop their advance at the Sutlej river (the eastward tributary to the Indus). That is, they would stay out of the Punjab and Kashmir.

Left to themselves, the Punjabis became increasingly anti-Muslim. They no longer reached out in friendship to Muslims but laid ruinous taxes on them (causing a famine in 1832); they banned the distinctive Muslim call to prayer and closed down the major mosques; and they again pushed to the fore the distinctive totem animal of the Hindus, the cow, making slaughter of it a death penalty. These and other measures fell with particularly severity on the inhabitants of Kashmir.

This was the situation when Ranjit Singh died in 1839. His death opened, as so often in Oriental monarchies, a period of virtual civil war in which the members of his family and courtiers fought one another for his legacy. Seizing their opportunity, the British moved to dismantle the Sikh empire. Trained in imperialist tactics as they stormed, bribed and intrigued their way across India they usually found natives who were willing to help them-- for a price.

Shrewdly calculating his price, one of Ranjit Singh's followers, Gulab Singh, made himself available just when the British most needed him. When the British demanded reparations for the First Sikh War, which had destroyed Ranjit Singh's empire, Punjab's then rulers could not pay. So Gulab Singh covered the deficit in exchange for ownership of Kashmir. It was a bargain. Discounting the value of the land, based on tax revenue, he paid only about 3 English shillings in the currency of the time[5] for each person. In the Victorian English of the era, the 1846 Treaty of Amritsar specified that "the British

---

5 Kashmir Legal Documents quoted in Wikipedia; the exchange rate of the silver Nanak Shahi rupee (minted in Srinagar in 1819) was about 1 shilling sterling. Each one of the remaining, independent principalities minted its own currency. Because Kashmir was an active commercial center, all the currencies of Afghanistan, the [British] East India Company, various Indian principalities, the Punjab and others circulated in its markets and particularly in Srinagar (Charles Baron von Hugel, *Kashmir Under Maharaja Ranjit Singh,* Annotated by D.C. Sharma, 70.)

Government transfer and makes over, forever, in independent possession, to Maharaja Gulab Singh and the heirs male of his body" Kashmir. Thus, from 1846 when the Hindu/Sikh[6] Gulab Singh "bought" the Muslim population may be dated the problem of Kashmir.

As the Christian Copts did for the Muslim rulers of Egypt, so the Hindu Pandits[7] worked for the Sikh rulers of Kashmir. The then British intelligence agent Sir Claude Wade explained the nature of the arrangement to the Sikh ruler Ranjit Singh in these terms: the Pandits knew Persian, formed an official class and had a tradition of administration, so "the rulers had to depend on them for the assessment and collection of land revenue, then the main source of income to the state." Like Egypt's Copts so Kashmir's Pandits were also "squeezed" by the rulers so to avoid imprisonment, "they extorted as much as possible from the poor cultivators."[8]

As *maharaja* of Kashmir, Gulab Singh repaid the British by supporting them in suppressing the great 1857 Sepoy rebellion. That was his last act of state. Not interested in practical affairs, his descendants relied heavily on the Pandits to extract revenue from the Muslim peasantry: they monopolized the sale of everything from opium to raisins and the provision of services from prostitution to grave digging. As they did in the other Indian princely states, the British tolerated the *maharajas'* eccentricities provided they left serious decisions to their British "advisers." The Kashmir rulers were delighted. This arrangement enabled them to enjoy all the pleasures wealth could buy without bothering with ruling. For them Kashmir was an earthly paradise.

III

In the years following the First World War, the Kashmiri Muslim

---

6   I am simplifying somewhat: Gulab Singh was a Dogra, that is a member of an ethnic group with its own language, Dogri (now recognized as one of the national languages of India), which had converted to Sikhism at the time of Guru Nanak. While some Dogras had inhabited the Jammu area of Kashmir, most were from the Punjab as was Gulab Singh.

7   As used in Kashmir, the word Pandit indicated a member of the large social group, composed of several castes, numbering well over 200,000, which was typified by positions as clerks, tax collectors and civil servants. In India, proper, the word was an honorific for a man learned in Hindu scripture and law and was the official title of the religious guide to the Supreme Court.

8   Wade reporting to the then advisor to the Governor General Sir William Macnaughton; William Moorcraft, MS EUR D. 264 p. 38 cited by Hugel, *Kashmir,* 53.

society began to awake politically. Newly aware that they were being exploited, workers in the silk industry organized a strike – the first that Kashmir had ever experienced. When it was brutally repressed, the strikers petitioned the British viceroy of India for redress of their grievances. Instead of considering their demands, the viceroy turned their petition over to the then ruling maharaja who decided to hang them. Generously, the Viceroy ruled hanging to be excessive, so the maharaja just jailed and tortured them.

Jailing and torture of the workers was at least temporarily effective. The strikers gave up, their grievances unmet. But a decade later the Kashmir police compounded what was originally an economic grievance by introducing the religious issue. Fearing subversion, they attacked what they thought was the dissidents' headquarters in a mosque. Police violence thus made what had been the cause of a small section of the population into what, in the measure of the times, was a national issue. From that police raid can be dated the awakening of the belief that Islam itself was in danger from the Hindu government. Violent protests broke out throughout Kashmir and were met by police gunfire. These clashes constituted what has been described as "the founding moment of Kashmiri nationalism." In short, the Kashmiris began to experience in the 1930s the same sentiments of religious nationalism – Muslim versus Hindu -- that were already rampant in India.

Partly, of course, religious and ethnic tensions arose from and certainly were exacerbated by the vast disparity in living standards between the Hindus and Muslims. Even the resident British adviser was shocked by the conditions of the Muslim population. As he wrote,[9] it was "absolutely illiterate, working in poverty and...practically governed like dumb driven cattle."

Poverty also had a major impact on intellectual life. As Sumantra Bose remarks[10] until 1924 no newspapers were published in Kashmir and "Apart from the mass illiteracy due to a paucity of even primary education for Muslims, the maharaja's government regarded any semblance of a free press and public opinion as subversive and regularly tried to prevent newspapers and journals published in Lahore by émigré Kashmiris from reaching the kingdom."

9   Quoted in Tariq Ali, *The Clash of Fundamentalisms.*
10   In his excellent book, *Kashmir: Roots of Conflict, Paths to Peace,* (Harvard, 2003) 17-18.

A contemporary of Nehru and a fellow Pandit, the Kashmiri journalist, Prem Nath Bazaz, also focused much of his commentary on the appalling poverty of the Muslim population. "Dressed in rags and barefoot, a Muslim peasant presents the appearance of a starving beggar...Most are landless laborers, working as serfs for absentee landlords." The Muslim peasants were borne down by indebtedness often inherited generation after generation and compounded by usury. In poverty, weakness and illiteracy, they often were forced to work without compensation to pay off even imaginary debts of long-dead ancestors.

Bazaz, who was a Socialist as well as a supporter of Kashmiri independence, was arrested by the newly formed Indian government in 1947 and held in prison for three years. He was arrested again in 1955 for writings "prejudicial to the security of India." When he was released, he broadened his critique to discuss the plight of the whole Kashmiri society and the Indian occupation in a number of powerful works including *Azad Kashmir, a Democratic Socialist Conception* and particularly in *The Untold Story of Kashmir: Democracy Through Intimidation and Terror*. Together with another major figure who was influential in Kashmir's legacy in the modern period, he founded a significant journal on Kashmiri society and politics, *The Voice of Kashmir*. And, himself embodying the complexity of Kashmiri politics, he edited and printed the journal not in Srinagar but in Delhi.

Also illustrating the complexity of the Indian-Kashmiri relationship was that the 1955 ruling of the Indian High Court on Bazaz's petition for release rested on a British pre-independence ordinance. Promulgated in 1931 it gave the then British Governor General authority to bypass the partially-free Indian legislature;[11] ironically, under the Empire, it had been used to imprison such Indian leaders as Gandhi and Nehru for agitating against British rule. Inherited from the British, it was used by the Indian government against Kashmiri dissidents who, as I shall point out, were imprisoned in numbers reaching the proportion of a whole society. And, despite India's proclamation of freedom and democracy, the High Court

11   "The Governor-General, may, in cases of emergency, make and promulgate Ordinances for- the peace and good government of British India or any part thereof, and any Ordinance so made shall, for the space of not more than six months from the promulgation, have the like force of law as an Act passed by the Indian Legislature..."

judge not only refused Bazaz's petition for release but held that "It is against the public interest to disclose to you the names of these persons [he was alleged to have incited], the nature of their activities or the manner of the assistance given by you, or to give you any facts or particulars..." of the charge. The judge also held that Bazaz could legally have been arrested on the charge that he *might in the future* engage in acts prejudicial to the safety of India as defined in the Preventive Detention Act. Prem Nath Bazaz thought of himself as a guide to a new Kashmir – and indeed he was – but it was certainly not the Kashmir he sought.

In addition to Prem Nath Bazaz, two other Kashmiri men of Pandit origin would play major and conflicting roles in that tragic struggle: in Kashmir, the Muslim Shaikh Muhammad Abdullah,[12] whose family had converted to Islam in the Nineteenth century, came to personify Kashmiri nationalism while Jawaharlal Nehru who remained a Pandit Hindu became one of the leaders of Indian nationalism.[13] Except for their Kashmiri origin, the two men could hardly have been more different: Muhammad was literally a man of the people, having had to work at menial tasks to pay his way into local schools, with little exposure to the non-Indian world, formally educated as a chemist in the newly formed Indian Muslim University of Aligarh and, while tall, was physically unprepossessing while Nehru was a wealthy, urbane Brahmin, a product of the finest English education at Harrow and Cambridge and strikingly handsome. However, they shared two characteristics: they both would be frequent guests in prison and both became revered as leaders of their peoples. What was truly remarkable was that, after they met in 1937, they also became friends. That friendship almost saved Kashmir.

Like many leaders of nationalist movements, as I witnessed in Iraq, Syria, Egypt and Algeria, Shaikh Muhammad Abdullah began what became his political career with a small discussion group. Gathering together only about a dozen like-minded young men, he helped to focus their hopes and

---

12 His name is confusing. His given name was Muhammad. The second name usually is the name of a father or, sometimes, a clan, tribe or location. It is often treated in the Indian sources as a family name. I have fallen back on the classical form, using his first name and his honorific, *Shaikh*. Where in doubt, I use his entire name as his son and grandson followed him as major politicians.
13: Among the coincidences and ironies in the story of Kashmir is that what I find to be the best book on its recent history and society to be written by the grandson of Nehru's great rival for Indian leadership, Subhas Chandra Bose, Sumantra Bose. Bose, *Kashmir: Roots of Conflict, Paths to Peace* (Harvard, 2003).

angers on the issues that were then also energizing the educated youth of India. And from this modest beginning, he created what was first called "the All-Jammu and Kashmir[14] Muslim Conference" in 1932. Two years later, it was renamed the "All-Jammu and Kashmir National Conference." The difference was significant. Its program had attracted a number of Hindu members who also wanted Kashmir's ruling clan, the Dogras, to step aside so that Kashmir could become Azad [Free] Kashmir. To reach a common ground, the movement had to substitute nationhood for religion. Again, this was an echo of the Muslim-Hindu struggle within the Indian nationalist movement and, indeed, among nationalist movements throughout much of Africa and Asia.

The Kashmiri "Conference" had barely taken hold as a political movement – although Shaikh Muhammad had already served six months in prison and had been released to great acclaim by both Muslims and Hindus in Srinagar -- when the Second World War virtually froze Indian politics. Only when the pressing danger of an invasion of India by Japanese-supported Indian forces ended,[15] attention turned back to domestic affairs. Then, the National Conference immediately became Kashmir's largest political party. In 1944, chafing under British rule and the local authority of the *maharaja*, the National Conference took a symbolic step toward independence by proclaiming a flowery version of the American declaration of independence, "We the people...in order to perfect our union...to raise ourselves and our children for ever from the abyss of oppression and poverty, degradation and superstition, from medieval darkness and ignorance...do propose and propound the following constitution..." Eloquent words, but they did not assuage the festering sores of extreme poverty and communal exploitation. Partition would soon rub salt into the infection.

In 1947, when the British prepared to leave South Asia, the fate of Kashmir was undetermined. As the titular ruler of a princely state, its

---

14   I have simplified by using the name Kashmir. Jammu was the second city and originally a separate city-state. It was combined with Kashmir when it was sold by the British to Gulab Singh in 1846, but the dual name was often continued as it is for this organization.
15   It was Subhas Chandra Bose who inspired and led the Japanese-supported attempted invasion of India by the Indian troops who had been surrendered to the Japanese by their British commander in Singapore. On Subhas Chandra Bose see Sugata Bose, *His Majesty's Opponent.* (Harvard, 2011).

maharaja had been given by the British rulers authority to decide whether to join India or Pakistan. The British excused their lamentable role in the events at the end of their rule by alleging that they "assumed" that the *maharaja* would be guided by two considerations -- the wishes of the Kashmiris and "proximity." Neither shaped his choice. Probably most Kashmiris favored joining Pakistan or at least opposed joining India. Moreover, Kashmir fit what would become Pakistan better than India since they had a common frontier, a common river system in which the Indus and its tributaries were the arteries of the lifeblood of Pakistan and much of Kashmir's commerce was sent to or through Karachi.

However, joining a self-proclaimed Muslim state, Pakistan, would have made no sense for the *maharaja*. Joining India was also unattractive because at that time its self-proclaimed socialist leaders were decidedly opposed to the continuation of princely ownership of property. So, *Maharaja* Hari Singh equivocated.

There was, theoretically, a third choice: independence. But it was only theoretical. Neither India nor Pakistan wanted to "lose" Kashmir. Shaikh Muhammad Ahmad, having again become prime minister, publicly proclaimed the desire to Kashmiris for independence, but neither India nor Pakistan was willing to consider independence. They still are not.

Not trusting the *maharaja* to make the politically and geographically sensible choice and not approving the idea of an independent Kashmir, the leader of what would become Pakistan, Mohammed Ali Jinnah, decided to send that part of the army which Pakistan had inherited from the British *Raj* into Kashmir. But, the British would not allow him to use his English-officered regular troops. They argued that unless or until Kashmir had become a state, use of the army would be an act of war. So, lacking any better military option and determined not to lose Kashmir, Jinnah sent an irregular force of Pushtun tribesmen with some Pakistani officers and soldiers to secure the state. The Pushtuns, in their accustomed mode of warfare, as the Pakistani historian Tariq Ali wrote, "embarked on a three-day binge, looting houses, assaulting Muslims and Hindus alike, raping men and women and stealing money from the Kashmir treasury."

Jinnah had created a "no-win" fiasco and terrified the Maharaja who concluded that further equivocation might result in his murder. So he appealed to the new Indian government to come to his rescue. In response, Nehru seized his chance: he replied that India would save him but only if he chose union with India. He did so quickly. In response Nehru dispatched an Indian army regiment to occupy Srinagar. The still operative British administration, which had stopped the Pakistanis, did not stop the Indians. They quickly secured most of Kashmir including the best part, the Valley.

At this point, far too late and without means of enforcement, the last British Viceroy and first Governor General, Lord Louis Mountbatten, weighed in on the dispute: the Indians, he proclaimed, must consult "the will of the people, being ascertained by a plebiscite after the [Pushtun] raiders had been driven out of the state." Convening his whole cabinet to be sure of unity on this critical issue, Nehru promised to hold that plebiscite and, at the request of the *Maharaja*, sent troops to drive out the Pushtuns.[16]

That move only intensified the battle for Kashmir. The Pushtuns named themselves the "Army of *Azad* [Free] Kashmir" and managed to hold on to about a quarter of the *Maharaja*'s domain. (The small sliver of *Azad Kashmir* and the "Northern Areas" shown on the map below.) Indian forces moved in and occupied the lion's share, 85,806 square miles including the major city, Srinagar while Pakistan managed to get about 33,000 square miles. The population was roughly in proportion to the surface area: roughly two-thirds in the Indian controlled area and one-third in the Pakistani controlled area. China would later acquire a part of each of these two zones, from Pakistan by negotiation and from India by force.

Both India and Pakistan complained to the UN Security Council about events in Kashmir. In response, first in January and then in April 1948, the Security Council called for[17] the withdrawal of the irregular forces sent into Kashmir by Pakistan to be matched by the withdrawal of Indian

16   Signing the Accession agreement, so that Jammu and Kashmir became legally part of India, did not much help *Maharaja* Hari Singh. In 1949, the Indian government forced him to give up power and leave the Indian occupied part of the state. He died in Bombay (now known as Mumbai) in 1962.
17   Resolution 47 (1948), document no. S/726, dated the 21st April, 1948.

forces "progressively to the minimum strength required for the support of the civil power in the maintenance of law and order [and they]...should not afford any intimidation or appearance of intimidation to the inhabitants..." The Council then agreed to appoint a Plebiscite Administrator "for holding a fair and impartial plebiscite including, for that purpose only, the direction and supervision of the State forces and police."

It was not to be: on October 22, 1948, the first Indian-Pakistani war over Kashmir erupted. At the request of India, the United Nations worked out a truce which translated into de facto partition; it came into effect on January 1, 1949. The de facto partition, of course, did not solve the question of Kashmir. Kashmir entered a sort of limbo: unwilling to acquiesce but unable to persevere, the Kashmiris, often with Pakistani encouragement and sometimes with Pakistani help, continued to demonstrate against the Indian occupation.

A stalemate had been reached; it remains today: Nehru repeatedly reaffirmed his solemn promise to hold a plebiscite but took the position that no plebiscite could be held until the Muslim (Pushtun and Pakistani) forces withdrew; in response, shortly before his death Muhammad Ali Jinnah proposed that both sides withdraw to allow the plebiscite. But Nehru rejected this and no plebiscite was ever held. Indian-occupied Kashmir remains occupied and was proclaimed to be a state in the Republic of India.

It wasn't only Kashmir where Indian determination on the unity of the subcontinent was effected. What Nehru did in Kashmir was a part of the strategy he applied to the rest of India. First, he ordered an attack on the little coastal state of Junagadh whose ruler had opted to join Pakistan on August 15, 1947. The seizure was carried out almost exactly as Pakistan had acted in Kashmir, by government-inspired and government-armed bands rather than by the regular army. Pakistan demanded that India withdraw its forces and allow a plebiscite; Nehru refused.[18] Then in September 1948, Nehru sent

18   India refused to allow the then Maharajah's choice of union with Pakistan and put the little state under sanctions, cutting off fuel and all transport and postal connections with the outside world. In desperation, the Maharaja and his administrative body sought accommodation with India. In another of the ironies of the India-Pakistan-Kashmir historical tangle, it was the father of the later Pakistani Prime Minister Zulfiqar Ali Bhutto (and grandfather of Prime Minister Benazir Bhutto) who arranged for surrender of the state to India.

two divisions of the Indian army to conquer Hyderabad (whose ruler was a Muslim but whose population was mainly Hindu). So fierce was the resistance that it took the army four days to capture the country although it had no standing military force. Nehru also sent the Indian army into Goa, still a Portuguese territory, years later, in December 1961.

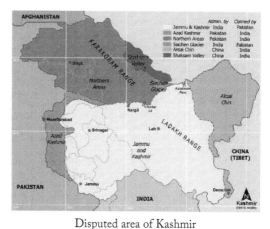

Disputed area of Kashmir

http://www.lib.utexas.edu/maps/middle_east_and_ asia/kashmir_disputed_2003.jpg

Both the United States and Britain reacted by asking the Security Council to condemn India for this invasion of Goa, but the Soviet Union vetoed the resolution. Like Kashmir, Junagadh and Hyderabad, Goa became part of India.

What Nehru and all his successors feared was that if a plebiscite were allowed in any Indian state, the fragile union might break up. These and other tragic aspects of the British withdrawal dominated Indian thinking on Kashmir. Contrariwise, for their part, so central was the issue of self-determination to Kashmiris, that their main political party took as its name, "the Plebiscite Front."

More than anyone, Gandhi was disgusted by the flow of events in the process of partition. He blamed Hindu intransience for the "decay and decline" of political decency and announced that he would again fast to protest the Hindu persecution of Muslims, saying "Death for me would be a glorious deliverance rather than that I should be a helpless witness of the destruction of India, Hinduism, Sikhism and Islam...Just contemplate the rot that has set in in beloved India." As I have mentioned, he even threatened to move to Pakistan although he had spent much of his life opposing the Muslim separatist movement. His was a lonely voice. Viciousness, fanaticism and stupidity were evident on all sides. Gandhi was among the victims. He was shot down in his garden by a Hindu terrorist on January 30, 1948.[19]

Gandhi's death was a stunning blow to India, but ironically it almost saved Kashmir. In the shock of the loss of Gandhi, Hindu extremism was temporarily weakened but, partition opened old wounds and created new hatred. Vast movements of refugees did not bring peace or security. Moreover they transferred to Kashmir the division that had put India and Pakistan at loggerheads. But Kashmir had already started to move toward a different future.

IV

The Kashmiri who sought a path through the labyrinth we have already met. Shaikh Muhammad Abdullah emerged from his second incarceration in the *Maharaja's* prison just days before the *Maharaja* wrote to Lord Mountbatten "that it is my intention at once to set up an interim Government [pending accession to India] and asked Shaikh [Muhammad] Abdullah to carry the responsibilities in this emergency..." Little noticed by most at the time was that each party to "this emergency" had staked out a position that would set the future course: the *Maharaja* was bowing out; the British had decided that Kashmir should go to India; Nehru was determined that it should do so; Pakistan's Muhammad Ali Jinnah felt cheated by the British and outsmarted by the Hindus; and Shaikh Muhammad Abdullah had made up his mind that the only sensible solution was not independence, as he had so long sought, but some sort of union with India. For the rest of his career, he was to be the, occasionally reluctant, standard-bearer for Nehru's policy.

Initially, Shaikh Muhammad rode the wave of his popularity and his decision not to press for independence was apparently not widely known or understood. He used his prestige to enable him to try to build a bridge between India and Pakistan. But, since he had decided that independence was not a viable option and knew that Nehru would not accept anything less than Indian sovereignty, he had nothing to offer Pakistan. Despite that reality, he thought he saw a dim light at the end of this tunnel so, as prime minister from March 17, 1948, he moved to raise a sort of national guard

---

19 Among the vast literature on these days when Gandhi tried to stave off the terrible events of the religious war, Louis Fischer's little book *Gandhi* is simple but heart-felt.

to defend Kashmir in what apparently he thought would be the proximate withdrawal of Indian armed forces and the achievement of some degree of regional autonomy.

That did not happen. But what did happen was perhaps much more significant. It was that Shaikh Muhammad used his authority to institute a number of domestic social and economic reforms that he had advocated from his first days in the "National Conference," fifteen years before. He began a program to divide the great (mainly Hindu) estates among (the mainly Muslim) peasant farmers, opened new schools and hospitals and even created a university. In sum, he created a new class of Kashmiris, richer, better educated and more capable than their fathers. In doing so, however, he also encouraged aspirations that would not be met by the Indian policy toward Kashmir.

Bowing as far as Shaikh Muhammad judged the Kashmiris would tolerate to the inevitability of Indian power, the National Conference proposed actions to implement what the Indian Constitution termed Kashmir's "special status:" Kashmir offered to turn over to India control of foreign and military affairs, provided it could keep control of its domestic programs. Shaikh Muhammad would go no further to meet the demands of the right-wing Indian Hindu party (the precursor of today's Bharatiya Janata Party, the BJP[20]). For seeking what Nehru judged a dangerous degree of autonomy, Nehru arranged Shaikh Muhammad's dismissal as prime minister in the summer of 1953, Ironically, in the interwoven events of Kashmir's story, the man who dismissed him was the then exiled Maharaja's son who had become sadr-i riasat (head of government); he was again arrested, charged with conspiracy against the state and hurried off to prison where he languished for the next eleven years.

When Shaikh Muhammad was let out of prison in 1964, a million people, practically the entire adult population of Srinagar, turned out to welcome him home. He then made one last major effort to win over Prime Minister Nehru to a compromise with which India, Pakistan and the Kashmiris could have lived. He thought he had conceived a workable formula

---

20   Although the fit is not exact, the BJP is roughly the equivalent of Israel's Right-wing Likud Party.

and went to Pakistan to discuss it with the then Pakistani President Ayub Khan. Ayub agreed to join him to discuss it with Nehru in Delhi. He was on the way when news came that Nehru had suddenly died. He felt that his best hope to bring peace had gone with Nehru. Shaikh Muhammad is said to have wept.

He was not trusted even in weeping. In 1965, he was interned for three years and internment and then exiled from 1971 to until 1973; and his party, the Plebiscite Front, was banned. Apparently dispirited and perhaps desperate, he met with Nehru's daughter and successor Indira Gandhi and reached a deal in 1974 with great personal and political consequences: it was that he would give up on behalf of Kashmir the demand for a plebiscite. In return, Mrs. Gandhi agreed that Kashmir would be given a larger degree of self rule (as allowed in the Indian Constitution, article 370). On this basis, he returned to the office of Chief Minister of the state. With one short break, he was to remain in office until his death in 1982.

What had happened in between 1974 and 1982, as Pankaj Mishra has written,[21] is that he became "what other men before him had been: a satrap of the Indian state in Kashmir." In effect, although Mishra does not draw the parallel, Shaikh Muhammad was willing to play the role of the Dogra *maharajas*.

Among the casualties of the growing struggle was thus the image of the man who had done so much to improve Kashmir. Shaikh Muhammad could claim to be the father of his country and the benefactor of his people. As I have pointed out, it was he who really began the nationalist movement and he who undertook Kashmir's first program of social, economic and intellectual upgrading. But he had been forced into a Faustian deal: he decided, and perhaps really believed, that Kashmir must give up all hope of independence, stay apart from Pakistan and submerge itself into the Indian mass. Thus, as Pankaj Misra has written,[22] "The grave of Sheikh [sic] [Muhammad] Abdullah, eight years after his crowded funeral [in 1982], was to require round-the-clock protection from vandals." In the maelstrom of the insurgency, there was no room for a compromiser, even the father of his country.

---

21 "The Birth of a Nation," *The New York Review of Books*, October 5, 2000.
22 "The Birth of a Nation"

V

During the late 1980s and 1990s Kashmir lived in a permanent depression and a political limbo. Shaikh Muhammad was followed by his son Farouk; both proved to be too independent for Indian Prime Minister Indira Gandhi who installed a Hindu governor. That governor then purged Muslims from government and in highhanded and violent ways virtually singlehandedly created the insurgent movement. By 1990, small groups of Kashmiris, often equipped by Pakistan and trained in the tactics learned in fighting the Russians in Afghanistan, were slipping back into Kashmir to harass the Indian administration.

When the Hindu rightist party, the BJP came to power in 1998, it announced its platform for multicultural, ethnically and religiously diverse India as "one people, one culture, one language" and set out to stifle the aspirations of non-Hindus. Repression was the order of the day: one of the leaders of the BJP was quoted as saying, "Give the security forces a free hand and the Kashmir problem would be solved in two weeks." The security forces were given nearly a free hand, but their brutal tactics only worsened public security and alienated the majority from the Indian administration. Security vanished. Meanwhile, the economy first stalled and then deteriorated.

The economy depended heavily on tourism and, because of the increasingly violent struggle between the Indian army and the inhabitants, the number of tourists fell from "around 7,000,000 in the pre-militancy days to a few thousands. It has been estimated that the state lost 27 million tourists from 1989 to 2002 leading to a tourism revenue loss of $3.6 billion."[23] India partially subsidized the economy but itself faced many competing claims on its resources. So the majority of the Kashmiris continued to live without electricity, safe drinking water and sewage facilities. Unemployment, already high (as in the rest of India), soared partly because, in the growing insurgency, the state had become virtually the only significant employer. About one in four Kashmiris lived below the Indian poverty line. This contributed both to growing hostility to the Indian occupation and to an explosion of mental

---

23   Debidatta Aurobinda Mahapatra and Seema Shekawat, "the Peace Process and Prospects for Economic Reconstruction in Kashmir, *Peace & Conflict Review* 3/1, 2008.

health problems. In the period 2003-2006, 45,000 people entered Srinagar hospitals with psychiatric problems.[24]

Probably the most systematic, informed and reputable study of Kashmir in the period around 2005 was made by the Dutch branch of Médicins sans Frontièrs.[25] Its report, based largely on interviews, covers the period 1989 to 2006. The findings can only be described as appalling:

> ...almost half (48.1%) of the respondents said they felt only occasionally or never safe...people frequently reported crackdowns (99.2%), frisking by security forces (85.7%) and round-up raids in villages (82.7%). In the same period, damage to property (39%) or the burning of houses (26.3%) was considerable. Interviewees reported witnessing (73.3%) and directly experiencing themselves (44.1%), physical and psychological mistreatment, such as humiliation and threats... one in six respondents (16.9%) were legally or illegally detained. A shocking finding is that torture appears to be widespread among those detained (legally or illegally): 76.7% said they were tortured while they were in captivity... nearly one in ten people (9.4%) lost one or more members of their nuclear family because of the violence. A third (35.7%) indicated that they had lost one or more extended family members.

The Report continues: "Sexual violence is a common strategy used to terrorise [sic] and intimidate people in conflict, but in Kashmir it is an issue that is not openly discussed. Nevertheless, 11.6% of interviewees said they had been victims of sexual violence since 1989. Almost two-thirds of the people interviewed (63.9%) had heard over a similar period about cases of rape, while one in seven had witnessed rape."

Much of the evidence was, literally, buried: although the relevant UN official, the Special Rapporteur on Extrajudicial Executions, was denied entry to Kashmir by the Indian government, an unofficial group known as

---

24: *Ibid.*
25 *"Kashmir: Violence and Health."* 2006.

the International People's Tribunal on Human Rights and Justice in Indian-Administered Kashmir (IPTK) claims to have documented in one small area "2,700 graves in 55 villages and three districts in Indian-administered Kashmir between 2005 and 2009. The numbers are staggering: 2,373 graves were found unmarked, 151 graves contained more than one body; while 23 graves held between three and 17 bodies."[26]

The International Committee of the Red Cross (ICRC) told Andrew Buncombe of *The Independent*[27] that "it had complained so many times to the authorities that it had concluded that the Indian government condoned the actions." The ICRC rarely discloses its findings to non-governmental organizations or the media, but it briefed officials of the US Embassy in New Delhi. Reports on its findings by the Embassy to the State Department were passed to Wikileaks.[28] The Embassy dispatches revealed that of the 1,491 prisoners the ICRC managed to interview,

> In 852 cases, the detainees reported ill-treatment, the ICRC said. A total of 171 described being beaten and 681 said they had been subjected to one or more of six forms of torture. These included 498 on which electricity [electric shocks] had been used, 381 who had been suspended [hung] from the ceiling, 294 who had muscles crushed in their legs by prison personnel sitting on a bar placed across their thighs, 181 whose legs had been stretched by being "split 180 degrees", 234 tortured with water and 302 "sexual" cases...The ICRC said all branches of the Indian security forces used these forms of ill-treatment and torture, adding: "The abuse always takes place in the presence of officers and ...detainees were rarely militants (they are routinely killed), but persons connected to or believed to have information about the insurgency.

These activities in spirit if not always in exact language were authorized

---

26 *Aljazeera*, "The Disappeared of Kashmir," April 18, 2011.
27 The report also quoted a spokesman for Human Rights Watch, saying that the Security Forces' actions "can range from beatings, to severe torture, and even extrajudicial killings."
28 Jason Burke, "WikiLeaks cables: India accused of systematic use of torture in Kashmir," *The Guardian*, December 16, 2010.

by the September 10, 1990 "Armed Forces Special Powers Act (AFSPA)" aimed at those "adversely affecting the harmony amongst different sections of the people [and/or those engaged in] activities directed towards disclaiming, questioning or disrupting the sovereignty and territorial integrity of India or bring about cession of a parts of the territory of India..." The act authorized any Indian non-commissioned or commissioned officer to use such force as he deemed necessary and to "arrest, without warrant, any persons...against whom a reasonable suspicion exists that he has committed or is about to commit a cognizable offence and may use such force as may be necessary to effect the arrest." In pursuit of these tasks, all personnel are to be granted immunity from prosecution.[29]

The Act was published; the actions were not. But two days after the Embassy cables were published, the chief minister of Kashmir insisted[30] "that the use of torture...is a thing of the past." There is no authoritative information on this claim, but in 2012, the chief minister is reported to have said that the AFSPA must be continued in force and as recently as March 2013, Kashmir was put again under curfew.

Insurgency and counter insurgency were the twin poles of Kashmir life during most of the last half century. As I have suggested, Kashmir has been a sort of eastern Palestine, a tragic result of imperialism and its heir, competing nationalisms, in which the original inhabitants have been nearly crushed. Each party to the events has seen itself in the right: the Indians believe that the letter of the original (British) law has been observed; the Pakistanis hold that Britain and India violated the terms of the devolution of the British rule both in law and spirit; and an increasingly large portion of the people of Kashmir believe themselves to be the victims. So we can now ask, what lies ahead?

29 The first Armed Forces Special Powers Act (AFSPA) was passed in 1958 by the Lok Sabha granting special powers to the armed forces in what the act terms as "disturbed areas" in the states of Arunachal Pradesh, Assam, Manipur, Meghalaya, Mizoram, Nagaland and Tripura. It was later extended to Jammu and Kashmir as The Armed Forces (Jammu and Kashmir) Special Powers Act, 1990 in July 1990.
30 Andrew Buncombe, "Kashmir torture is a thing of the past, says India," *The Independent* December 18, 2010. The chief minister Omar Abdullah is the grandson of Shaikh Muhammad Abdullah.

VI

We can peer through the gloom with only blurred vision. Many things are not what they appear to be or look very different to the sundry participants. But a few features stand out clearly enough to suggest the topography of the struggle. I will separate as far as possible the situation and views of India, Pakistan and Kashmir. I turn first to India.

The fundamental observation, as will appear from what I have written, is that no foreseeable Indian government will give up Kashmir. Even though Kashmir is a major drain on the Indian economy and has involved India in three wars with Pakistan and one military conflict with China, all Indian leaders for the last half century have feared that any devolution of Indian sovereignty in Kashmir would risk the break up of the Indian Republic. Preserving the unity of the Republic remains the fundamental objective of all the major Indian political groups. They are willing to preserve it at all costs.

The second, observation, one sometimes not appreciated by those who focus only on current events, is that the historical context in which Indians view current issues includes the use of "divide and rule" tactics in the British Indian Empire and the trauma of the separation of Pakistan and Bangladesh. These deeply imbedded memories have further emphasized Indian obsession with unity.[31]

Third, those Indian leaders with whom I have talked and/or whose statements I have read, believe that India is on an upward path, getting stronger, richer and more able to implement such policies as it deems to be in its interest. Thus, there is little support for any form of compromise on Kashmir. On this issue, I find no significant difference between the "liberal" Congress Party and the "radical right" Bharatiya Janata Party.

Fourth, India also feels itself strengthened internationally as a result

---

31   I have illustrated this in the case of Prem Nath Bazaz and for the attitude toward the peasantry, see David Hardiman (ed.), *Peasant Resistance in India, 1858-1914*, Oxford, 1992.

of years of astute public relations in which its much heralded dedication to democracy has been turned into a national asset. It mines this asset with a large, active, heavily subsidized and dedicated lobby in Washington.[32] One result is that for some years, the US government has been actively engaged in supporting Indian counterinsurgency programs in its other "front," the struggle against the Naxilite-led rural poor of India itself, and facilitating Indian nuclear development. During the past decade, a significant change has come about also in India's relationship with China. While the Tibetan issue and disputes over small pieces of isolated mountainous areas have caught most of the headlines, trade between the two countries has increased from $5 billion in 2002 to $75 billion in 2011. As a result of these trends, India feels itself far less isolated than at any time since independence and confidently expects soon to be awarded a seat on the United Nations Security Council.

Many Indians, particularly in the security forces but also in the Bharatiya Janata Party, believe that India is winning or, if given free rein, could win the war against the insurgents in Kashmir and, therefore, that any compromise would be a sell-out of India's sovereignty and national interests. Those who remember the past will see the parallel to the bitter dispute in America over who "lost" China and over withdrawal from Vietnam. Indian politicians are probably not braver than most others and admitting that the struggle for Kashmir has not succeeded will not be popular.

Those, as I see them, are the main viewpoints underlying India approaches to Kashmir. I now turn to Pakistan to list the key determinants of events there.

On its side, seeing Kashmir, as was discussed at the time of partition, not only as a geographically "logical" part of Pakistan and also as a fellow

---

32   *The Indian Express,* Feb 10, 2013: reported that Indian-Americans, Indian- led companies and companies doing business with India spent about $212 million in lobbying activities in the House and Senate through the US-India Political Action Committee (patterned on the Israel lobby) while the Indian government paid directly to its lobbyist about $5 million since the end of 2005 according to *The Times of India,* April 22, 2013. It had a firm based of action, as *The Pakistan Observer* noted on June 16, 2011 because there are 2.2 million people of Indian descent resident in the USA and *The Washington Post's* Mira Kundar wrote on September 30, 2007, "Forget the Israel Lobby. The Hill's Next Big Player Is Made in India." The article says that "Following consciously in AIPAC's footsteps, the India lobby is getting results in Washington -- and having a profound impact on U.S. policy" The group works through former American Ambassador to India and Kissinger Senior Fellow at the Council on Foreign Relations, Robert D. Blackwill, as its paid lobbyist.

Muslim society, Pakistan has remained focused on Kashmir as the ultimate test of its sense of nationhood. It was, after all, to be an Islamic nation and the "fall-back" homeland of all South Asian Muslims that Pakistan was created. As recently as fifteen years ago, the then Pakistani government, under the man who has just been reelected, Nawaz Sharif, tried to reestablish the *Sharia* as Pakistani law. Islamic nationhood remains the fundamental assertion of Pakistani national policy.[33]

In the cause of what it sees as its raison d'être as a nation-state, protecting Islam and fellow Muslims, Pakistan has fought three wars with India. It was defeated in each war. This has had three effects that affect its approach to the Kashmir issue: first, in the fear of the much stronger India, it has devoted a large part of its gross national product (GNP) to its military services; second, it has acquired a nuclear weapons capacity large enough to balance Indian conventional armed superiority; and, third, in default of adequate conventional armed forces and at the request and with the assistance of the United States (initially to embarrass the Soviet Union in Afghanistan) it has financed, trained and encouraged a paramilitary force of *mujahidin*.

None of these three ventures has accomplished the objectives set out for them: in terms of conventional power, the Pakistani army is and will remain inferior to the Indian army; nuclear weapons, which both Pakistan and India have, have everywhere proven unusable offensively and serve only as a deterrent; and guerrilla warfare in Indian occupied and incorporated Kashmir, while forcing the Indian government into expenditures it can ill afford and encouraging hostility to the Indian occupation, has not resulted in a solution to the Kashmir problem acceptable to Pakistan.

Will these considerations make a deal with India possible and, if so, on terms attractive to Pakistan?

More than in India, where the issue of Kashmir is less acute or at

---

33 Those who have focused on Israel will see parallels: the "fall-back" homeland for Jews, the imposition of religious law, the inheritance of British imperial laws and regulations, the vivid memory of traumatic events, the wars with neighbors and the influx of refugees.

least not so outstanding, the Pakistani political leadership, and above all the Pakistani Army, would suffer unacceptable ignominy by a perception that it had failed in its proclaimed task of protecting that part of Kashmir it controls or perhaps even from admitting that it cannot – ultimately at some undisclosed date -- liberate all of Kashmir. So far, the army has blamed failures on the political leadership.

Those who remember the bitter struggle in and between France and Algeria will find parallels. The professional French Army and particularly its Armée Secrète "Praetorians" came close to destroying the French civilian government.[34] Even in an "advanced" European state, civic institutions are often fragile. In Pakistan, where civic organizations are more fragile than in France, there is more danger of military dictatorship. Pakistan does not have a Charles de Gaulle, and Nawaz Sharif can hardly forget his fall from power, imprisonment and exile when his civilian government lost control over the army and security forces just fourteen years ago. He has tried to blame his fall on one general, Parvez Musharraf,[35] whom he had appointed to command, but he must know that one general alone could not have seized power. The current crop of generals are, after all, the protégés of Musharraf and his colleagues and they work within the same system as the previous commanders. A shrewd calculation of the realities of military power and civilian weakness must suggest to him the danger of an another coup – there have been three since independence -- if he does not meet enough of the expectations of the military and security services.

These expectations focus on the wide range of activities and the generous subsidy allotted to the army and the security services. They are the "sacred cows" of Pakistani politics. They currently draw approximately 18% of the government budget – considerably more than the combined expenditures on development and infrastructure improvement -- and expect to increase

---

34 I speak with some competence on these matters as I was head of the US government task force on Algeria in the bitter last days of the war, in close contact with both the rebels and he French government on a daily basis.

35 *The Guardian*, May 13, 2013, Jon Boone, "Pakistan election winner..." Invited on Monday to publicly slap down the military establishment, Sharif played it safe, saying he had "never had a problem with the army" and that the 1999 coup was the work of Musharraf alone." He repeated this assertion in an interview with the Indian newspaper, *Hindustan Times*, the next day saying, "the army was not in favour [sic] of what Musharraf did...the army will report to the PM, who is the boss."

this to 31% this year. They have expanded their activities (somewhat like the Iranian Revolutionary Guard) into a wide range of the Pakistani economy. And, regarding the environment in which they operate as a virtual war over Kashmir with India, they have played a pivotal role in Pakistani politics, including overthrowing governments which have not met their demands. Finally, they alone have mobilization, movement and projection of force capabilities that, at least in the past, have not been controlled by any civil government, including the previous government of the incoming Prime Minister Nawaz Sharif.

Most competent observes have pointed out that the incoming prime minister must make his deal with the military and the security services. As of this writing, it is not clear that he has done so. He has, however, met with the chief of the army general staff, General Ashfaq Parvez Kayani. According to one Indian newspaper,[36] reporting from the Pakistani capital, General Kayani told – warned? Instructed? Ordered? -- Nawaz Sharif "to take [only] gradual initiatives [with India and] with utmost caution." The director general of the powerful Inter Services Intelligence (ISI),[37] General Zahir ul-Islam,[38] has "invited" the new prime minister to attend a briefing at his headquarters on Pakistani security. The general is known to take an expansive view of the role in the intelligence service in all aspects of Pakistani affairs and, among other past duties, is known to have commanded troops in Pakistani-occupied Kashmir. He too is thought to be very cautious on Indian relations. Both men and their respective organizations are rumored to approve of Nawaz Sharif but are thought to have been disturbed by some of his electioneering speeches.

How much latitude these services have given to the *mujahidin* guerrillas is not, of course, public knowledge but the evidence suggests that the main *mujahidin* groups believe they and the formal military are in agreement on Kashmiri policy.

---

36   *The Indian Express, India Today,* May 19, 2013
37   The ISI was founded by an English general who was seconded to the Pakistan government in 1948 and has played a major – and often autonomous -- role in Pakistan's domestic and international affairs over the years. It might be compared to a combination of the CIA and the FBI.
38   General Zahirul-Islam is a graduate of the US Army War College and is a professional army officer. He is touted as a probably chief of the army staff when the current head retires. See *The New York Times,* July 31, 2012, Declan Walah and Mark Mazzetti, "Pakistan's New Spy Chief..."

In a recent statement, one of the *mujahidin* leaders, Syed Salahuddin, head of the United *Jihad* Council and leader of the *Hizbul Mujahidin*, warned Nawaz Sharif that "no government would be able to survive in Islamabad if it abandons the 'Kashmir cause' and warned the new regime not to make the 'mistake' of pursuing friendship with New Delhi at the cost of Kashmir... No government in Pakistan, whether it is Nawaz Sharif or anybody else, will remain in the chair if it abandons the Kashmir cause."[39] Whether he was speaking with the consent or approval of the military cannot be known, but he apparently thought he was because this has been a persistent theme of his proclamations and has not been refuted by the military.

In January of this year, Syed Salahuddin laid out his views on the strategy of the Kashmir conflict, saying,[40] that "those calling for settlement of the Kashmir issue through peaceful means were in fact deceiving the innocent Kashmiris, adding that an armed struggle was the only way to resolve the dispute...experience of the past 65 years should convince any one that only a strong and target-oriented armed struggle across India-held Kashmir could win freedom from Indian occupation... about 150 rounds of talks with India had failed to produce anything." He also drew attention to the power of armed struggle for having forced foreign troops to quit Vietnam, Algeria, Libya, Afghanistan and Iraq and was then forcing American forces to withdraw from Afghanistan. In contrast, he continued "the on-going Pakistan-India talks and confidence-building measures" favor Indian strategy. His view was repeated the same day by the quasi-official *Pakistan Defence Forum*.

What Nawaz Sharif will try to do is still unclear. He is known to be an economic and political conservative and is personally an enormously rich businessman. He has said that his major concern will be the Pakistani economy which is grievously rundown.[41] The new prime minister is also the leader of the Islamic party and certainly is committed to promoting Islamic affairs, including institution of the Islamic legal system, the Sharia. Despite electoral rhetoric some Pakistani observers believe he has not changed his

---

39 *The Nation*, Lahore, Pakistan, May 17, 2013.
40 *Dawn.com*, Karachi, Pakistan, January 6 and *Pakistan Observer*, Islamabad, January 28, 2013.
41 *The New York Times*, May 18, 2013, Declan Walsh, "Pakistan, Rusting in Its Tracks."

position on these issues.[42] Paradoxically, his reputation and position may give him unusual freedom of action. As a rightwing Punjabi his patriotism cannot be questioned according to one astute Pakistani observer.[43] In short, if he wishes to push toward an accommodation with India -- somewhat like President Nixon going to China – he has more latitude than a liberal.

On the issue of support for the *mujahidin,* he said in the run up to the election, "If I become prime minister I will make sure that Pakistani soil is never used for any such design [as a terrorist attack] against India." Then, after he was elected, he told[44] an Indian journalist that "the jihadi elements… have to be reined in."

In recent years, international support for Pakistan has dramatically declined. The ending of the Cold War and decline of the importance of the military alliances (CENTO and SEATO) created by US Secretary of State John Foster Dulles have made it less important to the US. US rapprochement with India in the last two decades have shifted America's aid and support. And with the projected withdrawal from Afghanistan, America will depend less on transit through Pakistan. Many issues plague the relationship -- drone bombings of Pakistani territory, squeezing of supply routes to Afghanistan and Pakistani support for the Taliban in Afghanistan. Not so dramatic but in the same direction are moves made by China. China has been a military supporter of Pakistan, but its major economic interests lie with India. Whether the Chinese will continue to be a major arms supplier if this policy hurts their trade with India is undecided.[45] If not, Nawaz Sharif will certainly have trouble meeting the expectations of the military and security services. Thus, it appears that we are at what may be a turning point in Pakistani-India relations with fundamental implications for Kashmir.

Consequently, Mr. Sharif's announcement that he plans to resume talks with India over Kashmir[46] has to be greeted with hope but also with caution.

---

42   *The Guardian,* Jon Boone, May 17, 2013, "Nawaz Sharif: rightwing tycoon who has won over liberals – for now.
43   *The Guardian,* May 13, 2013. Jon Boone, "Pakistan's new prime minister…"
44   *Hindustan Times,* May 14, 2013, Harinder Baweja, "We will not allow Kargil, 26/11, terror from Pak soil."
45   *The Guardian,* May 19, 2013, Ashok Sharma, "Chinese premier heads to India to boost ties"
46   *India Today,* May 12, 2013.

Negotiation is, after all, a theme that has periodically been announced by Pakistani leaders over the years. Mr. Sharif is certainly putting on a brave face in his initial appearances. He was quoted, even before the election, as saying[47] that "Kashmir was not an 'obstacle' in India-Pakistan ties..." That is clearly not true, but he went on to say, what is true, that it is "a very important issue which needs to be resolved 'peacefully' to the satisfaction of both countries and the Kashmiri people..."[48]

Can he do it? He has shown that he can mobilize enough public support to be reelected, even after making clear that he wants to ease away from Kashmir or perhaps to end the war altogether. But the events of the last half century, with one military coup after another, also suggest that the ability of the people to organize to protect either their civil rights or their electoral decisions is weak.

My hunch is that unless or until the new government can give the public more of a stake in an improving economy it will remain weak. A change in the context in which the new Nawaz Sharif government must operate will require both noticeable improvements in the socio-economic scene and an accommodation of the military.[49]

So I turn now to the Kashmiris.

The Kashmiris are the weakest of the three parties to the dispute: consequently, they are more acted upon than actors in their own cause. Leaving aside both Pakistani-controlled and Chinese-controlled Kashmir, I will focus on what is likely to happen in Indian-controlled Kashmir.

The chief minister of Kashmir is the third generation of the Sharif Muhammad Abdullah family, Omar Abdullah. Like his father and his grandfather, he is dedicated to Indian sovereignty in Kashmir. As I have mentioned above, he keeps his family in New Delhi, spends most of his time outside Kashmir and, according to foreign observers, most Kashmiris regard

47   diaji.com, in a CNN-IBN dispatch dated May 6.
48   In an interview with Karan Thapar on CNN-IBN.
49   *The Guardian*, May 13, 2013. Cyril Almeida, "Nawaz Sharif must mend Pakistan's three fault lines.

him with contempt.[50] He is, consequently, almost certainly unable (and probably unwilling) to take any position not approved in advance by India and certainly not to press for Kashmiri autonomy, much less to propose Kashmiri independence. No other figure has emerged from the years of insurgency to contest his position. I predict, therefore, that there will be no change of substance, although there may be cosmetic changes, in Kashmir's status.

I say this despite the argument (with which I largely agree) of Shabir Choudhry, the director of the Institute of Kashmir Affairs, that "time has shown that the strategies adopted by both countries were inappropriate, not only did they failed to find solution but brought misery and destruction to the region. Both India and Pakistan need to have new progress on this front. The starting point is to accept that Kashmir is not [only] a territorial dispute between India and Pakistan. Kashmir belongs to the Kashmiri people and they alone can decide its future. India and Pakistan are, of course, parties to the dispute, but it must be remembered that the Kashmiris are the main party..."

I see no evidence that either the Indians or the Pakistanis are thinking along these lines. I believe that both states will continue the "two-state solution" even though in itself it is not a solution.

What might be a solution; that is, what might change is the nature of the conflict? I see two possible impulses: the first is that continuing the present impasse is both expensive and tarnishes the reputation of India. The second is that the Kashmiri people have shown in nearly three generations of warfare that they will not give up. The resistance movement in Kashmir has drawn on Pakistani support, it is true, but it has long since developed its own momentum.[51] Thus, while Chief Minister Omar Abdullah has urged Pakistani Prime Minister Nawaz Sharif to restart the peace process,[52] that is unlikely to be, in and of itself, a game changer with the Kashmiri people. While he has not spelled out his position, I presume that he hopes that if peace talks begin, India will withdraw most of its army of occupation and

---

50 *The New York Times,* September 22, 2010, Jim Yaardley, "India adds olive branch..." wrote that "Mr. Abdullah's popularity has cratered."

51 Time, August 30, 2010, Jyoti Thottam, "Kashmir's new warriors. Their cause is not independence or union with Pakistan, but the ouster of India's military from their homeland."

52 Hindustani Times, May 17, 2013.

violence will subside.

This has been said several times in the past. In September 2010, an Indian delegation headed by the Home Minister and four other members of the Lok Sabha (India's equivalent of House of Representatives) from the major parties visited the headquarters of the Kashmir Liberation Front and asked "What is the way out? What is the way to stop the bloodshed?"[53] A *New York Times* reporter, seeing the level of security on the streets of Srinagar, with one of the witnesses called by the Indians having been stopped "every few hundred meters with machineguns," commented that "If the delegation had come to reach out to Kashmir, it was extending its hand through barbed wire."[54]

And the hand could not reach very far through the barbed wire. Most of the militants who are still alive have been in prison for years and must be presumed to be out of touch with the current generation of fighters. And, even if they were in touch, and free to do so, would they proclaim a message of peace? Analogies with other resistance movements give mixed answers: hatred must be very deep and virtually universal. As I have recounted, almost every Kashmiri family has been hurt and humiliated by Indian soldiers. But, at least some evidence points to the willingness of survivors of similar experiences to turn to a new page. This has been evident – although it must be admitted, often not clear or secure -- for example, in the Philippines, Eire, Kenya, Vietnam and Algeria.[55]

Perhaps more important, one of the effects of "successful" counterinsurgency is the destruction of the organization of the insurgents. So, as the Russians found in Afghanistan and I believe the Indians will find in Kashmir, if no one remains who can speak authoritatively for the insurgents, fighting will go on. Can anyone speak for them? Certainly the current India-supported Kashmiri politicians cannot. Negotiation thus becomes almost impossible or, if undertaken, not effective.

---

53 *International Herald Tribune*, September 22, 2010, Jim Yardley, "India adds olive branch to its Kashmir strategy."
54 Ibid.
55 See my *Violent Politics: A history of Insurgency, Terrorism & Guerrilla war.*

The only path I can envisage through this conundrum is unilateral – not negotiated – actions by India and Pakistan. India would have to lead. It would have to declare that the struggle was over, that Kashmir would be accorded the maximum amount of autonomy allowed by the Indian Constitution, that generous compensation would be paid for damages, wounds and deaths, that an amnesty would be proclaimed, that a major infusion of development funds and other economic assistance would be provided and that it was progressively – with all deliberate speed -- withdrawing its troops. Pakistan, informed well in advance of the Indian plan, would have to respond in like measure, with the additional moves of progressively scaling back all support and encouragement for the guerrillas and opening the border between Pakistani controlled Kashmir and Indian Kashmir. As tensions slowly decreased, both sides would agree to a free election – not a referendum which India would not allow -- and promise to honor its results. Just listing the necessary measures gives an indication of how difficult moves toward peace would be for all the parties. But I see anything less to offer little hope.

To this day, Kashmir is the unresolved issue of Central Asia. Without agreement on its politics, religion and society, and even its geography, the problems of India, Pakistan and Afghanistan will remain in turmoil. The human and material costs have been immense. There is a glimmer of hope today, but that hope has a chance only if India and Pakistan – and their foreign friends and supporters – develop a full understanding of Kashmir, its people and its history. To make a small contribution to that end has been my aim in this short paper.

May 21, 2013

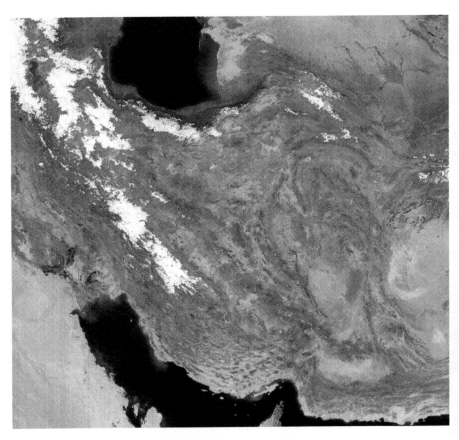

NASA Satellite image of Iran

CHAPTER 11

IRAN: DANGER AND OPPORTUNITY

I wrote the following analysis of the dangers of war and opportunities for resolution of the "Iran Problem" five years ago. I wish it were more "dated" than it is. For the last five years, we have skated on the brink of war with Iran. Even today we are not far from the brink. So, while the names of some of the participants have changed, the issues remain distressingly familiar. The dangers I then foresaw are still with us while the opportunities I then identified have yet to be exploited. A second reason argues for the inclusion of the essay as written: while Americans may forget what was happening five years ago, the Iranians certainly do not. Rather they will define the general attitudes of the public in both countries. Moreover, those events inevitably form the "mindset" that the officials, diplomats and "experts" will take into current moves toward war or peace. Thus, while dated, they are a key part of today's "possible."

Cassandra and Yogi Berra are an unlikely pair, but I hear both of their voices today. Cassandra, like some of us, was cursed to be always disbelieved as she correctly predicted the future while baseballer Yogi Berra will be remembered for his penetrating insight into the flow of history, "This is like deja vu all over again."

It is through the unlikely medium of *U.S. News and World Report* that Cassandra speaks. The March 12, 2008 issue gives us "6 signs the U.S. may be headed for war in Iran." The first tip the magazine highlights is the firing of Admiral William Fallon. While Fallon is hardly a "dove," he apparently – to judge by hints he gave in an interview with Thomas Barnett published in the March 2008 issue of Esquire – had argued that an attack on Iran made no military sense. If this really was his judgment, he obviously was not the man to be "CINC [Commander-in-chief] Centcom." That is, if the Bush administration really is intent on an attack.

Among other straws *U.S. News and World Report* found in the wind blowing out of Washington was the projected trip by Vice President Dick Cheney to what the magazine correctly described as a "logistics hub for military operations in the Persian Gulf," Oman, where the Strait of Hormuz constitutes "the vulnerable oil transit chokepoint into and out of the Persian Gulf that Iran threatens to blockade in the event of war."

Here is where Yogi Berra begins to come into the picture. As the *U.S. News and World Report* notes, "Back in March 2002, Cheney made a high-profile Mideast trip to Saudi Arabia and other nations that officials said at the time was about diplomacy toward Iraq and not war…" It was, as we now know, one of the concerted moves in the build-up to the already-decided-upon plan to attack Iraq. Is Cheney's 2008 trip "like deja vu all over again?" That certainly is the inference drawn by *U.S. News and World Report*.

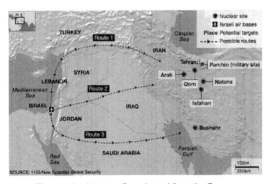

The multiple ways Israel could strike Iran.

Then, *U.S. News and World Report* also introduces the Israeli card. It reports the widely held belief that the Israeli air attack on Syria, analyzed by Sy Hersh in one of his insightful pieces of investigative reporting on February 11, 2008 in *The New Yorker*, was *not* what it was proclaimed to be, an attack on a presumed nuclear site, but a means to force the Syrians to activate their anti-aircraft electronics – as America used to do with the Russians – to detect gaps along what might be a flight path from Israel toward Iran.

Why a flight path across Syria? Because it is one of the three possible routes for an attack on Iran (as shown in the BBC World News map from *New Scientist Global Security* on this page) as Israel has been threatening and urging the US to make. Israel has US-supplied long-range fighter-bombers and tanker aircraft that could reach all Iranian targets and return along any of three possible routes. Turkey might not allow the use of its airspace and using Jordan's airspace, as Israel did in its June 7, 1981 strike on the Iraqi nuclear facility at Osiriq, might seriously weaken the Jordanian regime which Israel would like to keep in place, at least for the time being. So, presumably Israel would regard the flight path across Syria as involving the lesser risk.

U.S. News and World Report also drew attention to the stationing of a guided missile destroyer off the Lebanese coast as another indication of preparations for war. The article does not explain why but points out that the destroyer has an anti-aircraft capability; so, the inference is that it would shoot down any Syrian aircraft attempting to hit Israel. That move suggests that the US was seeking to prevent the possibility of Iran retaliating for an Israeli strike.

Israel is not alone in threatening Iran: a major part of the US Navy is deployed in and around the Persian Gulf. These ships are armed with the whole array of weapons that were developed to fight the Soviet Union in event of "general war," and they are backed up by aircraft that can be supplied by some 14 bases the US has built in Iraq. The numbers are stunning and include not only a vast array of weapons, including nuclear weapons, cruise and other missiles and hundreds of aircraft but also "insertion" (invasion) forces and equipment. Even then, these already deployed forces amount to only a fraction of the total that could be brought to bear on Iran because aircraft, both bombers and troop and equipment transports, stationed far away in Central Asia, the Indian Ocean, Europe and even in America can be quickly employed.

Of course, deploying forces along Iran's frontier does not necessarily mean using them. At least that is what the Administration says. However, as a historian and former participant in government, I believe that having troops and weapons on the spot makes their use more likely than not. Why is that?

It is because a massive build-up of forces inevitably creates the "climate" of war. Troops and the public, on both sides, come to accept its inevitability.

Standing down is difficult and can entail loss of "face." Consequently, political leaders usually are carried forward by the flow of events. Having taken steps 1, 2 and 3, they find taking step number 4 logical or even necessary. In short, momentum rather than policy begins to control action. As Barbara Tuchman showed in her study of the origins of the First World War, *The Guns of August*, even though none of the parties really wanted to go to war, none could stop the process. It was the fact that President Kennedy had been reading Tuchman's book just before the Cuban Missile Crisis, I believe, that made him so intent on not being "hijacked by events." His restraint was unusual. More common is a surrender to "sequence" as was shown by the 1991 Gulf War and the 2003 invasion of Iraq. It would have taken a major reversal of policy – and considerable political bravery -- to halt either invasion once the massive build-up was in place. No such effort was made then. Will it be now? I think the odds are against it.

In fact, moves are being made, decisions are being taken and rationale has been set out that point in the opposite direction. Consider just a few of these in addition to what *U.S. News and World Report* highlighted:

First, the strategic rational for preëmptive military action was set forth in the 2005 *National Defense Strategy of the United States of America*. It proclaimed that "America is a nation at war...[and] will defeat adversaries at the time, place, and in the manner of our choosing...[rather than employing] A reactive or defensive approach...Therefore, we must confront challenges earlier and more comprehensively, before they are allowed to mature...In all cases, we will seek to seize the initiative and dictate the tempo, timing, and direction of military operations." In short, as Henry Kissinger pointed out in *The International Herald Tribune*, April 14, 2006, it is an assertion of the intention to engage in preëmptive or "first strike" warfare. So, the process that began in Afghanistan and was then carried to Iraq and (on a smaller scale) to Somalia points toward action against Iran.

Second, why Iran? Among the reasons that the Bush administration has proclaimed are that Iran is supporting terrorism by supplying arms, training and encouragement both to anti-American insurgents in Iraq and to anti-Israeli Hizbullah militants in Lebanon and that it is moving toward the acquisition of nuclear weapons.

There is reason to doubt each of these contentions. Iran actively supported the American attack on the Taliban (and against the drug trade) in Afghanistan and evidence on Iraq is, at best, sketchy. On the nuclear issue, a National Intelligence Estimate (NIE) reported in November 2007 the consensus of all 16 of the American intelligence agencies "with high confidence" that Iran is not actively seeking to develop nuclear weapons.

However, there are real psychological or political motivations. President Bush proclaimed on January 29, 2002 that Iran was part of the "Axis of Evil." He and others have conjured the memory of the seizure of the American embassy and taking of our officers hostage and have condemned the lamentable Iranian government record on civil liberties and particularly on the treatment of women. With Iraq under occupation and presumably incapable of mounting a credible threat outside its own territory and with North Korea immune to attack (beause it already has nuclear weapons), Iran is the major perceived adversary capable of doing what *National Defense Strategy of the United States of America* termed "adopting threatening capabilities, methods, and ambitions...[to] 1) limit our global freedom to act, 2) dominate key regions, or 3) attempt to make prohibitive the costs of meeting various U.S. international commitments."

Decoded and applied to Iran, the *Strategy* paper defines Iranian actions as disrupting American objectives in the Middle East and has the potential to dominate what is believed to be the largest still-only-partially-developed pool of oil and gas in the world.

Thus, as defined by the *National Defense Strategy of the United States of America*, Iran is an obvious target.

Apparently, President Bush's firing of Admiral Fallon was meant to signal to the Iranians that "all options remain on the table." This is the publically proclaimed policy of the Bush administration and has also been adopted by the Democratic Party aspirants to the White House, notably even by Barack Obama who recently said, "all options, and I mean all options, are on the table."

Leaving aside the issue of international law – which defines the conditions under which military action is *defense* (and so is legal) rather than *aggression* (and so is illegal) and which, having been adopted by the United States government, is American law also -- is a preëmptive military strike against Iran feasible? Allegedly, Admiral Fallon did not think so.

The reasons are both evident and unambiguous. They include the following:

First, the Iranians would resist. However they may feel about their government, Iranians are a proud and nationalistic people who have suffered for generations from meddling, espionage and invasions by the Russians, the British and the Americans. They are even less likely than the Cubans (as the organizer of the CIA Bay of Pigs task force, Richard Bissell, predicted) or the Iraqis (as the Neoconservatives fantasized in 2003) to welcome foreign intrusion. If attacked, they undoubtedly would fight.

But surely we would overwhelm them. No, not so surely. While the United States could almost certainly quickly destroy the Iranian regular army, as it did the Iraqi regular army, the Iranians are better prepared for a guerrilla war than were the Iraqis. They have in being a force in being of at least 150 thousand dedicated and appropriately armed members of the *Pasdaran-e Enqilab* (Revolutionary National Guard) on land and at sea (stationed along the Persian Gulf coast) a numerous assortment of small, maneuverable and missile-armed speedboats. Use of the boats would probably be suicidal for the crews but it would be a miracle if they failed to inflict heavy casualties among the American fleet. They almost certainly could interdict oil tankers.

Second, war is always unpredictable – except that it is always worse than expected. No contemporary statesman thought that the First World War would last more than a few months. The cost is also always underestimated. Before the American invasion of Iraq, Secretary of Defense Donald Rumsfeld thought it would cost only about $50 billion; his deputy (and later president of the world bank) Paul Wolfowitz thought it would cost *nothing* because the Iraqis would pay for it; and when Larry Lindsay, the White House economic adviser, predicted it might cost $200 *billion*, President Bush fired him. Estimates now run between $2 and $6 *trillion*. To shield this reality from the public, the Bush administration resorted to massive borrowing abroad – U.S. Treasury obligations amounted to $2.7 trillion as of early this year and are now higher – and to a massive increase -- up 70% during this Administration -- in national debt.

Almost no casualties were expected in Iraq; now American dead number about 4,000 and a realistic figure for various categories of "wounded" – officially put at about 20,000 – actually runs in the hundreds of thousands. Just coping with the American wounded is expected to cost half a trillion dollars.

A sober viewer, if there are still such in the White House and the Pentagon must see that while Iraq is a small country Iran is large, diverse and populated by about three times as many people as Iraq. The costs, human, material and monetary would certainly be a multiple of those suffered in Iraq. It is not unlikely that war with Iran would effectively "break" the American volunteer army and bankrupt America.

Given this unattractive scenario and Iran's difficult terrain, military planners have reportedly emphasized their intent to use mainly or even solely "surgical" air strikes. But the fact that CENTCOM has positioned ships to "insert" troops may be taken as a tacit admission by military planners that air strikes alone would be unable to destroy either Iran's nuclear facilities which are believed to be widely scattered, often located in heavily populated urban areas and/or in protected underground locations.

Almost certainly, military commanders would demand permission to follow up air strikes with some form of "boots on the ground." Presumably and at least initially these would likely be Special Forces, but, inevitably (I would assert from my observation and study of past military adventures) some of these forces, even if intended only for limited action and quick withdrawal, will get caught and have to be rescued. *Thus, what is planned and begun as restricted action is extremely unlikely to be containable.* Sensible military staffs must be aware of this. Whether or not their civilian bosses are aware or are willing to understand is another question.

Military action against Iran would probably "spill over" into a wide area. What is done to and in Iran is likely to result in military, paramilitary and terrorist responses by Iranians and others outside of the immediate theater of combat. Consider the following:

First, Iraq. The Iraqi government, although installed by the United States, is predominantly culturally and religiously allied to Iran; in the shock of an American invasion of Iran, it would almost certainly take action or be unable to prevent action against American personnel in Iraq. Guerrilla forces of Muqtada as-Sadr's "Mahdi Army," now observing a ceasefire, would turn on the Americans;

Second, Lebanon. What the Hizbullah forces in Lebanon could do other than firing rockets is, to me at least, unclear, but a renewed round of savage fighting with Israel would appear likely;

Third, in the wider Middle East, those governments allied with or thought to be subservient to the United States (Jordan, Saudi Arabia, Bahrain, Qatar and Egypt) might be overthrown by their own military;

Fourth, throughout the Islamic world, Muslims of all sects and political persuasions would probably turn against the United States so that much of Asia and Africa would be convulsed and Americans and American interests would suffer; but

Fifth, it is the economic consequences of an invasion that are, perhaps, the most predictable and the most damaging to America. Iran produces about 8% of the world's flow of energy and roughly 40% of the world's energy is conveyed by tanker down the Persian Gulf. Iran's own production – and possibly much of the Saudi production which is worked by Saudis of Shia persuasion – would be drastically curtailed or even halted, and as a result of naval action tankers are likely to be laid up or sunk in the Gulf. With oil already at over $105/bbl, the price is likely to soar with the predictable result of a major world economic catastrophe. *Just for the United States, every $1 rise in the price of oil diminishes the national income by some $3 billion.*

Such might be the results of a decision to attack Iran. But, what if the current actions and pronouncements are just threats, intended only to frighten the Iranians into doing what the United States wants? Is that better for us? Consider these points:

First, to be effective, threats must be credible. I imagine that the Iranians must view our threats in something like the scale I have just set out. If they have, I imagine that they will have concluded that the United States government would have to be mad to attack Iran when the costs of doing so are so evident and so large. In short, they probably would have reached the same conclusion Admiral Fallon is said to have reached.

Second, what if they believe our threats? Having received a credible threat to destroy their country, the Iranians almost certainly would seek as rapidly as secretly possible to acquire the only sure means to deter such an attack: possession of a nuclear weapon. This also was the conclusion that Mohamed ElBaradei of the International Atomic Energy Agency (IAEA) reached, as he told the Argentinian newspaper *Clarin* on November 29, 2007. Thus, a policy of threat that falls short of actual attack must result in precisely what the United States seeks to avoid.

Third, suppose I am wrong and the threat works and the Iranians promise never to try to develop a nuclear weapon. What could the Iranians do that would satisfy the United States' demands? Absent a large and intrusive American presence, how could an Iranian government prove that it does not have or at least seek nuclear weapons? Proving a negative is logically impossible and any Iranian attempt to do so would probably politically impossible for Iran.

Fourth, since we must assume that both the Iranian and American governments will realize the logic of these points, I think we must conclude that a policy of threat would slide almost inevitably into conflict.

Moreover, war does not occur only by design. During the long years of the Cold War, many of us worried over the danger of accidental war. Dozens of incidents illustrated the danger – and at least some were avoided more by luck than by cleverness. One in which I was personally intimately involved was averted during the Cuban Missile Crisis. As careful as we on the Crisis Management Committee then were, we could see that an unpredictable and even a rather trivial event could happen and could have disastrous consequences. One I luckily caught was this: one of our destroyers was positioned above a Soviet submarine, intent on embarrassing the Russians when the submarine ran out of air and to surface. When I received notice of the situation, my mind went back to the June 28, 1914 assassination of Austrian Archduke Francis Ferdinand at Sarajevo. I could imagine a sailor throwing a bottle and his Russian counterpart firing a pistol. Accidents happen despite all attempts at control: most are immediately contained as was the submarine incident in the Missile Crisis, but luck cannot be guaranteed. War is a weapon with many triggers.

Of course, we must factor into our estimates the fact that some Americans, notably the neoconservatives who have set much of the policy of the Bush administration, have actively espoused a war policy.[1] Their position has been encouraged and echoed by the current Israeli government. Less known is the fact that the American and Israeli "hawks" have their counterparts in the Iranian government, as the former Iranian ambassador to the United Nations admitted to me privately. Consider their positions as they put us squarely on the brink of war:

First, the neoconservatives. They began almost twenty years ago to advocate what has come to be called "the long war," in the vortex of which the world would be recast. One of them, the former CIA Director James Woolsey, tried to be optimistic, saying he hoped this world-wide and cataclysmic conflict would not last more than 40 years.

Second, the religious fundamentalists. Christians, Jews, Muslims and

---

1 See, for example, Norman Podhoretz's article "Stopping Iran: Why the Case for Military Action Still Stands," February 2008 *Commentary*.

Hindus share an eschatological vision. Indeed, each faith includes groups who actually *yearn* for apocalypse during which time the world is destroyed to be reborn as a messiah or *mahdi* or Vishnu appears. To the "true believers," hurrying toward the end of the world is a race not toward horror but a fulfilling spiritual experience in which it is only the enemies of the true faith who will suffer -- as St. John so graphically portrays in *The Revelation*. In their version of messianism, the Shiis believe that the righteous will be delivered from the tyranny of the corrupt and the earth will be filled with justice and happiness. For the fundamentalists, "fatalism" is the wrong word. They do not just accept destiny but often seek to pre-empt it. This attitude may shape at least some Iranian attitudes toward the terrible destruction that would come from an American attack. My impression is that the Iranian Shia fundamentalists, presumably including their *mujtahid* leadership, believe that the ensuing war would hasten the way toward the Last Day when the Twelfth Imam, *The Mahdi*, would reappear to cleanse the world of evil.

If the *mujtahid* leadership, which of course espouses the central dogma of Shiism, holds these views then a policy of threat or even of brutal military action will produce effects different from those we thought shaped the attitude of the Russian leadership during the Cold War. Then, we shared with the Russians a salutary vision of horror -- as set out, for example, in Cormac McCarthy's recent novel, *The Road*. The absolute need to avoid war was the ultimate brake on us and them because both of us knew that if we really went to war millions, perhaps hundreds of millions, of people would be made refugees, wounded or incinerated. But, if one really believes in the Last Day, then this brake is loosened. Thus, I think we should factor into our calculations on American policy toward Iran, a reaction very different from that we expected from the Russians.

Moreover, even among secular Iranians, I detect a belief that while America would win battles it would lose the war, that over time, Western society, seen as corrupt, materialistic and selfish, would give way, exhaust itself or retreat to its home ground while those who have no place to which to retreat would be kept "pure" by their very poverty and so, inspired by their faith or nationalism, cannot and will not surrender. War unending would be the likely result.

213

Thus, even short of a nuclear Armageddon, the "Long War" advocated by the Neoconservatives would spread misery, violence, starvation, disease and death. The "fabric" that holds societies together would be shredded so that a chaos even the great English philosopher of civic danger, Thomas Hobbes could not have imagined would become common over much of the world. The worst affected would be the poor nations but even rich societies would be corrupted and crippled. Reacting over a generation or more to fear of terrorism and the emotional "blow-back" of war, they would lose faith in law, civil liberties, indeed civil society in general. Strong men would come to the fore proclaiming that survival justifies giving up the civic, cultural and material good life. Step by step along the path of the long war, we could fall into the nightmare George Orwell laid out in his novel *1984*.

If this is even a remote and unlikely danger, and I believe it is far more than that, we would be foolish indeed not to try to find means to avoid taking any steps –- of which war with Iran would be not a step but a leap -- toward it. So what might we do to avoid war and still meet our need for security? I begin with the nuclear issue:

Since obviously means should be tailored to the issue to be solved, we must begin by asking why Iran would want nuclear weapons. If I were an Iranian, I would point to President Bush's formulation of the "Axis of Evil." I would note that Iraq did not have nuclear weapons and was virtually destroyed while North Korea which had them and was left in peace. Having a nuclear weapon is the surest form of defense in our dangerous world. There are, of course, other reasons for becoming a nuclear power – access to advanced technology, national prestige, cheap power, etc. – but the bottom line is national defense.

It follows that threats must encourage the Iranian leadership to acquire a nuclear capacity. If I were an Iranian, that is what I would certainly advocate. And, if America attacks Iran, even if it manages to completely destroy all the production facilities and kill all the technicians, as an Iranian I would do all in my power to beg, borrow or steal a bomb. Recall the decision of another government. When Pakistani Prime Minister Zulfiqar Ali Bhutto learned of India's acquisition of the nuclear bomb, he said that Pakistan too must have one, regardless of the ruinous cost, even if it meant having nothing to eat but grass. Go a step further. We can be sure that that would be the aim of any future Iranian government. It was, after all, also the aim of the government of the Shah, and had he lived a few more years the current Iranian government would have *inherited* nuclear weapons. So, threats and certainly any military action can only be ultimately self-defeating even if apparently temporarily successful.

The second question we should address is what is the consequence of Iran acquiring a nuclear weapon and what we should do about it. There are, I suggest, four interlocking answers:

First, from personal experience during the Cuban Missile Crisis and from my study, I firmly believe that the existence of nuclear weapons *anywhere* constitutes a danger to people *everywhere*. Thus, we should do all we can to get all nations to phase them out with all deliberate speed. For the first half century of the nuclear age, as McGeorge Bundy wrote in *Danger and Survival*, we have been both prudent and lucky, but we have little reason to think we can count on either luck or wisdom as former Secretary of Defense Robert S. McNamara ultimately concluded.[2]

Second, if Iran acquires a nuclear weapon, it will not be able to use it or threaten to use it aggressively for fear of an almost certain attack. This has been true of all the nuclear powers -- the US, the Soviet Union, China, India, Pakistan, Britain, France, North Korea and Israel. While dangerous and costly, Mutually Assured Destruction (MAD) has worked. Ironically, this ultimate weapon is employable only as a deterrent. Therefore, I think that the near hysteria evoked by the nuclear issue as applied to Iran is overblown or as put forward even meretriciously by some.

Third, if Iran does acquire a weapon, it is likely that other countries in the area would follow its (and Israel's) lead and move toward acquisition. These might include Turkey, Saudi Arabia, the richer of the Gulf states and conceivably even Syria. Today, since the technology is known and available, acquisition is largely a matter of allocation of resources and in changed

2   In "Apocalypse Soon," *Foreign Affairs*, May/June 2005.

circumstances might be achieved without having to actually make them.

Fourth, it seems to me that this course of events, which I judge to be predictable offers us a rare opportunity to move toward nuclear sanity. We must not forget that *crises are also times of opportunity*. This could be so crucial to our life on this planet that I will dilate on it:

The reason why states acquire nuclear weapons (as distinct from why they seek to acquire nuclear technology) is fear of attack. The Soviet Union acquired the bomb because of fear of us, China did largely out of fear of the USSR, India and Pakistan did out of fear of one another, Israel did in fear of the Arabs. However, *as more and more states acquire weapons, parity or balance is replaced by growing unpredictability*. Arguably, Israel, for example, gained security when it alone in the Middle East had the bomb. But *if, as I believe is inevitable, other states acquire them, its security will be diminished and its danger increased. Therefore*, arguably, since it already has the strongest army and air force in the area, *it would be to Israel's interest to create a nuclear-free zone in the Middle East.* It is probably not possible to force the Israelis into such a policy, if it is directly solely at them, but overall considerations I have mentioned argue that the United States should revert to the policy we espoused in the 1960s which foresaw the elimination of nuclear weapons worldwide. *The Iranian crisis could thus be a catalyst in a move toward a safer world.*

Since attack or even threat could lead to disaster, and since it is to the fundamental interest of the United States to move toward peace, a part of the solution to the Iranian "crisis" should involve the revocation of the 2005 *National Defense Strategy of the United States of America* which causes other nations to fear us and which is more likely to embroil us in wars than to enhance our national security. Highlighting this issue, the Iranian crisis thus gives us an opportunity to readjust our goals and our means of action.

Included in our means of action is an awesome military force, which we have painfully learned does not always and necessarily enhance our security and well-being but can, itself, be a cause of danger and impoverishment. This is the lesson of history: great powers seldom fail on the battlefield but often lose sway by exhaustion, hubris or economic collapse. Our military machine is grossly out of proportion both to our needs and to what the world will peacefully tolerate. And some pieces of it, particularly the legacy of Secretary Rumsfeld, the "Special Operations Command," are a clear and present danger to us. As we recognize the dangers inherent in the Iranian crisis, we can use the opportunity for a clear-headed reëvaluation of our *real* security needs and best means to achieve them.

The Iranian crisis also gives us the opportunity to come to grips with reality: we should by now have learned, the neoconservatives to the contrary, that we cannot remake other cultures in our image and should not try to do so. The harder we press, the more ugly the process becomes both for us and for them. Specifically in Iran, our threats bring out the worst in the ruling group. Once the pressure is removed, Iranians will have the breathing room to reaffirm their often-expressed desires for "the good life." Then a more humane order will have a chance. That is the course of events we have seen, for example, in Vietnam. It has not become our version of a democracy but has matured in a way acceptable to the Vietnamese and in accord with our security aims.

Solving the Iranian crisis also should give us a chance to reëvaluate the international structures we have built. We can see that the International Atomic Energy Agency (IAEA) has made a major contribution to our security and well-being. It has served our purposes not by being our rubber stamp but by being professional and independent. But, American administrations of both parties have purposefully made all the organs of the United Nations weak and have deliberately picked weak men to lead them. We would be well advised to use the process of solving the Iran crisis to reconsider how international institutions could be more effectively used to enhance our national interest.

In conclusion, I believe that we are at one of those rare points in history when great nations find themselves, as Shakespeare put it so memorably as the changing of the tide:

There is a tide in the affairs of men,

Which, taken at the flood, leads on to fortune;

Omitted, all the voyage of their life,

Is bound in shallows and in miseries,

On such a full sea are we now afloat,

And we must take the current when it serves,

Or lose our ventures.

I hope and trust we will use the tide of the Iranian "crisis" to lead on to fortune rather than getting bound in shallows and miseries; it is truly a time both of dangers and opportunities.

March 18, 2008

CHAPTER 12

REFLECTIONS ON "WEIGHING BENEFITS AND COSTS OF MILITARY ACTION AGAINST IRAN"

I have been reading "Weighing Benefits and Costs of Military Action Against Iran" -- a paper based on a series of meetings organized by Ambassadors William Luers, and Thomas Pickering and put out on the internet in the last few days.[1] I salute Luers and Pickering who have done yeoman work on Iranian-American relations both in a sequence of previous articles and here. I hope you will read their Paper.

Because the topic is so important, perhaps nearly vital to us all and because the Paper was aimed at the largest possible American audience, it should be the beginning of rather than the end of a debate. The authors call for this: "Our hope is to encourage more informed and objective discussion of the military option by policy makers, the public, and the press." I decided to accept their invitation to comment. I ask your (and their) indulgence and would appreciate your reaction

The importance of this Paper, which is substantial, lies primarily, I believe, in the publicity it will, hopefully, generate to foster a reasoned approach to the issue of American-Iranian relations. Its weaknesses, which are several, arise primarily from its narrow focus. I regretted the lack of a weighing of the pros and cons of military action in the scales of American values and laws, both of which I will briefly consider below, and Iranian culture, religion and experience. As the authors point out, the Paper's focus is restricted to "costs and benefits of military action." Also, with the prejudice of the historian, I find the Paper skewed by a lack of, or insufficient attention to, history.

---

1 www.wilsoncenter.org/sites/default/files/IranReport_091112_FINAL.pdf. September 11, 2012

Who's who: Probably you do what I do first: look to see who writes or endorses a demarche Some 32 people signed it. Obviously, the men who originated the project, Bill Luers and Tom Pickering, attempted to get together a group, at least some of whom American readers would recognize as serious, experienced and able. Having attempted to assemble a group for the conference I chaired this year in Washington on "Affordable World Security," I know how difficult a task that is and I commend them for their effort. Practically every educated American will find a few names he or she will recognize.

A few words on the participants: I find only one person among them who I believe knows Iran intimately. So, not surprisingly, there is little appreciation of Persian culture, religion or politics. Some of the authors have been deeply affected either or both professionally or personally by the Iran "problem." One was in charge of the abortive Carter administration mission to rescue the hostages, one was fired for opposition to current policy and another is known to have accepted payments from a dissident terrorist organization, the Mojahedin-e Khalq. The opinions of others may have been shaped by their involvement in American policy. Lay readers, who cannot be expected to know much about them, should have been given somewhat more than just the signatures of the participants in order to evaluate the group's opinion. I certainly did not know all of them, and I doubt that others will. Their backgrounds matter.

The Paper's signers are divided among backgrounds: 8 are or were diplomats; 3 were senior non-diplomatic government policy officers; 7 have military backgrounds; 3 are current or former senators; 2, academic administrators; 3, foundation presidents, 1 each, a banker, businesswoman, financial expert, business school professor, and former journalist. Given the American system of "career migration," most fall in multiple categories.

Who's Not Who: It is easy, of course, to lament the absence of others. Rightly, the organizers feared that a larger group would be unwieldy, but in the emphasis on "insiders" a few "outside" voices needed to be heard. I didn't hear them. It would not have been impossible to include at least one critical journalist. I think of the Leveretts, Flynt and Hillary Mann Leverett, Sy

Hersh or Gareth Porter. And why no Congressman? Admittedly there are few who could offer informed comments, but regardless of their intelligence (or lack of it) several play significant roles in the formulation of American policy.

Three "slots" are notably unfilled: 1) a constitutional lawyer who could have commented on how any course of action affects our system of law, 2) an authority on Shi'a Islam on how it affects the Iranians and (3) an experienced former intelligence analyst who now could speak freely and could discuss how we know what we know and whether we know what we think we know. On the latter issue, I think of several members of the organization of "Veteran Intelligence Professionals for Sanity,"

Sponsorship of the Paper is impeccable: the Woodrow Wilson Center and the Rockefeller Brothers Fund.

To get at the fundamental question posed in the Paper, allow me an analogy: think of the assumed Iranian nuclear danger as an onion. Should it be peeled or sliced? The Paper focuses on slicing, that is, military action. An alternate, not here considered, is peeling. That is, negotiating. But there is a more fundamental question which is only briefly dealt with here and is hardly ever brought up in the media: is there really an onion?

It was the failure to ask the last question, the existence of the problem or crisis – that is, the danger to US national security posed by the existence of a nuclear weapon in the hands of the ruler of a hostile country – that led to the disastrous American war in Iraq. Iraq had none. Is there one in Iran? In December 2007, the 16 US intelligence organizations, gathered in the National Intelligence Council, produced a National Intelligence Estimate (NIE) judging "with high confidence" that Iran had no weapon and showed no sign of planning to produce one. After an intense period of further investigation, the essential element of the 2007 NIE was reconfirmed in 2010.

The signers of the Paper maintain that "While there is no evidence that Iran's Supreme Leader has decided the country should develop a nuclear weapon [and it is significant that he issued a religious ordinance, a *fatwa,* "prohibiting the production, stockpiling and use of nuclear weapons (Iranian Foreign Minister Kamal Kharrazi, "We're not building a bomb," *International Herald Tribune,* February 5-6, 2008)], many observers believe that Iran's leaders want the country to be capable of making a bomb if they perceive one to be needed." I believe the signers of the Paper are right, as I wrote in my 2009 book, *Understanding Iran.* Having a nuclear *capacity* but not going for a bomb, "breaking out" in the current jargon, is the de facto policy of a number of other countries including Japan, Brazil, Argentina among others. The question is whether the Iranian regime has come to the conclusion that it needs a weapon in order to defend itself. That question is not fully addressed in the Paper.

So crucial is this issue to American policy on war in Iran that a brief look at the history of Iran's flirtation with nuclear activity is necessary. It is not dealt with, as I believe it should have been, in the Iran Paper. (David Patrikarakos in the *London Review of Books,* December 1, 2011 and in the June 18, 2009 *New Statesman,* based on interviews with the founder and first head of the Iranian Atomic Energy Organization, Akbar Etemad.)

In the Eisenhower administration's "Atoms for Peace" project America gave Iran its first nuclear reactor. Initially nothing was done with it. Allegedly, it was hardly uncrated. But, on July 1, 1968, the Shah's government signed the Nuclear Nonproliferation Treaty (NPT) apparently as a gesture to reassure the world that its intentions were peaceful. It is significant in today's events, although never discussed in today's media or in the Iran Paper, that from that time, Iranians have regarded the NPT as unfair.[2]

It was the dramatic rise in oil prices in 1973 that promoted Iranian interest in nuclear affairs: the Shah decided that oil was too valuable to burn to generate electricity and that Iran should develop nuclear energy. (That remains the policy of the current regime.) Moreover, the Shah agreed with

2   The founder and first head of the Shah's nuclear agency, and a determined enemy of the Islamic Republic, Akbar Etemad, commented. "We should never have signed it. It was not a fair treaty...Only small countries joined – Burkina Faso, Nicaragua, the Fiji Islands. The countries that actually had a chance of getting nuclear power – India, Pakistan, Israel – they stayed out. Only we signed."

other Third World rulers, including India's Indira Gandhi, that nuclear technology was the key to modernization, that is, to becoming a "First World" nation. (That remains the policy of the Iranian and the Indian governments.) Iran signed agreements to buy reactors from West German and French firms and Westinghouse.

In public, the Shah said that Iran did not need nuclear weapons because its army was strong enough to implement his policy of hegemony over the Gulf area and he feared precisely the issue facing the current government: as he told Akbar Etemad, the quest for nuclear weapons would be dangerous because it "might actually force others to go nuclear and wipe out our conventional arms advantage." But, continued Etemad, "he also said that if things ever changed – if our security was threatened – he would give the order."

What changed was the Revolution and the Iraqi invasion. The 1979 revolution brought to power an Islamic theocracy that opposed nuclear weapons and in 1980 Iraq invaded. The war was devastating for Iran. It suffered at least 250,000 casualties. And the war dragged on without resolution. Finally, the effective ruler, Ayatollah Khomeini, decided to accept a cease fire because, as he said, his military commander informed him that Iran would need to build a nuclear weapon to defend itself. To do so, he said, would be like drinking poison. Nuclear weapons, he ruled, were unclean, sacrilegious, illegal.

In the following years large numbers of young Iranians studied in the West and many became physicists or technicians. Apparently, the Iranian regime then began to dabble, with Pakistani help, in the nuclear weapons field. At least by 2003, however, it stopped. Intense investigation by the CIA, the Israeli intelligence agency, Mossad, the British intelligence agency MI-6 and the International Atomic Energy Agency (IAEA) led them to conclude that after 2003 Iran did not pursue acquiring a nuclear weapon. The US National Intelligence Council has recently reconfirmed this finding and its appreciation is shared by both MI-6 and Mossad. (See *The New York Times*, March 18, 2012, James Risen, "Iran's Nukes: What US

Intelligence Really Believes.")

What disturbs some observers is that the logical course for Iran is to get a nuclear weapon as quickly and as secretly as possible. That is what we, the Russians, the Israelis, and others have done. As Israeli Defense Minister Ehud Barak reportedly said recently (according to Seumas Milne in the December 8, 2011 *Guardian*), "if he were an Iranian leader he would 'probably' want nuclear weapons." Going even further, the noted Israeli military historian/ strategist Martin van Creveld said in 2004 (according to Ralph Nader in the January 12, 2012 *Reader Supported News*) , that Iranians "would be crazy not to build nuclear weapons considering the security threats they face." So sure are some writers that this logic is compelling that they "cook" the evidence: In the January/February issue of *Foreign Affairs*, Matthew Kroenig wrote that "according to the IAEA, Iran already appears fully committed to developing a nuclear weapons program..." That is simply not true. (*IPS*, September 12, 2012, Gareth Porter wrote that the latest IAEA report "reveals that Iran has actually reduced the amount of 20-percent enriched uranium available for any possible 'breakout' to weapons grade enrichment over the last three months rather than increasing it.")

I turn now to the structure and substance of the Paper.[3]

The quest for both brevity and range naturally affected the writing. Failure to put events or statements about them in context repeatedly presented problems. I found myself saying "yes, but..." or questioning how the choice of words would affect the argument.

For example, the authors' first point in "Shared Understandings" (page 7) is that "a nuclear-armed Iran would pose dangerous challenges to U.S. interests and security..." The non-specialist reader, for whom this Paper is intended, would probably read this to mean that Iran is either now or soon is going to be nuclear armed whereas the 16 US Intelligence agencies are sure this is not the case, and, as I have said, their appreciation is shared by

3 Where something is controversial, I will cite a source. I should mention that as a part of my therapy, following my 4th operation for cancer this year, I have "read myself" back into Iranian affairs. I have gone back over, and summarized, hundreds of press and other clippings, government and "think tanks" papers, and notes dating from the time I finished my book *Understanding Iran*. I will not, however, burden this comment with more than a perhaps crucial few citations.

both MI6 and Mossad. The authors of the Paper acknowledge this, but I fear that the non-specialist reader will be left with the impression that Iran already possesses nuclear weapons since he or she will have been given that impression over and over again in media reportage.

Another example: the authors' second point in "Shared Understandings" is that "Iran has twice in the past attempted to expand its nuclear program secretly [and its actions are characterized by] evasive responses to questions about the past record of deception [and its regime has prevented the IAEA from gaining] full access to Iran's military facilities. "The choice of words – "secretly," "evasive" and "deception" – suggest, subliminally at least, that the Iranians are wily, deceitful people who cannot be trusted. If so, then anything short of war will be unavailing. The "onion" should be sliced.

A more balanced statement would indicate, *on the negative side*, that no nuclear power has opened its facilities to inspection during the period of acquisition and few have done so even after acquisition. To my certain knowledge (as the Member of the Policy Planning Council responsible for the Middle East and cleared for all nuclear information) , Israel would not allow even its close ally, the US, to access any information on its nuclear-weapons facility at Dimona in the 1960s. Nor, of course, did China and the USSR open their facilities or allow observation of their tests – which is why we built the U-2 spy plane. India, Pakistan and Israel, to take just those in Iran's "neighborhood," have not joined the NPT, and Israel does not even admit to having nuclear weapons. It is thought to have 300 to 400. India and Pakistan each are thought to have over a hundred.

On the positive side, after the Shah joined the NPT, this regime has stayed in. It also has allowed what must be admitted to be a surprising degree of access to its facilities, even when its government believed that the inspectors from the IAEA were infiltrated by intelligence "moles" from the CIA (*Christian Science Monitor,* April 12, 2012. Scott Peterson, "Iran nuclear talks Why the trust gap is so great: Part of the reason for Iran's distrust lies in the CIA's infiltration of a UN weapons inspection team in Iraq in the 1990s.") and when it believed that the inspectors were gathering information to be used in an attack on Iran.

These and other problems of context and balance, could have been, at least in part, ameliorated if not solved by short factual asides. For example, on the second point:

"As have all the other states that were acquiring nuclear capacity, including the US, Britain, the USSR, China, India, Pakistan and Israel, Iran sought to restrict outsiders' access to its programs. We believe it should have allowed more. However, it is significant that neither India, Pakistan nor Israel, Iran's neighbors, is a signatory to the NPT nor allows IAEA inspections."

Journalists have frequently quoted Iranian officials, particularly President Mahmoud Ahmedinejad, threatening to "wipe Israel off the map." In fact, what he said was somewhat less bellicose although certainly not friendly: he said that Israel will "vanish from the pages of time." But the chances of understanding between Israel and Iran are little helped by a correction of the translation of his remark because, in reverse, Rabbi Ovadia Yosef, the spiritual leader of Shas, the ultra Orthodox sect which is the fourth largest party in the Knesset, said, (according to *The Jerusalem Post* August 27, 2012, as quoted by IPS correspondent Daniel Luban) "Destroy them God, obliterate them from the face of the earth...wipe them out, kill them." He had earlier proclaimed, "it is forbidden to be merciful to them [Iranians and Lebanese Hizbullah members]. You [the Israeli government] must send missiles to them and annihilate them." Little hope for peace there!

Missing from the Paper are two absolutely critical questions:

First, what is the logic behind Iranian actions? Unless the authors assume that there is no logic, it is important to ask what it is. Otherwise, there is no way to answer the main question posed by this Paper and highlighted in the opening section: what are "the potential benefits of military action?" Or, more pointedly, "will an attack be effective?"

Of course, none of us is privy to the thinking of the Iranian regime, but I suggest that we can infer four probable motivations in Iranian nuclear programing: 1) the Iranians are sensitive to history. In many conversations, officials have mentioned the contrast between what happened to Iraq, which did not have nuclear weapons, and North Korea, which did. Iraq was "regime changed" and nearly destroyed while North Korea was offered an aid program. One does not have to be sophisticated to draw the policy lesson: get a bomb.

2) Iranians feel surrounded by us. They are. In addition to the reinforced 5th Fleet in the Gulf and Arabian Sea, we maintain at least 35 bases near Iran's frontier. No part of Iran is more than an hour's flight time from one or more of these bases or from a carrier. (That is, roughly the distance from New York to Washington.) In addition we have remote bases such as Diego Garcia in the Indian Ocean and others in various parts of Europe and the Continental USA. Iranians turn their apprehension into a joke: "There are just two countries in the world that have only the US as their neighbor. The other one is Canada." We have the means to mount a devastating attack at any moment.

3) Do we have the motivation? The Iranians would have to be deaf and blind not to notice that day after day for years our government, members of the Congress, the media and powerful lobbies and advisers to our government such as the Zionists, the neoconservatives and the Christian Right, have kept up a steady drumbeat urging an attack on Iran.

4) More than just words, we have acted in ways that buttress the Iranian fear of attack. (Scores of articles substantiate this statement. The most complete account is the July 7 & 14, 2008 *New Yorker* piece by Seymour Hersh, "Preparing the Battlefield." More recent is David Rohde's September 19, 2012 article in *Foreign Policy*, "The Obama Doctrine: Obama's Secret Wars.") Iranians have been invaded and attacked by our drones, Special Forces and proxy terrorist unitswhich we have trained, paid and armed. With cyberwarfare, we and/or the Israelis have invaded their most protected areas to destroy their equipment. And, in a program of assassination, in which we were almost certainly complicit, senior Iranian officials have been murdered. The Iranian regime has been only sporadically successful in defending itself and its territory.

Sooner or later, as the former CIA director, General Michael Hayden, has pointed out (cited by Josh Rogin in the January 2012 *Foreign Policy*), senior officials of the US government concluded that if we keep hitting them, we are going to drive the Iranians to acquire nuclear weapons.

Short of acquiring weapons, the Iranian regime has at least three other reasons to acquire a nuclear capacity. 1) There are about 800,000 Iranians with cancer, to treat which they believe they desperately need atomic isotopes. No government, even a theocracy, can afford to ignore the urgent demand of such a large bloc of its citizenry. 2) Today's regime realizes that the Shah was right, oil at $100 a barrel is too valuable to be burned. So, Iran wants to do what France, Germany, England, Japan and other countries have done (and what Saudi Arabia and the UAE have announced plans to do), generate electricity by nuclear power. 3) Finally, as I have mentioned, under both the Shah and the Ayatollahs, Iranians are determined to become part of the "First World." They believe they must access nuclear technology to lift themselves out of poverty and "underdevelopment."

The second critical question, also not addressed in the Paper, is what are the political, legal and strategic paramenters around possible American policy?

The issue of threat has been extensively, if not always intelligently, dealt with in dozens of media accounts in recent years. It is a centerpiece in both the 1945 UN Charter and in the legal doctrine that emerged from the Nuremberg Trials. Both emphasize prohibitions of threat and recourse to war. The UN Charter was ratified by the US Senate and so is embodied in American law. That legal doctrine, which is or should be binding on us as well as on the Iranians, has been flouted for years, but devotion to law is something Americans would be wise not to give up because, as President Eisenhower memorably put it, "There can be no peace – without law. And there can be no law -- if we were to invoke one code of international conduct for those who oppose us and another for our friends." Onwards from Eisenhower's time, devotion to law has been periodically reasserted.

More dramatically, the American devotion to the rule of law has periodically been breached. As a consequence, the strategic strength of America has been weakened by the growing belief among peoples not only in Iran but also more generally among the 1.6 billion Muslims – a quarter of the world's population -- that America has become a rogue state, unbound by law and in its ruthless pursuit of hegemony a determined enemy of their religion. (A Doha Institute poll of Muslims in 12 countries found that 22% of the 16,000 responders thought the US was their major threat.) The widespread and violent reaction in the last few days to a silly film on the life of Muhammad is an indication of deep anger and disillusionment. I am sensitive to this, beyond what the polls tell me, because during my professional lifetime over the last half century, I often traveled freely in areas I can no longer safely visit.

And it is not only among Arabs or even Muslims that American rectitude has been called into question: Further afield, the Chinese government this year allowed the publication of an article in which an official of the Ministry of Commerce commented on US policy by saying "the numerous economic sanctions initiated by the United States... [will] create a serious humanitarian disaster... At the beginning of the founding of New China, the United States imposed a comprehensive trade embargo on China... The Chinese people have strong feelings about the humanitarian suffering caused by sanctions, and will never agree to impose the same suffering on the innocent people of other countries." (*Renmin Ribao*, January 12, 2012) India also is disinclined to follow American policy toward Iran and keeps buying Iranian oil despite the US push for boycott. (*Juan Cole Blog*, March 18, 2012, "India Trade Delegation Bucks US Sanctions on Iran.") More generally, the 120 nations that are members of the non-aligned movement, meeting in Tehran this month, unanimously criticized current American policy "to isolate and punish Iran."

Perception that America has lost "the hearts and minds" of a large part of the world has, apparently, begun to be shared – and feared – by Americans. Many now believe that despite our massive allocation of resources to "security," we are less secure today than we were just a few years ago. (As former CIA officer Haviland Smith wrote in the September 22, 2011 *Nieman Watchdog*, "America, 10 years after 9/11, is as vulnerable as ever."

Thus, the legal issue is neither abstract nor peripheral. It is apt to be central in the coming years and probably even earlier, should the decision be made to attack Iran.

Can America afford to put the legal and moral issues aside? I think not. One of the lessons the last half century of the history of Iran offers is that strength is not solely to be measured by the number and skill of soldiers or the amount and power of their equipment but also by a *perception* of rectitude. In 1979, Iran's army was regarded as world-class, but it collapsed before a shot was fired. Today, Iran's army is certainly not world-class but if, under threat or in the heat of action, Iranians rally to protect their religion, their way of life and their nation, or even the regime, outside military action may prove, as in Vietnam, Iraq and Afghanistan, more a danger to us than an effective policy toward them. I do not find this issue adequately dealt with in the Paper although the signers agree that "an attack would strengthen the Iranian regime instead of weakening it…"

The perception of just action or unjust aggression obviously impacts on another issue which the authors wisely do bring forward – an exit strategy. How to get out and leave behind more than ruins and graves should also be a critical determinant of evaluation of the military "option." And it should be considered before rather than after the action.

What is likely? The answer we get from previous wars varies according to the level of social and political organization. We "cut and ran" from Vietnam, famously flying out the last evacuees by helicopter, but we did not leave chaos behind. That was not because of what *we* did but because, having won the war, *the Viet Minh* had in place a shadow government that was ready to take over. We are finding the idea of getting out of Iraq and Afghanistan increasingly difficult to imagine because our military action shattered not only the *political structure* of the two countries but also their *social composition* (with massive exodus) and their *social "contract"* (with the violent displacement of the traditional Sunni Muslim order by a Shi'a Muslim order in Iraq and the imposition of a Westernized puppet kleptocracy in Afghanistan which has not been able to overcome regionalism or even to control its own security forces).

Weighed in the scales of these experiences what might lie ahead in Iran?

Optimists would note that the overthrow of Prime Minister Mossadegh in 1953 was followed immediately by the re-imposition of the Shah. If the present government were gravely weakened or overthrown during an invasion, is there a potential replacement? The Shah managed to stay in power 26 years. Would a successor to the current government be capable of a similar feat of longevity? Or at least stay long enough to obscure our withdrawal? Of course, we cannot know. But we can both assess the probabilities and make some reasonable guesses on the forces that would shape whatever political system survives. For what it is worth, my hunch is that a successor regime, perhaps after an initial period of chaos following a war with the West, would seek, probably even more actively than the present government, to acquire a complete nuclear capacity including weapons. As I have mentioned, this was also the opinion of the CIA under President Bush.

A successor regime, which the neoconservatives hope will be different, would be, in my opinion, almost certainly be much like the current regime. Whether I am right or wrong in this prediction, few can doubt that it would be committed to an active nuclear policy. Right, Left and Center, religious and secular, regime and dissidents, Iranians want to be part of the "First World." It is difficult to imagine a government that would just bow its head to the West. Consequently, the stated objective of ensuring that Iran *never* acquires a nuclear bomb, which in practical terms means its giving up virtually all knowledge of and ability to produce even non-military nuclear power, is, in my opinion, highly unlikely.

So, to get Iran to give up the nuclear option, even for the short term, what would have to be done?

The authors, rightly in my opinion, believe (pages 9-10) "that objective is unlikely to be achieved through a military action that relies on aerial strikes supplemented by cyber attacks, covert operations, and perhaps special operations forces." They predict that a military assault might set Iran back from an attempt to become a nuclear power – which our huge and lavish intelligence organization tells us they have so far *not* decided to become – perhaps for up to four years. Even achieving this relatively modest result might require repeated attacks and almost certainly would require the continued positioning of forces around Iran. Indeed, as the authors of the Paper and other commentators have observed, the attempt to control Iran might require the occupation of most or all of the country by American__ground forces . It is perhaps worth remembering that putting ground troops into Asia is a move that General Douglas MacArthur thought was madness.

Why? Because the occupation of Iran would almost certainly provoke insurgency.

Iran today has forces, many of which are already trained, equipped and ready for guerrilla resistance, thus the ability to mount what would be for us an unwinnable and ruinously costly war. As the Paper's authors write, "Given Iran's large size and population, and the strength of Iranian nationalism, we estimate that the occupation of Iran would require a commitment of resources and personnel greater that what the U.S. has expended over the past 10 years in the Iraq and Afghanistan wars combined."

We should try to estimate exactly what that statement means.

Although many of the costs of those two wars have been disguised, obscured or unreported, we are now beginning to get an overall view. It is horrifying. US dead in Iraq and Afghanistan amount to at least 7,000; wounded, to at least 100,000 plus almost half a million brain damaged or otherwise partially incapacitated soldiers who will require long term medical and financial support. Due to the analysis of Joseph Stiglitz and Linda Blimes, we can, at least, discuss monetary costs. Using standard accounting measures, Iraq and Afghanistan have so far cost perhaps as much as $6 trillion dollars or more than a third as much as our national debt.

The cost of destruction in Iraq and Afghanistan has so far not even been guessed. The single battle of Fallujah was a small-scale Stalingrad with the city reduced to rubble. The figures for casualties are impossible to add accurately, but about 3 million casualties would not be far off with wounded perhaps that many or more. Additionally, about 3 million Iraqis (of whom 1.3 million are in Syria) and 3 million Afghans (of whom 1 million are in Iran) fled their countries.

So, if the Iran Paper is accurate in its prediction, an attack on Iran might lead to the displacement, grievous wounding or death of 12 million or so Iranians and a monetary cost to Americans of an amount perhaps as large as the current American debt of c. $15 trillion.

Even if these figures are exaggerated and the cost would be half that much, could the US, as rich and powerful as it is, afford a war on Iran? Given our already large debt – itself unsustainable in the opinion of some economists and many politicians -- it is at least problematical that, America could borrow enough to carry out a war policy toward Iran. Worse, current lenders might call a part of their existing loans.

In addition to these human and material costs would almost certainly be what might be called "foreign policy costs." The Paper's authors believe, and I agree, that "Iran would retaliate, costing American lives; damaging U.S. facilities in the region; and affecting U.S. interests in Iraq, Afghanistan, the Gulf, and elsewhere. Iran would draw on its extensive conventional rocket capability and IRGC anti-ship missiles, small submarines, fast attack boats, and mine warfare in the Gulf. Iran might attempt to close the Strait of Hormuz [through which passes about 20% of the world's energy] and cause a significant spike [-- some analysts predict $200 or more/barrel --] in oil prices..." This alone would cause chaos. "Gas[oline] prices would soar, economic recovery would stall worldwide, and European nations now struggling to deal with unprecedented unemployment levels would watch the eurozone collapse..." (wrote the former CIA officer Philip Giraldi in September 3, 2012 *The American Conservative*.)

.

Armchair generals have spoken as though the war could be managed in a sort of "surgical" fashion and contained to a small area of Iran. "A targeted U.S. operation need not threaten Tehran in such a fundamental way," wrote one analyst about regime change. "To make sure it doesn't and to reassure the Iranian regime, the United States could first make clear that it is interested only in destroying Iran's nuclear program, not in overthrowing the government." As the bombs rain down, Iranians are likely to miss this delicate distinction! (This fantasy is laid out and advocated by Matthew Kroenig (in the January/ February issue of *Foreign Affairs*, "Time to Attack Iran. Kroenig was partially countered by Colin H. Kahl in the next issue.) But those who have seen war know that it is always unpredictable and, that once begun, it is likely both to become less controlled -- Kroenig has obviously not read Tolstoy or Stendhal on the uncontrollability of warfare -- and to spread.

Consider just Iran's "neighborhood." We know that the Lebanese Shi'a political movement, Hizbullah, has a large rocket force – said to number 40,000 to 50,000 – targeted on Israel. (*Time*, August 31, 2012, Karl Vick and Aaron J. Klein, "Exclusive: U.S. Scales-Back Military Exercise with Israel, Affecting Potential Iran Strike.") Hizbullah's rockets are said to be relatively primitive and inaccurate, and Israel is believed to have the latest counter-missile equipment, but in such numbers, it is difficult to believe that they would not do considerable damage. Syria, also, would probably be dragged into the fray since it has a mutual defense treaty with Iran. Its rocket force is believed to be much more modern and accurate. The Israeli government is said to be taking civil defense measures such as issuing gas masks and checking out shelters, but is anticipating at least 500 casualties. (The estimate of Defense Minister Ehud Barak) but others, including the former Director of Israeli Intelligence Meir Dagan, believe that an attack on Iran would precipitate a "regional war that would endanger the state's existence." (*IPS*, February 4, 2012, Gareth Porter, "U.S. Leak on Israeli Attack Weakened a Warning to Netanyahu.") In Iraq, also, we should anticipate attacks on the 16,000 American soldiers, officials and private citizens still there. In Baghdad alone, there are several thousand Americans who would be virtual hostages.

In retaliation for Israeli, American and proxy assassinations and other acts of aggression, the Iranians have begun to mount their own state terrorism.

So far, they have not been so successful as the Israelis and the Americans, but in the event of full-scale war, they and their allies and coreligionists could probably make life very uncomfortable for us and our allies. Either directly from Iran or from Lebanon, Bahrain and Iraq, *jihadis* or *fida'is* (warriors of the faith) would be able to hit targets in many areas of the Middle East and beyond. As one able and experienced commentator put it, "A US or Israeli attack on Iran would turn that regional maelstrom into a global firestorm." (The *Guardian*, Dec 8, 2011, Seumas Milne, "War on Iran has already begun. Act [to stop it] before it threatens all of us.") I do not think that the Paper took this "cost" sufficiently into account.

The Paper takes note of the belief by some commentators that Iran might not retaliate for an attack. I find this wishful thinking to be a dangerous fantasy.

I base my opinion, in part, on a politico-military war game run by the US government in the Pentagon in the aftermath of the Cuban Missile Crisis (in which I played a minor role). In the ensuing game, I was the political member of "Red Team." When confronted with a "Blue Team" provocation – a devastating attack on a Russian city – we opted for general war. (I discuss this episode in my book *Understanding Iran*.) While Red Team realized that such retaliation was not in "our" national interest, we also realized that we could not survive as a government or even as individuals if we failed to act.

I feel sure that the members of the Iranian regime would reach a similar conclusion. And, even if personal survival were not their main motivation, I cannot see how they could simply turn the other cheek after what would be a devastating and humiliating attack. In short, the mistake in this wishful thinking scenario, as I pointed out in the 1963 Soviet-American game, is to confuse the "interest of state" with the "interest of government." Those interests are separate and are sometimes in conflict. When they are, history shows that the interest of government usually predominates. Let me consider this in the Iranian context:

The inevitable harm done by the attack on Iran will leave the population embittered, wounded, grieving, and probably without adequate food and shelter. (Dozens of reports and predictions paint a picture of the death of whole sectors of the population with near nuclear levels of devastation. For example, 2010 *Oxford Research Group*, "Military Action Against Iran: Impact and Effects.") Iran's Shi'a Islam is acutely sensitive to victimhood. The martyrdom of Iran's "patron saint," Husain, the grandson of the Prophet, 1,400 years ago is still today the most vivid emotional experience of Iranians. The casualties of the decade of war with Iran are living memories. But these are relatively remote in comparison to what would happen in the event of a modern blitzkrieg. Misery would shape the ruins. The influence of the radical right wing, already strong, would be greatly increased. The path to political reform would be blocked. And not only the extremists but a far larger slice of the Iranian population would certainly demand that whatever government survives – or emerges -- do everything in its power (or perhaps even beyond *its* power) to acquire a nuclear weapon. As the writers of the Paper correctly set out, "…a U.S. attack on Iran would increase Iran's motivation to build a bomb…" Under these changed circumstances, it is not beyond imagination that another nuclear state – Pakistan? North Korea? Even India? -- might be willing to help it.

Finally, on the issue of cost, I am increasingly worried about the impact of an exhausting, fear-inspiring and probably lingering war on American mores and civil liberties. Every war, even short and successful wars, have cost us some of our freedom and our trust in one another. In the aftermath of the Revolutionary War, the "Alien and Sedition Act" nearly poisoned the new republic; in the Civil War, Lincoln suspended the most precious piece of the heritage of English Common Law, the right of *habeas corpus;* in the aftermath of the First World War, the Palmer Raids were an obscenity that most Americans wished to forget; during the Second World War, the incarceration of American citizens of Japanese descent has left lingering scars; and during the Cold War, McCarthyism made us suspect and turn against one another. Today, as Dana Priest (*Top Secret America*) and Chris Hedges (*War is A Force that Gives Us Meaning*) warn us, we are rapidly turning our country into the "security" state of George Orwell's nightmare.

I can only imagine – and dread – what the result of a war on Iran would be. The cost in our liberty would at best be great and might even be fatal.

The Paper does not even consider this cost.

The bedrock of our political system is the Constitution. Declaring war is not the prerogative of the president but of the Congress. Past presidents have flouted this provision partly by the fiction that military action is not war. Presidents Bush and Obama have precedent for their actions. But, over our relatively short history, we have seen that succeeding generations have been horrified by what their forbearers did to weaken our national purpose. We have not reached the "end of history," and I believe we will eventually – hopefully soon – recognize we are on the brink of a wrong turn.

Embodied in American law are two major treaties: the 1928 Kellogg-Briand Pact which was ratified by the US Senate by a vote of 85 to 1 and the 1945 United Nations charter which was ratified by the US Senate by a vote of 89 to 2. These treaties aimed to avoid war by requiring negotiated settlement of international disputes and by prohibiting the threat or use of force. Passed by the Senate, they became binding American law. (Francis Boyle, Professor of International Law at the University of Illinois, personal communication of July 29, 2012, "...as a ratified treaty the UN Charter is the Supreme Law of the Land under Article VI of the US Constitution." Also see Richard Falk, "Why not Get the Law and Politics Right on Iran?" *The Chronicle of Higher Education*, April 6, 2012.) In turn, they formed the basis of the so-called Nuremberg Doctrine which was the centerpiece and proudest achievement of our defeat of Nazism.

In summary, these fundamental agreements hold that the threat or use of force against the territorial integrity or political independence of any state, except in clear instances of self-defense, ranks as a war crime. Since Iran cannot possibly threaten the United States, it is at least arguable that the military option is illegal.

This point was made clear by one of the signers of the Paper, former staff director of the National Security Council, Zbigniew Brzezinski. In the April 25, 2006 *International Herald Tribune* he wrote: "In the absence of an imminent threat...the attack would be a unilateral act of war. If undertaken without formal Congressional declaration, it would be unconstitutional and merit the impeachment of the President. Similarly, if undertaken without the sanction of the UN Security Council either alone by the United States or in complicity with Israel, it would stamp the perpetrator(s) as an international outlaw(s)...[Moreover,] an attack on Iran would be an act of political folly."

Another signer of the paper, a former *New York Times* editor and former president of the Council on Foreign Relations, Leslie Gelb wrote (in the January 17, 2012 *Daily Beast*) "We're doing this terrible thing all over again. As before, we're letting a bunch of ignorant, sloppy-thinking politicians and politicized foreign-policy experts draw "red line" ultimat. As before, we're letting them quick-march us off to war. This time their target is Iran."

We must carefully consider that what we do in the future may well have multiple and unforeseen costs that we cannot afford and remain a nation of free citizens respected by the whole world.

So what are the **alternatives to an attack on Iran?** I suggest these are the major categories:

1) **Negotiation.** Former Secretary of State, General Colin Powell, has said, "I think ultimately the solution has to be a negotiated one." (Quoted by Tony Karon in *The National*, April 4, 2010) But each side deeply distrusts the other. Thus, so far at least, negotiation has been sterile. As the Iranian-American commentator, Trita Parsi has written (*The Diplomat*, July 21, 2012), "...a long series of miscalculated escalations have brought the two states to the current deadlock. Iran and the United States are entrapped in a paradigm of enmity...both assume the worst about the other's intentions. The 'other' embodies almost pure evil [and] this mindset has created a self-fulfilling prophecy [thus] information that appears to vindicate the mistrust has been seized upon, while data that contradict it have been dismissed, neglected or disbelieved."

The record shows that the United States has been at least as obstructive as the Iranians. *The New York Times* commentator, Nicholas D. Kristof, summarized the American side in "Hang up! Tehran is calling," (*International*

Herald Tribune, January 22, 2007): "In 2003, Iran sent the United States a detailed message offering to work together to capture terrorists, to stabilize Iraq, to resolve nuclear disputes, to withdraw military support for Hezbollah and Hamas, and to moderate its position on Israel, in exchange for the United States lifting sanctions. Some diplomats liked the idea, but administration hawks rejected it at once...the State Department sent a cable to the Swiss ambassador in Tehran, who looks after U.S. interests in Iran, scolding him for even forwarding the package to Washington."

More recently in 2010, with the intense diplomatic help of Turkey and Brazil, Iran agreed to what was essentially President Obama's proposal on swapping nuclear fuel. Secretary of State Hillary Clinton pressed ahead on sanctions. Parsi again, "...Tehran read that as evidence that Obama's true intent was to sanction Iran regardless of what compromises Iran would agree to." Pointedly, Parsi asked, "Can Washington take 'yes' for an answer?"

On its side, the American government in both the Bush and the Obama administrations has viewed Iranian actions that seem to favor negotiation as ploys to delay action while Iran secretly moves to acquire a nuclear weapon. This interpretation has been vigorously pushed by the current Israeli government under Prime Minister Netanyahu.

Two men who experienced personally the low point in Iranian-American relations, when they were taken hostage, the chargé d'affaires and the chief political officer of the US embassy in Tehran, Bruce Laingen and John Limbert, warned (*Christian Science Monitor* January 17, 2012), that "America should not paint itself into a rhetorical corner. American presidents have said that a nuclear-armed Iran is 'unacceptable.' So, presumably, is a nuclear-armed Pakistan, India, or North Korea. The Berlin wall was also unacceptable. In all these cases, however, Americans remained smart and did not become captive to their own rhetoric." The message is that we should keep trying to create a "negotiating climate." To do so, we not only need to tone down our rhetoric but also to stop our harmful actions.

2) Keeping Iran in poverty and pain through what Secretary of State Hillary Clinton called "crushing sanctions."

Without going into detail, the record shows that sanctions – which were tried against the Mossadegh government in the 1950s and frequently implemented since the 1979 Revolution -- do not necessarily bring about beneficial change. As the former head of the London-based International Institute of Strategic Studies and current head of the German Institute for International Security Affairs, Christoph Bertram, wrote (*Centre for European Reform Bulletin #59*) "Sanctions will not work." They hurt the country's poor but not its rulers. And they create hatred. So, usually, they cause a nationalist reaction which is exactly what they were intended to stop. Moreover, they stifle the thrust of domestic reformers to bring about change. (See Thomas Endbrink, "Iranian Opposition Warns Against Stricter Sanctions, " *The Washington Post,* Oct 1, 2009.)

3) Weakening the Iranian state by acts of subversion and terror.

I have briefly described (above) what we have done to try to weaken the Iranian state by actions short of invasion. Subversion has not worked; our covert, violent acts have simply exacerbated relations and inflamed mistrust. "In March 2009, Iran's Supreme Leader Ayatollah Ali Khamenei publicly warned the Obama administration that Iran has intercepted communications between U.S. officials and *Jundallah* militants. (Flynt and Hillary Mann Leverett, *www.RaceForIran.com* November 3, 2010). 'Bandits, terrorists, and murder[er]s are in touch with American officers in a neighboring country,' he said. '[The Americans] say, 'let's negotiate. Let's start relations…[But] Change has to be real. You change and we shall change as well.'" Then in November 3, 2010, the US did designated *Jundallah* a terrorist organization. Unfortunately, just a few days ago it removed the listing of another terrorist organization, *Mojahedin-e Khalq.*

4) Since "pin pricks" have not worked, what about invasion? Leave aside the issues of cost and legality (which I have touched on above) and focus on effectiveness. As Milt Bearden, who ran the anti-Soviet CIA operations in Afghanistan, warned, *(International Herald Tribune,* February 7, 2007) "…in the past century, no nation that has started a major war has ended up winning it. Moreover, in the last 50 years, no nationalist-based insurgency against a foreign occupation has lost…" This should be a sobering observation. I find

that practically all those who know Iran and/or have studied the Vietnamese, Iraqi and Afghan wars agree with it. In my book *Violent Politics*, I show it in a dozen insurgencies.

5) Allowing Iran to acquire the bomb. If none of the other options has, or will, work in an acceptable fashion at acceptable cost, we may not have any choice but to endure the inevitable, eventual result, as we have done with the USSR, China, India, Pakistan, Israel and North Korea. What are the dangers and is there any conceivable benefit?

I see two dangers: first, Israel may unilaterally strike Iran. It could not "win" according to the Israeli Defense Force Chief of Staff, Noam Sheizaf who said "Israel has no military option in Iran. (*http://972mag.com/yedioth-idf-chief-of-staff-told-us-israel-has-no-military-option-in-Iran/YediothAhronoth* Newspaper: February 4, 2011), But it could begin a war that would almost inevitably drag in America.

Second, if Iran actually acquires a nuclear weapon, doing so may stimulate other countries (Saudi Arabia? The UAE? Egypt?) to follow. The spread of nuclear weapons should be avoided as much as possible. In my opinion, which I should admit was much formed by my experience in the Cuban Missile Crisis, nuclear weapons anywhere are a danger to people everywhere. So a wise policy would aim at disarmament. This, indeed, was the US policy 30 years ago. At the behest of the US, the UN Security Council passed Resolution 687 in 1981 mandating the establishment "in the Middle East a zone free from weapons of mass destruction and all missiles for their delivery." (Phyllis Bennis of the Institute for Policy Studies, private communication, January 16, 2012).

Despite the finding of a Brookings Institution Saban Center poll showing that "by a ratio of two to one, Israelis support an agreement that would make the Middle East a nuclear-free zone, (Noted by the then Saudi Foreign Minister Turki bin Faisal, private letter to Marina Ottaway on January 15, 2012, *turki@kff.com*.). But, no Israeli regime would give up its nuclear weapons so long as it has a monopoly.

The remaining policy option will occur in the inevitable change in the "context." That is, when sooner or later, in war or "peace," Iran also acquires a nuclear weapon capacity. At that point, a "grand bargain" including joint disarmament would be in Israel's interest, and a wise Israeli government would seek, at least, to explore it. So would a wise American government. The consequences of that recognition might be the best chance we have to avoid the tragedy of war in which all the dangers I have described above might come to pass.

September 23, 2012

CHAPTER 13

THE SYRIAN MAELSTROM

Turning from the danger of war in Iran to the horror of war in Syria requires a change of gears. I found this a difficult psychological jump. It was aided for me when Ambassador Chas Freeman kindly sent me Leslie Gelb's article on "How to save Syria from Al Qaeda." (*The Daily Beast*, February 24, 2013) Having profited long ago from Gelb's editing of The Pentagon Papers, I read his piece with care. Some of what Gelb wrote is similar to what a few of us have been saying for many months; much is not. Essentially what he advocates is that we should focus our attack on the more radical of the insurgents while aiding with non-lethal supplies their conservative Muslim counterparts. That appears unambiguous, but Gelb has left out what seem to me crucial aspects of the Syrian dilemma. So let me broaden the issues he raises and think through them with you.

Press reports out of Syria have focused almost entirely on day-to-day combat as seen from the side of the forces opposing the government. Many of the reports do not stand up under careful scrutiny. But, judged as a media "event," the insurgents long ago won the war.

Since the insurgents have obviously not won, those governments in the Middle East and Europe that deplore the regime of Bashar al-Assad have sought means to help them. Conservative Arab states, particularly from the Gulf, have poured arms and money into Syria. Covertly, the CIA and other intelligence services have not only helped the rebels but have set up camps to train them on how to use weapons and what tactics to employ. In effect, they have tried to copy the insurgent campaign organized in Afghanistan against the Russians in the 1980s.

Not surprisingly, they face the same dilemmas their predecessors faced in Afghanistan. First, they do not know much about the rebels, but what

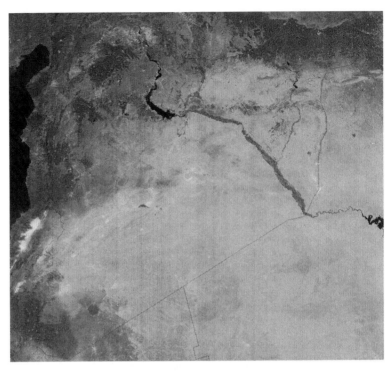

Syria NASA Satellite image

they have learned shows that the rebels are bitterly divided among themselves in hundreds of mostly tiny groups. Some seem to be "moderates" while others are certainly extremists. Their objectives and their means of action vary from secular nationalism to uncompromising religious fanaticism. Many are not Syrians but come from all over the world to act out in Syria their cause Indeed, a striking aspect of the "Syrian problem" is that it assembles so many outside actors and interests -- ranging from Russia through Iran and Iraq to the largest political faction in Lebanon on the side of the existing regime and on the side of the rebels including an unlikely coalition of the conservative Gulf states, Israel, America and the European Union.

Can any sense be made of the Syrian maelstrom?

To put the question in policy terms, does it make sense to offer solutions to the Syrian maelstrom before we really understand it. More pointedly, what are the essential features of each of the participants, their objectives and fears, their strengths and weaknesses and their conflicting beliefs? I think we are far from answering such basic questions so in this essay, I will attempt to analyze these complex and often obscure issues.

I begin with what the press portrays as the line up of actors and issues. Who are the actors and what are they fighting about.

It would be convenient to think of the war as being about simple objectives. Generally, that is what the press accounts have given their readers. The Assad regime wants to stay in power and the rebels want to throw it out. There is, of course, some reason behind that "macropolitical" view, but as I shall point breaks down into numbers of "micropolitical" issues, causes and justifications.

Broadly speaking, the two principal adversaries are the regime that has ruled Syria for the past 32 years and the hundreds of separate and often mutually hostile groups of rebels. The regime is usually characterized as representing an off-shoot of Islam, the Alawis while the insurgents are portrayed as orthodox (Sunni) Muslims. But, as we shall see, these categories are only approximate. The Assad regime includes large numbers – indeed most of its army – of Sunni Muslim Arabs. It is supported by virtually all of the minorities including the Christian community. So far, only one significant group has managed to be more or less neutral or at least guided by different objectives. That is the Kurdish community, which is also mostly Sunni Muslim, but it has has been attacked by the rebels because they are not Arabs and by the Government because they are using the chaos of the war to try to achieve at least autonomy if not full independence.

Before the war began, the Syrian population was about 23-24 million of whom about 9 in 10 were Muslims. The rest of the resident population was divided among a number of religious and ethnic groups, Orthodox and Catholic Christians, Shiis, Alawis, Ismailis, Kurds, Druze and others. Mixed among them were about half a million refugees from Palestine and roughly the same number from the Iraq war. Today, and at least temporarily, all these numbers are changing. Upwards of 2 million Syrians – and mostly of course among the minority communities -- have fled abroad. Millions more have been displaced from their homes but remain in some part of Syria. In short, it is frivolous to consider the Syrians, as the media usually does, just the "good guys" and the bad.

And Syrians are not the only actors in the war: consider the outsiders and their interests. Begin with neighboring Israel. A weakened, perhaps fragmented formerly "frontline" state which can no longer serve as a source of hope for the Palestinians. This was Israel's goal in the Iraq war and it was achieved. Almost any conceivable outcome of the Syrian conflict will achieve it there.

Meanwhile, in neighboring Lebanon, the society will suffer a deep trauma no matter who "wins." This is particularly likely if the outcome is a continuing epidemic of violence. The fragile consensus among Lebanese Shiis, Sunnis, Druze, Maronites, Greek Orthodox, Greek Catholics, Armenian Gregorians, Armenian Catholics, et al -- held together but apart from one another by what the French scholar Pierre Rondot termed *l'espirit communautaire* -- has already frayed and could erupt in civil war. Indeed, as refugees pour into Lebanon, it is being transformed into virtually a Syrian province.

Defeat of Assad's regime will be welcomed – and has actively been promoted with money, arms and military training for the rebels -- by Jordan, Qatar and Saudi Arabia because, among other reasons, they believe it will enable them to steal the thunder of their own internal oppositions. Bahrain's minority government is already engaged by a sort of "trans-denominational" echo of Syria. Egypt is a special case. While the Muslim Brotherhood regime shares with the Syrian Muslim opposition, at least in theory, a stake in the Islamic political revival, I believe Egyptians will increasingly question and perhaps oppose the regime's affinity with the Syrian Muslim fundamentalists.

On the contrary, Iraq and Iran appear to be fairly solidly in Assad's camp; so a defeat of his regime will perhaps serve to further isolate them from the European-American camp and their conservative neighbors. Understandably, they are trying to prevent that from happening. Russia and China are ambivalent. Their own, long-term interests lead them to give Assad some support. Russian, particularly, would be very disturbed by a Muslim Fundamentalist and aggressive victory that conceivably could disturb the large Muslim minority – about 1 in 6 or 7 of all inhabitants – in the Federation, the Caucasus and the former Soviet Central Asian republics. No Russian government, moreover, would want to be frozen out of the Middle East.

What about America? The remaining neoconservatives in government, the media and a number of "research" organizations want to "regime change" Syria and to redefine or perhaps subdivide the country. But, those of Mr. Obama's advisers who at least partly agreed on the neoconservative line some months ago seem now to be having second thoughts. It apparently has finally dawned on them that, if America continues to fight Muslim fundamentalists almost everywhere else — the latest being Mali -- supporting them in Syria with arms and money may not be smart. So the latest statements and hints out of Washington suggest that they are trying to have it both ways: giving the Syrian dissidents just "non-lethal" help. Doing so, however, will not end the war, but it will solidify the anti-American feelings of both Assad and his opponents and almost inevitably will morph into directly supplying arms and money, as we are encouraging Jordan, Saudi Arabia and Qatar to do. Ultimately, it will probably lead by "policy creep" to American intervention. That could be another trillion-dollar venture.

Let us be realistic: there is no completely satisfactory policy for America at this point except to try to help find a way to end the tragic loss of life and destruction of the country. As the UN negotiator Lakhdar Brahimi has argued, it can only be by negotiation.

What lies behind that assertion? Experience should have taught us that the major objective of any intelligent strategy must be to prevent destruction of people, institutions and both natural and man-made wealth. Destroying is easy. Rebuilding is hard. As we should have learned by now, armed intervention by outsiders is dangerous, costly and often fails; it must be taken only in self defense. That, indeed, is the law of America. Intervention is often advocated only because of the ambitions and fears of politicians and generals. Generals want to exercise their professions, win promotions and gain prestige. Political leaders want to avoid the "Chamberlain analogy," that they failed to act when they could have "won." No leader today wants to "lose" Syria any more than his predecessors wanted to be charged with "losing "China or Vietnam – which of course were never ours to lose. Allowing scope and time for evolution is derided as a "do-nothing policy." Americans tend to leap before looking. 6 of each 10 of us wanted to invade Iraq despite the lack of any threat to America. We began the slide into Mali when few of us even know where it is. In the urgent call for action, we give little thought to what comes after. We should. Rebuilding a shattered *governmental structure* is difficult, costly and slow. Rebuilding a shattered *social structure* is much *more* difficult, much *more* costly and is likely to take at least a generation. So every effort must be made to achieve a ceasefire, use it to foster the formation of a consensus in favor of reform and help to rectify the problems that led to the war. In these processes, the *beneficial* role of outsiders, even the rich and powerful, is limited.

Compare Syria to Iraq to bring into focus these points: Saddam's Iraq was socially and economically more progressive than Assad's Syria. Iraq had launched programs in health, education and social affairs far in advance of other Arab countries. Under Saddam, Iraq was a secular state. Remember that he was enemy number one to Usama bin Ladin who offered to raise troops to fight him. Both regimes rested on the base of minority communities – Sunni Arabs in Iraq and Alawis in Syria. Neither regime, like the Chinese, Saudis, Bahrainis, and others, would tolerate free politics. Assad's Syria was less socially progressive, in part because it was much poorer. But that regime had a remarkable social program including a more encompassing healthcare system than America's and free universal education. Like Iraq, Syria engaged in imprisonment, repressions and torture. That was the regime's ugly face. Usually it did not bother us. We embrace several regimes in other parts of the world whose tyranny is far more egregious than either the Iraqi or Syrian regimes. Tyranny was not their real "sin" in our book.

Focus for a moment on Iraq. The real issue in Iraq, which was seldom discussed at the critical time, was that as long as Saddam's regime survived, the Palestinian people could believe that they had a chance to win independence. To destroy that belief was, of course, the reason the Israelis and their neoconservative allies pushed for regime change. But since they could not publicly justify the invasion by this objective, they brought forward the phony issue of weapons of mass destruction. Behind this shield, the real objective – removing Iraq as a significant Middle Eastern nation-state -- could be accomplished.

To launch the attack, all that was missing was a suitable "trigger." As some of you know, I went out to Baghdad just before the invasion and tried to work out with Deputy Prime Minister Tariq Aziz a way to remove the triggers. Aziz rightly countered my suggestions by saying the Bush Administration was determined on war and nothing the Iraqis could do would stop them. (See my account of our discussion in my collection of essays, *Distant Thunder*. Also see Ray McGovern's review of George Tenet's new book, *At the Center of the Storm* and Valerie Plame Wilson and Joe Wilson's article in the February 27, 2013 *Guardian* on the rush to war.)

So we invaded, regime changed and created lasting chaos. Incidentally, we also cost the lives of hundreds of thousands of Iraqis and destroyed much of the country's infrastructure; our losses include from 2,000 to 4,500 soldiers dead (the numbers are still in dispute) , hundreds of thousands wounded (physically and/or mentally), at least $1 trillion -- perhaps as Joseph Stiglitz and Linda Bilmes have calculated, as much as $3 trillion.

What did these huge costs buy and who gained from them? Ironically, the two strategic "winners" were Israel and Iran. The Israeli objective had been accomplished. The *fahilu'l-Arab* ("champion of the Arabs)" Saddam was gone. So, the Israelis believed or hoped that the Palestinians would finally have to recognize that they must unconditionally surrender. The Palestinians didn't -- in part because Israel had failed to facture Syria into their equation. And the Iranians, who had fought a long and bloody war with Saddam, were equally glad to be rid of him. As a bonus, we virtually gave them Iraq by installing a new regime made up of fellow Shiis, many of whom had spent their adult years in Iran, spoke Farsi as their main language and sought objectives similar to those of their Iranian partners.

For itself, America had only losses, party because it had no coherent strategy and no clear concept of feasible goals. Although much lauded by our military, even the tactics failed. The Sunnis, Saddam's base, were our enemies so we hit them as hard as we could – the destruction of Fallujah became the symbol of our power. But then we got nervous about the Shiis. As was to be expected, they certainly did not share our goals or care for us. To try to keep them in order, we began to arm the Sunni Arab tribesmen and pour out money to rent – we could not buy – their loyalties. They gladly took the money and went their own ways. In urban Iraq, General David Petraeus took credit for his counterinsurgency in reducing inter-communal violence, but the reason for this reduction had little to do with his much publicized program. What happened was that ethnically mixed neighborhoods ethnically cleansed themselves. As the weaker populations were driven out, or eliminated, there were fewer murders because there were fewer targets. We sat on top of this process, thinking we were in control, but in fact we were largely irrelevant. Indeed, we hardly understood what was going on in the country – only one person in our occupation government (my former student Ambassador Hume Horan) was fluent in Arabic and knew Iraqi history and society – and our only tool was the hammer. Finally, we realized we could not restore what we had broken, both the good and the bad. Everywhere, chaos reigned supreme. And so, finally, we packed up and left.

How does this relate to Syria?

With the prejudice of a historian, I believe one must dig into at least the recent Middle Eastern past to answer such questions. Only if we know what has happened can we understand what caused Syrians, who had long lived under repressive regimes, to revolt at this particular time and comprehend the nature of their revolt.

Dought extent from 2006-2009

http://reliefweb.int/sites/reliefweb.int/files/resources/
B76DB80A434B1E3985257607005566BF-map.pdf

We don't have to look far for a cause. From 2006 to 2010, Syria suffered through an unprecedented drought that devastated much of its rural society. Rain averaged less that the bare minimum needed for agriculture and groundwater tables fell so low that farmers could not reach them. Cattle died by the thousands and farmers were forced to eat the see they had put aside to plant in the next season.

But then, like most other governments, the Assad regime didn't do enough of what it could have done to mitigate the damage. Blinded by foolish pride, it did not press hard enough for international aid even in food stuffs. So thousands of frightened, angry, hungry and impoverished farmers flooded into the *bidonvilles*, the slums around the cities. They had lost not only their lands and incomes but also their hope. Hundreds of thousands of Syria's farmers gave up, abandoned their farms and fled to the cities and towns where they had to compete with the refugees Syria had taken in from Palestine and Iraq for almost non-existent jobs and severely short food supplies. Outside observers including UN experts estimated that between two and three of Syria's 10 million rural inhabitants were reduced to "extreme poverty." They became the "tinder" of revolution.

Still Syria did not immediately catch fire. To understand why it did not and also why it eventually did, we need to appreciate the political/ideological/ emotional process that had been occurring all over the Middle East since the Second World War. Look first at Egypt which was the leader.

When outside observers investigated the Egyptian economy at the end of the Second World War, they were shocked to find that Greece, just emerging from years of exploitive and brutal Nazi occupation, could more easily feed Egypt than Egypt, which had not suffered from the war, could help Greece. The long-term and common plight of the Egyptian poor was measured in terms of starvation. As the economist, Doreen Warriner who was sent out by the British government to investigate, wrote, "the conditions of his [the Egyptian peasant's] life are of unrelieved horror... There is no standard of living; anything lower would be death..." Why was this true? Warriner pointed out that the peasantry was "an almost slave population..." with 97% of the farmers owning the same amount of land as the upper ¼ to ½ of 1% of the owners. Britain, still regarding Egypt as the lynchpin of its Middle

Eastern policy, was worried: the Egyptians might revolt and so endanger the then nearly vital Suez Canal and the huge British military base on its banks.

But the Egyptians did not revolt. (I wrote a thesis at Harvard in 1951 trying to explain why and more or less predicted the 1952 *coup d'état*.) They just kept on suffering. Why they did not revolt had, I think, two causes: first, because the Egyptians, unlike today's Syrians, were accustomed to their condition and, second, because they did not have the means, physical or psychological, to revolt. The established forms of social interaction and political accommodation remained intact. More important, the Islam they knew was an otherworldly faith that preached the fatalistic dogma that what is, is God's will.

The only large-scale manifestation of anti-British sentiment had occurred at the end of the First World War. Then a relatively small group of Egypt's privileged class demanded a voice in the Paris Peace Conference to plead the cause of independence. They were easily diverted, squelched or accommodated.

What changed was that after the Second World War, a few of the younger, urban, middle-income civilians and officers tried to understand Egypt's weakness and figure out what to do about it. Even then, what stirred them was less Egypt's domestic malaise than its defeat in the 1948-1949 Palestine war. In the aftermath of that war, a group of young officers and some civilians seized power and turned to nationalism as a panacea. That was the initial message of Nasser's book, *Falsifa ath-Thaurah* (*The Philosophy of the Revolution*).

When Nasser fastened onto nationalism, he strove to make two changes in its program. First, he greatly expanded public education, tried to create a new kind of Egyptian peasant and industrial worker (whom in an earlier essay I called "the new men"), tried to slow down population explosion and began land reform. He quickly learned (as he and I several times discussed) how difficult such programs were to implement. And second, motivated by his experience in the Palestine war, he directed his policy away from *wataniyah* (single territory nationalism) toward *qawmiyah* (pan-Arab nationalism). Soon that policy shattered on two rocks -- the interests of other Arab rulers and the military power of Israel. After being rousingly "unified," Syria and Egypt quickly split and, with the Egyptian Army sucked off into the Yemen war, Nasser overplayed his hand. The Israelis quickly punctured his pretentions. Then, after his death, Sadat and Mubarrak muted both parts of his message and focused on getting rich in Egypt. Corruption reigned supreme.

So the frustrated radicals of the nationalist movement said, "we told you so. Nationalism is superficial. We must entirely recast our society." Socialism seemed to many to provide more effective answers. But, what passed for socialism, little more than a slogan, in turn failed to satisfy. It brought neither power nor dignity. In Egypt and elsewhere the slogan "socialism" just masked greed and corruption. Worse, regimes in Egypt and throughout the Arab World stunted or quashed the growth of institutions – parliaments, the judiciary and the media -- that might have balanced the military and reined in the *nouveaux riches*. With nothing hindering them, these groups merged and took over regimes. Egypt had a new pharaoh. There were princes and kings everywhere, some crowned, many just rich. Nasser's army became a plutocracy; the civilian "new men," like the pashas of old, enriched themselves; and the peasants got nothing but the scraps. Disillusion was pervasive.

Meanwhile in Libya, professing to be revolted by what other Arab rulers were doing, Muammar Qaddafi proclaimed himself Nasser's acolyte. And, to give him his due, he carried out a major program of social and economic reform. Rightly criticized for his regime's corruption and oppression, what caused the revolution was that he carried out the social and economic reforms too well. He turned the backward village of Tripoli (as I had seen it in 1963) into a modern city with electricity, clean water and better housing while giving the people free healthcare and education. In short, he raised the *capacity* of the Libyans. Unintentionally, he also engendered *new political expectations* which, like most rulers in Africa and Asia, he thwarted. Frustrated in their quest for participation and angered by the Libyan "military-profiteering-governmental complex," the Libyans revolted, adding their push to the momentum of "the Arab Spring."

So, disillusioned with nationalism and state socialism but partly empowered by a higher standard of living that failed to satisfy their desire to run their own lives, many began to ask, "what unifying, energizing set of ideas and aspirations was left?" Democracy? Not very likely. New dictatorships? Probably. But for ideological guidance? Only Islam. It is Islamists we now see wherever we look. And not in Syria alone. So let us examine them.

Who are the Islamists? What are their strengths? What are their ideas? Who will follow them? What will they lead their followers to do? We now have a great deal of empirical evidence -- in a widely varying range of societies with differing historical experiences -- on which to draw, yet I find that few scholars and officials are seriously trying to answer these questions. Consequently, we often fly blind into new crises or are guided only by what we want to hear.

Look first at who they are. At the death of Muhammad, the Quran had not been written down. His initial followers were being killed in wars or dying of old age. So attempts were made to piece together the text of the Quran and to gather a record of Muhammad's sayings and actions (much as was done for the New Testament and the "Sayings of Jesus" by early Christians). As in Buddhism, Zoroastrianism and Judaism, these attempts generated disagreements. Memories differed, and because written Arabic displayed only consonants so variations were inevitable. To try to resolve them, within a few years adherents devoted their lives to collecting and commenting. A single text was declared to be canonical and variants were destroyed. But they remained known to scholars and rival leaders. So, over the centuries, a new profession of commentators rapidly proliferated. Their commentaries and resurrections of variants (*tafasir*) of variants were spread by hundreds of religious seminaries which furnished teachers for the world's first major universities and tens of thousands of village schools as well as law courts where judges were expected to be scholars of Islam. At each age, a few of the outstanding scholars (*mujtahids* or *mullahs*, as the Iranians call them) have become the acknowledged leaders of their people. The best known in our times is, of course, the Iranian Shia Ruhollah Khomeini.

So what is the source of the Islamists' strength. Why do any of their peoples follow them? The most obvious answer is that echoing the pronouncements of the *mujtahids*, their lower level colleagues, the teachers in primary and secondary schools, the *muallims*, put into practice the Jesuit saying "Give me a child for his first seven years and I will give you the man." They molded generation after generation all over the Middle East. That is why those in the forefront of the Islamic struggle today are called, and often are, students *(taliban)*. This is not a new development. Over two centuries ago, the ruler of the little principality of Swat in what is now Kashmir raised an army of *taliban* to fight against Sikhs and the British. (André Singer, *Lords of the Khyber*); indeed, throughout Islamic history, students were a ready source of militants since they were of the right age, already assembled in sizeable groups and fired with religious enthusiasm. They remain so today.

Not only to them but also to the general public, I suggest Islamic leaders have four things to offer. The first is a firm, lucid and explicit ideology that especially the poor, rural and formerly-rural urban people find familiar. This is as true of Egypt and Syria as of Afghanistan or Iran. That non-Muslim minorities, the educated and privileged (and we foreigners) find aspects of it "medieval," retrograde or ugly is beside the point. It is the only system left in much of Africa and Asia after the disillusionment with nationalism and state socialism. And, like it or not, it encapsulates the beliefs and practices – many of which are indeed pre-Islamic – of the mass of the populations in these lands.

Second, Islam proclaims itself to be a coherent way of life. Unlike the New Testament and more aimed at governance than the Old Testament, the Quran embodies a system of laws. The system, the *shariah*, is believed by Muslims to be God's ordinance while the laws of the West and the Westernized natives are portrayed as ephemeral, unjust and illegal. That does not necessarily mean that "pure" Islam is either unbending or that it cannot incorporate and so gain strength from aspects of nationalism and socialism. Even its more radical ideologues accommodate outside ideas and practices, but such borrowings are not allowed, at least theoretically, to "contaminate" Islam's beliefs and practices. A century ago, the split between the two caused the creation of parallel legal systems. Renaissance Italy, even under the domination of the Church, did much the same with the adoption of commercial law in parallel to Church law.

The third advantage Islam offers its adherents is that, as practiced by the Muslim Brotherhood among other Sunni and Shia groups, including Hamas, Hizbullah and followers of various groups we lump together as al-Qaida, it embodies a social program that addresses perceived needs: Since all men are brothers (*ikhwan*), they have obligations toward one another. Thus, where Muslim movements hold sway, they usually attempt "grassroots" social programs. More dramatically, they proclaim in action their hostility to regimes they see as corrupt, exploitive and indifferent to their people. The Quran-ordered treatment of mankind as brothers also gives them a way to counter the propensity of an essentially tribal people to fragment. As the great medieval sociologist Ibn Khaldun put it, Islam "turns their faces in the same direction."

The fourth strength of Islam arises from the justification for revolution against the un-Godly. If revolution is justified, it must be won. Struggle is not only morally and legally right but religiously obligatory. And, as Muhammad himself found, there is no surer way to win adherents than struggle for a cause. Thus, becoming a jihadi (a "striver" in God's cause) or a fidai (one who sacrifices himself for a cause) or a mujtahid (a witness to the true faith) is a powerful attraction. So, on entering the field of battle in Syria, such people as soldiers or suicide bombers have sought the approval of religious leaders. Look now briefly at what they believe and what motivates them.

The common word used of revolution-friendly Islam is *salafiyah*. Even native Arabic speakers often would tell you that it means simply "reactionary." But the concept is far more complex. The word *salafi* in classical Arabic means a person who stands both in the rearguard and in the vanguard -- Arabic delights in such contrasts. The logic of the apparent paradox was brought out by the teachings of jurisconsults from the beginning of the "impact of the West." In the Eighteenth century they began to search for means to protect their civilization. Some argued that "real" strength had to be derived from fundamentals as laid out in the Quran and elucidated in the practices of the Prophet and his intimate circle (the *Hadith*). Weakness, they believed, came from the innovations and perversions that encrusted Islam and Islamic society in the long dark ages.

I have suggested elsewhere that the movements of "purification" inspired by such men as the Arabian Ahmad ibn Abdul Wahhab, the Algerian/Libyan Muhammad bin Ali al-Sanusi, the Sudanese Muhammad Ahmad al-Mahdi, the Iranian activist Jamal ad-Din al-Afghani and the Egyptian theologian Muhammad Abduh resembled in this fundamental aspect the movements set off in northern Europe by Luther and Calvin. They shared a belief in the authority of the word of God as set out in the original texts. Their task was to go back to discover the "pure" message. However much they differed, they were in this sense *salafis*. Not only the Muslims but also the Protestant Christians enforced a draconian, Biblically-based legal code, complete with lashings, burnings and stoning to death for such crimes as adultery and blasphemy. Some, like the New England Puritans and the "enlightened" Muslims, eventually relaxed. Others held firm. So I turn to the recent expression of their ideas among Muslims.

The inspiration for the current version of Islamic *salafiyah*, and particularly for its militant wing, has come mainly from the Egyptian, partly-American-educated polemicist and *Alim* (religiously learned man) Sayyid Qutub. Feared as a bigot and a subversive, he spent about twelve years of his life in prison when, at age sixty, he was hanged by President Nasser for sedition. During his life especially in prison, he wrote commentaries (*tafasir*) on the Quran as many clerics have done. But he also wrote widely on early Islamic society, Islamic law and the foibles and failures of Western society. Some of his writings were, judging by the terms of Islamic literature, remarkably innovative. As a group, they have attracted a mass readership throughout the Islamic world and have apparently influenced men as opposed to one another as the leaders of the Taliban, the Saudi Establishment, al-Qaida, the Iranian and Iraqi *ulema* and now the various and competing groups of Syrian militants. His works deserve our attention.

Qutub did not use these words, but I read his works to be motivated by much the same judgment as the secular nationalists: his people are now weak and must find their way to dignity and strength. He differs from the secularists in believing that they can find it only in returning to first principles whereas the secularists wanted to forget the past and rush into Western-style modernity.

Qutub understands this urge and partly, only partly, is prepared to accommodate it. He concedes that the West is materially strong and argues that the East must also become materially strong. That is justified, he points out, because God appointed mankind to be his agents to control and exploit the Earth. But, he argues, Westerners have perverted God's intent. In its blind race toward materialism, Western society has become spiritually weak. It has lost sight of what wellbeing really means. In his view it is precisely the turn away from spirituality that is the great failing of Western culture. It is not just that a life without spirituality is barren – which he concluded from his residence in America – but that it loses the coherence of the whole Divinely-created and -mandated system. The attempt to make up for the loss of spirituality by individual good works or such constructs as participatory democracy are, he believes, wholly inadequate and, worse, they are a false trail leading away from true religion. With them, he argues, there can be no compromise.

Reacting to his period of study and residence in America, he argues against wasteful consumption, perverted sex (which should, he believes, be oriented only toward the birth of children) and greed. Putting together all he found to detest about America, he compared it to the pre-Islamic Arabian period of "ignorance"[of God's way]," *Jahaliyah*, which was reformed through the actions of God's Messenger, Muhammad. In this way, he essentially categorizes the West, not Islam, as the retrograde society. Thus, to move ahead, he argues that today Muslims must reinstate the pattern and practices of the new order created by Muhammad. That is, *salafiyah* is their path: they must go back to the original pattern, Muhammad's community, in order to correct its excesses and move ahead.

As a historian, I have to say that Qutub's reading of Muhammad's new order is not quite what I and other scholars believe the years immediately following the establishment of Muhammad in Yathrib (now known as Madinah) to have been. There was a great deal of dissidence, infighting and greed. Moreover, it lasted only a few years. However, not only for Qutub but also for virtually all Muslims, it was the Golden Age. What really mattered was that, in their view, "pure" Islam was coherent, all-embracing, just, available and God-given.

Moreover, Islam's basic demands were easy to understand: affirmation of the unity of God (*tawhid*) and denial of any sharing (*shirk*) of his majesty; men are not to exploit one another (so taking of interest, *riba*, is forbidden); they are enjoined to help one another (so everyone must pay a welfare tax, *zakat*); all must abide by the law (*shariah*) where explicitly laid out in the Quran or exemplified by the actions and sayings (*hadith*) of the Prophet; Muslims are forbidden to kill one another because they are brothers, (*ikhwan*); if possible, they should perform the pilgrimage (*hajj*) in which as many Muslims from all over the world as possible assemble to express their faith, exemplify their unity and draw strength from one another; and Muslims are commanded to struggle (perform *jihad*) in the cause of God (*fi sabili'llah*) to create the community (*ummah*) He had ordered.

The rules for Muslims were clear. But only for Muslims. Despite the widely held idea that Islam was spread by the sword, Qutub rightly points to the Quranic injunction that *belief* is both personal and free; each man is legally allowed to chose his own way. Thus, the "People of the Book [the Bible]," Jews and Christians, and later, the Hindus, were to be accepted peacefully into the Islamic world as protected communities. Only if what an individual or a group does is deemed detrimental to Islamic society are restrictions to be imposed. This is an issue posed by the Syrian rebellion – have the Alawis – a heretical sect of Islam embodied in an ethnic community – harmed the Islamic community? The Syrian *jihadis* answer that it has. Therefore, suppressing it is legal. If the West supports them, is it too acting illegally and deserves to be fought?

It is the latter point that comes into focus in Western views of militant Islam. If one views the West as an oppressor, which, where they exist, polls indicate that probably most Africans and Asians do, then believing Muslims must target them. As the Quran has it (Surah II/190-193, my translation),

> Fight in the cause of God those who fight against you [that is, defend yourselves], but do not initiate hostilities. Verily God does not love aggressors.
>
> But [if such people are the aggressors] kill them wherever you encounter them and expel them from where they had expelled you, because tyranny is more insufferable than fighting...
>
> And fight them to the death until subversion is no more and the religion of God is established. But if they surrender, do not attack any but the evil doers.

We may take these words as essentially the marching orders of the *jihadi*. For him, the West, its local agents, Israel and such deviants as the Alawis, not Muslims, are the aggressors. They are charged with having dispossessed Muslims from their homelands, oppressed them with tyrannies and attempted to corrupt their faith. So it is moral and legal to fight them, if necessary to the death. Only if they desist can peace come. This battle cry is memorized, along with the rest of the Quran, by young students in tens of thousands of religious schools all over the Islamic world.

If they believe themselves under attack, how can they fight? Obviously, they cannot match the West in armies, tanks, aircraft and most of the sophisticated tools of modern warfare. This is the dilemma faced not only in the Muslim world but all over Africa and Asia as well as, from time to time, in Europe and the Americas (as I have spelled out in my book, *Violent Politics*). Generally speaking, people who believe themselves to be oppressed have found two answers: insurgency and terrorism. Insurgency can be employed when a foreign army is in occupation of a territory and the native people grow to hate it. Then the insurgents can grow to fairly large numbers because they draw support from the people. The insurgents are rarely able to fight set-piece battles but usually rely on hit and run tactics. Many of these will be what we call "terrorism," but terrorism can also be carried out by individuals (such as suicide bombers) and groups of fighters far from their national bases. This was the nature, for example, of the 2003 attacks on the World Trade Center and the Pentagon. It is a tactic that has been employed not only by Muslims but by Christians in America, Jews in Israel, and many other people. It is highly likely to be repeated because it is hard to prevent and often accomplishes the mission of those who employ it.

So where does that leave us today? Are we back to something like the time of the Crusades with Holy War against Islam and a *Jihad* against us? There are many Muslims and Christians who believe so. I do not. I confess that I fall within the category Qutub found to be most dangerous: I believe that the human spirit can be nourished by humanism (*insanniyah*). I also believe that most of Asians and Africans are motivated by relatively mundane things like peace, security, dignity and wellbeing rather than by eschatology. Eschatology will always attract some people and in times of brutal war, massive plague and wide-spread misery, many people. So, evidently, thought must be given to avoiding such events. To me, this suggests two courses of action – a tactic in the short range and a strategy in the long range.

The tactic must be to stop the mayhem in Syria. It is very late to try to do this, but it is still possible. Indeed, in one way or another, it will eventually happen. To speed it up, outsiders must not provide arms to anyone as this will enable the fighting to continue. Negotiation will be difficult because, unlike the Afghan resistance to America but similar to the Afghan resistance to Russia, the Syrian resistance has no unified structure. Moreover, any agreed ceasefire is likely to be violated by the rebels both because their combatants are scattered and not under control and because passions are high. So it will not be clear who can speak for the rebels or enforce what their – usually absent – assumed leader agree to. On the contrary, as long as the Syrian regime stays intact, negotiating with it will be easier. Thus, the aim of some foreign powers, including the United States and the European Union, to regime change it and kill or exile Assad are self defeating. So a truce, the initial step, when achieved must be enforced by a well-funded and adequately manned multinational peace-seeking effort led by members of the Islamic World. Under no circumstances should we or other Western powers intervene. Such intervention will fit exactly in the Quranic injunction quoted above even if, at least initially, it favors the insurgents. It will almost certainly cause splits in both the regime and the insurgents and exacerbate what is already a vicious ethnic/religious genocide.

261

Then, the intelligent strategy must be to stay out of insurgencies wherever they threaten to occur and help to head them off before they start. We should make a high priority of avoiding or ameliorating the actions or conditions that have caused a relatively small portion of the Islamic world to turn to extremism. We must take note of what the affected peoples know well: that they are still suffering from the residue of colonialism. These legacies of the past include poverty and lack of a sense of empowerment. Much of the fault rests on native governments which are often seen as corrupt, tyrannical and unpatriotic. Such attitudes combine with the generally held belief that the West projects force, brutality and tyranny. Particularly against Islamic society. It is demonstrable, I suggest, that these are the "lessons" today's *jihadis* draw from the wars in Iraq and Afghanistan. As the Quranic verses quoted above suggest, they believe that they are the victims not the aggressors.

Changing the nature of our relationship will take time and cannot be hastened by force. A close look at each of the flash points of the last half century or so will reveal that the application of pressure produces a reaction in which extremists flourish. When force is removed, and time is allowed, evolution has a chance. There is much to evolve. So we need to buy time. And we need to use the time intelligently and humanely to everyone's advantage.

March 4, 2013

CHAPTER 14

WHENCE LIBYA?
WHY LIBYA?
WHITHER LIBYA?

Since March 2011 when this essay was written, the civil war in Libya – intensified by American and other foreign interventions against the regime of Muammar Qaddafi – has played out various trends I then anticipated. First was that the regime collapsed. Its collapse did not bring the peace, justice and freedom desired by Qaddafi's enemies. Libyan society slid into anarchy and its previously thriving economy slid into ruin. The crucial oil industry came almost to a standstill and virtually all government services in health and education ceased. Moreover, when the army that Qaddafi had created, drawing heavily on the Saharan nomadic Tuwareg, fled from the insurgents, they nearly overwhelmed the state of Mali (the subject of my next paper). What had happened was that no constructive thought had been given to what could replace the structure of the Qaddafi regime. Or, rather, everyone had thoughts -- and nearly everyone had guns -- but there was no effective reorganization. So the events I have described here continue to dominate the Libyan scene.

Since the Libyan regime was established by a coup d'état in 1969, Americans and Europeans -- with a three-year intermission from 1986 to 1988 -- found it acceptable enough to recognize it, sell it arms and buy its petroleum. In that one interval, on April 15, 1986, the American government under President Ronald Reagan attempted to kill Colonel Muammar Qaddafi by bombing his residence and did wound his wife and killed about 75 Libyans including his adopted infant daughter. Two years later, Qaddafi retaliated by bombing an American airliner. That attack

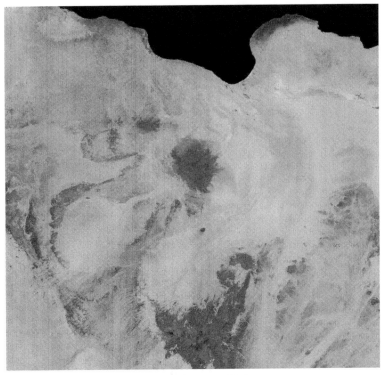

NASA satellite map of Lybia

killed 270 people including 190 Americans, among whom were at least four intelligence officers. These were just the major events; there were many others. Of course, Americans and Libyans took very different views of them. But both sides eventually smoothed over their angers, and relations again became profitable and "correct" on both sides, as they remained until early this year.

So, what is the basis of those attitudes and the causes of those actions? Who are the Libyans anyway? And what is the position of Qaddafi among them? What motivates the Libyans? What governs their action? And what is likely to be the outcome of the revolt, the regime's resistance to it and the Western intervention?

With the prejudice of a historian, I find that seeking answers to these questions requires at least a glance at the past. That is the aim of this essay.

* * *

Let me reveal my prejudice. As it happened, I was in Tripoli a few years before the coup. I had been sent by our government to figure out what we should do with the huge airbase we had rebuilt (from Italian and German days) and were running to train pilots assigned to NATO. Secretary of Defense Robert McNamara wanted to close it down. I concluded that he was right. One look at the base convinced me, as I reported back to the Policy Planning Council, that the base made a coup against the pro-American, decrepit and very corrupt monarchy almost inevitable: on one side of the base were scores of the latest jet fighters and bombers (ours) while across the tarmac were half a dozen puny trainers (theirs). Any Libyan nationalist, particularly a military officer, like then Lt. Muammar Qaddafi, was bound to want, at least, to "level the playing/air field." That is what he eventually did by throwing out the old king and bidding us goodbye.

The Libyans were ecstatic. Those then alive had grown up on tales of generations of greed, violence and humiliating foreign rule. So what was the historical substance of those memories?

For centuries, "Libya" had been a loose collection of poor outposts of the Ottoman Empire on the Mediterranean coast. The Ottoman Turks wisely confined themselves to minimal government. That suited the nomads in Cyrenaica and the deep interior who were opposed to the very concept of government. In the coastal towns and villages, such resistance to Ottoman rule as existed was both feeble and sporadic. While probably not "popular," the Ottoman Turks were at least fellow Muslims and, over the years, the garrison in Tripoli had become fathers of many of the inhabitants. Merchants and artisans occasionally voiced resentment over the level of taxation and abuses of arbitrary administration, but the Libyans had yet to discover that exciting and lethal elixir, nationalism.

Nationalism, however, had already been discovered by other Ottoman populations. One by one, the several Balkan ethnic groups and the Greeks had broken away from the Empire. Everywhere in Europe nationalism was in the air.

265

Among the late comers were the Italians. Only half a century after they had achieved a formal union, the Italians had become assertive nationalists (or, more accurately, revanchists); that is, they had begun to dream about repossessing the Roman Empire. This dream got them into a war in 1911 with the decrepit Ottoman Empire which still occupied much territory that had been Roman.

Right across the Mediterranean – which the Italians were coming to think of as our sea, *mare nostra* -- was the collection of Ottoman port-towns. At that time, few outsiders knew anything about them, but Italian antiquarians thought that in Roman times, at least some of them had been agriculturally rich. Led by this dubious view of history, Italian politicians saw them as answers to the quest for imperial glory for themselves and agricultural land for the poverty-stricken Italian peasants. By the early years of the 20th century, Libya had become an Italian national obsession.

The other European states, particularly Britain and France, were slightly more realistic. While they were trying to turn similar imperial dreams into reality elsewhere in Africa and Asia, they had no serious objections to an Italian push into a more or less empty piece of North Africa between Britain's Egypt and the Sudan on the east and France's Tunisia, Algeria, Morocco and central Africa (modern Niger and Chad) on the west and south. The reason for their indifference was their evaluation of the "the prize." Libya hardly seemed worth the effort to collect it.

Italy paid no attention to their views and in 1911 belatedly joined the race for North Africa by sending an expeditionary force of 35,000 men with whom it assumed it could overwhelm the garrison of 7,000 Ottoman Turkish soldiers. Neither the Italians nor any of the other Europeans then thought much about the natives. At least for the Italians, that proved to be a major mistake: there was a remarkable invigorating movement among the Libyans, the *Sanusiyah*.

The *Sanusiyah* or Sanusi Brotherhood was a powerful example of what is known in Islam as a *Salafi* movement. *Salafiyah* ("Salifi-ism") is difficult concept for outsiders to comprehend. The word itself comes from the verbal "root," *salafa*, that means "to take the lead" but also "to keep pace with" and "to return to origins." Westerners usually place the emphasis on "return," that is, on backwardness. But the sense is "return to first principles" and, as defined by Muslim thinkers, the implication is "in order to advance." If this seems awkward or unlikely, consider the European counterpart. Protestant reformers in 16ᵗʰ and 17ᵗʰ centuries also thought that "purifying" the present by going back to origins was necessary to be able to advance. That concept sparked the great commercial and intellectual revolution in Holland, Belgium and North Germany. The *Salifis* were not so interested in commerce; their aim was to recapture the power and dignity of the days when Islam was a world leader. They believed that by stripping away the shroud of dark ages, they could advance toward a magnificent future.

One of several revivalist movements in 18ᵗʰ and 19ᵗʰ century Islam, the *Sanusiyah* was founded by the scholar, poet and mystic Sayyid Muhammad bin Ali al-Sanusi who was born in what is now Algeria in 1787. After study in Fez, he left in haste when the authorities became disturbed by his revolutionary pronouncements.

On his way east toward Mecca, al-Sanusi moved from town to town along the North African coast, through Egypt and into Arabia, preaching and gathering adherents. After two long periods of study in Mecca and having worked with other *Salafi* groups, al-Sanusi had achieved sufficient fame by 1837 to found the order that bears his name. Leaving Arabia, he intended to return to Morocco but stopped in Tripoli when he learned of the French invasion of Algiers.

Thus, having spent years in fear of Moroccan, Egyptian and Arabian religious and secular authorities, and now worried about the incursions of Europeans, he found himself, one might say by historical accident, in Libya. There, he decided to establish his new religious organization in as remote an area as he could find. He picked the hump of Libya sticking out in the Mediterranean, Cyrenaica. But, since the northern part of Cyrenaica is relatively well watered and relatively densely inhabited, he moved south to where the cultivated land fades into the Sahara. In the then-uninhabited oasis of Jaghbub, he established a *zawiya*. The word is usually translated as "lodge," but more accurately it means a settlement focused on a mosque.

To Jaghbub came devotees and students from the core of Africa and, as they graduated, they established new *zawiyas*. Through his teaching and their proselytizing, a religious society was born. This community overlaid the Bedouin tribal divisions so that, in a way similar to what the Prophet Muhammad had done a millennium before, al-Sanusi was able to effect a supra-tribal community of "brothers," *ikhwan*. And just as the Prophet Muhammad had found, the Bedouin who became his followers were content to leave mysticism and theology to him and his acolytes but gave him intense loyalty because his cause seemed to them to take on transcendental purpose.

By the end of al-Sanusi's life, about 150 *zawiya*s had been created in oases scattered across the landscape from Tunis in the West across what is now Libya through Egypt to Mecca in the east. The expanse was enormous. Measured in the means of contemporary means of travel – by camel caravan -- it was months wide. So it could be held together only by an active religious organization and a shared faith. To promote these, al-Sanusi created a religious university to which students flocked from all over the Islamic world.

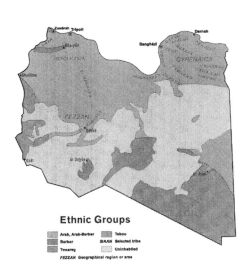

Ethnic Groups

Arab, Arab-Berber Tebou
Berber SIAAN Selected tribe
Touareg Uninhabited
FEZZAN Geographical region or area

For years after al-Sanusi's death, the order prospered and, as it did, its effects were increasingly felt by the French (who had moved into West and Central Africa), the British (who controlled Egypt) and the Italians (who after 1911 had begun colonizing the Libyan coast). All three saw the *Sanusiyah* and the tribesmen it inspired as obstacles to imperial ambition.

*   *   *

So what was the "Libya" in which this Sanusi-led coalition was based? We can describe it roughly as Caesar summarized that other object of Imperial Rome, Gaul. As Caesar wrote, *Gaul est omnis divisa in partes tres.* Libya similarly could be divided into three: Cyrenaica (including Benghazi), Tripolitania (including Tripoli) and the vast steppe and desert interior.

In the early years of the 20th century, the only real city was Tripoli which then had a population of about 40,000 while the main eastern town, Benghazi did not reach 16,500 until 1911. Smaller towns and villages were scattered along the coast. European travelers reported that most of the townsmen were not natives but recent arrivals. They included Arabs from Egypt and Algeria, *qulaughla* (Turco-Arabs), *shawashna* (Negro-Arabs), a few European *renegrados* (converts to Islam and/or refugees) and Jews.

The steppe and desert interior supported the other and much larger division of the population. Most of these people were semi-nomads who lived part of the year in spring-fed oases where they raised millet, vegetables and dates and around which they herded sheep. The true nomads, the people the Arabs differentiate by their reliance on the camel, ranged widely from the Nile all the way to southern Morocco. They had to move because only by nomadism could people and animals survive in the desert. This was because the Sahara does not receive enough rainfall to sustain agriculture or sufficient grass, brush and water in any one place to feed camels and the people who are their parasites. Rain, being both scanty and sporadic, set the pattern of life.

This pattern of life, as throughout the steppe and desert lands of North Africa and the Middle East, gave rise to a particular way of life, tribalism. Generally far from any form of government, each group of people had to be small because resources of water and fodder could not support many. This group of kinsmen is what we call a clan. In Libyan Arabic it is called a *bait* -- literally, a household, the family with whom one sleeps. Groups of clans, a tribe (Arabic:*qabilah)*, could gather in temporary congregations only in the rainy season, if rain actually fell which it often did not. Most of the time, each *bait*, composed of perhaps 50 to 100 men, women and children, was on its own. To protect what little it had, it either was prepared to fight fiercely

269

or it died out. It was the intense loyalty of members of a *bait* – *asabiyah*, as the great medieval North African historian and student of the nomads, Ibn Khaldun, identified it -- that enabled it to survive.[1]

What was politically important about the *Sanusiyah* was that it afforded an acceptable way for groups that were necessarily hostile to one another to "turn their faces in one direction," as the Arabic expression has it, and unite against foreigners. That is precisely what had given Islam its Bedouin-based power in the time of the Prophet Muhammad.

* * *

We associate the attempt by Italy to create an African empire with Fascism and Mussolini, but the attack on Libya began 12 years earlier. Indeed, it was there, on November 1, 1911 that the Italians invented the new kind of warfare which we are still employing -- aerial bombing -- when an Italian pilot tossed a grenade out of his plane at a Bedouin. That episode illustrates the disparity between the forces, but still the Italians lost some 8,000 men and wasted roughly half of their gross domestic product on their venture into Libya that year. It did not much impress their local opponents, but the Italians moved to establish the legality of their invasion by resurrecting the ancient name "Libya," aiming to show that it was, after all, Roman.

The Italian invasion and the Turco-Bedouin-Sanusi resistance morphed into the First World War. In that great conflict, Libya was a backwater, but it was not unimportant to either side. In 1915, Italy declared war on Austria and joined the Allied side. Although it became bogged down in the ghastly "White War" with Austria where the Italians lost nearly a million men, the Italian government did not dare to pull back from Libya for fear of being charged by Italy's virulent journalists with lack of patriotism. So the

---

1   Beginning my research for a doctorate in the Lebanese mountains some 60 years ago, I became a close friend of Stella and Emrys Peters who had just completed two remarkable studies of the Bedouin of Cyrenaica. Stella's was on the concept of the *bait* while Emrys, who would later become Professor of Social Anthropology at Manchester University, had made the most complete analysis yet done of Bedouin society. A posthumous collection of his writings survives as *The Bedouin of Cyrenaica* (Cambridge: Cambridge University Press, 1990). Then, later when I was a student at Oxford, I became a close friend to their teacher, Edward (later Sir Edward) Evans-Pritchard, then Professor of Social Anthropology and previously, during the Second World War, a Political Officer in Cyrenaica. This had resulted in his book, *The Sanusi of Cyrenaica* (Oxford: Clarendon Press, 1949). These friendships much influenced not only my views of Libyan affairs but also of the craft of the historian. I owe a great deal to the inspiration of all three of these remarkable scholars.

government sent over another 20,000 soldiers. (Ironically, Benito Mussolini, then still a socialist, was put in jail for urging dock workers to oppose the invasion. He soon abandoned socialism and came out in favor of the Libyan war.)

Beset by still-formidable Ottoman forces and fearful that the *Sanusiyah* might stimulate dangerous uprisings among its thousands of followers in Egypt, the British made common cause with the Italians in Libya. At the same time they were beginning relations with the *Sharif* of Mecca and covertly attempted to hedge their bets by trying to initiate talks with the *Sanusiyah*. In Libya as further in the Middle East, British double dealing proved to be a poor substitute for honesty. Their attempt soured the relationship with the Italians and won them no friends with the *Sanusiyah* against whose colleagues they were fighting in Egypt.

Meanwhile, the Ottoman Empire was fighting for its life. Having already lost Egypt, it was desperately holding onto the Levant and the *pashaliks* that became Iraq. The Turks thought that in Libya the Sanusi-inspired tribesmen might, at least, create a diversion and thus relieve British pressure on their eastern front. So, they smuggled arms into Cyrenaica (even by submarine) and sent officers to teach the tribesmen how to fight in a more modern way. But by 1916, reeling from defeats in the Middle East, the Empire had few resources left and so recalled most of the remarkable officers it had sent to Libya.[2] The few remaining Turkish soldiers and their Bedouin allies were attacked by the relative vast 35,000 man British army in Egypt, by a smaller French colonial army driving north from central Africa and by the Italians along the coast.

For the tribesmen, the Italians were the nearer of their three enemies. The war, in their eyes, was local: it was to defend their way of life, their religious brotherhood and their dignity against the European intruders. Early in the war, the *Sanusiyah* led this struggle, but when the leadership split, one faction, led by the man who later became King Idris, began to

---

2 Among the officers who served in Libya were two of the most important of the later Turkish leaders, Ismail Enver, who would become the Turkish equivalent of prime minister and would lead the resistance to the Soviet conquest of Central Asia, and Kemal Atatürk, as he became known, would become the president of post-Ottoman Turkey.

play the British game. Judging that his followers had no hope of defeating the Italian-British-French coalition, he began – like other Arabs in Egypt, Lebanon and Arabia – to negotiate with the British.

As the First World War ended, the major issues in Libya were unresolved. But the Libyans were exhausted. So, with British help, Idris began negotiations with the Italians. To have someone with whom to deal effectively and to end the fighting, the Italians were forced to recognize the *Sanusiyah* as a de facto government and to recognize Idris as *amir.* In short, the Italians did what the British were doing in Transjordan and Iraq, using a local notable a façade for their rule. He would get a title, a handsome allowance and various marks of prestige while the coastal peoples would be offered limited self-rule and even Italian citizenship. Provided, of course, that he could deliver Libya to Italy.

Idris could not. Knowing that, he equivocated as long as he could. By 1923, the incoming Fascist Party, led by Mussolini, decided to force the issue; so the second phase of the Italo-Libyan war began. For the Fascists, Libya became a test of their right to rule. To be sure of victory, they committed still more soldiers who were armed with the latest equipment, from the European campaigns, machine guns, armored cars and aircraft.

Against this modern European army and then more or less abandoned by the *Sanusiyah* leadership, the Bedouin could employ only classical guerrilla tactics. They probably never had as many as a thousand men under arms at any one time. But their war against the Italians – in which the coastal, settled peoples played no part -- was to last for a decade, from 1923 to 1932. Students of insurgency will find nearly exact parallels to Iraq, Afghanistan and other African and Asian conflicts.[3]

Mussolini's Marshal Rodolfo Graziani used all the tactics of counterinsurgency to break the insurgents -- favoring the coastal people,

---

3 As I have set out in my book, *Violent Politics* (New York: Harper Collins, 2007 and 2008). In Libya, the guerrillas called themselves the *muhafaziyah* or, roughly, the "Defenders." In Arabic, the word is more loaded with meaning than the translation: another form of the same word used of those who memorize the Quran and so embody the essential values of the faith.

whom the Italians called the *sottomessi* (the submissive), empowering Quislings, playing off the leadership of the *Sanusiyah* while punishing, starving, "regrouping" (Graziani's invention) or killing the tribesmen they called the *ribelli*. Graziani was a master of this brutal game. He built a barrier to cut the Bedouin off from their migration and supply routes into Egypt, filled in and cemented or poisoned their water wells and dug metaphorical *solci di sangue* – channels of blood -- among the tribes, hoping that they would defeat one another.

Unable to stand against large well armed formations, the insurgents learned new tricks. They stole and carried identity cards to pretend to be "reconciled" to Italian rule, struck without warning and at night – it is from such tactics that we got the expression "guerrillas own the night" -- concealed their weapons and pretended to be just herdsmen in daylight or when outgunned and forced the *sottomessi* to shelter them, furnish intelligence and give them supplies. Even when the leadership of the *Sanusiyah* abandoned them, the tribesmen fought on. Indeed, they created for themselves a new form of the *Sanusiyah* under the leadership of one of the least known of the great anti-imperial patriots, Umar al-Mukhtar. Like the leaders of the Afghan Taliban, he was both a man of religion, an *alim* (or as the Afghans would say, a *mulla*) and a warrior, a *mujahid*.

Under al-Mukhtar's leadership the revised Sanusi brotherhood proved to be a flexible bond, responding with arms when possible, fleeing when nearly overwhelmed but never giving up. Of Bedouin background and also a Sanusi "brother," he became Libya's hero. In a decade of almost daily fire-fights against the Italian army, it fair to say that Libya itself was born. But it also nearly died. In desperation, the Italians decided on a campaign of genocide. Putting nearly the whole Bedouin population in concentration camps, the Italians slaughtered the herds on which the Bedouin lived and killed tens of thousands of men, women and children. Finally, they wounded, captured and hanged al-Mukhtar.[4]

The long campaign of infiltration, bribery and assassination has left a bitter residue: to the generation of the 1960s, Qaddafi's generation, it

---

4 A Hollywood version of his life and death, *A Lion of the Desert*, was made in 1981 and starred Anthony Quinn, the Mexican actor who routinely portrayed all darker-hued foreigners.

appeared as a clash of Africa versus the West, the poor versus the rich, the weak versus the strong, Islam against Christianity. Fertilizing that crop of hatred were the bones of about two in three of the Bedouin population. This is the national epic on which young Muammar Qaddafi grew to manhood. He would proclaim his coup d'état in the name of Umar al-Mukhtar.

* * *

The decade of unremitting war had turned Libya into an empty husk. This was precisely what the Italians intended as they wanted to send Italians to inhabit it. But, even the Fascist state had difficulty persuading Italians to settle in Libya. Finally, only about 100,000 went, and most of them, despite all the help they were given by the state, left as soon as they could.

The big influx of Italians was in the army. So fragile was their hold on Libya in the 1930s that the Italians stationed a quarter of a million soldiers there – ironically their need to garrison Libya enabled them, when they declared war on Britain in June 1940, to attack the 86,000 troops the British had in Egypt. Their overwhelming numerical advantage lasted less than a year because in February 1941 the whole Italian 10th Army surrendered. Thereafter, it was the Erwin Rommel's *Afrikakorps* that did most of the fighting. After the great battle of al-Alamain, the British moving along the coast and the French coming up from central Africa had captured all of Libya by February 1943. Ironically, the British then found themselves administering what remained of the colonial Fascist state.

In 1945, the victorious Allies met to decide what to do with Libya. The United States wanted to turn it over to the United Nations; the Soviet Union demanded that it become the Libyan "trustee;" France wanted to turn it back to the Italians; the Italians wanted it back; and the Russians, hoping that the Italian Communists would assume power, changed course and adopted the Italian option. As the Cold War began to dominate thinking of the Western powers and the surge of the Italian Communists petered out, the British swung over to the French plan to return it to Italy. But this idea evoked memories of too-recent and too-painful events so "The Libyan Problem" was turned over to the United Nations. There it was decided to give the country independence and to bring back from exile the surviving Sanusi leader who had spent the war under British protection in Egypt. He would become King Idris I.

Idris's rule was marked from the beginning by petty tyranny, corruption and charade. No outsiders then much cared. This was, at least partly, because Libya didn't seem worth much consideration. It then produced nothing of any serious value, it had a total population smaller than most Western cities and it posed no threat to anyone. Weighed in the balance of all the other world problems, it drew no attention.

But then the US Strategic Air Command rediscovered the air base. Located just outside Tripoli, the old Italian-German-RAF-American field was within bomber range of the Soviet Union. Moreover, with Libya's nearly perfect flying weather, it also was an ideal place to train NATO pilots. So the Americans took over the field and enormously expanded it, eventually placing nearly 5,000 Americans in it. It was described by the then American ambassador as "a Little America...on the sparkling shores of the Mediterranean." It was upon seeing it, as I have mentioned, that I became convinced that a government that had turned it over to the Americans could not itself long continue. It didn't, but the airfield itself did continue. Ironically, it would later be used by the Soviet air force and still later (on April 5, 1986 and in March 2011) would be bombed by the United States.

The airfield was not the only attraction of Libya to postwar foreigners. Stimulated by the discovery of oil in Algeria, French, British and American companies began to search for oil in Libya. In one of those curious "might-have-beens" of history, the Italians had come close to finding oil in the late 1930s and had the Afrikakorps taken up their research, they could have solved the shortage of fuel that was the major cause of their defeat.[5] (Allegedly, they thought the curious oily taste of water in the wells on which they drew was because the British must be trying to poison them.) It was 17 years later, in 1959, that Esso struck the first field and 2 years later opened a pipeline to

---

5   The British had broken the German codes and so could exactly pin-point and sink supply ships sailing from Italy. It was largely because they were in danger of running out of fuel for their tanks that the Afrikakorps narrowly missed taking Egypt and cutting the Suez Canal.

the little Mediterranean port of Brega. Other discoveries quickly followed.

As oil flowed out, money flowed in. The relatively enormous inflow of money greatly increased the capacity of the coterie of officials around King Idris to enrich themselves. As the late American journalist John Cooley observed,6 "Concession brokers and influence peddlers operated in the near fringes of the royal court. The sudden infusions of huge amounts of cash were dramatic in a poor country that, by some estimates, had only a forty-dollar per capita income as it completed its first years of independence...For poor tent-village-dwelling families like that of [Muammar Qaddafi's parents] Abu Meniar and Aissha al-Qaddafi, this was rubbing silt into the wounds of poverty."

The disparity between rich and poor multiplied by corruption, the empty puffery of the leadership, the government's pandering to foreigners, its weakness and petty tyranny were all too evident in the Libya in which Muammar Qaddafi grew to manhood.

*　　*　　*

During his long reign in power, Qaddafi evolved from the young revolutionary who overthrew the aging monarch until finally becoming an aging (and virtual) monarch himself. He has always presented a puzzle to outside observers. He is not an easy study. My aim is not to pass judgment, but to try to understand how he sees events so that we can predict what he will do. Clearly, it is important that we understand as much as we can if we are to deal effectively with Libya.

In my time in Government in the early 1960s, the CIA attempted to psychoanalyze rulers of other countries. Buried somewhere in its vast headquarters building in Virginia, was a team of "shrinks" who, at vast distance, with no personal contact and depending only on diplomats', agents' and journalists' reports, tried to understand their proclivities. The analysts probably worked assiduously. I never saw their reports, but I think most of my State Department colleagues found them merely amusing. However, it does

---

6　*Libyan Sandstorm* (London: Sidgwick & Jackson, 1983), 47.

not seem to me to be beyond the wit of man to understand enough about what influenced Qaddafi to get a reasonable view of his thought and perhaps to predict his likely actions. These are the points that strike me:

Qaddafi told us in his first pronouncement, announcing the coup, that he was guided by the hero of the war against the Italian Fascists, Umar al-Mukhtar. This was no abstract identification since he proudly proclaimed that his father was a companion of al-Mukhtar. What al-Mukhtar meant to him and to the cadets and young officers of his generation, I suggest, came to two main points: al-Mukhtar and the tribal *ribelli* were the true nationalists and no matter how terrible their ordeal they did not surrender.

Like al-Mukhtar, Qaddafi and most of the young officers were of tribal origin. Surely, from tales told by relatives and friends of the vicious Italian campaigns that came close to wiping out their people, they imbibed a deep suspicion of foreigners – not only the Italians who still sought to control Libya even after the end of the Second World War but also the French who occupied the Fezzan (the vast interior) until 1955. Under the pallid skins of all Westerners, they suspected, beat the heart of imperialism.

So how does this translate into current events? After all, to us, our intervention seems justified (by Security Council resolution 1973) and certainly moral (to protect the rebels who at least initially were unarmed civilians). To Qaddafi and his supporters, it seemed different. Is there any substance in their feeling?

They know, because it was leaked to the press, that the British had a plan (code named "the Radford Plan,") to intervene in Libya to prevent precisely what Qaddafi did, overthrow the monarchy. Like most Middle Easterners, the Libyans generally believe – those opposing the current regime, happily, and those upholding it, angrily – that Western secret agents are constantly being infiltrated into the country. In recent days, these beliefs have been certified: a British MI-6 team was caught red-handed in a most embarrassing way while the US government has acknowledged that it has CIA operatives and Special Forces troops now on Libyan soil. So, whether we like it or not, what is often derided as Arab paranoia is grounded in both history and current events. The Libyan government must ask how could such agents be effective? The answer is 'only if supported by some Libyans.' Absent local supporters, foreign agents don't survive long. It is obvious today that their supporters are the rebels against the regime.

So the question arises, how did Qaddafi identify these rebels. Obviously, he had a view different from ours. To us the rebels may seem incipient democrats, although, we really do not know much about them because they seem to be a very loose collection of individuals and groups. We are so unsure what they stand for that we have found it necessary to warn them not to engage in killing innocent civilians – or, we hinted, we would also attack them. But they appear to share one attribute: they want a role in running their lives beyond what Qaddafi is willing to allow.

To Qaddafi, I believe, these non-tribesmen seemed unpatriotic agents of foreigners. By the men of his father's generation, Qaddafi would have been regaled with tales about the people the Italians called the sottomessi, the settled, coastal people, who contributed to the Italian conquest and occupation. I suspect that he must have viewed his opponents as essentially the same group. Moreover, I imagine that he was furious over what he must have regarded as their lack of appreciation for what he has done for them. When I visited Libya in 1963, even Tripoli was a city of slums with many of its houses made from scrap and most without running water or electricity. When he took power, Qaddafi enormously improved the lives of the settled, coastal people. Today, they live beyond the dreams of their fathers and grandfathers. Finally, I suspect that Qaddafi saw their revolt not so much as a quest for participation in government (which we believe it is) as proof that they are just another generation of collaborators with foreigners who want to gain unfairly from Libya's oil. Whether this is true or not is to some extent irrelevant: I think those views are what has governed his action.

In addition to Umar al-Mukhtar, the second "role model" for Qaddafi, as he told us, was the Egyptian leader, Gamal Abdul Nasser. At the time of the coup, Westerners were as hostile to Nasser as they later became to Qaddafi, but to most Arabs, Nasser was an almost supernatural figure, orator, guide, font of inspiration and movie star wrapped in one. Qaddafi adored him. Indeed, in the first moments of the seizure of power, he and his colleagues wanted to turn Libya over to Egypt and themselves become Nasser's lieutenants. That this did not happen was apparently because Nasser, having been burned in the abortive merger with Syria (the United Arab Republic) and his intervention in Yemen (which set up his defeat by Israel), did not want deep involvement in Libya.

Nasser was, of course, an authoritarian ruler. There are few living rulers in Africa or Asia who are not. Qaddafi was certainly an authoritarian figure. Worse, he was a true believer. He was sure, I think, that what he was doing was right and that those who oppose him do so for selfish, unpatriotic motives. This made it difficult for him to contemplate sharing power – just as it does for the leaders of Iran, China and many other countries. We think that representative government is inherently universal, but in fact it was a fragile concept; it took centuries to grow in the West and often broke down even there. It suffers in much of the rest of the world from the heritage of imperialism, the lack of popular non-governmental organizations, lack of experience, poverty and other problems. We must hope that it will grow, but the growth is very slow and often takes forms very different from ours.

To Qaddafi, what was important about Nasser, I think, came down to two points: he was a true nationalist and he was not corrupt. Qaddafi carried out his coup for the same reasons Nasser carried out his. What has happened over the years since then in both Egypt and Libya is less edifying. Nasser's successors, Anwar Sadat (whom Nasser despised) and Hosni Mubarak wallowed in corruption; evidence is growing that Qaddafi himself or at least his family have evolved from the Nasserist to the Sadat-Mubarak pattern.

The Israel-Arab conflict also played a part in Qaddafi's intellectual and emotional development. Libya had a significant Jewish population in the 19th century, but I find no indication that Qaddafi had contact with those few who remained in Libya after the 1948-1949 Palestine war. Rather, I think, he shared the emotional commitment of most Arabs, particularly those at a distance, to the Palestinians. He probably equated

President Gamal
Abdal Nasser of
Egypt (right) with
the Leader of the
Libyan Revolution,
Muammar Qaddafi

http://en.wikipedia.
org/wiki/File:Nasser_
Gaddafi_1969.jpg

the Israelis to the Italians: both colonized Arab lands and both used overwhelming military force against its defenders. Multiplying these deeper feelings, I think, would have been the Israeli defeat of his hero, Gamal Abdul Nasser in the 1967 war.

And what about terrorism? President Reagan memorably referred to Qaddafi as "the mad dog of Africa." His attack on a nightclub in Berlin and, above all, his blowing up the Pan American aircraft over Scotland were strongly and rightly condemned. But, Qaddafi hardly invented terrorism. The CIA practiced it to the fullest extent in his youth and early days in power. It tried to murder Nasser, did murder Lumumba, overthrew governments, and engaged in various kinds of black propaganda and "dirty tricks," seeking as the US government admitted, to overthrow his regime. As President Reagan said, he wanted Qaddafi to "go to bed every night wondering what we might do." From the point of view of most of the world's weaker peoples, the distinction we draw between such government actions as our shooting down an Iranian passenger plane and their planting bombs on one of ours is specious. Both are certainly horrible.

Some things American governments did not choose to do directly but wanted to have happen was sometimes done under their auspices and often with their connivance by Israel. Israel routinely carried out "operations" in the Arab countries in which it murdered Arab leaders. It also shot down or at least caused the crash of a Libyan commercial airliner in 1973, killing 108 people. Israel had its own agenda, of course, and even turned on its American patrons as when, in 1954, its agents set fire to an American government building in Alexandria to try to turn the American government against Nasser and when in 1967 it attacked and tried to sink an American Naval ship in the Mediterranean. The British MI-6 and the Soviet KBG also joined in, indeed virtually invented, this dangerous game.

Finally, there were mercenaries, like the "Dogs of War" led by the English soldier-of-fortune and former commando, Colonel (later Sir) David Sterling. The group associated with Sterling tried to overthrow Qaddafi's government and kill him in the summer and fall of 1970. Ironically, it was the British, Italian and American intelligence forces that then squashed this freelance (and partly-Moroccan-funded) attempt. But the very success of the "formal" intelligence services in suppressing the mercenaries must have convinced Qaddafi, if he needed any convincing, that the real world more resembled the fictional world of Ian Fleming's "OO7" than the law-abiding world proposed by Thomas Jefferson or Alexander Hamilton. As even President John F. Kennedy repeatedly showed, the excitement and seeming effectiveness of a "James Bond" was addicting. Qaddafi certainly became addicted.

Being one himself, Qaddafi was fascinated by revolutionaries. He identified with and contributed to a number of revolutionary groups including the Palestinian *Intifada*, the Basque ETA, the Irish IRA and the Philippine Moro Islamic Liberation Front. But, of course, he did not create these organizations. They grew on native soil. And, where he moved over from financial and propaganda support to "dirty tricks," he often employed foreigners – including former CIA and US Special Forces officers.

Espionage can be a profitable game – at least temporarily – for those engaged in it, but it is a dirty game that corrupts those who employ it, deludes otherwise reasonable leaders and poisons international relations. Moreover, its record of "success" is very near zero. It needs to be abolished everywhere by everyone. Qaddafi certainly has been guilty of many wicked acts, but he joins a notable crowd of statesmen including our own. As with nuclear arms control, we would do well to begin with ourselves in the quest for getting others to go straight. In the meantime, we are right to punish those who engage in it.

There is another, brighter, side of Qaddafi's record. Qaddafi poured Libya's oil money into projects to uplift his people. Under his regime, Libya evinces a remarkable record of development in almost every aspect

– education, health care, infrastructure, job creation – and usually with a commendable sense of social justice. Some of the projects were grandiose. One, particularly, was to build a massive pipeline to bring water from aquifers from Kufra oasis, deep in the Sahara, to the settled people on the coast. Libya is often described as "Egypt without the Nile" so, having the money and the water, Qaddafi moved to change geography. "The Second Nile" as it was termed, has often been derided as the Libyan equivalent of building a pyramid and showed Qaddafi's madness. But, as a matter of fact, the project was first proposed not to Qaddafi but to the Libyan monarchy by the highly successful and eminently practical American oil man, Armand Hammer. Moreover, today the Spanish government is planning to do exactly the same thing, build a massive pipeline to bring water from a river in the north of Spain to the parched farmers in the south. Perhaps the pipeline is not so clear an example of Qaddafi's flight from sanity.

To manage Libya's one major resource, energy, Qaddafi essentially continued the very intelligent policy devised by the monarchy. It had aimed to create competition among a number of prospecting companies; thus, no one company could dominate and so set the scale of its production not on the needs of Libya but according to its own world-wide marketing needs as, for example, British Petroleum (then known as AIOC) had done in Iran. Under the monarchy this was accomplished by dividing the country into a large number of lease areas and opening bidding on them to a wide variety of American and European oil companies. Qaddafi carried this policy to the next logical step: as oil was discovered he moved cautiously to increase the government involvement in production and refining by purchase or nationalization. What Libyans could not do – handling the highly technical work of field maintenance – he left to foreign companies. It is notable that the essential features of his program were copied by most of the oil and gas producing countries throughout the world.

In political affairs he was less pragmatic than in economic matters. Like the rulers of other authoritarian states, China, Egypt, Syria, Iran and others, Qaddafi was not willing to allow participation in governance. His people could live well, even get rich, but they were not to be allowed to challenge his authority. There is a joke that sums up the situation: 'when a dog ran all the way over to Tunisia, the Tunisian dogs were baffled. Why, they asked did he come? After all, they pointed out, they had no more to eat than dogs elsewhere. It was not for the food, the migrant replied. He came to bark.' "Barking" was not allowed in Libya but having a voice in their national affairs is what the younger generation insisted on doing.

If these influences give some hints on Qaddafi's youth and, in part, during his years as Libya's ruler, one should ask "what happened to him" that caused him to appear bizarrely costumed and erratic in behavior later in life? The usual explanation is that he went insane. Another widely quoted witticism explained how his practical policies meshed with his bizarre behavior -- "he may be insane but he is not crazy."

Of course, losing one's mind sometimes happens to rulers as it happens to other humans. And to modify the great English historian's dictum that "power corrupts and absolute power corrupts absolutely," one could say that the sycophancy with which statesmen, and particularly absolute rulers, are surrounded promotes eccentricity that occasionally borders on lunacy. But that answer seems to me inadequate. I confess I do not have a satisfying answer. But the more interesting question, I suggest, is directed at what he was doing in Libya rather than how he was dressed. The answer there, it appears, was that he was a victim of his own success. He got to be too rich, became too much of a king and like many men occupying supreme power began to believe his own myth. In short, aging, he became the King Idris he had struggled as a young man to overcome.

As, as he did, he narrowed the circle of his advisers and listened only to praise. Thus, as I infer from the press, he was genuinely shocked when those he thought he was leading and whom he had so much helped to better their lives, demanded more and loved him less. I imagine that he really had concluded that much of their motivation is foreign inspired. Given his upbringing and his experience, Qaddafi will undoubtedly attach much, perhaps excessive, importance to the role of foreigners. The long history of Western intervention, dirty tricks and subversion will be at the forefront in his and his supporters' thoughts. We would be wise not to strengthen his evaluation.

*   *   *

So what is likely to follow when the bombing stops? At worst, the fighting will continue. I do not see Qaddafi meekly surrendering. I think he will fight to the death. If he survives the onslaught in which we and the European Union as well as the rebels are launching, my hunch is that Qaddafi will hark back to his Bedouin mentor, Umar al-Mukhtar, and wage a guerrilla war. And what about his enemies, the insurgents? I see no sign that they will unite sufficiently to form a coherent and lasting government. Thus, at least a period of chaos is likely to follow. I suspect that this chaos will energize rather than quiet Qaddafi's loyalists among the tribes. Perhaps it will not happen quickly, but it will be latent from the beginning. Libya, we must realize, like Afghanistan, is a tribal society and the tribesmen are Qaddafi's people. It will be very difficult or perhaps even impossible for the opposition, which is made up of coastal people, to cope with the people of the vast interior. The cost to the Libyans will be enormous.

Then there is the question of legality: even if they deploy overwhelming force, do the Western states and particularly the United States have the right to "regime change" Libya? Already questions are being posed by the "other" powers, particularly Turkey, but also China and Russia, on the extent and purpose of the UN Security Council resolution. If the questions are simply ignored as they were in Iraq, the cost to the already weak sense of a comity of nations will be heavy. Just at a time when we need more than anything to work together on the great and urgent challenges of surging population, declining natural capital of water and productive land and dangerous climate change, the consensus will fray.

And then there is the monetary cost to Britain, France and the United States. Accurate and inclusive figures are impossible to get, as they still are for Afghanistan and Iraq, but we are told that the war has so far cost – probably at minimum – the United States alone $100 million a day. Not only America, mired in foreign debt with associated domestic problems, but France and Britain are struggling with severe economic shortfalls and are cutting back on programs that many of their peoples regard as essential for an acceptable pattern of life. The attack on Libya has already added about $20 a barrel to the cost of oil. If that price is sustained, the ripple effect will derail attempts to cut back on "dirty" fuels, coal and shale oil, and so hasten the process of climate change. Libya is more than a straw on the already faltering camel's back.

And what follows this "straw?" The press is already drawing attention to the similar autocratic regime in Syria; Yemen is in virtual revolution against another strong man whom the US is unlikely to keep supporting; the majority population of Bahrain has been repressed, at least so far, by Saudi military intervention; the war in Iraq is by no means over; nor is the war in Afghanistan. And beyond these nearby issues, what about the regime in Myanmar (Burma) which surely is far worse than Qaddafi's or the Ivory Coast where the arguments for "humanitarian intervention" are far stronger than in any of the other countries. Where will it stop? Foreign policy specialists of my generation used to think that there could be no more Vietnams, that we had learned our lesson. But we did not.

It also is worth considering that leaders of some of these countries will ask themselves whether it is wise to follow Qaddafi's decision to give up nuclear weapons. Would he be under attack today if he had gone ahead and developed them? I think it unlikely. That is surely not the message we want to give to those nations that can but have not yet gone nuclear.

*   *   *

Finally, what is the alternative today in Libya? At this point there are no attractive or easy alternatives. That was true in Vietnam and Iraq; it is certainly also true of Afghanistan. So the easy thing is to keep on doing the same thing. But doing the same thing also causes the costs to rise and only rarely produces conditions conducive to policy change. A more sensible course of action is to try to stop digging the hole into which one is falling.

Supplying arms to the insurgents and bombing Qaddafi's army may lead, indeed is likely to lead, to more protracted and more bloody engagements. "Leveling the playing field" will only enable the "game" to go on. That will mean more misery, more destruction, more death. Rather than furnishing still more arms to the rebels – after having sold so many for so long to Qaddafi – it is certainly worth exploring whether peace-seeking might still be possible. Negotiation may not work, but it is always preferable to killing. Both sides (and we) have something to gain – and much to lose if we do not try. Attempting to jump into a "quick fix" is probably not going to work and is apt to create new problems. Moving with "all deliberate speed" is the best course and probably will involve a cooling off period to quiet inflamed passions. We have the tools to enhance the preconditions of peace during such a period. We should keep in mind the purpose of diplomacy: negotiation is not needed when people agree; it is needed when people don't. The cost to the Libyans, to us, and to the world community of nations is simply too high not to try.

March 31, 2011

CHAPTER 15

MALI'S QUICKSAND

With America still deeply committed in Asia, a new war has erupted in Africa. And, according to Secretary of Defense Leon Panetta, it is very serious. In his last days in office, he warned (http://news.yahoo.com/us-helping-hesitant-mali-intervention-075210491.html) that the rebels in Mali "are a threat to our country, they are a threat to the world." Even before this warning was sounded French President François Hollande launched a 3,000-man military invasion of its former colony. As it did in Vietnam, America is lending France logistical support to help it accomplish the goal French Defense Minister Jean-Yves Le Drian described as "the total re-conquest of Mali."

Privately, some European statesmen, even in France, hear in those remarks and actions an echo of the first steps toward the multiyear campaigns in Vietnam, Iraq and Afghanistan. Are they right?

First, is what Mr. Panetta has said credible? Could the Malians pose a danger to "the world?" Or even just to America?

The facts make his remark appear almost ridiculous. Mali is a poor, land-locked, backward country of which about 65% is deep in the vast Sahara desert, and less than 4% is arable. Half of the fifteen or so million of its inhabitants subsist on about $1 a day. Only one person in three is literate.[1] Mali has no modern army or air force and certainly no ocean-going navy. More important, the inhabitants of Mali are now bitterly divided, literally at one another's throats.

Moreover, Mali is an "artificial" state, put together by the French at the

---

1 Library of Congress, Federal Research Division, Country Profile: Mali, January 2005.

NASA image of Mali

end of their colonial rule in 1960 from part of what used to be known as the French Sudan. Nine in ten Malians are black Africans while one in ten belong to a biracial community known as the Tuwareg.[2]

The majority black population in today's Mali is divided linguistically, religiously, ethnically and culturally. About half are "Mandes," most of whom can communicate in *Bambara,* but they too are divided into various communities, speaking more than forty languages or dialects. About half of the Tuwareg are also black -- descendants of former slaves who are known as *Eklan* in *Tamasheq,* the language of the Tuwareg. The other half are a lighter skinned people of Berber descent. None of these people are deeply committed citizens of what is today Mali; most cling to identifies shaped by villages with weaker but overarching cultural distinctiveness. It follows that the over-used term "artificial" for the state has at least social validity.

In Mali, as elsewhere in Africa, the creation by the departing imperial power of a single state on top of a multi-ethnic society has been a major source of domestic instability and hostility. Artificial state formation is one of the perhaps inevitable but certainly pernicious legacies of imperial rule. And Mali has not had either the time or the stability to overcome it.

---

2   As with religion, language in much of central and western Africa is derived from Arabia. The word Tuwareg (spelled in the Western media Tuareg) comes into the Tuwareg dialect of Berber, *Tamasheq or Tamaheq.* from Arabic. It is the plural noun derived from the Arabic verb *taraja,* meaning "to be veiled." It stuck with the people since the distinctive dress of the men includes a face veil, an adaptation to desert heat, dust and solar power. Like the Middle Eastern Bedouin, the Tuwareg are nomads and are dependent on the camel for much of their food and drink. They are widely scattered because no one area can give their animals sufficient and constant fodder or water. Consequently, the nomads always number far fewer than settled peoples. The best guess today for the Tuwareg is about 1 5 million of whom about half are descendants of black slaves, the *Eklan.*

Even more a source of dangers is the residue of imperial map drawing. The Tuwareg peoples are scattered among five African states. Traditionally, they ranged freely over the broad band of territories known as the Sahel which were later carved into parts of Mali, Niger, Algeria, Libya and Burkino Faso.

Depending on rainfall for their camels and opportunities for trade for themselves, groups of them moved about sporadically all the way from the Atlantic to the Red Sea. The only boundary they knew was grazing opportunity. Not many could congregate in the mainly waterless wastes so they were drawn into contact with the settled peoples to whom they provided transport, from whom they got food grains, tools and textiles and upon whom they periodically preyed. We may think of them as the bedouin of Central Africa.

The Tuwareg are not alone in being widely scattered. So too are the Mandes. They are majorities or significant minorities in all the neighboring countries -- Niger, Senegal, Sierra Leone, Benin, Burkina Faso, Benin, Côte d'Ivoire, Chad, Gambia, Ghana, Guinea, Guinea-Bissau, Liberia, Mali, Mauritania and Nigeria, Creation of these separate states in the final stages of French rule divided Mandian society but created new political problems and opportunities.

One of the possible opportunities and also dangers, which is now being discussed and may soon be realized, is for Mali's neighbors to intervene militarily on behalf of its Mandian majority government in its civil war.

II

The "Mali" that first captured the attention of Europeans was believed to be the source of what Europe then desperately lacked – gold. Toward the end of the Middle Ages, European economies produced little they could sell to pay for luxuries they imported from China, India, the Levant and Egypt. Thus they suffered from the same problem as many countries today, a balance of payments deficit. What they wanted they could buy only with precious metals. Silver was not a good alternative to gold and, in any event, their silver mines were nearly exhausted. The "florin," the first gold coin minted in Europe since antiquity, was the favored medium of exchange, but not enough florins could be minted due to the declining mineral resources. Traders knew that somewhere in West Africa was a source of gold. To find it, Florentine explorers set out – much as Marco Polo's family and other Venetians went to China – for Timbuktu. The first man we know by name was Benedetto Dei who apparently reached that fabled city in 1470.

It was not for another 80 years that much was known about Timbuktu. In 1518, a Spanish Muslim who had lived in the Moroccan city of Fez was captured by Christian pirates and presented to Pope Leo X. Al-Hassan ibn Muhammad, known in Europe as Leo Africanus, was able to describe Timbuktu. He paid particular attention to what Europeans most needed, gold. Its merchants, he wrote routinely used gold coins and its king had ornaments of solid gold of which some weighed over a thousand pounds. Europeans were fascinated: Africa, they believed, was literally golden.

Yellow gold was not the only lure: "black gold," played an even more important part in the European incursions into Africa. In the early Renaissance, few wealthy households in Europe were without *blackamoors* – pages, porters, cooks, maids, mistresses and, sometimes like Shakespeare's Othello, soldiers. They also worked the fields that produced the sugar for which Europeans had developed a new taste. What motivated Prince Henry the Navigator was less geographical curiosity, as we were taught in school, than the quest for cheap labor, and Columbus got some of his inspiration from his father-in-law who was growing sugar cane on a plantation on the Azores. So it was that in 1441 Europeans carried out the first slave raids in West Africa.

In the Seventeenth century, France took its first steps toward acquiring an African empire by establishing trading posts in what is today Senegal. But France focused its major efforts elsewhere; Africa was relatively unimportant. Then the French lost much of their empire during the Napoleonic wars. They got back in the game of empire in 1830 when they invaded and conquered Algeria. Algeria consumed their interest in Africa for decades.

It was not until the end of the Nineteenth century that France plunged deeper into Africa, creating what came to be called its "Second Empire." At its height, the empire (including the Americas, Asia and metropolitan France) amounted to nearly 10% of the land area of the Earth, smaller only than the British Empire. Conquest and rule was justified in French eyes by what the English called "the White Man's Burden." As they conceived it, France had a *mission civilisatrice* -- in which the benighted natives would be brought into French culture and even be marginally introduced into the French metropolitan political structure. They created the French Sudan as a separate colony in 1890 and a decade later divided it into separate colonies.

French policy in Africa was one of the changes brought about by what had amounted to a civil war between the adherents of Marshal Philippe Pétain in Vichy and General Charles de Gaulle's "Free French" during the Second World War. When de Gaulle became president of France, he renamed the former empire the *Union française* and allowed it increased autonomy. Moving further toward independence, the *Union* evolved into the *Communauté française*. And from 1960, that arrangement was allowed, as Karl Marx would have said, "to wither away." While the status of the member states was not formally abrogated until 1995, what was then know as the Mali Federation (formed from what became Senegal and what became Mali) proclaimed independence. Senegal seceded the following year and shortly thereafter the remaining part of the Mali Federation changed its name to Mali. On the basis of this precedent the "veiled people" in 2012 proclaimed a separate state they called Azawad.

Today's Tuwareg people, perhaps a million and a half strong, are driven by religion, energized by ethnic hostility and empowered by experience. While Muslims, their interpretation of Islam differs from that of the relatively rich and settled people of the south, the Mandes, with whom, long before the advent of the French, they traded, performed services for and with whom they occasionally clashed over water and land. The great Niger river is both the frontier and the goal: while the Mandes remained along and south of the Niger River, the Tuwareg ranged northward from the river over the deserts.

It was the rise and fall of Muammar Qaddafi's Libya that brought this relatively peaceful arrangement to an explosive end. The Qaddafi regime was poor in manpower and felt itself blocked in its relations with the eastern Arab countries. So it reached south into Africa with aid programs and recruitment. Being of Bedouin background himself, President Qaddafi was attracted to the Tuwareg: they would pose no challenge to his rule, were natural survivors in an environment like his and were what the British in another context called a "martial race." Many Tuwareg spent years in the service of Libya. There, they were subsidized, trained, armed and used by President Qaddafi. They fought bitterly and well to protect his regime to the very end. When Qaddafi was defeated, those who escaped made their way back south toward the Niger River. While we have yet to hear the voice of an agreed leader, it is clear that they believe their safety cannot be assured any longer in either the north or the south but requires a homeland in between, in the vast Sahara desert. Poor as it will be, Azawad is their "national" objective.

To thwart that objective, and apparently with little attention to the complexities of Malian historical experience and current reality, French President François Hollande decided on January 11, 2013[3] to intervene militarily on behalf of the just-installed regime, itself the product of the latest in a litany of coups and dictatorships.

III

So what do we need to know of the political history of Mali?

The first president, Modibo Keïta, determined in 1960 to separate his country from France and moved to establish relations with the Soviet Union. He attempted to organize his state as a "socialist" republic with only one political party, his. In neither activity was he successful: Mali was too insignificant to draw much attention or support from the Soviet Union and the economy deteriorated so fast and so completely, impelled by a devastating six-year drought, that he was forced to reconstitute ties with France.

---

3   As David E. Sanger & Eric Schmitt reported on January 23, 2013 in *The International Herald Tribune,* "...some officials [of the Obama administration] say they believe the French went into Mali hastily, in the words of one official 'before they understood exactly what they were biting off.'"

After only eight years of independence, Mali suffered its first coup d'état when a group of military officers installed one of their leaders, Lieutenant Moussa Traoré, as chairman of a "governing committee" (somewhat like the Free Officers committee in Egypt led by Gamal Abdul Nasser). Then, after six years of rule, in 1974, the leaders of this coup issued a constitution proclaiming a "centralized democracy." It was affirmed, and the now General Traoré was elected (with no opposition) president in 1979 with 99% of the popular vote. It was obvious that the newly legitimized government did not quite measure up to the proclaimed election tally since, within a year, Mali's student population and dissident army officers revolted and three times tried to overthrow Traoré's government. But the students and officers were no match for the newly empowered security forces and were arrested, imprisoned or otherwise disposed of.

Widespread corruption among the close supporters of the Traoré regime, exacerbated by austerity measures imposed on the faltering economy by the International Monetary Fund (IMF) fomented occasionally violent popular demonstrations. The government tried to meet public anger by deflecting the demand for popular participation in the political process with attacks on the Tuwareg. Additionally, while Traoré's *Union Démocratique du Peuple Malien* (UDPM) remained the only legal party, a clever change in voting procedure gave the appearance of political diversity. Multiple candidates, but only from the UDPM, were allowed to contest some of the parliamentary seats. The ruse was, of course, recognized and increased rather than calmed unrest. In response, the regime opted for violent repression, with troops firing on demonstrators, but in 1991, agitation spread beyond the students and junior army officers to civil servants. It was the representational process itself that was the main loser: well over half of the eligible voters simply abstained from voting; indeed, Mali had the lowest voter turnout of any West African nation.

Capitalizing on popular dissatisfaction, a new group of army officers led by Amandou Toumani Touré seized power and arrested the incumbent president. After abolishing the old constitution, the officers wrote a new one that allowed the formation of political parties. The *Alliance Pour la*

293

Démocratie au Mali (ADEMA), by then the only unified and coherent group, won the ensuing election. The election was generally believed to be "free," but the Supreme Court of Mali threw out half a million votes – about one in five or six -- as fraudulent. The ADEMA candidate, Alpha Oumar Konaré was installed in office and managed to stay there for two terms. Then, following complex jockeying for power, the former leader, Moussa Traoré, reemerged after a relatively open and free election in 2002 as president.

Under Traoré's second administration, corruption reached new heights. As the American anthropologist Bruce Whitehouse wrote (*The London Review of Books* August 30, 2012), the president "maintained a veneer of progress," but underneath, he diverted millions of dollars of aid funds to his own use while his officers "often skimmed off their soldiers' ammunition and pay." Even grants made to fight AIDs, Tuberculosis and Malaria, Mali's crippling health problems, were stolen. Using their new power, as in Afghanistan, favored insiders seized the property of those too weak to defend it, while judges "sold favourable verdicts to the highest bidders." Whitehouse quotes a popular Mali saying that "a fish rots from the head."

A Malian journalist, quoted by Mr. Whitehouse, castigated not only the leadership, but the whole society for corruption: "Corruption is for everyone," he wrote. In addition to the "big time thieves," he ticked off "teachers [who] trade exam grades or exam answers for sex or money...lawyers and judges who settle their cases among them before trial, having sold the verdict to the highest bidder...in short, when we talk about corruption in Mali, 98% of the population does it." The comparison to Afghanistan is startling. The simple fact is that under a corrupt regime, people must cheat to live.

Unlike Afghanistan, Mali has been given little foreign aid, and much of what could have benefitted the population has been stolen. Thus, today, it ranks only 182 of the world's 187 nations (UN: *Human Development Report 2013*). Not only is the population poor, but it suffers from malnutrition and inadequate hygiene. According to the latest more or less reliable figures, the government spends about $4/person per annum on public health measures. With only five physicians for each 100,000 inhabitants and few medical facilities, what impact medicine might have made is further diminished by corruption. As the journalist I just quoted remarked, doctors routinely treat only those who slip them money under the table while nurses sell medications stolen from patients for whom it was prescribed. Not surprisingly, Malians suffer a high incidence of cholera, hepatitis, meningitis, and tuberculosis among water-borne and other diseases.

In this environment, those of the Tuwareg who had settled along the Niger River were the main victims. And victims not only of corruption but of police and army brutality. The record, according to Bruce Whitehouse ("Bridges from Bamako," bruce.whitehouse@lehigh.edu) shows "torture and summary execution of prisoners" dating back to the formation of the Republic in 1960. Added to such practices, which presumably fell mostly on the poorer Tuwareg, the educated and relatively affluent Tuwareg increasing voiced their anger at being effectively excluded from decision making and representation in the regime.

IV

Perhaps we would not have heard much about Tuwareg dissidence had it not been for the events, described in a previous essay, in Libya. As Glen Greenwald wrote (*The Guardian*, January 14, 2013), "much of the instability in Mali is the direct result of Nato's [sic] intervention in Libya." The "Arab Spring" forces that overthrew Qaddafi, with massive support from the EU and the USA, focused their anger on his foreign supporters among black Africans and Tuwareg. They fought hard for the regime and when it fell many were massacred; the survivors packed up their arms and left.

As Professor Hugh Roberts of the International Crisis Group has written (*The Financial Times*, January 14, 2013),

The Sahel's terrorism problem dates back no further than 2003 – the West's global war on terror gave birth to it; the west's part in the destruction of Muammer Qaddafi's Libya aggravated it; and France's decision to pursue another war in Mali is expanding it.

The Tuwareg reaction was the, at first slow and tentative attempt to create their own state by insurgency.

Whether Tuwareg militancy caused real fears or was merely a cover for intervention by the military -- or both -- a new group of army officers carried out yet another coup d'état in March 2012. Ironically, the coup came just a month before elections were to be held and in which President Traoré had declared he would not run. Although not much discussed, it is noteworthy that the leaders of the coup were beneficiaries of an American training mission and, presumably, were more competent than their predecessors. But they were not capable of controlling their troops or the semi-official thugs who in the aftermath of the coup looted government offices, private houses and shops, stole cars, TV sets and computer equipment, broke into safes to seize cash and raped women and even one another.

As Adam Nossiter reported (*The New York Times,* March 22, 2012), the coup's leaders were obviously ill-equipped to govern the country. At their head was the American-trained Captain Amadou Sanogo, whose spokesman displayed its plans and attributes "in halting French, stumbled over the junta's moniker and was surrounded by humble-looking soldiers in the uniforms of enlisted men or low-ranking officers [as he] announced on state television that Mali's Constitution had been 'suspended' and its institutions 'dissolved.'" (A photograph of the group by *Reuters* appeared in *The [Toronto] National Post*.)

Reaction to the coup from abroad was startling in its uniformity. The White House issued a statement saying that "the United States stood by 'the legitimately elected government' of Mr. Traoré." It also suspended aid to Mali four days after the coup. French Foreign Minister Alain Juppé announced that France was suspending diplomatic relations. The UN Security Council demanded "the immediate restoration of constitutional rule and the democratically elected government." The chairman of the African Union Commission issued a statement that the African Union "strongly condemns this act of rebellion, which seriously undermines constitutional legality and constitutes a significant setback for Mali and for the on-going democratic processes on the continent." Other African states followed suit and some called for military action against the coup leaders and their soldiers. The regional grouping, the Economic Community of West African States put troops on alert and issued an ultimatum that if constitutional government was not restored immediately, it would close Mali's borders and block its assets in member states.

Perhaps because of the furious reaction of other governments, the coup leader, Captain Sanogo, announced that he intended to enter negotiations with "our brothers," the Tuwareg, and invited them to peace talks. (*BBC News* March 24). Further, he promised free elections "in which we will not participate." At the same time, Sanogo moved to kill the presidential guard, which had remained loyal to President Traoré and had tried to launch a countercoup. Allegedly not only the guard but uncooperative politicians and businessmen were hunted down, tortured and assassinated. The numbers were not so large as in other countries because Mali is a small country and offered fewer targets to the new junta.

In December the junta forced the resignation of the more or less neutral prime minister whom they arrested and incarcerated at a military base. By installing a prime minister of their choice, Django Sissoko, the junta appeared to consolidate its hold on the government. Not surprisingly, however, the bitter rivalries within the ruling group and between the civil servants and the coup leaders made military action against the Tuwareg almost impossible. One episode shows what was happening. Lydia Polgreen reported (*The New York Times*, January 24, 2013) the experience of a Malian soldier. He had just successfully engaged a Tuwareg unit and radioed for reinforcement to consolidate his position. On being told that his "fellow soldiers had already fallen back, beating a hasty retreat...[he] did what other soldiers had done as the fighting intensified: He stripped off his uniform, waded through an irrigation canal and melted into the town's civilian population...'we barely escaped with our lives.'" As Ms. Polgreen goes on, "Beyond fleeing in the heat of battle, hundreds of Malian soldiers, including commanders of elite units trained by the united States, defected to the rebels..."

V

Into this mess strode the beleaguered French president. François Hollande, who, struggling with an ebbing mandate and with approval ratings down to 40%, suddenly announced that he would send armed forces, partly drawn from the Foreign Legion, to fight "terrorists elements coming from the north..." Predictably, his approval ratings surged to 63%. However, as Stephen Smith reported (*The London Review of Books*, February 7 2013), former Foreign Minister Dominique de Villepin sounded a grave warning:

> Let us draw lessons from a decade of lost wars in Afghanistan, in Iraq, in Libya...In Mali, we will fight blindly for lack of clear war objectives. And we will fight alone for lack of a solid Malian counterpart. Their president was ousted last March, their prime minister in December, a divided Malian army has fallen apart; on whom shall we lean?

Indeed, it could be worse than M. Villepin suggested. Activities by the Malian soldiers and their officers, Ms. Polgreen (cited above) suggests, "have rekindled longstanding doubts about whether it [the coup-installed regime] can – or perhaps even should – be left to hold on to the gains French troops have made." Massacres of prisoners, anal rape of army soldiers at gun point by their comrades and other atrocities as well as widely reported acts of incompetence, desertion (by about 1 in 4 soldiers of Mali's 7,000-man army) or cowardice indicate a poor return on the more than $550 million the US spent over the last four years to train the Malian and other West African armies. The omens bode ill for a quick and successful war resulting in a better Mali.

However, the Obama administration and the French government have ruled that the current military government is legitimate, and have said that they intend to support it with whatever it takes to "win."

VI

We have been told the same as we got deeper into Vietnam, Iraq and Afghanistan. We are told that we really have no choice because its fall into the clutches of the insurgents would endanger us all. The "domino" theory is no longer respectable, but it must linger in the minds of some militant strategists. If we "lose" Mali, what will happen in Senegal, Niger or, worst of all, Nigeria? And what will happen to us? The nightmare scenario is Mali as the "heart of darkness."

Is this a real danger? The sequence of events I have recounted above and the current situation suggest that we should be at least cautious in evaluating such fears and in our responses. What we know about our Malian allies – like what we knew about our Vietnamese allies -- is not reassuring; As the former French Foreign Minister asked, we can hardly hope to rely on them. Our answer in Vietnam, Iraq and Afghanistan was that we would do the job of governing for them. The record is clear, it did not work.

We know less about the Tuareg. Is it conceivable that their grievances can be sufficiently assuages to make peace? Is there enough of a coherent movement among them with whom the African Union or the United Nations could make an acceptable accommodation? Would such an accommodation undermine French and American objectives? We are told that their most impressive organization, *Mouvement National pour la Liberation de l'Azawad* (MNLA) has been infiltrated and partly sidelined by another group or groups calling themselves "al-Qaida in the Islamic Maghreb." Is that true and if so what does it mean?

As Andy Morgan reported (*The Guardian* April 3, 2013), "...most Tuareg do not even begin to see themselves as Islamists, terrorists or gunrunners and are dismayed by their new starring role in the 'global war on terror.'" And Hugh Roberts of the International Crisis Group (cited above) has charged that those "pompously renamed al-Qaeda in the Islamic Magreb in 2007" owe...much to manipulation by Algeria's intelligence services. The country's [Algeria's] Islamist insurgency had been going for 11 years with no overspill to the south; and virtually no terrorism in Algeria's Sahara region."

Roberts concluded that the Islamists were "a constant nuisance but never a serious threat to any state in the region, let alone Europe...[but] as the International Crisis group...[warned] 'a misconceived and heavy-handed approach could tip the scales the wrong way.'"

Today, the few competent observers believe that the radical wing of the Islamists have drained away much of the sympathy for them (or more accurately the hatred of the population for their opponents, particularly Mali's army and police). Popular disgust over draconian penalties – carried out by both the Tuwareg and the coup leaders -- for civil and religious disobedience is widely known. Many Malians appear to wish a plague on both their houses.

If we correctly identify the problem, is there only one solution – military action? Would it not be wise to explore all the options? From what I read, the objectives of both sides sound like they would be sufficiently met by some form of federation. At the least, this option should be fully explored before we rush into military action.

If we opt for military action, what does this choice portend? At minimum, it seems to me, it suggests an open-ended, problematical, expensive and certainly long-term commitment. Reading pronouncements from the Obama administration and the Hollande administration, I hear echoes of Indo-China: the French are clear that they are on a losing wicket and want to get out with honor while the Americans are already moving to take their place. Vietnam redux.

As Eric Schmitt quoted (*The New York Times*, March 19, 2013) a counterterrorism specialist at the Africa Center for Strategic Studies of the National Defense University in Washington, he said that "an ongoing commitment will be required." The Americans and, above all the French, hope that their role can be taken over by African troops, mainly from Chad, and perhaps operating under a UN mandate. But, as in Vietnam, the projected numbers keep escalating: France initially sent in 750 soldiers, then reinforced them with 2,500 more. Now there is talk of a "heavily-armed rapid response force" of 10,000.

As the counterinsurgency forces grow in number, so do the guerrillas.

As Stephen Smith (cited above) observed, "all over the north throngs of unemployed young people have started to make a living from jihad and sharia enforcement. War and religion have become a sustainable way of life for them...[one can be] a Taliban [sic.] by day and a smuggler [of cigarettes, weapons and drugs] at night...The French intervention may well give them purpose and greater coherence."

So, as Peter Tinti and Adam Nossiter report (*The New York Times*, February 18, 2013), the militants are not just hiding out in the mountains but have taken up posts in the dozens of villages along the Niger River and even the major city of Gao where they blend into the local populations so that the foreign soldiers "can't tell the difference between them and the population." Indeed, many of the *jihadis* are themselves native and are hidden by relatives. Apparently, many of the younger and more dedicated *jihadis* are religious students (*taliban ul-Ilm*).

Drawing on his experiences in Iraq and Algeria, Ambassador Chester Crocker predicted (*The New York Times*, Op Ed, March 7, 2013), "a very long struggle for control of the Sahel – the trans-Saharan badlands that stretch from the Atlantic Ocean to the Red Sea." Thus, whatever else may be involved the very success of an anti-Tuwareg, anti-Islamist war in Mali is almost certain to impact on the surrounding African states. In the worst case, which may be also the likely case, what has begun in Mali will spread among Africa's many weak states whose societies are at least partly Muslim.

As we should have learned from our past wars, intervention is easy, but getting out is often difficult. This is partly because natives who lack sophisticated equipment and large armies fight as guerrillas. Trying to defeat such foes in Vietnam, Iraq, Afghanistan and Somalia, Americans have suffered tens of thousands of casualties, hundreds of thousands of wounded and trillions of dollars. When supported by their own people, guerrillas are virtually undefeatable.[4]

In the spring of 2013 we began to see these tactics at work: Tuwareg

---

4 I offer case studies of a dozen insurgencies in my book *Violent Politics* (New York: HarperCollins, 2007).

guerrillas, thought to be already defeated, attacked Mali's second city, Gao, on the Niger River. Meeting resistance, they dispersed. Their move was not "defeat" but wise tactics. The tactics of the guerrilla. They strike, fade away and return to strike again.

The harder the native forces are pressed, the more likely they are to accept help from foreign jihadis who profess to share their aspirations and angers. Since they are relatively few and have neither armies nor territory, such foreigners often fight as terrorists. Those with similar grievances will hear the Tuwareg call. Indeed, that call will energize more foreign Islamic fighters because they will see the war in Mali as a war against Islam and so, regardless of their ethnic backgrounds, a war against them. We encouraged, financed and armed such forces in the Afghan war against the Soviet Union and suffered from them in their struggle against us. It is unlikely to be very different in Mali.

And the response, too, is predictable and indeed already partly underway: As Eric Schmitt and Scott Sayare wrote (*International Herald Tribune*, February 25, 2013), "Opening a new front in the drone wars against Al Qaeda and is affiliates, President Barack Omama has announced that about 100 U.S. troops have been sent to Niger to help set up a new base from which unarmed Predator aircraft will conduct surveillance...The new drone base will join a constellation of small airstrips that the United States has placed in Africa in recent years." Indeed, even before this move occurred, as David E. Sanger and Eric Schmitt reported (*International Herald Tribune*, January 23, 2013), the United States was aiding French military operations with aerial refueling. Such "refueling," they noted, "would bring the American involvement to a new level, directly supporting military attacks."

Thus, the quick response of the former colonial power has led to victories that may come to seem pyrrhic. The French and their American and European allies are apt to find that Mali is a bed of quicksand in which they can sink in unending and profitless war.

February 11, 2013
Revised to April 2, 2013

CHAPTER 16

THE ELUSIVE QUEST
FOR SECURITY

"Security is mortals' chiefest enemy"

Hecate in Shakespeare's Macbeth

As we worry over our quest for security today, few of us are aware that what we experience has been repeated over the ages time after time: security has always proven to be elusive and our ancestors failed repeatedly in their quest for it. So perhaps a short excursion into the past may provide a perspective worth considering because as George Santayana memorably wrote, "Those who cannot remember the past are condemned to repeat it."

* * *

Human beings are not alone in our quest for security: it is instinctive among all living creatures. Everywhere we look, we see animals banding together to attempt to protect themselves. Usually, land animals, birds and even fish in the open ocean mark out territories from which they attempt to exclude intruders. The drive to exclusivity in these territories is perhaps echoed in our times in gated communities: the attempt to keep people who are "not like us" out. Today, sanctuaries are more or less random in location, but among primitive peoples, they focused on a water hole or a grove of fruit trees or other source of their sustenance.

At least originally, human societies were small and the members were all kindred. As we have learned more about these groups, which lived the way our ancestors lived for well over a million years, they appear to have rarely been as large as a hundred people. More than that number could not have fed themselves within the range they could walk across in a day and so could access. Consequently, as they grew larger, groups were constantly breaking up with the weaker portions moving or being driven out to new territories. As they did, they lost touch with one another and often became rivals and enemies. So enmity and rivalry were built into the experience of our ancestors generation after generation.

While, of course, we have no records, we can infer from studies of animal behavior that intense hostility to foreigners and strong incentives to group loyalty shaped human society over something like the last 50,000 generations. Father to child, each generation believed that only group solidarity afforded a degree of security from ever-present enemies; so somehow and some time along this long enforcing experience, social and religious forces were generated to ensure group solidarity. As the great 14th century North African student of society, Ibn Khaldun, observed, the intense attachment of the individual to his group was the glue that made for internal security and also enabled groups to defend themselves against foreigners. It too, he believed, was instinctive – or in his words, God-ordained -- and could be violated only at the cost of destruction of the society.

* * *

Ibn Khaldun was writing about nomadic peoples, but, as the agricultural revolution began to take hold about 10,000 years ago, what had been little bands became more numerous and outgrew kinship ties. The members became less motivated to protect one another than to protect their neighborhoods. Cultivated fields were now the focus of their investment and consequently, the source of their sustenance. Croplands could be abandoned or lost to enemies only at the cost of famine or oblivion. So these defined areas acquired a sanctity that was often encoded in religion and became the objects of intense devotion. This may be taken as the origin of nationalism.

We know, historically, that the effect of this transformation was first manifest in the growth of little states, neighbors to one another but also strangers to each other's gods and loyalties. For them achieving security meant keeping infiltrators from neighboring societies at bay. And the obvious way to do it was by turning dwellings into forts and extending them by building walls. First, little villages like Jericho and then even large cities, began to be encased in stone. About 7000 BC, Jericho's ten-acre plot was surrounded by a massive wall. The cost was enormous. Jericho had only about 2,000 inhabitants. That yielded a work force, at a maximum of about 200; so each worker had not only to carry out the productive tasks of the economy, farming and herding, but also to build and then maintain the town wall. It has been calculated that each adult worker had to quarry, carry and place, without machinery or animal power, about 50 cubic meters of rock and earth. We cannot accurately measure the cost in terms of gross domestic product (GDP) but the task must have amounted to at least a quarter of the labor of the community.

Even at that huge effort, walls didn't save Jericho. We know that the inhabitants were killed, carried off or ran away and were replaced by invaders time after time, so that their successors had to build or rebuild the town's walls 20 times.

We see this enormous outlay of resources and the desperate fear that drove it on a large scale first among the dozens of cities in the Tigris-Euphrates valley. By 2500 BC Uruk had a double wall over 20 feet high and six miles long. No matter what the cost, the inhabitants thought they must build it or be enslaved or killed. That same conclusion was reached in later centuries in hundreds of cities and towns during the "warring states" periods in Greece, India and China. As societies grew in number and became increasingly dependent on their lands, war became endemic, and societies were desperate to find means to achieve security. Walls were at least temporarily effective and often were the only available means of defense.

What Jericho began has been carried forward over the centuries, at probably a comparable cost and for the same reason, the quest for security. As one town created a relatively safe redoubt, its neighbors felt compelled to follow suit. Town and wall merged; indeed, the town virtually became its wall. We see this in Egyptian hieroglyphic writing, the ideograph for town was a wall; similarly in Chinese, the words for city, *ch'eng* and *shih*, arise from the characters for wall.

The most massive and famous fortification, of course, is the complex of forts and walls the Chinese called the barrier, the *Ai*, and we call the Great Wall of China. It was constructed in an effort to keep out the inner Asian nomads, just like the Roman Emperor Hadrian tried to keep out the Scottish tribesmen with his wall on the northern frontier of Roman Brittan. Neither accomplished its purpose.

Following the barbarian invasions of Rome, the descendants of the barbarians themselves as well as the surviving natives carried on with wall building, surrounding their new towns with the huge structures whose remains we see today. Medieval Europe had no unfortified towns: it was a walled society.

Virtually everywhere and century after century, wall building was thought to be the key to security, but the cost was often unsustainable. The quest for security, as Shakespeare has Hecate say, caused its own defeat. We see this in miniature in the struggle between two Italian city-states, Florence and Sienna: the cost of building and maintaining its wall literally bled Sienna to death. It could not maintain the productive economy that the wall had been built to protect.

Is all this only antiquarian interest?

No, it is more contemporary that we like to think. Consider the amount of wall building in the 20th century -- in the 1930s, Italy tried to seal off Egypt from Libya with mine fields and barbed wire to starve the Libyan insurgents while France dug the Maginot Line to block the German army; then in the 1960s, Russia/East Germany tried to cut ties with the West with the Berlin Wall while France tried to isolate the Algerian resistance with a wall separating the militants from Tunisia; with walls, America is trying to block Latin American immigrants and India similarly is trying to prevent Bangladeshis from entering. Today, the most impressive feature of Israeli-occupied Palestine is a massive concrete wall.

Common to all these efforts at achieving security in stone or concrete are two features – they were ruinously expensive and they did not work.

* * *

Israeli separation barrier at Abu Dis, June 2004. This picture shows a portion of the barrier being built by Israel in the West Bank. http://en.wikipedia.org/wiki/File:AbuDisWall.jpg

Probably already in Jericho and certainly later, rulers recognized that walls provided only a temporary barrier, indeed often just a psychological barrier. To be even partially effective, they needed to be manned. Jericho's builders had to be not only its masons and farmers but also its army.

The logical next step, as societies got larger and commanded more manpower, was to reach beyond the wall with armed force. Jericho's 200 masons/soldiers/farmers probably did not venture beyond their wall, but the thousands enrolled by Uruk and other growing city-states could and did. Their aim was to weaken, disable or ultimately conquer the potential invader. The survivors in this Darwinian contest among the city-states were those societies that carried war to their enemies. Armies became massive and war became the industry of the state.

Even genocide ultimately failed. This was both because some subject peoples survived to fight again but more importantly because the survivors became integrated into Assyrian society. While the defeated states were

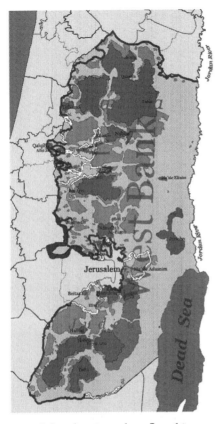

Map showing where Israel is building walls.

"regime-changed" they, individually or in small groups, underwent a transformation of their culture and their perception of themselves. In effect, as the Assyrians exploited their labor they turned the subject peoples into "Assyrians" who became their farmers, craftsmen and even their soldiers. The converted aliens soon came to believe that power and enjoyment of its benefits no longer needed to be an Assyrian monopoly. Once this transformation happened, Assyria, despite its powerful army, sophisticated government and elaborate security policy, collapsed, leaving behind only massive ruins to decorate museums.

Even genocide ultimately failed. This was both because some subject peoples survived to fight again but more importantly because the survivors became integrated into Assyrian society. While the defeated states were "regime-changed" they, individually or in small groups, underwent a transformation of their culture and their perception of themselves. In effect, as the Assyrians exploited their labor they turned the subject peoples into "Assyrians" who became their farmers, craftsmen and even their soldiers. The converted aliens soon came to believe that rule and enjoyment of its benefits no longer needed to be an Assyrian monopoly. Once this transformation happened, Assyria, despite its powerful army, sophisticated government and elaborate security policy, collapsed, leaving behind only massive ruins to decorate museums.

Impotently, the native Assyrians watched their former serfs and mercenaries erect a new empire in their place. This was a theme to be played out time after time – by Persia, Greece, Han China and others – until, a thousand years later, Germanic tribes would replace the Romans.

* * *

As state after state has found, armies are blunt instruments, often wielded by the blind to bring about what was neither expected nor desired. Indeed, the military often transformed those who wielded it. Historically we see this over and over again. Regard China and Rome. Both had populations of about 50 million people and both set out to conquer their worlds. After their defeat by the Gauls in 391 BC, the Romans recast their society as an army and set about conquering the 60 or so other states of the Italian peninsula. Over the next century, Rome had only about 5 years without a war. We do not know the cost in monetary terms, but in terms of lives, enslavement of other peoples and destruction of other societies it was enormous. It also led, as it had earlier in Assyria, to the replacement of the sturdy peasants who had made its victories possible by imported alien slaves.

In China warfare among the 100 or so petty states began as a game: during the so-called *Ch'un Qin* period it was like the tournaments of Western Knights: beautifully dressed rulers rode to the event in their carriages and retired before anyone got hurt or rain threatened their costumes. But gradually it became serious. By the 5th century BC, in the *Chan Kuo* or "Warring States" period, many of the populations in the traditional states had been massacred, and the survivors were desperate to find ways to achieve security. Three of the ways they tried, and which remain with us, are striking: a new profession was created, the strategist who professed to know how to achieve security. Standing aloof but claiming vast knowledge, he offered his sage advice to the practitioners. This "expert," profilerated now into legions, remains with us today.

The second innovation was the contribution of the state of Lu. In 594 BC, it instituted the first tax on land to support its army. Now such taxation is universal and absorbs ever increasing amounts of money, talent and industrial capacity. It has obviously also created sharp political debate that has virtually replaced the focus on the achievement of sustainable security.

But it was the third transformation that is most striking: warfare became truly total. The defeated could not surrender. When they dropped their weapons, they were slaughtered. As the victors raped and burned vast areas of China, whole societies perished. Since the armies of the remaining states were nearly equal, the ruler of the state that ultimately won, Qin, transformed his society, purging the aristocracy and creating a controlling bureaucracy. But what was really crucial was that independently he hit on the same formula as the contemporary Romans – transforming aliens into allies or clients and ultimately into citizens – and encouraging agriculture with new land grants and handicraft industry for weapons and other equipment. It is perhaps not too much of a stretch to say that Qin created the first military-industrial complex. These new ventures culminated in the creation for the first time of a unified Chinese state in 221 BC. China had staked out the road to security through monopoly. That has ever since remained a central doctrine in Chinese national policy.

* * *

While, relative to China, medieval Europe was miniscule, it too was beset by the terrible costs of war. Armies were then organized not on the Chinese scale of hundreds of thousands, but by squads of three men, two men-at-arms and a page. Even these tiny formations were ruinously expensive, each costing as much in a day as a skilled artisan earned in a week. Consequently, perhaps 80% of the revenues of many Italian city-states went to the military, and when states mounted campaigns against their rivals, they were economically defeated even if they were militarily victorious. A single campaign might cost 10 times their yearly revenue. So it was that in the 14th century, Florence created the first Western tax, the *catasto*. It proved unable to keep up with the cost of defense; so soon Florence created the first known institution of a public debt. Our current debate over the bite of taxes and the size of the debt can thus be seen to go back to medieval Florence and was caused by the same need: to pay for the army.

The Italians were deeply disturbed by these pressures, and sought to learn how better to handle the issue of security. Their hunger for guides unconsciously echoed that of rulers in ancient China, one of whose many "itinerant strategists," Sun Tzu, was avidly consulted as the warring states rulers fought to the death.

Less well known were a similar class of advisers to the warring states of India. The most famous of them, Kautilya (a.k.a. Vishnugupta), speaks less clearly to Westerner than to "oriental" rulers. Divided as the Indian, Persian, Turkish and other dynasties were by the offspring of multiple marriages, Kautilya begins his analysis of state power, danger and the quest for security in the harem. To us, this is exotic, but when he speaks of war, he speaks to us: in warfare, he warned, there is no sure benefit even in victory. And, victory does not always go to the strong. So the prosperity of the state and society is more likely in peace. Wherever possible, peace is the wisest option. Driven often by ambition and sometimes by fear, few rulers have heeded his advice.

In Medieval Europe, we all know of Machiavelli, but his *The Prince* was only one of scores of "Mirrors for Princes." They were early members of what has grown into a virtual industry with pundits and would-be strategists, even journalists, producing vast numbers of books and articles advising the practitioners on how to engage the world.

It was long before the Western version of the strategists had any access to an academic grounding. The credentials of most consisted almost entirely of residence abroad; few knew much about the history or culture of "their" countries and practically none knew the languages. A more solid grounding was long in coming. The first course in international affairs, a rather perfunctory effort and restricted to a comparison of France and Germany with occasional notes on Russia, was offered by Columbia not until 1917. It took Yale and Harvard 8 years to catch up. And really solid courses on world affairs did not begun until after World War II. The number of Americans who could speak or write languages other than English could have sat in one lecture hall. In my area, the Middle East, it was said that there were five native Americans who knew Arabic.

But the Cold War changed all of that: programs blossomed all over the country and students were subsidized. Special programs were established to train men and women to listen to broadcasts of suspect nations and so had to be given courses in a wide variety of languages. Unfortunately but understandably their vocabularies had to be geared to their tasks so they skipped over culture and even politics to discuss the hand grenade, the Kalashnikov and the road bomb.

From this "tactical" beginning, studies proliferated into such strategic issues as coups d'état and revolutions. One issue that has attracted much attention in recent years is counterinsurgency. That study is what made the reputation of General David Petraeus. I have analyzed it in my book Violent Politics. Petraeus began his work academically with a Princeton doctoral thesis, but then narrowed his focus to the challenge of defeating insurgents. Unknowingly, he fit within what is really a rather long tradition of "how to win..." books, of which the ancestor in Western literature was the work of the 16th century Spanish strategist Bernardo de Vargas Machuca. Machuca told his government how to defeat the Indian guerrillas in the New World. The plan he advocated may have helped the Spaniards, but what actually defeated the Indians was smallpox. Unfortunately for Petraeus' war plan, smallpox which was the counterinsurgency that defeated the Indians has virtually died out. But this did not prevent his plan from being implemented in Iraq and Afghanistan at vast cost in treasure, lives and the chance for settlement.

More benign, George Kennan has become an icon in the field of foreign affairs. He first caught high-level attention for his analysis of Soviet society in "the long telegram." (Less well known is the work of Kennan's Russian counterpart, Ambassador Nikolai Novikov, who similarly analyzed American society.) Sadly, even insiders and professionals like Kennan saw their analyses misinterpreted or distorted. In his better known article in *Foreign Affairs*, Kennan laid out the essence of a policy of containment: contain, that is, by generally peaceful means, or occasional "dirty tricks" (which he also advocated) any outward thrust by Soviet forces while allowing Russian society to grow, transform or fester. But, as it was interpreted, his doctrine encouraged a reliance on the military and gave a major push to the militarization of American society so deplored by President Eisenhower in his farewell address.

The gap between perception and action deeply worried a few of the modern strategists led by the then chairman of the policy planning council, Walt Rostow. He saw the prior efforts at planning as a formless mass. So he launched a different program: to construct a sort of pyramid in which individual issues and separate countries would be grouped and arranged in a hierarchy of importance. For example, Iraq would be viewed as a sort of building block in the structure of the Middle East and in turn the Middle East was to be seen as an adjunct to Europe. At the next level, Europe, Asia and the Americas were fitted into the sides of the pyramid, at the apex of which was America whose aims, fears and ambitions radiated through the whole structure.

Implicit was the idea that security could be achieved both by arranging that the pieces of the pyramid fit together. This model of the world in action would divide the fundamental from the peripheral and so guide practitioners to act in ways that enhanced security rather than just monitoring the flow of events or reacting to crises. Rostow brought to his plan his experience in World War II when he lobbied for concentration of bombing: scattering of bombing, he wrote, did little to impede the German army. But when the target was narrowed to bridges, and they were destroyed, the German army was unable to move. Similarly, he argued, the entire weight of the United States must be directed to where it would really make an effect. What the "targets" of this policy thought or did was of little moment. They could be forced into line by the overwhelming power of America. That was the policy America took to Vietnam.

This theory took little account of historical, cultural and psychological dimensions. It did not take into account why Vietnam, for example, did not just accept French rule and benefit from French largess or why it fought so tenuously against the American occupation. In short, the emphasis was on us, what we did or could do, rather than on the dynamics of what the Vietnamese saw as a national struggle. The policy led enormous cost to both the Vietnamese and the Americans and failed in it central objective, blocking the spread of Communism to Southeast Asia.

*　　*　　*

In parallel to the attempt to build analytical and theoretical models of policy, governments have devoted much energy and other resources to the building of bureaucratic means to carry out the policies. One of the most interesting examples of institution building was the Chinese establishment of an admiralty in 1132. For its time, it was an enormous institution which soon grew to 20 squadrons with 52,000 men. Kublai Khan inherited and greatly expanded it so that he was able to mount an attack on Japan with 900 ships in 1274. (The Spanish Armada that figures so strongly in Western history was composed of only 132 ships.) It was a very impressive entry into naval warfare, but it led nowhere and certainly did not increase Chinese security. Nor, of course did the smaller Spanish armada.

Financial pressures and the need to recruit Swiss mercenaries for his depleted army forced King Francis I of France in 1529 to build the first of a new style, essentially the style we have continued, diplomatic service. To him can be credited the first office of foreign affairs, the *Conseil des Affaires*. His great rival Charles V soon followed suit, but it was not until 1782 that the British created their Foreign Office. Foreign affairs was to become bureaucratized.

At first, and often still, the diplomatic personnel who were the instruments of this new bureaucracy were not highly regarded – far less highly regarded than their military counterparts -- and had little impact on national policy: the word "ambassador" is derived from the Celtic *ambactus* and went into Old English as *ambeht*. It meant just "servant." Even at a post abroad, the ambassador was an isolated figure, often neglected (and frequently not paid) by his own government and forbidden contact with natives; everywhere he was regarded as a spy.

In the military sphere, the new category of official, whose members were soon to be gathered into a general staff, carried more weight than the diplomats. This was the contribution of Prussia. After their defeat by

314

Napoleon in the battle of Jena in 1806, Prussian strategists, partially led by Carl Von Clausewitz and invigorated by the emotional thrust of nationalism popularized by Johann Gottlieb Fichte in his "Message to the German Nation," transformed their tiny state into a virtual army. One in each 4 young men became a soldier and the half-a-million-man military organization absorbed 90% of government revenues. The soldier became the ideal German and the General Staff set national policies. War and the preparation for war was not, as Clausewitz had written, "policy by other means;" rather the reverse was true: policy was war by other means. The military became the rationale of the state and, indeed of the whole society. Clausewitz's Prussia became Germany and its policies led directly to the great world wars of the 19th and 20th centuries. Rather than increase German security, however, it set off the move toward the near destruction of Germany in two world wars and the terrible events of the Nazi period. What had seemed to its inventors the guarantor of security became its nemesis.

*   *   *

At the end of World War II, the United States and the Soviet Union found themselves in what they thought was a completely new world. Few if any in either government were aware of previous attempts to achieve security; so, as Santayana warned, they were condemned to repeat some previous failures. They did so, however, under new labels and in new guises. We begin to see this clearly in the administration of President Truman.

In the American government, the quest for new means of action, better intelligence and a freer hand for the President led to the formation of what has grown into vast new bureaucracies including the CIA and the NSA and soon would become even larger by the addition of semi-governmental, former governmental and private contractors. Today, this assemblage is larger than most of the states in the United Nations and cannot be completely counted much less completely controlled. Whether the "national security state" has contributed to the achievement of security is at least questionable, but the government, urged rather than questioned by the legislature, threw itself into the new – to them -- policy direction.

Institution building was "in the air." Every problem seemed to call for a new office. And transferred to foreign affairs, and meant gathering all the allies, clients and associates of America into a grand anti-Soviet alliance. This became the *idea fixe* of Secretary of State John Foster Dulles. He aimed to surround the Soviet Union with virtual walls made up of alliances – NATO, CENTO and SEATO – each becoming an adjunct of America but each with its own bureaucracy and each functioning in its area almost like a superstate. NATO has more or less survived, in a rather different form, but CENTO, a.k.a. the Baghdad Pact, did more than any other factor to promote insecurity in the Middle East. Despite or because of them security remains elusive.

In a flurry of invention and contrivance, the United States got itself organized for the role it began to play. But, oblivious to history, it borrowed from the past. Consider such old timers as the division of the world into spheres of influence: that was a traditional British policy, and it was put into play by Winston Churchill even before the end of the War. He proposed to Josef Stalin – and Stalin wisely accepted – a division of Europe into spheres of dominance. Britain was to get Greece and the Soviet Union to get Eastern Europe. Long before the Yalta Conference, where allegedly weak and traitorous Americans gave away Europe, it was Churchill who planted the corner stone of the Iron Curtain. Attempting to cancel or modify Churchill's move would shape American policy toward Europe for nearly the next half century.

Britain also convinced the American government of the validity of a concept invented by South African General Smuts: the domino theory. Smuts argued that if a state anywhere "fell to Communism," all its neighbors would soon also fall like a row of dominos. This is the concept that drew America into the war in Greece (which was a sort of dry-run for the later Vietnam war) and explained and justified the emphasis on the infusion of resources into Italy, France and Germany. Fear of collapse of the row of dominos was the motivation behind a series of policies put into place all over Asia as well. Insecurity was seen as the reality and the quest for security was an almost visceral reaction.

The action that has had the longest-lasting effect on security was also set in the first years after the end of the War. Britain was disputing control of the oil of Iran with its newly elected government. The Iranians, newly awakened to their national interests and led by the first freely elected leader in their history, Muhammad Mossadegh, were demanding greater participation in the oil industry. The British threatened and bribed Iranian officials and even closed down the fields and refinery. The Royal Navy menacingly appeared off shore. Nothing worked. So the British sent an emissary, the senior MI6 (foreign intelligence) officer for the Middle East, Montgomery Woodhouse, to Washington to convince the Dulles brothers, John Foster at the State Department and Allan at the CIA, that Iran was another domino, falling to Communism, and could be saved only by "regime change." (The term had not yet been coined.) The Dulleses were enthusiastic and sent Kermit Roosevelt of the CIA to mount a coup. It succeeded but proved to be a Pyrrhic victory: Mossadegh was overthrown, the Shah reinstated, but the Anglo-American intervention left a bitterness, suspicion and hostility to the West, and particularly toward America, that still underlie Iranian attitudes and actions.

*   *   *

Where other means of action failed to produce desired results or were impossible to undertake, rulers and their generals have always found changes in weapons technology attractive: the bronze sword gave way to the iron blade, the long bow to the cross bow and so on down to the machine gun and the tank. More recently, the rocket replaces artillery and the drone the piloted aircraft. The arms industry would have us believe that warfare can be made virtually into a board game with distant control, no casualties and uniform results. Nothing is more seductive to professionals and laymen alike.

Believing in this new form of safe, secure and victorious warfare, in the last 5 years, the US has spent at least $2.59 trillion on "defense," a large part of it on weapons, and plans to spend 5% more in the coming 5 years. Its new emphasis is on the drone and the targeted killing of enemies, some of whom may be American citizens. So what are the results?

An independent survey in 2007, the latest available, of hundreds of such missions by an official research organization, the "Counter-IED Operations Integration Center," found that   attacks accelerate after assassinations and drone attacks: in the areas where the 'hits' had taken place, bomb attacks had gone *up* by as much as a fifth. Not *down* as was the advertised objective. The marvelous new technology not only did not stop attacks but, as we now know in Afghanistan and Pakistan, has created a bitter reaction to America that may unhinge American policy. Ever improving weapons do not appear to have enhanced the quest for security.

*   *   *

So what remains to be tried?

In 1931, under the auspices of the League of Nations, a number of European intellectuals decided to form an organization to seek to find the causes of war and the means to achieve security. They had reason for alarm. That was the crucial year in the rise of Nazism and all over Eastern Europe Fascist movements were in the ascendant. America was oblivious and a large part of the English ruling class was enthusiastic about this new source of world order, totalitarian governments and mass militant right-wing parties. Churchill famously thought Mussolini to be the greatest man of the time. And slightly later, Edward VIII (as the Duke of Winsor) often gave the *Heil Hitler* gesture in public. Little European nations, like Greece, were creating "order" on the Nazi pattern. Some saw these moves not as creating order but preparing for war. But who could offer any insight into the dilemmas posed by human nature and see the shape of the growing storm clouds? Either encouraged or condoned by the already nearly moribund League of Nations, Albert Einstein took up the task of trying to decide what forces were at work.

In his open letter of July 30, 1932, (often referred to as the essay "Why War") Einstein asked, "Is there any way of delivering mankind from the menace of war...[which] has come to mean a matter of life and death for Civilization as we knew it; nevertheless, for all the zeal displayed, every attempt at solution has ended in a lamentable breakdown."

Einstein began by recognizing that there was no institutional means of action then available. The League of Nations had no means to enforce its decisions, so it was little more than a debating society. As for governments, "...my first axiom [he said, is that] the quest for international security involves the unconditional surrender by every nation, in a certain measure, of its liberty of action – its sovereignty that is to say – and it is clear beyond all doubt that no other road can lead to such security." The ambitions and fears of rulers were simply too powerful for this to happen.

Moreover, ambition of rulers and avarice of "purely mercenary" groups, amounting virtual governments were "active in every nation; they were composed of individuals who, indifferent to social considerations and restraints, regard warfare, the manufacture and sale of arms, simply as an occasion to advance their personal interests and enlarge their personal authority."

How does this minority sway the majority who stand to lose by insecurity and warfare? He answers that "it has the schools and press, usually the Church as well, under its thumb. This enables it to organize and sway the emotions of the masses, and make its tool of them." While recognizing the power of these elements, he believed that "strong psychological factors are at work which paralyze" efforts at peace seeking Consequently, Einstein turned from institutional answers and sought to deepen the inquiry: what were the human factors that blocked the road to peace and security? It is evident that people are ready to be led "even to sacrifice their lives." This must be "Because man has within him a lust for hatred and destruction." What can be done about this? Einstein decided that the best person to address this question was Sigmund Freud.

In his answer, Freud touches on human evolution – then not well known – and concludes that over the long span of the human experience force was the arbiter in all disagreements or disputes and that the end desired by the winner "is most effectively gained when the opponent is definitely put out of action – in other words killed." Any lesser result, such a sparing the victim for forced labor, "rankles in his victim [and so] forfeits to some extent his personal security." Genocide is the most logical policy.

The only long-term hope, Freud believed, is "first, the creation of … a supreme court of judicature; secondly, its investment with adequate executive force. Unless this second requirement be fulfilled, the first is unavailing… [and] any effort to replace brute force by the might of an ideal is, under present conditions, doomed to fail…there is no likelihood of our being able to suppress humanity's aggressive tendencies." But, he remarked, the chance that the current "judicature" being given power is nil. Security could not be achieved by the impotent League of Nations.

Freud was not a historian and thought in more or less rigid or absolute categories, but it is worth pointing out that the deep psychological forces he described must have been set over the 50 thousand or so generations of experience being passed to the young; it is only in the last 100 or so generations that even sporadic attempts have been made to modify the long heritage of violence.

Surely, this effort must be greatly strengthened and expanded if we are even to have a hope of success in our quest for security. But it is a slow process, little understood and little supported, and to which relatively little attention is paid. So where does all this leave us?

* * *

So it is that after this long record of failure we are now slowly beginning to turn toward the things that really matter in the lives of peoples around the world, health, education, access to an adequate amount of food. These we, in the relatively secure and relatively affluent West, understand. What eludes us is an emotional issue with which we seldom emphasize: the desperate demand of peoples, particularly in the formerly colonial and despised parts of the world for respect for their beliefs, their customs and their territory.

As we have learned at vast cost, it is the ability to "be themselves" which even more than the physical basics of life that has driven the militants in Algeria, Vietnam and Afghanistan. So it is likely that the road to real and long-term security must, as Freud and Einstein agreed, begin here with us, in our own attitudes, as well as in our willingness to share at least some portion of the good things of the earth. This is, admittedly, a slender reed on which to base policy, but it is also clear that our quest for security by other means has failed. If we are wise enough to admit this, perhaps we can make a new start and develop a more knowing, sensitive and comprehensive approach to security.

March 25, 2012

George Polk reading a dispatch for CBS News Radio

CHAPTER 17

GREECE, THE MURDER OF GEORGE POLK AND THE MODEL FOR VIETNAM

The Greece in which George Polk was murdered was a battleground. Historically, of course, Greece had always been. Metaphors of war are perhaps the most persistent themes in Greek art and literature. Classical Athens knew peace for only about a dozen years in the two centuries of its greatness. And when they were not fighting, raping, pillaging, enslaving and killing Greeks in rival city-states (*poleis*), Greeks were plotting against, exiling or killing their fellow townsmen. Our word "ostracize" comes from the Greek custom which allowed citizens to write the name of one of their fellows, whom they envied or feared, or simply disliked, on a fragment of a pot (Greek: *ostra*) to vote to banish him from the *polis*. Our word "politics" has a brutal provenance.

What makes Greece outstanding, indeed unique, is not that the Greeks were more bloody minded than others but that they so magnificently memorialized their hostilities. All nations fought wars, but Homer raised war to art; many suffered through terrible civil wars, but Thucydides makes their experience a text for all future statesmen; and while many empires have exploited their subjects only Pericles turned the fruits of imperialism into the Parthenon.

After its days of glory, Greece became the plaything of others. Rome both sat at the feet of the Greeks and knocked their legs out from under them. Augustus rebuilt Rome to Greek canons of beauty in Greek marble but then filled Rome with Greek slaves. Tens of thousands of Greeks were forcibly resettled in Italy, and those who were left behind lost their freedom and often their lives: for example, when Corinth tried to rebel,

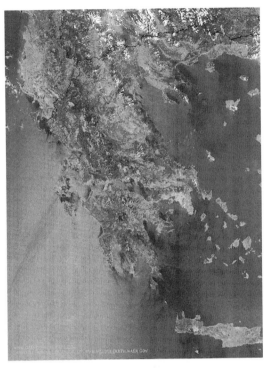

NASA image of Greece

the Romans exiled, enslaved or killed the entire city population and resettled the city with Italians. Indeed, when one tallies all the invaders and settlers since classical times, it is doubtful that there could be much Greek "blood" in modern Greeks.

But Greeks and others have tended the myth of the Greek past. The myth so strongly colors foreigners' attitudes as to have become a strategic national resource. We can see it as a significant cause of English support for British policy toward the eastern Mediterranean.

Lord Byron put to song this ideal. In it, Greece's splendor acquired an ethereal quality, an essence that had never been destroyed but merely concealed under the dust of unfortunate centuries. Neither the often sordid and brutal history which Thucydides lays before us nor events of the last 2,000 or so years ultimately matter. The "Greece" we see is just the physical manifestation of an ideal of beauty and freedom to which the proper response of educated and decent human beings must be *philhellenism*.

However much this view pervaded the universities, and set a tone in literature, art and architecture (and not only in Britain but in Germany, Italy, France, Russia and America), it usually gave way in British government circles before other realities. The reality that usually counted most was Russia's imperial thrust southward.

In this "great game," Britain had two chessmen, one was a valiant warrior (the *rukh*), India with its Sepoy army, while the other, the Ottoman Empire, was rarely more than a pawn, a peon or simple foot soldier. Indeed, the Ottoman Empire, the "sick man of Europe," seemed always about to fall off the board. At nearly all costs, British statesmen, at least until the First World War, agreed that it had to be kept alive as a barrier to the Russians. The British were willing to plunder it in the south, as they ultimately did of its Arab provinces, but they were wary of hurting it in the north.

When both the Ottoman and the Russian empires collapsed at the end of the First World War, Britain shifted its strategy: it decided that it could afford to more or less forget about the Balkans.

Then came the Second World War. The source of danger shifted from the northeast, Russia, to the west, Italy, and to the northwest, Germany. At first Greece held its own against the Italians, but the Germans quickly and brutally demonstrated Greece's vulnerability. In a curious way, that brought the two strands of Nineteenth century thought together and transformed them -- Britain had a number of classicists who knew Greek well enough to operate there clandestinely under the Nazi occupation and British statesmen transferred to Greece the role of blocking northern encroachment which their grandfathers had assigned to the Ottoman Empire. To explain and justify the shift, whatever the current reality, Greece began to be idealized as a bastion of freedom.

My brother, George Polk, who was then the chief CBS correspondent in the Middle East, was murdered in Greece in 1948. He had the misfortune to be reporting on Greece when four trends that had begun long before came into focus. To understand why he was murdered, it is necessary to understand them. Having done so will also lead us on to see the beginnings of ideas and actions that would lead America into the Vietnam war a decade later.

First were the political events within Greece immediately before the war; second, flight of parts of the royalist government to Egypt where, under British protection, it was recognized by Britain and the United

States as the Greek Government-in-Exile; third, the rise of the anti-German resistance movement in Greece; and fourth, British strategy in the Eastern Mediterranean. I will now briefly describe them.

* * *

First, before the Second World War, during the 1930s, Greece lived under the iron fist of the Metaxas regime. Ioannis Metaxas himself and the policies he effected differed from those of Hitler and Nazi Germany mainly in that Metaxas (who had studied at the Prussian war college and had unbounded admiration for all things German) was Greek. In the prewar years, he had tried to remake the Greeks into modern "Aryans" by imposing upon them a Greek version of Nazism with additional flourishes borrowed from Fascist Italy. Adopting the title *Arkhigos* – as close as Greek could come to *Fuhrer* or *Duce* – he enforced the greeting of a raised arm salute. For Hitler's Third Reich read Metaxas's "Third Hellenic Civilization." What Hitler had hoped to do with the next generation through the *Hitlerjugend*, Metaxas tried to do with his *Ethnikí Orgánosis Neoléas*, (EON). Greeks were to be purged of all corrupt ideas in which Metaxas sweepingly included parliamentary democracy, a free press, women's rights and even the Boy Scouts. The books of a wide range of authors were banned and burned. Those unfortunate enough to be caught opposing him, by the Greek equivalent of the Gestapo, were exiled, sent to concentration camps or shot.

In one of those curious turns of politics, it was Mussolini and Hitler who made this unattractive regime part of the "Free World." What happened was ironic but also enormously important: it was ironic because Hitler was opposed to the attack. In October 1940, Mussolini threw his ill-equipped army into Greece apparently to show that Italy was a full partner to Germany and that he was the equal of Hitler. It was one of the most important events of the Second World War because, when the attack failed, Hitler had to rescue the Italians and doing so threw off the timetable for his assault on Russia. Without the attack on Greece, the Germans would have been able to avoid the fearful Russian winter. Thus, while Metaxas's regime would certainly have hated to help the Russian Communists, it deserves some credit for the salvation of Russia. They paid a heavy price for this contribution to the defeat of the Wehrmacht.

Whatever else it was, Metaxas's regime was nationalistic; so when the Italians attacked Greece in October 1940, the Greeks went to war...more or less shoulder to shoulder. Initially, they did well against the Italians but quickly collapsed when the Wehrmacht attacked in April 1941.

Then, second, in the British-organized withdrawal the upper echelons of the government and a part of the Greek army fled into exile in British-occupied Egypt. Most of the middle and lower echelons of what had been the Metaxas regime, especially the various formations of the police and virtually all of the civil service, however, remained in Greece. During the Axis occupation, almost all of these groups worked actively with the Germans, Italians and Bulgarians. At the top, the Germans were able to form a puppet government composed of Metaxas's remaining ministers. They converted parts of the former political police into quasi-military formations, known as the Rallis Security Battalions, that were armed and directed by the Germans. They were notorious for rounding up and shooting Greek hostages.

Meanwhile, in Egypt, the British subsidized – and supervised -- the royalist government-in-exile. Despite its previous commanding position in Greece, that government apparently had hardly any contact with its native land; there is no record, for example, of the British expecting it to perform even intelligence gathering, much less sabotage or guerrilla raids against the German occupation forces there. For these purposes, the British used their own soldiers and intelligence agents, among whom were a number of scholars of classical Greece. But, without local support, they could do little. Not that targets were lacking: the Germans were plundering Greece of everything from food to heavy equipment, even including merchant marine ships. As Mussolini commented to his foreign minister, "The Germans have taken from the Greeks even their shoelaces…"

So complete was the victory and so thoroughly planned was the occupation that the Germans were getting ready in just over a month, in May 1941, to launch from Greece a new campaign aimed at the British-controlled oil fields of Iraq and Iran and the Suez Canal.

Third, in desperation as the Germans achieved victory after victory, Churchill sought to "set Europe alight" by helping to set up and arming a resistance movement in the Nazi-occupied areas. Whether or not this was a wise or even an effective policy may be doubted. In the few countries where the Underground became operational, it probably would have done so without British help. The National Liberation Front *Ethnikon Apeleftherotikon Metopon* (EAM) was formed in February 1942 not only with no help from the British but even without their knowledge. Even earlier, individual acts of bravery against the Germans gave Greeks the feeling that they were deciding their own fate. Neighboring Yugoslavia is the prime example of a country where the partisans were able to form a government that survived; Greece is an example of where they nearly did.

This upsurge of self-determination was an entirely new development to which the British were as profoundly hostile in Greece as they were to similar movements in Egypt, Palestine, Iraq and India. It was not just, although this was a factor, that the British did not much care what the natives wanted, but that in Greece, as in much of Europe, it was the Left that proved most successful in rallying people into the Underground. For Churchill, "Left" was just a euphemism for Communism to which he was profoundly hostile.

However, during the worst days of the war, in Greece as in Yugoslavia, the British were grateful for the Left-led Underground, even when it was dominated, as in Yugoslavia, or strongly influenced, as in Greece, by Communists. In both countries, the British tried to foster the rival Underground movements of the Right but gradually came to realize that it was the Left that was doing the fighting. The Rightist partisans in both Yugoslavia and Greece compromised themselves by often collaborating with the Germans, Italians and Bulgarians. In Greece, the EAM – which enrolled at least half a million (and claimed two million) members

-- controlled most of the country and tied down several German divisions with guerrilla warfare while the only significant Rightist group (under Napoleon Zervas) was more or less confined to one province in northwestern Greece and was at best a reluctant ally to the British.[1]

By July 1943 the EAM had won a place in the British-led Joint General Headquarters in Cairo. Since this group was charged with coordinating resistance to the Germans, membership in it made of EAM a de facto ally of the British. And since EAM was fighting for liberation and actually administering large areas of Greece under the noses of the Germans, unlike the government in exile in Cairo, it was as close as there was to a pro-allied government *in Greece.*

As the price for its cooperation, EAM set out two demands: it wanted the king to promise not to return to Greece before the Greeks voted in a plebiscite to determine their future government and in the meantime it wanted to participate (by holding the ministries of justice, interior and war) in the Cairo-based Greek government. The British (with President Roosevelt's agreement) refused and forcibly returned the EAM delegation to Greece. Its members went back convinced that the British were merely using them and that it had determined to reimpose upon Greece the old royalist regime. They were right. Churchill was determined to have a "friendly" government in Greece.

Whatever doubts the EAM delegation may have still had when the British cut off aid to EAM and stepped up aid to Zervas's small right-wing group. EAM countered this move by formally proclaiming what was already de facto a government of the occupied territories. Learning of this, elements of the Greek forces in Egypt mutinied and demanded to be placed under the EAM government. In riposte, the British sentenced some of the mutineers to death (at Churchill's personal order) and put many others into prison camps.

The EAM action and the Royal Army "mutiny" enraged Churchill.

---

1 The British officer in charge, Colonel Montgomery Woodhouse who later played a major role in fomenting the MI6-CIA coup against the Iranian Prime Minister Mossadegh, recounts that, having failed to win over Zervas with a "fortune in gold," he had to threaten to denounce Zervas to the Gestapo, to get him to engage the Germans even on a small scale.

He described them as "treacherous, filthy beasts" and "miserable Greek banditti." But the British position was not conditioned only by Churchill's personal hostility to Greek Leftists.2   Even if in the short term, the Greek Leftists were allies of a limited sort, he concluded, they would be enemies of Britain in the long haul. In this way, they were worse – more "treacherous" -- than the obvious enemies. Indeed, during most of the prewar period, Churchill had been more sympathetic to Franco, Hitler and especially to Mussolini (whom he called "the greatest lawgiver among men") than to their victims. One knew where he was with them whereas with the Left one could never be sure. But, underlying this personal predilection, there was the long view of his reading and experience. That view solidified and focused his personal angers and fears.

This leads to the *fourth issue, strategy.*

The role of Greece in world (read: British imperial) strategy was a particular passion of Winston Churchill. At the time of the buildup to the invasion of Western Europe, he tried to divert the Allied, mainly American, invasion forces from Italy to Greece and, when he was unable to accomplish that, almost breaking up the fragile Anglo-American military structure in the process, he threw all the British forces that could be spared into the Greek campaign. Indeed, as we shall see, he was prepared to make a pact with the Devil himself to secure control of Greece. We must ask why this was. After all, Greece was a small and poor country, without significant wealth in resources, industry or highly trained people. It would almost certainly be a net drain on the already depleted English economy. And its people in 1943-1944 evinced no desire for British suzerainty. What was Churchill thinking?

It was Russia as a rival empire that dominated Churchill's thinking. It wasn't just Russia's espousal of Communism although that gave the contemporary Russians a powerful weapon. But, for centuries before the advent of the Commissars, it was the Tsars who threatened the British Empire. In whatever form they took, the Russians had to be stopped. So

---

2 They, however, were some of the demons (which he called his 'black dog" or depression and anger) that drove him into occasional paroxysms of rage and occasional sullen withdrawals. Some psychiatrists believe he suffered from bipolarism.

barriers must be erected and maintained. The British Empire had been engaged in this task in Churchill's memory and in the stories of British statesmen and warriors he imbibed as a child. They were the glory of the Empire. And what was past had a modern sequel: oil and money. He had been engaged in getting the British government into the oil business. Otherwise, it could not maintain the Royal Navy. And without oil, there was little money. Then the glorious empire would be threadbare indeed. The current threat was not just Germany, which was a real and present danger, but ultimately it was still the old threat, Russia. It had to be headed off before the threat became irreversible. Otherwise the Russians, their sinister movement and their willing local friends would seize the oil fields of Iraq and Iran. Then there would be no stopping them. That would give the Indians and other natives the option of breaking with the British Empire as the great anti-British Indian leader, Subhas Chandra Bose, was trying to do. So the battle had to be joined in the north, as far from the heart of the empire as possible. Greece was the cork in the Mediterranean bottle which alone, Churchill believed, could keep the evil Russian genii locked up.[3] In the age of aircraft and radio, it was an oddly antiquarian view of strategy, but it was the British and, for a time, the American view. It suffices to explain, I suggest, why the British were so determined to hang on to Greece.

Churchill found two means of action: the first was to buy off the Russians and the second was to destroy their Greek potential allies.

Buying off the Russians was one of the most remarkable actions of Twentieth century international affairs. It came to fruition in 1944: in May Churchill had Antony Eden propose to Soviet Foreign Minister Vyacheslav Molotov a swap -- a free hand for the Soviets in Rumania in exchange for a British free hand in Greece. Then, he followed this demarche with a visit to Stalin in October where he enlarged his offer to include Hungary and Bulgaria. "I pushed this [offer on a piece of paper] across [the table] to Stalin, who had by then heard the translation.

3: Churchill was willing to accept Communist control of Yugoslavia as he told his chief political officer, William Deakin, but not in Greece. The reason, I believe was that Churchill did not regard Yugoslavia as an actor in Middle Eastern strategy whereas Greece, on the sea, with a fleet, and with a merchant community in almost every Middle Eastern city could be, he thought, a mortal threat.

(Churchill wrote in *The Second World War*). There was a slight pause. Then he took his blue pencil and made a large tick upon it, and passed it back to us. It was all settled in no more time than it takes to set it down."

With Russian acquiescence, Britain was ready to take on the EAM. I turn now to the British invasion, the destruction of the EAM and post war chaos.

* * *

At daggers drawn with the British and sold out by the Russians, the EAM was kept in the dark by them both. Not knowing that a pit had been dug under its feet, it was proud that by then it was virtually running "free Greece" and, other than Yugoslavia, was the most effective and largest Resistance movement in Europe. It had won the support even of the conservative Orthodox hierarchy and most of the senior army officers who had remained in Greece. With between one and two million members it certainly was the national institution.

At this point, it appears, for the documents (if there were any) are not available, that the Soviets sent a message to the EAM leaders altering them that they had made a deal with the British and warning that unless they reached an understanding with the British, the British would crush them. Isolated, feeling betrayed and exhausted by the underground war, the EAM caved in and agreed to place its military force under the British-supported royalist Government-in-exile. That was the opening the British were looking for. And in October of 1944 some 6,000 British troops and the remainder of the Royal Greek army-in-exile arrived under the command of an English general.

As they retreated, the Germans had left chaos behind them -- Greece was starving, there were no jobs and the currency was worthless. What remained of the functioning bureaucracy and the police was deeply compromised by collaboration with the Nazis. The society was bitterly divided, loyalties were conflicting and suspicion was deep. In this explosive mixture, the British struck a spark by attempting to disarm the Underground (who had become legally a part of the national army) while leaving the collaborators free and, in many cases, armed.

Push came to shove in the central square of Athens on December 3, 1944. The police fired into crowds of demonstrators, and in reprisal EAM units attacked their posts. EAM was careful not to attack the British, but British troops were quickly caught up in the fighting. The push of the British and the shove of the EAM threatened civil war.

A last minute cease-fire was worked out in the first days of 1945 and a month later a more comprehensive deal was reached (in Varkiza) in which EAM agreed to turn in its weapons while the government proclaimed an amnesty, promised to prosecute collaborators, guaranteed various fundamental freedoms and agreed to hold a plebiscite on the monarchy before general elections.

Almost before the ink was dry, this compromise broke down. Vigilante bands (particularly of an organization known as *X* and the so-called "National Guard" began hunting down and killing the now unarmed EAM members. The relatively moderate right-wing government of General Plastiras fell and Greece collapsed into a sort of "guided" anarchy. Mass executions of the veterans of the Underground dispirited the survivors and terrified the moderates who tried to stand aside. In this climate of violence, elections were finally held; not surprisingly, the Right won an overwhelming victory. The Left, foolishly as it turned out, abstained. A far-Right-wing government was formed by Constantine Tsaldaris (of whom more later) who fostered massive arrests and summary executions of his opponents.

By October 1946, Greece was plunged into civil war. And a bitter and divisive war it was. Since Thucydides, Greeks have not been known for their kindness to one another, and, if this time cities were not razed and populations enslaved, what happened was almost as vicious. Even by the standards to which, lamentably, we have become accustomed, the Greek war became especially savage.

Both sides had major disadvantages. The Government was a loose coalition gathered around a hard core. Much of the civil service and virtually all of the police were at least disliked by those who had hated the Italians and Germans. The (originally German) royal family had never been particularly popular and continued to be regarded as alien; at the minimum, sitting relatively comfortably in Cairo it had not shared with the people the rigors of the occupation The various ministers, some recycled from the Metaxas period, were thought to be little more than puppets of the British. Corruption was endemic everywhere and was blatant at the higher reaches. Some of the leaders, like Tsaldaris, were preparing their getaways because they knew that most Greeks feared and disliked them.

The Left was also a loose coalition around a hard core. No longer energized by the fight against the Occupation, it rapidly unraveled so that, in the end, it was little more than the Communist minority. Like the Right, so the Left had become the party of the extremists. After the initial clash with the British in 1945, EAM lost all of the urban areas but remained relatively strong in the countryside. That was not a secure base. By tradition the Greek peasantry was both religious and conservative; so, once the unifying nationalist issue of the German occupation was removed, the Left was never again able to build a dedicated following. When I first visited Greece in the spring of 1947, it was jokingly said that the rebels had been "confined" to the mountains -- that is to about 70% of the country -- but the joke had a hard edge. In the mountains, the Left became isolated from the people as it had not been during the war. No matter how much they feared the heirs of Metaxas, the Greeks did not want the Communists as their rulers. And the people were exhausted, hungry and desperate for some degree of peace. The Left did not offer surcease in any of these.

It was this tragic mess, for which certainly it had to take a large measure of blame, that in the early days of 1947 Britain decided to turn over to America.

The British, at least those officials resident in Greece, were convinced that their policy was going to win, but, in London, the more sober leaders realized that they could not pay even for a victory. The British officers and intelligence agents on the spot were not pleased with the election of the Labour Government and were strongly opposed to its policy of dismantling the Empire. They were also annoyed to see the Americans, whom they regarded as naïve, inexperienced, brash and of dubiously political reliability, take control. But the Atlee Government told them that they had no choice -- they were broke.

The Truman Doctrine was announced in March 1947 to help "free peoples" resist subversion by armed minorities, and the Congress authorized $400 million in aid for Greece. America began to take responsibility, but, well into 1948, the only effective foreign presence was British. A large British police mission continued to dominate the Athens and Salonika security forces at least through the first half of 1949. In the period critical for my present purposes, the Americans were only getting organized. The CIA, which would later play such a role in Greek affairs, was then just being created out of the debris of the wartime OSS. Americans had money but little knowledge and few ideas; the British had no money, considerable knowledge and just one idea.

1947 and 1948 were, therefore, difficult times in almost every sense: there was little public security, virtually no justice, not much work, no trustworthy currency and even considerable tenseness in the relations between and responsibilities of the British and the Americans.

The resident British officials regarded themselves as realists about Greece. They knew the government was shaky, corrupt and inept; that was the reality, but the existing regime was the only one they had so they were determined not to let it fall. The Americans also saw the corruption, weakness and ineptitude, and they were dismayed. Some, including George Polk, found it not to be the sort of government America should support. He detailed his observations in an article in *Harpers Magazine* in December 1947 that caused the Greek government to request that CBS recall or fire him. In subsequent reports, he detailed corruption on such a monumental scale, and at the very center of the government, that he believed it could not win the civil war or, if it won, having such an ally would be a defeat rather than a victory for America. It is to George Polk's métier as a journalist that I now turn.

*   *   *

What set George apart from many of his fellows was a deeper commitment to the role of the independent journalist. He was an extremely patriotic man, believing deeply and firmly in those credos and institutions which for the last two centuries had made America unique. For him America was not just a nation but was also an ideal. For that he had fought. The first flying officer ashore on Guadalcanal, America's first counterattack in the Second World War, he flew in combat throughout the Guadalcanal campaign, was decorated for bravery and was so badly wounded that he was retired rather than discharged from the US Naval Air Force.

Almost as important as that experience was, there were others. Already before America entered the war, he had worked as a newspaper man in China and France and saw Japan and Germany during their mobilization and the first periods of combat. Then as the war ended, he returned to journalism and so went from combat against the Japanese to watching a part of the Nuremberg trial of the major Nazis. These experiences were seared into his memory and his credo. He remarked to me and others that we simply could not have fought so hard and so painfully merely to see the world go back to what it had been in the 1930s. We certainly could not idly suffer new totalitarians of whatever kind to arise to again threaten our liberties. And, since the fate of the world was increasingly in our hands, we must galvanize ourselves to protect them. At minimum, we must applied high standards to our own actions.

George did not (as I did) aspire to government service or politics. He had gradually, and not without failures and shortfalls along the way, made himself into a topflight journalist. That was his calling. And he spent a good deal of time defining its responsibilities.

It was the role of the responsible journalist, he insisted, to question, to search, to probe those in power. That task, he recognized, required a subtle tension between professional responsibility and official irresponsibility -- the journalist must follow his own dictates, he believed, even when, indeed precisely when, they ran athwart those of government. If, as he saw a number of his colleagues do, he tailored his activities to fit those of officials, even those "on our side," the journalist either had no value or became merely a toady.

George believed deeply that our freedom and the quality of our contribution to world affairs depended, in no small part, on the willingness of the responsible journalist to stand outside the comfortable and safe precinct of officialdom and take both criticism and risk in his pursuit of truth.

Viewed from the perspective of many American officials, this was naïve and troublesome. Naïve because no journalist could ever know all that secret and massive sources of information could reveal. I confess that during my years in government service, especially in times of crisis, I was occasionally annoyed at sometimes naïve journalistic intrusion. And many officials found journalists troublesome because revealing one's better forgotten mistakes could damage one's career.

Standing outside with a detached and sometimes critical approach -- this special kind of journalistic irresponsibility -- was not in the British imperial tradition. Britain had for generations controlled, generally economically and efficiently, large areas of Asia and Africa. Its officials often knew the languages and customs of the subject peoples and had set rules of the "game" which were accepted by all but a few troublemakers. The prime rule was that politics, in the sense we know it in America and England, was not allowed or, at least, was never to be allowed to interfere with strategy or administration.

Into this orderly china shop then came American bulls. They came in two breeds. Those in official positions were callow and naïve, it is true, but they were grateful for British tutorial. This was especially true in the intelligence services whose new officers literally sat at the feet of the British masters: the Americans aped British manners, took over their "buzz words" and accepted their "tradecraft." If Americans as a group tended to emphasize economics more than the British, and put their trust in money, that was (the British understood) because America was nouveau riche, was trying to apply to the world its domestic experience and because it lacked the political skills which running an empire had given to the British. Where disagreements were evident, they arose, in the British view, because the Americans had not yet appreciated the realities of the colonial world or the requirements of suzerainty. Given time and expert advice, the Americans would perform adequately.

The worm in this apple was not the incompetent or brash official, who could be set right, but the outlaw -- the American journalist. British journalists, at least those common in the Middle East, were usually members of the club. They literally supped at the table of colonial government and had learned not to bite the hand that fed them. Many were former officials -- *The* [London] *Times* correspondent in Cairo, for example, had been a brigadier in military intelligence. Many of those who covered Greece were alumni or, in some cases still covert members, of the various intelligence services. Except perhaps on the issue of Palestine, in which domestic English opinions were of major importance, the English journalist played a role that was more ancillary to than apart from British administration.

The few American journalists then in the Middle East had been much affected by the Second World War. By and large, they were (or seemed to my youthful eyes) an uncommonly able group. Some were certainly lazy and incompetent, but the more memorable ones, like Homer Bigart of *The New York Herald Tribune*, had come from a school in which reporters were suspicious of "city hall" and got their stories by persisting in asking unwelcome questions. Their cynicism had an iconoclastic bent which served to bring out more than a smug officialdom found convenient to reveal.

George did not come from the same school as Bigart and, man for man, there was no one he admired more than the British. He found them understated, brave and well informed. But he did not admire or condone their casual contempt for and occasional brutality toward "the natives."[4] Tyranny infuriated him in what might be described as an old fashioned or even naïve way.

Ultimately, it was the moral imperative to seek a saner and freer world that set George apart. He insisted that it also set America apart. It meant, at minimum, that we could not support oppressive and corrupt governments or colonialist policies even when such policies appeared convenient. If this was or appeared to be naïve, he did not particularly care. He thought, and I certainly agreed (and agree) with him that without a clear and operative sense of who you are, what you stand for and what you oppose, no policy other than war can, for long, be "realistic." Thus George might be described as a "hardheaded idealist." In a sense, of course, that made him far more dangerous -- because more effective and incorruptible -- as a journalist.

These attitudes already affected his approach to the Egypt of King Faruq. The British had put Faruq into power and were keeping him there despite the terrible misery of his people. But it was when George came to Greece that the issues of corruption and oppression became more personal. In Greece, by the time George arrived, it was America that was paying the bills, sponsoring the politicians and getting ready to fight the civil war. So, with American connivance, corruption, lack of commitment amounting virtually to treason and vicious anti-democratic tendencies were evident. Many such actions were carried out by people who had actively supported the Nazis during the war. But as George saw, they were "on our side." That was a set of issues which George

---

4   None of us then knew much about what MI5, which dealt with the colonies, was doing. Only now, 60 years later, has its role been documented. See, for example, Calder Walton's *Empire of Secrets*, published in 2012.

could not, either as a journalist or as a politically sensitive American, avoid. Finally, his feelings boiled out in an article he wrote for December 1947 *Harpers Magazine* which, as I mentioned caused the Greek Government to put pressure on CBS, whose chief Middle Eastern correspondent he had become, to get him fired or recalled.

Map of Greece showing Salonika in the North.

In the months after the publication of the *Harpers* article, George received numerous death threats. Having received a few myself, I know that it is an unnerving experience. When I was threatened with assassination by a lone, mentally deranged young man, while I was President of the Adlai Stevenson Institute of International Affairs and Professor of History at the University of Chicago, I called in the FBI, Chicago and University police. It never occurred to me that they might be involved. I had at least that comfort. But George, of course, did not. In the conditions prevailing in Greece in 1947 and 1948, no one, not even the prime minister, could trust all of the virtually autonomous security services and their informal or parakratic "friends." A foreign journalist was defenseless.

But that was not the worst. A week before he was murdered, George had confronted the sometimes Greek Prime Minister Constantine Tsaldaris with proof that Tsaldaris was profiteering on American aid money and was illegally depositing it in his personal account in the Chase Manhattan Bank. From a personal point of view, this was dangerously naïve, but George believed it to be his professional duty to track the story to the source. He had to give Tsaldaris a chance to refute what might be only a rumor. Tsaldaris did not try to refute it, but he was furious that George knew of it.

George was due to leave Greece in May 1948. CBS had discussed with him his becoming chief correspondent in Washington. That offer was, apparently, widely known in Greece; indeed, he informed Prime Minister Tsaldaris, in their unpleasant encounter a few days before his murder over Tsaldaris's illegal acquisition and export of American aid dollars, that he intended to take that post. He even said that he would use it to make known his views on Greece. Tsaldaris was furious, and George was, to say the least, indiscreet.

*   *   *

Before leaving, however, he decided to take a last look at northern Greece which, as he wrote me, he worried might become a new battleground that could lead to a world war.

Like other journalists in Greece, George had discussed with many people getting what then was the journalist's plumb in the Greek pudding, an interview with the leader of the guerrillas, General Markos Vafiadis. Whether this was a serious hope, much less a plan, became a central issue in the investigations of his murder. Before he left Athens, George had told various people that he had no good leads on the story.

We know the following: George left Athens on May 7 for the northern Greek town of Kavalla. When the plane touched down in Salonika, George got off. I understood that he did because the plane was having engine trouble. (George was still having the terrifying nightmares of burning to death in a plane crash -- from being caught in the wreckage of a bombed plane and being shot down on a rescue mission during the Guadalcanal campaign and from a recent wreck in which he was a passenger on a private plane in Lebanon.) Edmund Keeley (*The Salonika Bay Murder*) maintains that the Kavalla airport was inoperable due to a heavy rain, and that the flight was canceled when it was due to take off from Salonika. In any event, the stop in Salonika was not planned. That is an important fact as it makes it certain that George did not go to Salonika "on his way to see Markos" or had set up contacts in Athens to do so, as has often been said.

Finding himself unexpectedly in Salonika, he did what all journalists do, attempt to find a story. One, on which he had been gathering material, was the abduction of Greek children by the guerrillas and the other was, of course, the possibility of setting up a meeting with the guerrilla leader in his mountain retreat. He asked everyone he saw for information about these two issues. The children abduction charge was then being monitored by a United Nations organization, so gathering information on it was both easy and noncontroversial. Visiting the guerrillas was neither, but I think George would have known that Salonika was not a good entry into guerrilla territory. (Parenthetically, I mention that George's friend Homer Bigart shortly thereafter started his celebrated trip to the camp of Markos through Yugoslavia.) And all those who have talked of meeting George say that they made the point that Salonika was the least likely point of entry to guerrilla-held Greece.

Among the men he met during the two days before his death was the British sometime intelligence officer and then "information" officer, Randall Coate. Coate was just the kind of man George always sought out, a quiet, withdrawn person who knew much: he had served as a British liaison officer with the Underground during the war. (Having often seen his counterparts in Egypt and Palestine, George had advised me to find this sort of man when I went to a new place.) Coate was generally esteemed the best informed man in northern Greece.

There are several odd things about the Coate story. First, Coate was abruptly reassigned and left Salonika six days after George was murdered and two days before his body was found. Even his secretary was transferred a few days later. Perhaps these are just coincidences, but it does seem odd timing and, after so many years spent becoming an expert on Greece, Coate was moved to Oslo, Norway. Second, we also know that George's body was found about 400 meters from Coate's apartment. Third, it is likely that George and Coate spent some hours together, probably at Coate's apartment, the evening George was shot.

The only person to interview Coate after George's murder, until Kati Martin briefly met him years later (*The Polk Conspiracy*), an American Embassy official in Oslo, reports Coate as saying that "he [Coate] might well have been the last person to have met Mr. Polk before the latter's death."

It is my suspicion that, at minimum, Coate gave George his last meal which was an unlikely menu for a Greek restaurant (officially said, based on the autopsy, to have been lobster and peas) and one which George apparently ate in what he thought were secure and relaxed circumstances. Moreover, the restaurant where the police said George ate his last meal is an outdoor taverna and, since that night a rain was falling, he must have eaten elsewhere.

Obviously, at the least, Coate was a key witness, but he was not called into the investigation nor into the trial. I have never been able to see Coate. He could not, of course, talk with me.

Colonel James Kellis, a US Air Force officer, a Greek American who of course knew the language and had been assigned to be General William Donovan's investigator, discovered that two known figures of the Piraeus underworld, associated with Tsaldaris and apparently with the British police mission, did travel to Salonika the day before George was killed. They were known to have been used for various "dirty tricks" before. And as , as I explained, they could not have traveled without the permission of the security forces and the permission or at least the knowledge of British intelligence. Donovan was annoyed by Kellis's investigation, although that was what he was brought to Greece to undertake; Donovan fired

Kellis and sent him out of Greece. The Salonika hit man or men slithered back into obscurity – no one ever was able to question them.

* * *

Here one must introduce the issue of motives and actors. First, why would anyone have wanted to kill George?

As an historian, I have been trained to look for the most straightforward answer. Here, it appears to me that it is that what George was writing, and would write upon his return to America, would harm the policy the killers wished to effect. Somewhat more forced, but certainly worth considering, is the answer that killing him would embarrass US-Greek relations to such an extent as to bring about a change in the Truman Doctrine. Finally, also forced, is the idea that killing him, if blamed on opponents of the Truman Doctrine, would serve to strengthen it. These, I believe, set out the parameters of motive for the crime.

The next question is who could have done it?

I think we can rule out a lone fanatic. It is evident that there had to be too much organization for that to be likely. Let me dwell on this point a moment. If we conclude, as I think we must, that George had not intended to go to Salonika and if we agree that it was he, not just any journalist, who was the target of the attack, then the killers had a relatively short time. Regard their challenge: They had to get permission to travel to Salonika and/or Kavalla. Even if they were reliable agents, they would have been unlikely to be given in advance a blanket permit. Of course, if they were not agents of some authority to grant permits they would have had to bribe, steal or otherwise obtain the permits or find some means of rapid ground transport. The only sure means was by air because, open to guerrilla ambush, ground travel was often impossible and was at best slow, dangerous and unreliable. But air travel was then tightly controlled by the government under the "guidance" of the British police mission. Next the hit man or hit men had to set up a place in Salonika rather than Kavalla, arrange some sort of meeting, carry out the murder and make arrangements to get away. All that had to be done in just one and a half days.

Two incidental points are also raised by these circumstances. The hitman had to notify his handlers of the required change of plans and probably communicate with his support. Such communication would have been by radio and would have been monitored by the British communications intercept group.

If we agree that only an organization could have carried out the murder, those who remain to be considered divide into four groups: (1) the Communists, (2) some organized but secret politico-military group, (3) some element of the Greek security organizations, and, finally, (4) the British.

With this in mind, look again at the motives:

(1) The Communists were seeing their position deteriorate as American aid, and military power, began to come to bear on them, but, according to Homer Bigart who visited them a month after George's murder, they still believed that they would win the war. A part of their campaign was to take their message to as wide a public as they could find. They also sought to differentiate the Greek government (which they fought) from the American people (whom they said they admired). They demonstrated this in returning American officials whom they had captured and in arranging for Bigart to visit them. These events centered on the time George was murdered. Even as late as the trial (spring of 1949) they arranged for me to visit one of their leaders in Prague. They wanted all the attention they could get. In their position, I would have done the same. I do not doubt that the Communists would have murdered George, or anyone else, if that had suited their aims. But, killing a journalist was not in their interest.

(2) I raised the question in 1949 of the possible involvement of the *X*. I felt that they certainly should have been investigated or at least

considered for their possible role. At that time, General Donovan and the AP chief correspondent in Athens, Socrates Chaklis (or Tsaklis), both scoffed at me, saying that there was no such organization, that it existed only in Communist propaganda to which I was naïvely susceptible. Of course, *X* existed. It is difficult to believe that either man could have been ignorant of it. It had recently (in January 1946) taken over control of a part of the Peloponnesus, and it was later to play major roles in the war against the British in Cyprus and the "colonels' coup" in Greece.

The *X* was one of the legacies of the Metaxas years. Little has ever been publicly revealed about it although, particularly because of the Cyprus war, much information on it must be available in the British archives. It was briefly discussed by the British intelligence officer, Nigel Clive (in *A Greek* Experience). A layman's view of it is graphically presented in the French movie "Z." *X* was a shadowy organization, made up of army and security officers, motivated by the semi-mystical, national and religious ideas Metaxas had drawn from Nazism and Fascism. Whether *X* was an independent group, which could act without the senior police and military commanders' approval, is doubtful, but certainly later, in well-known cases, it did perform the "dirty tricks" for which the regular forces chose not to take responsibility. Nothing was ever done to investigate its possible role. Donovan furiously warned me of dire personal consequences when I suggested that it should have been investigated.

(3) The Greek security forces were then divided into various discrete organizations. At least some cabinet ministers apparently did not have full knowledge of their activities and certainly appeared unable completely to control them. Dealing with them was particularly sensitive since most of them had been involved both in collaboration with the Germans, Italians and Bulgarians during the war and in the mass executions of the EAM in 1945. All of them, in some cases under different names, dated from the Metaxas regime. They demonstrated under Metaxas, under the Nazis, after the breakdown of the Varkiza Agreement (which should have ended the civil war and given Greece a non-Communist, moderate government), in the investigation of George's murder and finally under the regime of

the colonels, a uniform pattern. That pattern usually involved reliance on torture, summary executions, scant or no respect for the processes of the (already very lax) Greek civil liberties law to such an extent that, without exaggeration, they might be better characterized as sanctioned terrorists than police.

It was beyond contemplation that the weak, alienated and distant political figures in Athens could have carried out -- even if they had wished to do so -- an independent inquiry in which the very security apparatus could be examined. That is a difficult task even for well established governments in times of tranquility; in the Greece of 1948-1949, it was impossible.

However, not only was no attempt ever contemplated, but, to the contrary, even the Americans encouraged the very tendencies of the police toward fabrication of evidence and torture of prisoners. The CBS representatives, Winston Burdett and and John Secondari, the American consul general, Raleigh Gibson, the personal representative of the Secretary of State, Frederick Ayer, and General Donovan all became aware of the results of -- and contributed to -- American pressure.

One result of pressure to get a quick trial of a culprit who could be identified with the Communists. Thus, the chief of the Salonika Security Police arrested, held without charges, began torturing and dictated confessions (seven different ones were required as new facts emerged) to the Greek journalist who was later charged with complicity, Gregory Staktopoulos. The Greek authorities went along with the American demands for a speedy trial to close the issue, regardless of how it was done. This is clear even from the still-incompletely-revealed (and now partly destroyed) American official record.

At the time of the trial, I did not, of course, know of Staktopoulos's torture. It is a horrifying story -- revoltingly common to authoritarian regimes of both the Left and the Right. What I did then find out was that Staktopoulos had been a chameleon. To survive the violent swings of Greek politics, he had worked for the Metaxas regime, the Italians, the Germans, the Communists and the British (both for Reuters news agency and for a government agency). He was, in fact, the ultimate opportunist.

When I saw him again two years after the trial, when he should legally have been in prison, he was still in the Security Police headquarters. From his look and way of talking, I was sure that he was a dope addict. I interpreted this, at the time, as his being in league with the police. Probably I was wrong: Staktopoulos must have been desperate to get *to* prison and *away from* his tormenters in the Salonika Security Police headquarters.

All of this, incidentally, was later privately (though not officially) admitted by the Greek government. Staktopoulos was let out of jail but, ungraciously, neither pardoned nor given compensation for his false arrest, torture and imprisonment.

(4) Finally, I come, reluctantly I must say, to the British. I have the greatest respect for the English, as George had, and I have learned much, in my years at Oxford and otherwise, from them. But there is a well-known distinction between what an Englishman is and does in England and what Englishmen have done in their foreign affairs. Let me dwell on that a moment as I believe it is significant for what I will say later on the implications of George's murder.

The British, as I have already mentioned, found the Americans to be naïve and untrained for the "real" world. Many Americans, particularly in the incipient CIA, agreed with them. They looked with envy at what the British boasted of doing. In the murky world of espionage, their only rule was "don't get caught." What was routine in the vast colonial world Britain still controlled in 1948 is the subject of Calder Walton's *Empire of Secrets*. One of the reasons why the publication of Peter Wright's *Spy Catcher* so worried the English Government was that it revealed not only that espionage was routinely done abroad, but that it sometimes was carried out at home in England, even against the cabinet of the prime minister.

But surely, one may say, the British had already turned over to the Americans and had gotten out of Greece. No, that is not only not true for the period when George was murdered but was still not true a year later when I attended the trial. I was able to identify eleven English police agents at the trial. American diplomatic documents show that the large British police mission under Sir Charles Wickham was the hidden hand behind the Greek police "investigation." Even when, after the trial, I arranged to see Staktopoulos, a British police officer was present.

The senior member of this uncharacteristically large mission, Sir Charles Wickham, was arguably the most powerful figure in the nether world of "security" in Greece. He had been trained in political police work in the very hard school of Ulster violence (he was Inspector General of the Royal Irish Constabulary until he was assigned to handle Greek security matters in 1944). Because of his access to communications intercepts -- the "Ultra" code breaking of World War Two -- it is fair to say that no one moved in Greece without his knowledge. The British were even the source of information for the Greek government security services on the Communists. It would have been almost impossible for anyone to have gotten on the Athens-Salonika-Kavalla flight without his knowledge or even without his permission. Presumably for (among other reasons) fear of compromising this source of information, there was never any attempt to find out what the British knew about George's murder. Wickham had the means to find out; if he shared, as presumably he had to share Churchill's commitment to holding Greece at all costs, he had a motive to shut up a person who had already called into question the policy of upholding the royalist regime and who, if he went to Washington, might do considerable or even mortal damage to that strategy.

*　　*　　*

From the above, it is clear that three of the four possible culprits were not investigated. The investigation, such as it was, focused on only the Communists. And, despite every incentive and effort, the Greek Government made no case even against the Communists that would have been effective in any normal court of law. In fact, the only produced suspect, Gregory Staktopoulos, had to be forced to amend his confession repeatedly to account for such embarrassing facts as George's being away from Greece on the only occasions when Staktopoulos could possibly have met with him.

The police attempted to implicate George's widow, Rea, suggesting that, at a very unsophisticated nineteen years of age, she was a top Communist agent. A more unlikely "agent" particularly for the Communists, Rea being, if anything, a royalist, it is hard to imagine. They also attempted to implicate George's assistant, the *Christian Science Monitor* "stringer," Constantine Hadjiargyris, alleging that he had put George in touch with the Communists, to set up a trip to Markos, but they finally gave up this ploy.

In the end, the best that the security police could do was to concoct a story which, to be charitable, left most ends loose and dangling. Even at the time, immediately after the trial, one of the then ministers of the Greek Government, probably feeling sorry for my callow youth, took me aside and advised me that, of course, the trial was phony and it would be years before I found out what had happened, but I should take heart that someday I would find out "since Greeks cannot keep secrets."

The surprising feature of the trial itself was that it was so shoddily arranged. Jury selection was a farce. The defense attorneys were obviously acting on behalf of the prosecution. Key witnesses were not only not called but not even mentioned. Lines of inquiry which were evident even to me were not followed. And, with the only defendant "in the bag" it would have been so easy, I should have thought, to have a really impressive "show" trial -- like the Russians had in similar circumstances. In a sense, the trial was an insult to our intelligence. It must have taken a great deal of effort for an experienced lawyer like General Donovan to keep on his mask.

Several years after the trial, I returned briefly to Greece. Rea's father and uncle, of whom I was very fond, were then still alive. They asked me, curiously shyly I remember thinking, if I would like to meet a young man who was vaguely related to the family and who had been a newspaper man.

When he came to Mr. Coconis's apartment, he proved to be very thin, indeed emaciated, about thirty years old I guessed, although he looked much older, with a hacking cough. When we sat down, he told me his story. It was long and detailed, and I immediately wrote it down. This is the essence of it.

When Gregory Staktopoulos "confessed" to meeting George in Athens to set up a trip to Marcos, I discovered from my correspondence that George was actually in Cairo; so the two men could not have met. Staktopoulos then amended – or had amended for him -- his confession so that a Greek, identified only as "Yannis" (Johnny) was said to be the go-between in Athens. The description of Yannis could have fit half the population of Athens, and thus there was no way to check the alleged meeting against dates, places or contacts. I and everyone else then scoffed at this story. So, it seems, the police made a major effort to get a "Yannis" to fit the bill. He had to be, as Salonika Political Police Chief Major Mouskoundis pointed out in other contexts, able to speak English and to be someone who, on his credentials, George would trust. (These characteristics had constituted the "evidence" against Constantine Hadjiargyris.) The young man they allegedly picked was a former "stringer" or assistant to several foreign journalists, though not to George. He was an admitted former member of the Communist youth organization and was then available since he was a prisoner in the concentration camp on Mikronosis Island.

According to his story, he was brought back to Athens where a relative of his mother was a high official in the police. He was, he said, interviewed by this man who offered him a way out of the concentration camp if he would confess to being "Yannis." He was tempted, of course, but, when, upon being returned to his cell that night, he heard the banging of the tin plates of the prisoners as another group was being taken out to be shot, he decided he could not do it. The next day, he said, he refused and was taken back to Mikronosis where he was tortured nearly to death.

The story of "Yannis" was quietly dropped.

* * *

George's murder remains today almost as much a question as it was in 1948. No one has yet found a "smoking gun." Perhaps no one ever will. But there are two other questions which, over the long run, I think George would have thought were of much greater importance than who actually pulled the trigger.

The first was that George believed that in the defense of our liberties, the press, for all of its many, obvious and often infuriating faults, is a major line of defense. We see it lack so often in the events of Africa and Asia. As much as it often annoys the rest of us, it is far too valuable to be lost. However, the number of human beings in any calling, even journalism, who will risk their lives is bound to be small; so to keep it functioning as our watchdog we must constantly do what we can to allow, encourage and protect journalists. George's murder, seen in this light, diminished us all.

The Second is perhaps more controversial and tangential. It arose from the fact that the Communists lost the war. I want now briefly to examine this, because, in one of those curious cycles of experience, it later came to haunt me over the issue of Vietnam.

The common interpretation of the American victory in Greece was that George and others like him had been wrong, that the application of massive amounts of American aid had, ultimately, saved Greek democracy. The lesson of Greece was, thus, that *we* could win a guerrilla war even if our local friends were a corrupt, unpopular, anti-democratic lot if we were willing to go in and do the job for them. In Greece, we did -- with everything from an aid program to napalm dropped from American planes.

Greece, ultimately, became one of the arguments behind the American intervention in Vietnam -- the Saigon government might be corrupt, inefficient, undemocratic and unpopular, and we might not be able to make it work, but we could effectively replace it with our own people and win the war. With our Special Forces to "stiffen" the local army, our aid program to give hope of a better life, the British technique (evolved in the Malaya campaign) of the fortified village (made somehow grander by being called 'strategic hamlet') to keep out the "bandits," the French-inspired use of torture of suspected guerrillas (derived from the Algerian war and passed to us through Colonel Roger Trinquier's *La Guerre Moderne*) to gather information, the helicopter for mobility in the jungles and the M-16 light-weight rifle for our little brown brothers -- so the argument went in 1961 -- we would easily win the war *for* the South Vietnamese. A decade later, with 500,000 men involved, more bombs dropped than the grand total used in The Second World War, nearly a hundred thousand American casualties, and perhaps three million dead Vietnamese, it was clear that something had been "miscalculated."

I argued in the early 1960s that there were several miscalculations, but of these the most important was our failure to understand what guerrilla war is all about. It is, in essence, a form of violent politics. We never understood the politics of the war in Vietnam. Part of the reason, I think, goes back to what George was talking about in Greece.

What we failed to perceive in the Greek war was that it was not so much the government that won the war as it was the Communists who lost it. Up to the point of his death, I think that George was right -- the government he saw in Greece probably could not have won the war even with American aid. Even before George's death, however, a process had begun, and that process would defeat the Communists.

What happened (in summary) was that from the original wide popular consensus that constituted EAM during the national struggle against the German invaders, layer after layer had peeled off until only the Communists were left. Even that small minority was proving, as late as 1949 when I was in Greece, able to hold its own. Then it also fell apart over the issue of "national" versus Soviet-dominated Communism.

At that time, most observers believed that the guerrillas collapsed because Tito had closed his frontier and so denied the guerrillas supplies.

Of course, cutting off foreign aid was significant, but other guerrillas have won without resupply from outside. Even in Vietnam, where we made interdiction of supply routes a priority, I do not believe that the "Ho Chi Min Trail" was nearly so important as we then thought. But that it was, was the "lesson" we learned from Greece.

What Americans should have learned from Greece was different: two things were absolutely vital to the guerrillas in Greece, and they lost both. The first was solidarity in their ranks, and the Second was their ability to draw support from the people.

Ironically, Tito was both the model and the nemesis of the Greek EAM movement. The model because, posing as a nationalist, Tito was able to keep the loyalty of enough of his people after the fight against the Germans had been won. The nemesis because, in his break with the Russians, Tito established a new model for national Communism. He carried the Yugoslavs with him. But Markos, who tried to be both a nationalist and a Communist was not able to carry the Greeks with him. In the fight between the two wings of the Communist party, the "nationalist" faction under Markos Vafiadis and the "Moscow" faction under Nikos Zachariadis, the movement sundered.

The American government did not understand these processes when we evaluated our chances in Vietnam. They proved to be the essential missing elements -- we never found a way to separate the Viet Cong from the people; they had successfully fused nationalism, anticolonialism and communism long before we got involved in Vietnam. Intelligence reports indicated that when they came the Americans were viewed by the Vietnamese as just another kind of "French" foreigner. Even those Vietnamese who hated the Communists found it difficult to argue with their antiforeign feelings. And, rather than managing to defuse this issue, the Americans used tactics, like air strikes, search and destroy missions, relocation of villagers etc., and often, in the heat of war, committed acts that solidified the nationalist parts of the Vietnamese union.

Nor could America cause a split in the Viet Cong itself. We had not engineered the split in Greece, of course, but only benefited from it. As far as we could find out, there was never anything like the Markos-Zachariades division in Vietnam. There was nothing for us to exploit. At least until victory was in sight, the Viet Cong appeared to be monolithic.

Absent these two developments, all the other things we did proved either ineffective or self defeating. Not understanding what really happened in Greece, which is what George was trying so hard to achieve, we applied a false analogy to Vietnam and paid a fearful price.

*   *   *

Why after all these years, with so much water having flowed under so many bridges, why has George's murder not been laid to rest? I confess I am baffled. Everyone -- we, the British, the Greeks, even the Communists -- admitted to so much worse than the murder of one man; why is this case so special? Cannot the closets be opened and whatever skeletons they contain be allowed to fall out?

Apparently not. Both the American Government and the British Government still maintain a "Top Secret" classification on many, perhaps on most, of their documents relating to the case. After over sixty years! In 1948-1949 I was the youngest person involved and I am now 84. There cannot be many still alive who would be harmed by disclosure. And certainly all of the old policies have long since been scrapped. Yet, in recent years, it remained impossible for me to talk with the remaining key British official, Montgomery Woodhouse. Those few Greeks who might have known what happened are apparently now all dead. Nor can I today see the key documents. Those I have seen are mostly redacted (with key passages blanked out) and some have been illegally destroyed.

George was killed, I am reasonably sure, to keep him quiet and, perhaps, to serve as a warning to others. Homer Bigart, who was a brave and good man, made an effort to keep this from happening. I made an effort. Others did too. But none of us really succeeded. The fact was, as I have tried to point out, that for various reasons, including George's murder, we did not then and most of us still do not, understand what happened in that pivotal beginning of the Cold War. Perhaps if we had understood better, we might have avoided many costly and painful mistakes, have saved many lives, and have come out better in these last 63 years. That was surely what George's life was all about.

June 7, 1989
Revised, March 24, 2013

CHAPTER 18

LOOK BEFORE LEAPING

In "Inching Into Syria," in the June 24, 2013 New York Times, perhaps without meaning to do so, columnist Bill Keller drew attention to a variation of what used to be called in my time in government "mission creep."

He pointed out that President Obama has taken a few steps toward involvement in the Syrian maelstrom but then comments,

"It is hard to tell what has driven Obama even this far. Is it the prodding of critics like Bill Clinton, mocking the present's poll-minded caution? Is there a belated revulsion at the humanitarian catastrophe? A recognition that diplomacy backed by nothing much – which has been the White House answer until recently – is a fool's errand? Whatever the details, intentionally or not, Obama has raised expectations...[So] we should not as Bill Clinton put it in his recent excoriation of Obama's passivity, 'overlearn the lessons of the past.'"

Overlearning the lessons of the past is not something for which Americans are usually blamed!

So, at the risk of annoying either or both Mr. Keller or Mr. Clinton, I will ask what the lessons of the past really are? I see three that have been tallied in the cost of tens of thousands of lives of our young men and women, trillions of dollars of our increasing scarce dollars, delays or cancelations of projects to improve our health care, education, renovation of our means of production and our basic infrastructure. All this apart from damage to our ultimate safeguard, our national image throughout the world. And, finally, the damage done to other peoples.

The first lesson comes from perhaps the oldest experience in warfare: it is that not only is warfare unpredictable but that it almost always is worse than was foreseen. The kings and emperors who led their nations into the First World War told their peoples that the war would be short and inexpensive. Their decision – or stumble – almost destroyed Western civilization, produced the Russian Revolution, led to the rise of Fascism in Italy and may be said to have caused the rise of Nazism in Germany. In this sense, the moves made in 1914 echoed down to, at least, 1945. Later historians may call most these years "The Thirty Year War." The expenses are so varied and so large as to be incalculable. They could not have been predicted, but they were vastly more costly than anyone could have imagined when the first moves were made.

The second lesson grows out of the same series of events. You will probably recall that in 1914 none of the leaders of the major powers really wanted to go to war, but each of them convinced himself, or was convinced by the "hawks," who are always circling overhead on issues of national security, that military action would be short and relatively inexpensive. Indeed, early military action would forestall serious conflict. Those who wanted to increase pressure on their foreign (and domestic) adversaries argued that taking step A was just "prudent" and could be taken without serious consequences. If the adversary was aware of one's determination, he would back down. So, one could stop there. If he didn't, pressure could be increased gradually and under control. Of course, the adversary acted on a similar calculation. Each was determined to avoid what Mr. Keller called a fool's errand, "diplomacy backed by nothing much." Each Great Power had to show his determination with overwhelming or at least adequate force. Diplomacy faded into the background except as a ratcheting of threat.

I will come to the third lesson from the past – the last step in the sequence -- but now I ask you to focus on the word "ratchet" because I think it is a key element in the process of all international conflict.

I have several times written about it. Ratcheting comes down to a simple progression. Once step A is taken, step B becomes more likely. Then step C almost automatically follows and subsequent steps come to be seen as the only logical action to take.

During the Cuban Missile Crisis, President Kennedy was determined not to let America to be locked into the step-by-step process. He had recently read Barbara Tuchman's *The Guns of August* and was impressed by the fact that at the beginning of World War I the *process* itself had come to set the *policy* rather than policy determining action.

Prior to the Missile Crisis, Kennedy had a sharp – and for him a very personal -- lesson in the Bay of Pigs. Several steps had already been taken before he took office. He really didn't want to proceed with the Eisenhower administration project to invade Cuba, but he knew that if he aborted it, he would be attacked for being "soft" on Communism -- still in 1961 a very serious charge. He convened his senior advisers and asked for their opinions. Of course, he really didn't want their opinions but their support. All of them gave it with one exception: Chester Bowles. It happened that Dean Rusk was away and Bowles was acting secretary of state. Previously, he had been "cut out" of information on the CIA plan and was horrified when he learned of it. He spoke up at the meeting and Kennedy, who had his own plan -- the cynical one of letting the CIA trained and paid for Cuban team pay the price -- never forgave him. He soon found a means to get rid of him in the circles that really mattered in Washington.

Two subsidiary issues can be singled out from those events that have lasting consequence. Indeed, they are of critical importance today. One was the use of secrecy.

Although he was the number two man in the State Department, Bowles was not told about the planned action against Castro. Even more surprising was that the analytical division of the CIA, the Office of National Estimates upon which a president usually relies for informed opinion, was itself "cut out" of all information on what the covert action division was up to. Bowles found out about the scheme only because Secretary Rusk was out of town at the critical moment and the Office of National Estimates (DDI) found out about it by what amounted to espionage against its sister organization, the Office of Plans (DDP).

Mr. Keller's article in *The Times* illustrates the public aspects of the cost of secrecy. Bringing his account to the contemporary event in the Middle East, he remarks that he was told that "Qatar arranged a small shipment of surface-to-air missiles and the U.S. looked the other way." He probably is a good reporter, but what he wrote is simply not true. The fact is that our CIA has been supplying missiles and training to various of the Syrian opposition groups for months through Jordan and probably through other Middle Eastern countries. The Syrian government and the opposition, the Jordanian government, our European allies, the Israelis and the Russians obviously knew about this. The only people who didn't were the American public and journalists like Mr. Keller. Clearly, not knowing such things makes it difficult to have an informed public and, without an informed public, democracy is an inefficient form of government.

Not as obvious but also important is that having, as we have, layer upon layer of secrecy within government, achievement of coherent policies is difficult. In my time in government, even the officers (the so-called desk officers) in day-to-day charge of relations with most countries were not cleared for sensitive information and had to leave the room when important decisions were being made. Even within the Policy Planning Council, the members, all of whom ranked as the equivalent of major generals, were differentially "cleared." Some of us were cleared for nuclear weapons information, a few for "special intelligence" (code breaking) and others were not. We held or at least saw different parts of the "elephant." My "trunk" looked very different from the "tail" others saw. And, because of fear of Congressional attack, we were never able to discuss such crucial but sensitive issues as whether or not to recognize Communist China. To the best of my memory, we only once discussed the Vietnam war, and that meeting broke off after a few minutes because some of us sharply questioned whether our actions amounted to a policy.

Mr. Keller rightly highlights that problem in relationship to Syria. "What exactly is the strategy?" Or more pointedly, is there one? Does anyone in the government know what all the "players" are doing?

In my time in government, we tried, not very successfully, to handle this issue with interdepartmental task forces. The reason they did not always work well was that each government agency -- even the Department of the Interior -- had its own foreign policy with its own objectives. To say the least, it was awkward to force them into an overall single or national policy. The basic problem was that each of us began with an agenda and was determined to protect the position and interests of his agency. Some even tried to keep them secret. Once I had to threaten to go to the President to force the CIA to inform the interdepartmental task force on Turkish-American relations to tell it how crucial was the Turkish role in intelligence collection on Soviet nuclear arms positioning and testing.

Another time, when I was head of the task force on Algeria, I learned how hard it was to get the task force members to reverse course: I wanted them to come together not to speak *for* their own agencies but, having developed an overall policy, to go back to their agencies to speak for the whole government. It was not easy but the Algerian group became a sort of model in its time. That model would be very hard, apparently almost impossible, to apply now. Now arriving at a government-wide consensus is more complicated both because of the massive use of outside contractors (who are serving their own interests) and because of the push of special interest groups (which have their own agendas). As far as I can see no one is trying. So, regardless of legal, moral, and other issues, our policy is formless and often self-defeating.

When General George Marshall moved across the Potomac to become Secretary of State, he was appalled to find that the civil departments had no coordinating organization like the military had in the joint chiefs of staff. That was why he created what became known as the Policy Planning Staff which later under Kennedy was renamed the Policy Planning Council. To function, such a group had to have access to information, be free to express an opinion even on sensitive issues and to be listened to by those making decisions. These conditions may have existed under General Marshall, but they withered away under the following administrations. Information was restricted, expressions of opinion became personal rather than collegial and often reached no further than the chairman. By the time I resigned, the chairman's position had become so fragile that, although he was by statute the principal adviser to the Secretary of State, the then chairman, Walt Rostow was disinvited to the Secretary's weekly policy meeting.

President Kennedy made faltering and temporary moves to counter these trends. He upgraded the rank of the members and selected a few of us to serve more or less casually as "back stairs" advisors to his National Security Council, but he, no more than his predecessors, was willing to listen to advice. That was surprising because he entered office with the grim results of the Bay of Pigs attempted invasion of Cuba.

Kennedy did not learn from that botched job. True he fired the CIA Deputy Director responsible for the attempted coup but he also fired the man who had advised against it. And he did not consider the precedent when he began to sink into Vietnam. My experience and research leads me to believe that he never grasped the idea of *process.* For him, and for the government as a whole, each decision, each move, indeed each non-move was done in what computer people call "real time." Each day was separate from yesterday and tomorrow. Thus, American policy on Vietnam moved in regular and predictable steps from Eisenhower-Dulles step A (helping the French with limited logistical support and money), to B (training missions) to C (covert action by the CIA) to D (Special Forces and small numbers of other troops) etc. Never was there a time when stopping was a serious option. So we had years of war and thousands of casualties to no planned result. This process is what became known as Mission creep.

More recently have come a string of other comparable but smaller scale actions. Then again larger ventures -- Iraq and Afghanistan. Now comes Syria. Mission creep redux. And with the usual complications. It turns out that while we are still discussing what I guess is step B or C on Syria, the CIA has for months been at work on steps much further down the line, training, equipping and arranging the funding for some of the myriad insurgent groups. Interdiction of air space cannot be far behind. And, ultimately, our actions, our equipment and our troops will have to be protected by "boots on the ground."

Then what?

Answering or at minimum posing that question leads us toward the third major lesson of the past, along with the unpredictability of violence and the idea that having embarked upon actions designed to overthrow an adversary a government can stop when its leaders wish to do so. So let us at least pose the question of the last step in a sequence of acts. Let Mr. Keller begin.

He "asked a rebel commander named Abu Jarah how he imagined Syria after Assad.

"'Maybe Somalia plus Afghanistan,' he replied.

"That, I allowed, was a pretty horrifying prospect."

No one could argue against that conclusion, but is it predictable? My conclusion, and indeed the theme of this collection of essays, is that it is. It is unlikely but sometimes possible to "regime change" a country as the neoconservative hawks convinced President Bush to do in Iraq and Afghanistan. Then, by the application of overwhelming power and a great deal of money, a new regime may be installed as America did in both Iraq and Afghanistan. If this regime is pliant, doing so can be portrayed as a success – they do what we demand.

But, inevitably, there is a second part of the process as I have laid out in the essays in this volume on Afghanistan: the shattering of a regime is usually followed by the shattering of the social contract that unites the rulers and the ruled. That is the lesson I draw from the rhyme of "Humpty Dumpty." Once Humpty Dumpty is broken, no amount of power, money or foreign direction can "put him together again." Reconstituting an acceptable social contract is likely to be the task of several generations.

We did not have to address this issue in Vietnam because there the Vietminh was not shattered. It was ready and able to take over. Indeed, we got lucky there because the Vietnamese did the job pretty much as we had wished to have done; they even created a more or less capitalist regime. Iraq was different. Our invasion and the guerrilla war and counterinsurgency wars that followed did shatter the social contract. Consequently, the problem of Iraq is now larger and more painful than ever. If a part of our aim was to create a Western style democracy, Iraq today is at least as far from that model as it was under Saddam Husain. And, unleashed, the forces of repression and revenge have wounded, driven away or killed far more people than Saddam could have done. We converted a tyranny into a failed state without getting rid of tyranny. And, to judge by the incredibly inept handling of the Afghan challenge, no one has a view of a future of which we – or more importantly, the Afghan people -- would approve. There the worst is yet to come.

So what would "winning" be like in Syria? I predict it won't be what we think and say we want and is likely to be the very opposite: a shattered "failed" state or statelets, most or all of which will hate us and at least some of which are apt to host those who will seek revenge against us. Pretty much what Abu Jarah described to Mr. Keller – "Somalia plus Afghanistan." If we try to buy our way out, we will have to pour in billions of dollars we should be spending on teachers, students, schools, hospitals, roads, bridges, affordable energy, etc. at home. And there will come time when the Chinese may no longer agree to lend us the billions of dollars we ourselves do not have to pay for our senseless foreign ventures. At that time, we may combine the worst of foreign affairs with domestic poverty.

In conclusion, I emphasize the old fashioned idea that we should look before we leap. And we should recognize that in international affairs the first step is already part of the leap.

June 24, 2013

24379562R30210

Made in the USA
Charleston, SC
24 November 2013